15-99

INVESTIGATING TOWN PLANNING:
CHANGING PERSPECTIVES AND AGENDAS

South East Essex College
of Arts & Technology
Camarvon Road Southend-on-Sea Essex SS2 6LS
Tel: (01702) 220400 Fax: (01702) 432320 Minicom: (01702) 220642

OR 4/99
LR
SHL
SEC
711 INV X

Series: Exploring Town Planning

Series Editor   Clara Greed

INVESTIGATING TOWN PLANNING: CHANGING PERSPECTIVES AND AGENDAS

Edited by Clara Greed

Contributing Authors: Hugh Barton, Stuart Farthing, Clara Greed, Peter Hobbs, Christine Lambert, David Ludlow, Tracey Merrett, Nicholas Oatley, Kimberly Paumier, Derek Senior, and Geoffrey Walker

LONGMAN

Addison Wesley Longman Limited,
Edinburgh Gate, Harlow
Essex CM20 2JE, England
and Associated Companies throughout the world.

First published 1996

British Library Cataloguing-in-Publication Data

A catalogue record for this book is available from the British Library

ISBN 0-582-25834-0

Set by 8 in 10/12 pt New Baskerville
Printed in Great Britain by Henry Ling Ltd., at the Dorset Press,
Dorchester, Dorset.

CONTENTS

LISTS OF FIGURES, PLATES AND TABLES

THE CONTRIBUTORS

Hugh Barton Dip TP, MPhil, MRTPI is a senior lecturer in environmental sustainability studies in the School of Planning, and course leader of the MA/postgraduate diploma course in Town and Country Planning, within the Faculty of the Built Environment, University of the West of England, Bristol. He has a long-standing interest in environmental and energy issues, founding the Urban Centre for Appropriate Technology and Bristol Energy Centre in the 1980s. His recent research and consultancy projects have included the *The Good Practice Guide on the Environmental Appraisal of Development Plans* for the Department of the Environment, and contribution to the EU funded Bristol Energy and Environment Plan. Current projects are a book on local environmental auditing for Earthscan, and a design guide for sustainable development of the Local Government Management Board.

Stuart Farthing BA, MA, PhD, principal lecturer, previously researcher at the Centre for Urban and Regional Research at the University of Manchester, has been a lecturer at the University of the West of England (previously Bristol Polytechnic) since 1973. Teaching specialisms include housing and planning policy, and planning methods and research. He has undertaken extensive research in the field of town planning. Current projects include research on new housing developments, and local facility provision (PCFC funded); land supply for social housing (Housing Corporation funded). He has published widely and, for example, in 1994 authored three works on planning for housing developments, and has published in the *Town Planning Review* and *Journal of Property Research*. He holds a BA (Hons) in Geography from Nottingham University, an MA from Manchester, and a PhD from Reading.

The editor, Clara Greed BSc (Hons), MRTPI, FASI, FRGS, PhD, is a senior lecturer in town planning in the Faculty of the Built Environment, University of the West of England, previously working in the Department of Surveying, and in local government. She is the author of the first volume in this series *Introducing Town Planning*, editor of Volume II, *Implementing Town Planning*, and has published widely on built environment matters, including *Women* *and Planning* (Routledge, 1994) and *Surveying Sisters* (Routledge, 1991) on women chartered surveyors. She is a chartered town planner, Fellow of the Architects and Surveyors Institute, and a member of several committees dealing with education and practice issues in the built environment professions. She is a member of the CISC (Construction Industry Standing Conference) Planning and Strategy Group, which produced Part A (Planning) of the CISC map. This was prepared for the assessment of professional competence at NVQ levels 4 and 5. Currently she is involved in a working group developing NVQ standards for planning technician and support staff. She is interested in all aspects of equal opportunities issues, and is chair of the Faculty Access Initiative.

Peter Hobbs holds a BSc and PhD from the University of Reading. He is a chartered surveyor and member of the Society of Property Researchers. Prior to becoming a senior lecturer in the School of Valuation and Estate Management at the University of the West of England, Bristol, and course leader for the postgraduate real estate course, he worked in property market analysis and as a valuation surveyor during the property boom and slump of the late 1980s and early 1990s. His particular research interest is in the interface between town planning and the property market, and the role of town planning as one of the factors which determine investment performance. His research has been published in *The Economic Determinants of British Town Planning*, Pergamon, 1992, and he has contributed to many conferences including the RICS 'Cutting Edge' Conference series in 1995 and 1996. Currently he is working as the Research Manager at Boots Properties in Nottingham.

Christine Lambert is a reader in the School of Town and Country Planning at the University of the West of England, Bristol. She received a geography degree from the London School of Economics, and qualified as a town planner at the University of Wales. She has worked in planning practice and as a research associate and fellow at the universities of Birmingham and Bristol. Her recent and current research includes work on housing supply and finance, planning and social housing, and changing urban government roles and functions. She is co-author (with Glen Bramley and Will Bartlett) of *Planning, the Market and Private Housebuilding*, UCL Press, 1994.

David Ludlow is a chartered town planner with over 10 years experience in local government and planning consultancies. David is currently Director of EURONET, a European Economic Interest Group (EEIG) based at the University of the West of England, which links leading planning and environmental research consultants and institutes throughout the European Union. EURONET is undertaking research, supported by a variety of funding bodies including member state governments, local authorities and professional institutes, into the planning policy initiatives of the EU, facilitating the transfer of 'best practice' from the European experience and its application to planning systems. EURONET also provides the Scientific and Technical Secretariat for the Urban Environment Expert Group (DGXI) in the implementation of the European Sustainable Cities Project.

Tracey Merrett is a solicitor specialising in town planning and environmental law. She received an LLB (Hons) from Leicester University, and has worked both in local government and in a range of legal practices. She is joint author of the *Planning Service* (a loose leaf encyclopaedia of planning law) with Butterworths. She has published in *The Planner, Water Law, Environmental Protection Bulletin,* and other journals. She specialises in advising on planning applications, appeals, and compulsory purchase procedures; and has successfully represented several residents groups at public inquiries. She has advised on a variety of developments including offices, light industrial development, hotels, supermarkets, airports, and leisure uses. For example she acted for the County Hall Development Group in London co-ordinating the eight-week public inquiry on proposals to redevelop County Hall for hotel, residential, retail and office use, supervising the submission of all applications and instructing counsel and fifteen expert witnesses. She has headed an environmental law department for a major London solicitors and now works in the same field in Bristol.

Nick Oatley is a senior lecturer in Town and Country Planning at the University of the West of England, Bristol, in the Faculty of the Built Environment. He worked in the planning department at Bristol City Council for six years before joining the university full time. His teaching and research interests include urban policy and politics, and local economic development. He has published articles on Urban Development Corporations, City Challenge, and employment policies in local plans. He has a BA (Hons) in Geography from Exeter University, an MA in Geography from McMaster University in Canada, and a Bachelor of Town and Country Planning from the (then) Bristol Polytechnic, and he belongs to the Royal Town Planning Institute.

Kimberly Paumier has been involved in urban development issues over the past 15 years in both the USA and UK. She has gained this experience as director of a neighbourhood development organisation in Chicago, a leasing representative for a major US city centre shopping developer. She has also gained an understanding of how cities and towns develop through work with a land planning and market research firm in the USA. She moved to the UK in 1989 to manage tourism development studies for the English Tourist Board. Following this she was appointed as a project manager for retail development with Eurotunnel. She is currently City Centre Manager for Bath, a position which involves bringing the public and private sectors together to initiate changes and improvements to the city centre. She holds a degree in Urban Studies from the University of Michigan and an MBA from Loyola College.

Derek Senior has been at Leeds Metropolitan University since 1988, and is Professional Group Head for Urban Development and Planning. Previously he was course leader for the postgraduate RTPI planning course. His chief interests include development planning, planning legislation, local government, minerals and recreation. He has been involved in numerous short courses and CPD courses for planners, especially those involving training for public inquiries and hearings. He is also course leader in the Leeds Business School on a professional diploma in Planning and Environmental Law. He co-authored with Peter Robert a chapter on minerals in *Economic Activity and Land Use* (ed. P. Healey, Longman, 1991). Prior to becoming an academic, Derek spent twenty years as a chartered town planner in central and local government, and in private practice. He has worked for Liverpool CB, Cheshire CC, the Scottish Development Department, South Yorkshire MCC, and in his own consultancy. For over a decade he was group leader in South Yorkshire concerned with the policy and implementation aspects of minerals and environmental improvement. His experience includes mineral subject plan preparation, reclamation policies, AMA opencast procedures, submissions to the Flowers Commission, attendance at the Belvoir Inquiry, waste disposal liaison, and policy development for onshore oil and gas resources.

Geoff Walker BA, PhD is a chartered town planner and geographer living in Bath. He lectures in strategic planning and environmental resource management at the University of the West of England, and is currently Director of Studies for the Postgraduate Modular Programme in the Faculty of the Built Environment. His main lecturing, research, and consultancy interests are strategic-level development planning and management, and retail planning. His extensive practice experience covers both the private and public sectors. It includes planning consultancy in Birmingham and the West Midlands, local government in the South East, and consultancy in the South West. He has been a member of the executive committee of the South West branch of the RTPI since the early 1980s, which he has served as newsletter editor, programme secretary and, in 1992, branch chair. He makes regular contributions to local radio and television on retail planning matters.

PREFACE

The purpose of this volume is to look in more depth at the range of activities and perspectives which are generally perceived to compose that phenomenon called 'town planning'. In Volume I, *Introducing Town Planning*, readers were presented with a relatively straightforward, descriptive coverage of the subject 'as it is' with little room for debate or reflection on 'why it is as it is' or on 'how it might be'. The emphasis was placed upon developing an understanding of the statutory planning framework, and upon the key functions of development control and plan making. A broader contextualising perspective was provided as to the purpose and objectives of planning – to some extent – by means of sections which provided coverage of the history of town planning; identification of contemporary areas of policy concern, both urban and rural; plus a digression into an examination of some of the social aspects and community implications of town planning practice. It was decided to give space to the social dimensions of town planning because, it was considered, coverage of this controversial field would best serve as a vehicle to demonstrate to readers, especially to students new to the subject, that town planning, in spite of first impressions, is not purely a technical subject concerned only with physical land use plans and development control, but that it has wider dimensions too. One might have equally chosen the economic and environmental dimensions of town planning to demonstrate this breadth. It was considered that both of these key elements of modern town planning required more focused, and fuller treatment, and this will be provided in this present volume.

In Volume II, *Implementing Town Planning*, the aim was to produce a book which would illustrate the role of town planning within the development process, and would provide readers with actual site-related case studies which would demonstrate how the planning system worked in practice. This volume was directed at both students and practitioners whose main field is town planning, and at those involved in the wider field of the built environment studies, perhaps undertaking student projects, at intermediate level, on property development, estate management, housing, and general practice surveying courses. Although the examples in Volume II inevitably focused upon the more detailed aspects of land use planning – at site level – 'it goes without saying' that development happens on a particular site, in a particular locality because of a combination of governmental constraints and market forces which bring forth 'development' as an end product of complex economic forces and political processes. We have now reached a more advanced stage of study in Volume III, namely, *Investigating Town Planning*. This volume is intended for third-year students, first-year postgraduates, and those interested in understanding higher level urban policy and governance – of which town planning is one part – and in investigating further the forces which shape the built environment. The aim of this book is to delve deeper into the scope and nature of town planning, beyond the physical, spatial surface reality of daily planning practice. This volume attempts to take the reader 'behind the urban tapestry' so that students may appreciate 'the workings' of urban governance and policy making. The processes which generate the built environment are not mechanistic, and their investigation and interpretation are the source of much academic debate and political controversy. Therefore it will be found that some of the chapter contributions by the various authors are written more in the style of academic papers, such as one would find in a refereed journal on urban theory and policy. Less emphasis is put upon either procedural matters, or upon prescriptive policy guidance, but more is put upon theory and academic argument. The chapters provide valuable insights, and perspectives upon the current 'state of play' in town planning, and upon the wider environmental policy issues. The team of contributors is drawn mainly from the University of the West of England, Faculty of the Built Environment, and from colleagues with links with its School of Planning, and others in the vicinity. It may be argued that there is no longer one version of 'town planning' but many versions and perspectives, each with its own adherents and agenda. In seeking to capture this diversity and reflect fragmentation of the planning discourse within Volume III it is inevitable that different contributors will demonstrate quite different, and sometimes conflicting, views. Therefore it is up to the readers to develop their own analyses and judgements of the material presented in order to apply what they read to their own studies and situations.

PART I

INTRODUCTION

Chapter 1

THE QUESTION 'WHAT IS TOWN PLANNING?' REVISITED

Clara Greed

The scope of town planning

Town planning in Britain has traditionally and legally been perceived as being concerned with the regulation of physical land use and development, which has been implemented through development control and development plan procedures. The scope of town planning as a form of state intervention has been primarily spatial and geographical in nature. But many of the issues which have been of concern both to planners and to urban citizens have not been directly, or exclusively, 'spatial' in nature, but rather 'aspatial', that is related to social, economic, environmental or cultural trends, issues and problems (Foley *et al.*, 1964). The purpose of this book is to discuss some of the other types of 'planning' which have jostled for a place either within or alongside the realms of statutory town planning. Some of the more prominent among current contenders are environmental planning, economic planning, social planning for minority groups, and a resurgence of interest in architect-led urban design 'planning'. Indeed there nowadays appear to be many 'plannings' rather than just one 'town planning', each with its own jargon, discourse, objectives and disciples, coexisting uneasily with each other and with the governmental town planning system.

The purpose of this book is to focus in on a selection of these 'plannings' and to seek to unravel, and make sense of, the available discourses. Particular emphasis is put upon economic and environmental types of 'planning', and their relationship with physical land use planning, and with each other. This book seeks to delve deeper into the scope and nature of town planning, beyond the physical, spatial surface reality of daily planning practice, and to take the reader 'behind the urban tapestry' or to 'the other side of the screen' so that readers may gain an understanding of 'the workings' of urban governance, of which town planning is, arguably, one important component (Healey, 1988). The book not only investigates different types of 'planning' but also highlights the changing nature of planning agencies, and the different manifestations of those who call themselves 'planners', who, for example, nowadays, might include private sector urban investment analysts, environmentalists, traffic engineers, and city centre managers, as well as local government town planners. The processes which generate the built environment are not mechanistic, and their investigation and interpretation is the source of much academic debate and political controversy. Therefore the style of this book is more discursive and reflective than earlier volumes in this series. There is a greater emphasis upon theory, critique, and discussion, and less upon prescriptive policy guidance or statutory procedures.

Economic planning

The first section of the book is devoted to a consideration of different aspects of 'economic planning'. Economic planning has always been a strong contender for attention. In Volumes I and II in this series, as explained in the Preface, emphasis was put, respectively, upon describing land use planning, and upon considering the role of the planner in the development process in relation to site related case studies. It was presented as 'given' that development happens on a specific site, in a particular locality because of a combination of governmental constraints and market forces which bring forth 'development'. It may be argued that the demand for land use and development, in the first place, is generated by the growth in 'aspatial' human activities, and that the built environment is merely the end product of the process (Massey, 1984). For example, demands for new offices, business parks and industrial units may be a direct result of changes in the economic situation, whilst demands for new or different types of housing are also likely to be a reflection of changing demographic and social conditions (cf. Balchin and Bull, 1987; Rydin, 1993). It would seem more logical, therefore, to extend the scope of town planning to deal with 'cause' as well as 'effect', that is to seek to broaden urban policy making to introduce some element of control and direction on aspatial economic processes rather than simply seeking to control the spatial end product, which is like 'shutting the stable door after the horse has bolted'. In the post-war reconstruction period of the 1940s, when Britain was seeking to rebuild its industrial and employment structures, economic planning was accepted as a valid component of state intervention (as evidenced in the sentiments of the Barlow Commission, 1940; and see Greed, 1993, pp. 113–116 for background). But such measures were operated under a system of regional, rather than town, planning which has long since become defunct. Latent within discussions of the need for economic planning is the assumption, often informed by political perspective, that economic planners might do 'better' than the vagaries of market forces and the private development sector, which are often perceived as being motivated purely by opportunism and greed, in providing employment and balanced urban development.

In the past, enthusiasm for economic planning was more likely to be (but not exclusively so) associated with Labour governments in Britain and with 'socialist' economies elsewhere in Europe. In the cold light of the 1990s,

3

following nearly 20 years of a Conservative government which has favoured the importance of the private sector over the public, as the source of economic growth and prosperity, one might imagine that demands for extending the scope of town planning to embrace economic policy are inappropriate. On the contrary, as will be explained in later chapters, 'economic planning' in all but name has been a feature of Conservative government 'planning' policy. But, such economic intervention has usually been operationalised through agencies directly funded from, and responsible to, central government, such as the Urban Development Corporations, not through local town planning authorities. Although the government has ostensibly been committed to reducing state intervention, planning, and bureaucracy, in fact, it has, over the years, created a vast array of new *ad hoc* 'economic planning' type governmental bodies and urban policy initiatives, such as enterprise zones, and the Single Regeneration Budget. But the agenda of such initiatives has often been, arguably, one of commercial expediency rather than one of social welfare: job creation often appearing to be almost an incidental result of urban development programmes geared to facilitate property development.

The first chapter in Part II, following this introductory chapter (namely Chapter 2) is written by Peter Hobbs, a chartered surveyor, whose main field of practice is property market analysis, and who has undertaken research on the economic determinants of British Town Planning (see details of contributors). Chapter 2 provides a theoretical context to 'town planning' as seen from an 'economic planning' perspective. A primary theme discussed is the role of planning as a means of rectifying the failure and imperfections of the market in the allocation of resources. Unlike environmental 'green' planning, which has only come to prominence in recent years, economic planning has a long history which virtually pre-dates town planning. In Chapter 3, against this theoretical background, the evolution of planning practice is traced chronologically during the post-war period, with particular attention being given to describing the different phases and 'styles' of planning intervention which evolved in response to the changing economic conditions and trade cycles of the period (Hague, 1991).

Chapter 4 is written by Nick Oatley whose research interests include urban policy and politics, and local economic development (see details of contributors) and who has extensive experience as a local authority planner. The role of economic planning is investigated in relation to one aspect of urban governance, namely, planning for inner city areas. Emphasis is, again, put upon the historical background with particular reference to the different strategies adopted over the years towards urban regeneration policy. Attention is drawn to the related sequence of theoretical perspectives which have informed planners in tackling the urban situation, and this is linked to the impact of changing central government perspectives. The present situation, which evolved under the Conservative government of the 1980s and 1990s, is discussed, and the roles of such devices as special area designations and such initiatives as Enterprise Zones, Urban Development Corporations, City Challenge, and the Single Regeneration Budget, are evaluated in achieving effective urban economic governance. This chapter also shows how economic planning influences the physical nature of the city, and the chances of development, for, as Harvey commented, urban policy does not float in a spaceless vacuum (Harvey, 1973, p. 24) but the social, economic, political and physical elements of urban governance are inextricably linked. Therefore, economic planners may question the validity of aiming, primarily, at controlling the built environment itself, as against seeking to shape the economic forces which shape it in the first place. For example, trying to improve the inner city by 'cosmetic' housing rehabilitation projects, without a commensurate emphasis upon employment policy, may mean that the houses rapidly fall into disrepair again because of lack of adequate household income for maintenance. Alternatively the area may go 'up' in value as a result of such renewal policies, and become gentrified, thus the problem is not 'solved' but merely 'moved' as the original residents seek cheaper accommodation elsewhere.

Planning and housing policy

Chapters 5–6 comprise Part III, and investigate the development of town planning in relation to one specific land use, namely housing provision. This section continues the theme of discussing the scope and nature of economic planning, for housing is a key factor in the economy. Levels of housing provision, and the state of the housing market, in turn, affect a range of other economic sectors, such as levels of activity within the property market, public sector investment, employment within the construction industry, and household consumption and expenditure patterns (Ball, 1983). But, housing is also a major spatial, geographical component of any town or city. It is estimated that on average 70% of urban land is occupied by residential development, thus putting it firmly within the parameters of concern of physical, land use planning. So the field of housing may be seen as an important nexus point where physical and economic approaches to planning meet head on.

Chapter 5 is written by Stuart Farthing, who has undertaken extensive research on many housing issues, such as land supply for social housing, and factors influencing the nature of new housing development. This chapter focuses upon social housing. In the past, as described in Chapter 5, this was mainly composed of state, 'council' housing, but this has become a diminishing sector in the wake of central government initiatives to create a 'property owning democracy'. The chances of achieving meaningful 'planning for housing' are discussed in the wake of a shift from high levels of provision by local authorities themselves towards the provision of 'affordable housing' by a range of public, private and voluntary sector agencies. The respective roles of 'planners' and 'housers' are highlighted with particular attention to the role of the housing associations as the new main providers of social housing. Attention is drawn to the curious division in professional powers. It is observed that it is hardly logical, in seeking to 'plan' for housing in a comprehensive manner, that the responsibility for assessing demand for housing supply and geographically allocating and 'zoning' land for residential development is held by the planners, whilst the 'housers' are responsible for the management of housing stock and meeting social housing needs.

In Chapter 6, Christine Lambert, whose current research includes work on housing supply and finance, and changing urban governmental roles and strategies, looks at the topic of housing from the perspective of private housing provision *vis à vis* town planning policy. Nowadays, private sector housing provision, through owner occupation, is the larger sector. It is inevitable that comparisons will be made by the authors and, hopefully, by the readers between the differing 'planning' (or lack of planning!) approaches towards the public and private sectors. This public/private dualism is a key feature of the British housing situation. Yet, from the physical land use planner's viewpoint 'a house is a house' subject to virtually the same development plan and development control regulations whether it is public or private in tenure. Even if, in the past, some planners have remained 'blind' to the wider economic and social effects of physical land use zoning for residential development, undoubtedly, as the author explains, planning controls have had an effect on restricting land availability and thus upon housing provision and prices (Ball, 1983, 1988). Now that most new housing at least is likely to be private, rather than public sector generated, arguably housing requirements and provision are less easy to forecast or control from the planners' perspective. Indeed housing has become much more of a component in the market economy than a factor in public 'welfare' provision. But, as will be seen in the following section, another agenda is at work too in shaping housing policy. For environmental groups are demanding greater planning control over the location and layout of housing developments in order to create more sustainable cities. Thus economic, social and environmental 'plannings' coexist, arguably somewhat uneasily, within the field of 'planning for housing', and the reader will observe, from these chapters, the tensions this creates for town planners.

Environmental planning

Part IV is devoted to aspects of that other great contender 'environmental planning'. An emphasis upon the wider economic context of town planning enables one to understand the factors which generate the demands for land use and development in the first place (that is the 'causes' of development in the first place). In contrast, environmental groups have been more concerned about the 'effects' of land use and development (and of human activity itself) upon

the ecological system. The relationship between the 'new' environmental movement and the town planners has been somewhat fraught. Perhaps planners saw
themselves as the 'good guys' because they already imagined that they were
doing their best for the environment, and resented their world being turned
upside down by the new wave of 'greenies' who were often very critical of established town planning (Blowers, 1993). Significantly, in Chapter 2, Hobbs comments that the environmental movement has been the greatest challenge that
town planning has encountered in recent years. After all, in Britain 'town and
country planning' (to give 'town planning' its full title as enshrined in the relevant legislation) was 'always' concerned about protecting the countryside from
the worst effects of urban sprawl, and town planning has also had a strong 'conservationist' agenda for many years, in respect of both urban and rural issues.
But this was not seen as enough. Indeed what might be deemed perfectly
acceptable countryside land uses which under British planning law had not previously required planning permission, such as farming or forest development,
have now become the subject of scrutiny under Environmental Impact
Assessment regulations, which have come in 'on top of' the British national
planning system (Greed, 1993, p. 182) from the European Union.

In Chapter 7, Hugh Barton, who has a distinguished record in the field of
environmental and energy issues, and whose current research includes work
on local environmental auditing for Earthscan, argues the cause of environmental planning. The parameters of his concern may be seen as both representative of proponents of planning for sustainability, and as much broader
than the conventional ambit of 'town planning'. He itemises on his agenda
the issues of global climate, biodiversity, air quality, water, the Earth, and
minerals conservation. One could argue that since all these are 'physical' if
not 'geographical' elements they could be construed to fit into the existing
agenda of town planning. But, they are not 'earthbound', they are not
specifically related to a particular site or location, but embody a concern with
aspects of the global ecological system as a whole. Rather like vandalised public areas, such as corridors and lifts in blocks of flats, nobody has direct
ownership of 'air' or 'the biosphere', and so these common areas have not
been seen as being 'owned' by anyone and therefore have also been the subject of much mistreatment and abuse. The author argues strongly for greater
understanding, responsibility and thus regulation of the use of these global
assets. But can Britain do its bit towards saving the planet through the statutory planning tools available? Reference is made to the various legal measures
available, such as for example Environmental Impact Analysis. However, the
overall tone of this chapter would suggest that there is a need for more than
mere legislation, rather there is a need for a whole different attitude towards
environmental issues, and especially a need for greater co-ordination and
co-operation, and more 'effort', on the part of all those involved, especially
more commitment from government.

In 1995 the Environment Act was passed, which brought into force a wide
range of new environmental planning regulations as explained in Volume I

by the editor (in *Introducing Town Planning*, Edition 2, 1996). It should be noted that it is not the purpose of the author of the sustainability chapter (7) to cover the regulations *per se* but rather to discuss the principles. Those who require a detailed legal coverage of the 1995 Act should consult Ball and Bell (1995); and Lane and Peto (1995), and may also find Chapter 11 of this book of interest as to whether the new law will really work.

Because one theme of the book is to compare and contrast the different type of 'plannings' which compose the town planning discourse, it seemed apt to set a chapter on an earlier, but more nitty-gritty, site specific, form of 'green' planning directly in contrast alongside Barton's more global and visionary chapter on sustainability. In Chapter 8, Derek Senior takes one of the environmental issues of concern identified by Hugh Barton, namely 'minerals', and discusses the place of minerals planning within the context of statutory town planning legislation and environmental policy. 'Minerals' is an interesting topic to consider when looking at the range of different 'plannings', because it may be seen as acting as an arena where a range of different planning agendas, past and present, meet. Firstly, 'minerals' was always accepted as a valid component of physical land use planning, enshrined in development plan documents, and was an important issue in the past when extractive industry was a key component of the economy. Minerals planning, secondly, links directly to the world of 'economic planning', nowadays finding itself aligned to environmental planning. The economic emphasis was particularly strong in the past in defining the topic, when primary and secondary industrial production were seen as the cornerstones of the economic base of the economy, particularly under Labour governments. More broadly, traditional socialist economic theory and state planned economies saw 'mining' as a keystone to economic development, and were preoccupied with the nationalisation of raw materials, and with state control of the means of production.

Thirdly, traditional minerals planning legislation has met head on with the new environmental movement specifically in areas where there are, through a legalistic fluke, unexpired planning permissions for quarrying and mining, which are still in force. Typically the sites are located in areas which are, now, either seen to be of great landscape value, usually with some important species of flora or fauna in residence, or they are now alongside what have become gentrified, up-market, rural villages whose residents do not want to have to endure the noise of blasting or heavy lorries passing their houses. Presumably planning permissions for minerals extraction were given in the past, without restriction or time limit, because, particularly in the post-war reconstruction economy, raw materials were highly valued and society did not know about, or considered it could not yet afford to worry about matters of conservation or ecology. Similarly planning restrictions on farming development, as stated above, have been relatively lenient or non-existent until relatively recently, because like mining, farming was seen as a vital economic sector, beyond reproach or criticism.

Urban form and retail activity

Part V is at first sight not devoted to another type of 'planning' but rather centres on a controversial area of land use, namely 'retail development', although it has developed as a type of planning all of its own. However this is used as a vehicle to develop further discussion of the inter-relationships and relative impacts of the economic and environmental planning agenda raised respectively in Parts II and IV. Retail development is undoubtedly an aspect of 'economic planning' but in the past it might have been seen as a secondary issue, related more to 'consumption' and the service sector, rather than to 'production' (MacDowell, 1991). In reality, in the 1990s it is the source of more new jobs than more traditional 'industrial' sectors of the economy (although some purists would say these are not 'real' jobs). Although perhaps some traditional economic planners, obsessed with industry and 'jobs', may have not seen the retail sector as a key component of their strategy, the private property sector has certainly seen it as a major area for investment and development. Indeed another type of 'planner' has evolved who is mainly found in the private sector, involved in advising property developers on retail and other forms of commercial development (Price and Blair, 1989). It is one of the main forms (in some areas the 'only' type) of new urban development. But, the current nature of new retail development is often criticised by environmentalists because of its manifestation in the form of out-of-town sites which are based on motor car accessibility. Therefore, a discussion of changes in retail development brings the reader back to some of the basic, and unresolved issues more commonly associated with traditional town planning, such as urban form, land use, zoning, decentralisation, location, and transport policy. There is also a large social agenda associated with retail issues, relating to the decline of inner city retail locations and local district centres, disadvantaging the poor, elderly, and carless (Gilroy and Castle, 1995).

Geoff Walker, town planner and geographer, in Chapter 9, describes the development and current manifestations of retail development, and the government's response in terms of planning policy guidance, in which one can find echoes of both current economic and environmental agendas. Our cities have experienced immense change over the last 10 years or more as shopping facilities have moved out. Perhaps in the past town planners simply took shops for granted and underestimated the knock-on effect that car ownership, consequent central area car parking restrictions, and subsequent decentralisation of shopping facilities would have on the viability of the traditional central area. The author gives a historical perspective on the changes which have occurred in retail development, and considers the implications for city form and structure, and for transportation policy, using case studies. The problems of reconciling the demand for 'one stop' shopping complexes for the busy shopper with demands for car restraint and sustainability policy are evident in the discussion.

Chapter 10 also relates to the field of retail development, and city structure issues, but it is also used as a vehicle to introduce another type of 'planning' in all but name. Chapter 10 on city centre management is written by
Kimberly Paumier, who is the City Centre Manager for the historic Georgian
City of Bath in South West England, and who previously worked in the fields
of urban research, urban management, and tourism in North America.
Many of the issues which are of concern to her in Bath might be seen as
being town planning matters, or at least have become her concern because
of the lack of power or inability of the planning system *per se* to deal with
such matters. Her work centres upon creating the right 'image' for Bath,
and first impressions and 'all the little things' count. Tourists and other visitors are put off by parking problems, litter, lack of public toilets, limited
shop opening hours, problems of street crime and aggressive begging. It is
argued that these matters are important and should also be of concern to
town planners, particularly when the survival of the traditional town centre
is becoming so fragile because of the pull of out-of-town development.
There has been a tendency in the past for town planners to adopt a 'hit and
run' approach to town planning, in which once a scheme or plan is completed, the area in question is left to get on with it. In fact studies have
shown that there is an important case for ongoing maintenance, supervision,
surveillance, cleaning, and 'housekeeping' to keep an area in good condition. Therefore the role of the city centre manager is as important as that of
the high level strategic planner in contributing to the economic well being
of an area and its population.

The cutting edge of change

The final section consists of three chapters. In Chapter 11, Tracey Merrett, a
planning lawyer, gives a review of the current state of play regarding planning
law with particular attention to the question of the chances of environmental,
social, economic and other aspatial areas of the various 'plannings' identified
being incorporated into the statutory system. Case law and the related appeals
system is the cutting edge of progress in planning as to what can be achieved
in the future. Even if a policy is 'good', if it cannot be enforced legally it is a
non-starter. However, as demonstrated in the different chapters, 'planning'
and the wider concept of urban governance is not limited purely to the
parameters of town and country planning law. Economic planning measures
can be achieved by other means such as by direct central government initiatives, by a system of grants and loans, and through the taxation system. Wider
social objectives in planning might be achieved through negotiation and
bargaining with developers and representatives of the private sector over
planning gain, and by cooperation and partnership with voluntary and community groups. Some town planning policies might best be implemented
through other built environment related legislation and governmental

bodies, such as through housing legislation, environmental health measures, and through the work of highways departments.

Many of the new environmental regulations have been introduced into the British town planning system via the European Community (Union now). Indeed, many of the 'new ideas' about urban theory and town planning practice have emanated from Continental Europe. For example, in the field of transportation planning some of the ideas about traffic calming and new forms of public transport provision originated across the Channel. Likewise much of the impetus for the revival of 'urban design' by architect-planners might have been stimulated by the example of France. In the realms of 'social planning' many of the issues which concern the 'women and planning' movement and other minorities are echoed and reinforced by European planning colleagues (OECD, 1994). Therefore, in Chapter 12, David Ludlow, who is an expert on European Planning issues and director of the Euronet planning consultancy, presents an overview of the wider European context of town planning. It should be pointed out that 'town planning' as we know it is a very British, indeed 'English' phenomenon. In particular in England, and to some extent in other more north European cities (at least in the provinces) there is a preference for low density, suburban housing, and generally a more 'garden city' based approach to town planning (Hall, 1994, p. 31). In contrast, relatively speaking, a higher density, more concentrated city form, is a characteristic of central and southern European Union cities, accompanied by a greater emphasis upon medium to high rise apartment living (EC, 1990). Yet one might argue many of the issues are the 'same', relatively speaking, but they take on a somewhat different guise in different city form layouts and localities. Although urban policy specialists might be concerned with the 'same' issues as we are, they may not necessarily call themselves 'town planners' as the professional cake is divided up somewhat differently, and systems of educational qualification and employment differ somewhat.

Many of the town planning issues of concern cannot be limited to a particular urban location but are regional in importance, particularly in the realms of economic planning. Nowadays with the globalisation of economies and the enormous power of multinational companies to locate in whatever country they choose to get the lowest wage rates and the highest level of government incentives, one might see Britain as but one region of Europe, and on the extreme edge at that. At the same time regional economic disparities among regions within Britain may have increased as a result of European Union membership. For example, whilst London might be seen as retaining a favoured locational advantage for development as part of the Golden Triangle with Paris and Brussels, the (mainly Celtic) regions of Britain and France which compose the Atlantic Arc to the West may require more positive planning. In the future, effective town planning policy and implementation will only be achievable with reference to this wider European context. In particular it should be noted that many of the higher aspirations of British planners to achieve economic, social and environmental policy objectives may become more realisable with the context of 'Social Europe' than has been the case within a national system so centred purely on physical, land use planning.

In the final chapter, Chapter 13, the editor seeks to draw together the various threads from the different chapters, and to reconsider the state of play between economic, environmental, and physical land use town planning. It is argued that a key consideration which may determine the progress of all three agendas is the question of transportation planning. As highlighted in recent government consultation documents (Mawhinney, 1995) demands for traffic calming, and limitations in private car usage, must be set against the reality that most individuals, and indeed the economy itself, depend upon private road transport to get around. Restrictive measures to control the motor car, or reduce freight transportation by road, may be economically and socially detrimental, unless viable alternatives are provided. In the longer term relocation of the land uses and facilities which cause people to travel in the first place needs to be implemented as implied in PPG13 on 'Transport' (DoE, 1994a). The links between transport policy and governmental guidance on sustainability requirements are also discussed with reference to current policy documents. The economic considerations of implementing sustainability policies are weighed.

What might be seen as economically sensible within a nation-state economy might be seen as false economy by those concerned about sustainability issues for the whole of Planet Earth. For example much traditional economic planning has emphasised the importance of full employment particularly within the industrial sector. But if industrial processes are creating pollution, and workers are churning out short-life disposable goods manufactured from non-renewable resources, for sale in booming out-of-town retail centres, then although it might appear from production and consumption statistics that the economy is doing well, in global terms such statistics might been seen as indicators of ecological disaster. Clearly the issues are highly complex and cannot be resolved through land use planning changes alone, but require more fundamental cultural and political re-orientation. It should be noted that the 'social' aspects of planning, social planning, and for that matter 'women and planning' are not overtly prominent in this book (as some readers might have expected). But, undoubtedly certain types of social relations, and 'values' in respect of class, gender, and ethnicity considerations are latent within the way in which our cities, society and the economy are currently structured. These more complex cultural issues will be dealt with fully in a later volume. However, in the last chapter, some suggestions as to 'the way forward', in respect of the issues raised in this book, will be made for the consideration of the reader. It is difficult to come up with prescriptive policy suggestions, because the urban situation is constantly changing, and in the future the policy kaleidoscope will, no doubt, be shaken again by those politicians responsible for urban governance, and there will other new forms of 'planning', and city form, emerging as yet undreamt of.

Things to bear in mind when reading this book

Agendas and territories

As readers explore the various contributory chapters from the different authors, certain key themes and issues will become evident across the board. It may be helpful to identify some of these for guidance in this introductory chapter. (Unlike in the other two volumes in this series, at this level, no essays or project work have been provided in relation to each chapter.) Each author seeks to define the agenda, and to delineate the territory of the particular type of 'planning' which is being addressed. Many chapters contain an historical component, usually showing the changes which have occured in each decade since World War II. This enables the reader to understand the evolution of the 'planning' in question, and to appreciate why and when it came to prominence, and why it takes the form it does at present. Leading on from this some authors have sought to discuss the likely future development of the area, or to make recommendations as to policy solutions and governmental action. Putting all these agendas together, the reader will be struck by the contrasts and also the overlaps between the different subject areas. Also, because different authors are coming to their subject from different perspectives and have different objectives, readers will find that authors may either agree, or contradict each other, as to preferred solutions. This is because in town planning, to state a truism, there is no one right answer; your choice of solution depends on who you are, where you live, and what you want to achieve.

It is also valuable to look at the range of topics covered as a whole and to consider whether 'town planning' is fragmenting and breaking up as a professional entity or whether it is restructuring, metamorphosing, or even mutating, and thus experiencing healthy growing pains. Town planning may be seen as manifesting a shifting sequence of agendas as discussed by Hobbs in his introductory section. The town planning discourse may be seen as not having much content of itself – town planning can be anything you want it to be! As explained elsewhere (Greed, 1994a) the town planning discourse may be seen to be like a hall of mirrors reflecting and sometimes distorting the changing nature of outside academic movements and currently trendy issues. Indeed some apparently 'new' forms of town planning may in fact be 'old' discourses in different clothing dealing with perennial urban problems in the latest esoteric jargon.

Objectives

Different types of 'planning' have arisen because different interest groups have different agendas and objectives. It is important for the reader to attempt to identify the specific objectives of each type of planning discussed in the various chapters. Peter Hobbs in Chapter 2 provides some context as the rationale for planning in general, and identifies some of the objectives of town planning in particular. Attention is given to the traditional role of planning in compensating for the imperfections of the market in the allocation of resources, goods and services. Nick Oatley continues this theme in relation to urban regeneration and inner city policy, with reference to regulation theory, the objectives of the Welfare State, and the influence of Fordist and post-Fordist models of economic organisation (Murray, 1989). However, the demand for state intervention through town planning has also been fired by political ideology, particularly from the Left, by a desire for social reform and equality, and by the campaigning of community and environmental groups, as much as it has been driven by the persuasiveness of cool economic theory. In more conservative circles, town planning has also been seen as a prerequisite of setting out the 'playing field', to assist efficient operation of the property market in order to facilitate economic growth, and both national and individual prosperity.

A popular legitimation for planning, particularly in the past, was to argue that it was necessary because it would make cities 'better', and that planning would solve urban problems. For example town planning in the nineteenth century was meant to bring order in the place of chaos, hygiene in the place of disease. In the twentieth century planners have variously claimed to be able to solve traffic congestion, solve the homelessness problem, ensure full employment and protect the countryside from sprawl. Each new form of 'planning' claims to be able to provide the awaited salvation, and deeper insights than were available to previous benighted generations of planners. In reality it often seems that planners solve one problem and in the process create other new, unanticipated problems, as illustrated variously in the different chapters in respect of housing, transport and retail development issues. Alternatively the reasons for 'planning' have been seen as so 'obvious' and 'worthwhile' to the planners themselves that apparently there was no need to for them to justify their actions to the general public. It is important to stress that 'the people' who inhabit our cities are not a unitary group, and a policy which benefits one group may disbenefit another, and so in the final analysis city-satisfaction for the individual depends upon wielding enough power to get one's policy preferences adopted.

Levels of planning

'Planning' is an activity which can take place at various levels, and this is reflected in the content of the various chapters, in respect of which 'level' the different authors consider is the 'best' to tackle the aspect of planning policy under consideration. In terms of policy making agencies, the highest level is that of central government. Planning policy might be indistinguishable from general government policy on economic and political matters at this level. At the next level down, local authorities still have the main responsibility for the operational level of town planning. Healey prefers to speak of 'urban governance' rather than 'just' town planning when investigating the higher levels of urban policy making and management, in order to include all relevant policy realms such as those relating to economic activity, education, health, housing, taxation etc., and investment, which all contribute to urban development (Healey and Nabarro, 1990). Indeed some would see 'mere' town planners as essentially regulators rather than urban policy makers within the current political context (Thornley, 1993).

Reference to the higher levels of urban governance are evident in the content of the economic planning and housing chapters (Parts II and III). Some town planning issues are 'governed' by higher levels still such as by EU Directives, as in the case of environmental assessment requirements. National decisions may be influenced by pronouncements, and research findings, from international 'planning' policy agencies such as the OECD, or, for example, by the recommendations of the UN Agenda 21 programme (as will be explained in later chapters). But the actual implementation of these high level policies and directives may be achievable only through local level state agencies and authorities, through statutory development plans, national planning law, and through delegation and implementation at county and district levels of local government. Also increasingly 'planning' policy can only be achieved through working in partnership with the private sector or community groups, rather than operating exclusively within governmental structures. Ideas of the local state and local governance are reinforced by ideas of competition between areas for government funds. Structure and agency debates, latent within many of the chapters, all reflect questions of whether it is better to attempt to plan from a 'bottom up' grass roots, people-based perspective, or from a 'top down' governmental standpoint.

Inter-relationships and conflicts

The book team discussed, but were unable to reach a satisfactory answer to, the question of whether one could develop a diagrammatic typology, or continuum along which to align the different types of planning in evidence, in order to interconnect them and bring order to the diversity. For example it was suggested that different types of 'plannings' might be categorised simply into environmental or economic categories, and that this division reflected a red (economic and often socialist) as against green (environmental and often conservationist) dualism which runs through the recent history of town planning. Alternatively it was suggested that one might structure the different types of planning according to characteristics in a continuum or scatter diagram, between the four reference points of:

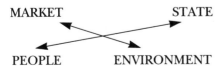

Alternatively it was suggested that planning policies are variously centred on dealing with: specific physical 'areas'; policy 'topics' (such as transport, housing etc.); current 'problems' (such as pollution, car parking); or (less commonly) particular groups of 'people' (the urban poor, ethnic minorities, women). In other words one might construct another set of reference points, and 'place' the different 'plannings' in relation to these, based on:

Dualist tensions within planning

The reader might consider this unresolved conundrum, as it is a valuable exercise in developing an understanding of the scope and nature of modern town planning. It was found that the different types of planning were not easily pigeon-holed, or located along some ideal continuum, but that their individual discourses were often made up of sets of alarmingly contradictory components. As an alternative, therefore, the reader may find it helpful to consider the following list of dualisms and to consider which dualistic tensions are most evident in the 'plannings' discussed in this book.

- red/green
- physical/economic
- physical/social
- social/economic
- physical/environmental
- social/environmental
- economic/environmental
- public/private
- state/market
- general/specific
- high/low
- top down/ bottom up
- long term/short term
- large scale/small scale
- master plan/incremental

Readers will no doubt find others.

PART II

THE ECONOMIC CONTEXT OF TOWN PLANNING

INTRODUCTION

This section comprises three chapters, in which the relationship between state intervention – as manifested in town planning – and the wider economic situation and property market context are discussed. Ironically, in Britain, within a mixed economy setting, town planning has generally been limited to controlling physical land uses, and has had little power to shape the urban economic factors which, arguably, create the demand for development in the first place. In Chapter 2 Peter Hobbs provides a theoretical context as to the rationale for town planning, and in Chapter 3 uses this as a basis for understanding the reasons why town planning developed in the way it did, with reference to an account of its development across the decades which comprise the post-war period. In Chapter 4 Nick Oatley retraces the evolution of planning policy with specific reference to the case of inner city regeneration, with attention being given to recent initiatives such as City Challenge and the Single Regeneration Budget. In the course of these chapters the reader should note that economic planning is not dealt with by the authors in isolation from other aspects of town planning, and in particular should bear in mind the impact that other 'plannings' – not least the challenge of environmental planning – has had upon policy approaches, and the possible links with social planning objectives. At this early stage in the book the reader should already be considering whether environmental and economic planning objectives (the green/red dualism) are compatible, in conflict, or mutually supportive in creating 'better planning'.

Chapter 2

THE MARKET ECONOMIC CONTEXT OF TOWN PLANNING

Peter Hobbs

The challenge of changing agendas

This chapter develops an explanation of British town planning which seeks to improve understanding of post-war changes in the activity and the implications of contemporary pressures for change. This explanation is centred on an investigation of the processes into which town planning intervenes, most particularly changes in the property development process. This involves tracing the major dimensions of change in post-war British town planning and relating these changes to the varying economic and property market contexts in which it has operated.

The need to develop such an understanding is, as explained in Chapter 1, more pressing than at any time over the past 15 years and, possibly since the mid 1940s. A number of factors have combined to suggest that British town planning is on the threshold of fundamental change. The potential significance of this change has been identified by a number of authors with, for instance, Begg (1991) arguing that:

> ... the notion of sustainable development marks a watershed in the evolution of town and country planning which potentially represents the greatest move forward since the Town and Country Planning Act of 1947.
>
> (quoted in Adams, 1994, p. 82)

The issue of sustainability coupled with changes in the context in which town planning operates means that:

> Over the next few years, the planning profession as a whole is likely to face an immense challenge in reflecting how best it can influence the production of the built environment in a market economy.
>
> (Adams, 1994, p. 69)

Within this context, it is important to understand the options that are available to town planning. This chapter examines the way material constraints have shaped the evolution of town planning in the recent past. An understanding of such constraints should be a critical issue in writing any new agendas for town planning in the late 1990s and beyond.

The scope of town planning for the purpose of this chapter is focused on the narrow, statutory definition preferred by Reade (1987), Rydin (1993) and Thornley (1993). This definition relates to the branch of government activity which influences the use, appearance, location, timing and density of land and property development and the relationship between uses. As we shall see, however, the range of measures for the control of the development process, and the institutional arrangements through which this control has taken place, has varied over time. For this reason, the broader context, in terms of other aspects of land policy and approaches to the provision of infrastructure, in which town planning policies have been devised and implemented, is discussed where relevant.

The economic and property market context is more broadly defined to include the organisation of the production and consumption of goods and services, and the level of activity involved in these processes. This definition involves more than simply the operation of the market, with an explicit recognition of the role of the public sector in producing and allocating resources.

The rationale and purpose of town planning

The rationale of town planning

In seeking to identify directions for change in town planning it is first necessary to establish the rationale of town planning, in other words, to understand precisely what town planning is seeking to achieve.

There are difficulties in defining the role of town planning, as one of the most enduring features about the process has been the tendency for planning concerns and activities to change dramatically over time. This process of continuous change has occurred despite the consistent promotion of formal planning goals to improve the rarely defined 'public interest'. The continuity and scale of change in the range of concerns and substantive activities in post-war British town planning have received wide coverage (Cullingworth, 1994; Greed, 1993; Reade, 1987; Rydin, 1993; Thornley, 1993; Ward, 1994). As has been colourfully observed by Reade (1987, pp. 113–114):

> Over the years, planners have donned one set of 'Emperor's new clothes' after another, now seeing themselves as designers of cities, now as 'systems analysts', now as 'allocators of scarce resources', now as 'urban managers', now as 'corporate planners', or 'social planners', or quantitative geographers, as analysts of 'social malaise', or even as bureaucratic guerillas, or 'planning aid' workers, intent on liberating oppressed minorities from official indifference. The guise most popular at the time of writing ... is that of promoters of entrepreneurial initiative.

Despite these changes in actual planning concerns, the activity has been carried out broadly within the same institutional framework and with the same formal planning goals. In institutional terms, British town planning has operated largely at the district and county levels of government within a legislative and national policy framework. The activity has not tended to control large expenditure budgets and was funded, up to 1981, entirely through taxation. Post-war British town planning has been essentially a regulative activity, covering most types of land development, with the notable exceptions of much agriculture and public sector development, in order to shape patterns of land use.

The formal rationale for planning control has been the improvement of the use and development of land in the public interest with much emphasis being placed upon the openness of town planning to the demands of the general public (Rydin, 1993). This control over development can be categorised into strategic land use allocations in terms of the quantity and location of land for different uses, and the more detailed control over the appearance, arrangement and density of development and relations between uses (Greed, 1993; Bruton and Nicholson, 1987; Pearce, 1992). This regulation of development has been exercised largely through the production of land use plans and development control.

Essentially, therefore, the post-war British planning has been characterised by continuity in the framework through which it has taken place, but within this framework, considerable change in its scope and emphasis. It appears, therefore, that the planning system has a high degree of adaptability, with, for instance, Healey (1992, p. 430) arguing that this:

> ... allowed the substantial shift to a narrow agenda in the early 1980s, to a negotiated project-based practice dominated by development values in the later 1980s, and to strategic concern for the integration of economic, environmental and social issues in the arena of managing land use and environmental change in the early 1990s.

This adaptability raises the question of precisely what determines town planning concerns at different points in time. The following section examines a range of different explanations of town planning to assess which perspective or perspectives might be the most useful in accounting for the evolution of the activity.

Explanations of town planning

The dimensions of change in the formal and actual concerns of town planning have been interpreted from a range of disciplines including economics, political science and geography (Barrett and Healey, 1985, pp. 6–12). This disciplinary-specific approach and the tendency to take different research traditions as mutually incompatible has tended to result in fragmented analyses of town planning. However, a more useful approach might be to understand the different traditions and perspectives on town planning as complementary in furthering an understanding of town planning. As Reade points out in an assessment of the range of social science explanations of town planning:

Though the various pieces of work on the subject focus often on quite different aspects of planning, and are indeed written from different philosophical and theoretical view points, it seems better to regard them as complementary rather than competitive, and to see all of them as valuable contributions towards our knowledge of this subject area.

(Reade, 1987, p. 118; see also Atkinson and Moon, 1994, p. 263)

The following brief review of five broadly distinct perspectives summarises the insights of each perspective in explaining both the role of town planning and the pressures for change in the town planning process. Each of these explanations is shown to have strengths and limitations in contributing to an understanding of the town planning process. On balance, it is shown that the most useful approach to explaining change in town planning is one that relates the planning process to the material circumstances in which it operates.

Theories of town planning practice

An underlying theme in British theories of town planning practice is the establishment of models or procedures to describe and prescribe for planning practice rather than to explain the activity. The emphasis in these theories has tended to be on the procedure or process of planning rather than the material reality of its consequences (Breheny and Hooper, 1985, pp. 1–14). This emphasis on procedure was strongest from the mid-1960s through to the late-1970s. But the relativity of planning theory and the failure to adopt a critical approach to the processes of land use change can be traced back to the 1940s and 1950s (Hebbert, 1977) and was pursued in practice and refined academically during the 1980s (Faludi, 1987; Hague, 1994).

Indeed, a number of commentators have observed that shifts in theories of planning practice over the past two decades have been associated with the retreat from the high public spending levels of the 1960s and 1970s (Harvey, 1985; Rydin, 1993; Yiftachel, 1989). The extent to which these theories and ideologies of planning practice have altered in response to changing material circumstances are explored later in the chapter. At this stage, however, it is clear that the relativity of theories of planning practice, and their lack of explanatory power, means they provide an inadequate context for attempting to explain contemporary pressures on town planning (Cooke, 1983a, pp. 64–66; Reade, 1987, p. 114).

Political, organisational and ideological perspectives

More analytical interpretations of town planning seek to explain planning through a range of pressures such as political, organisational and ideological factors. Such studies tend to emphasise the role of groups, individuals and ideas in bringing about change in town planning (Adams, 1994; Atkinson and Moon, 1994; Stoker and Young, 1993). These studies are helpful in increasing understanding of town planning but suffer from failing to explain many of the structural constraints on its operation.

Studies of the politics of town planning demonstrate that town planning, in shaping the pattern of land use, is inherently a political activity (Cox, 1984; McKay and Cox, 1979). Such accounts show that, with the exception of the betterment issue, there tends to be considerable party political consensus over the approach towards town planning at the national level. Similar conclusions are drawn at the local level of town planning where, due to the structure of local government, departmental or committee considerations are found to affect policy more than party political control.

These conclusions are supported by studies of the organisational aspects of planning, which demonstrate the strong role of central and local government bureaucracies, rather than politicians, in determining planning strategies and principles. Such studies reveal the limited scope for public participation in altering the principles of planning strategies, and the tendency of planning departments to pre-select information, thereby reducing the political input to planning decision making.

Despite such conclusions, studies of the organisational and political aspects of planning have also revealed the ability of community groups or interests to determine planning agendas and to shape planning outcomes. This was particularly the case during the late-1960s and early-1970s in reaction to the comprehensive development proposals and motorway building of the time (Loney, 1983; Wates, 1976), and again in the late-1980s and early-1990s in response to a variety of development proposals (Rydin, 1993; Shucksmith, 1990). These and other studies have demonstrated that in certain circumstances such interests and groups play a critical role in determining planning outcomes.

Analyses of town planning ideology at the national and local levels tend to reveal changes in the nature of planning ideology over time. They also reveal the general uncertainty over the role of planning which pervades planning practice, and the strong procedural basis to planning ideologies (Healey and Underwood, 1978; Hebbert, 1977; Reade, 1987; Yiftachel, 1989). These studies, in exploring the significance of individuals and groups in bringing forward new planning issues onto the policy agenda, demonstrate that it is individuals and groups rather than planning departments who determine strategies. Yet they also reveal constraints on the scope for individual action due to the working ideology and organisational approach of the department.

Research on the political, organisational and ideological aspects of town planning has contributed to an understanding of the variety of planning practices and the process of planning activity. Such research identifies inconsistencies in planning but fails to explain them coherently. It shows that party politics do not determine the planning process, that planning ideology is essentially procedural and relative, and that there is limited scope for individual planning officer action within the organisational approach of planning institutions. These conclusions raise the question of what precisely determines change in town planning. Such research also poses the problem of attempting to:

> ... generalise from detailed practices to statements about the characteristics of government intervention in land and development, about development processes, about forces which structure, shape or influence both, and about the purposes and effects of such interventions.
>
> (Healey, 1982, p. 185; see also Atkinson and Moon, 1994, pp. 7–10)

We shall see later that there has been considerable development in these approaches by linking them more explicitly to the material, or 'structural', context in which planning operates.

Town planning to rectify market failures

One of the perspectives that, during the 1980s and early 1990s, became more widely recognised as providing a rationale for town planning was that of welfare economics (Adams, 1994; Evans, 1985; Harvey, 1987; Reade, 1987; Rydin, 1993). Although politically and conceptually distinct from neo-liberal and New Right perspectives (Atkinson and Moon, 1994, pp. 11–15; Thornley, 1993), the rise of this perspective was based on changing material circumstances, most particularly the increasing economic and political emphasis being placed on 'market' criteria in the operation of town planning practice (Hague, 1991). Within this context, town planning came to be more explicitly identified with the regulation of various forms of externalities.

The principles of welfare economics rest on the neo-classical presumption that governments should intervene to achieve improvements in efficiency or equity by rectifying market failures. The property market is seen as a special case: a market with a specific series of market failures, particularly associated with externalities, such as the provision of public goods and imperfect information. Town planning is seen as a response to these problems, designed to ensure an acceptable form and scale of development (Adams, 1994; Evans, 1985; Keogh, 1985; Harvey, 1987; Reade, 1987; Willis, 1980). This is summarised by Evans (1985, p. 195):

> From a land-use planning framework the most important cause of market failure is the existence of externalities of one kind or another, either external economies or diseconomies. With respect to land use in an urban area external effects are endemic. Transactions between one party and another can rarely be 'private' in the sense that they affect no-one not a party to the transaction. Any development affects others, in its construction, its appearance, and its use.

Although welfare economics is normative and concerned largely with the reasons for town planning, it generates insights into resource allocation in the land market, into market failures, and the relationship between town planning and economic conditions. These insights, especially in helping identify and quantify externalities, might have considerable potential for the practice of town planning. Indeed, Reade (1987, p. 7) argues that perhaps the only valid case for planning might be '... the process of maximising the aggregate margin of positive externalities over negative ones, by "re-arranging land uses" ...' (see also Adams, 1994; Rydin, 1993).

Despite these insights, there are serious limitations on the ability of the welfare economics to provide an explanation of change in town planning. A fundamental limitation is the failure to capture the multicausality and complexity of the relationship between economic and planning change. A further limitation is the conception of planning intervention as standing outside the operation of the market and fulfilling a social reformist role as part of general state strategies for the alleviation of povery, unemployment and inequalities. This is based on the assumption that '... market-type relations and institutions are optimal for all individual and organisational goal-achievement' (Cooke, 1983a, p. 65) and will result in socially acceptable improvements. This conception of the role of the state and planning is fundamentally challenged by materialist interpretations. Scott (1980, p. 82), for instance, concludes a critique of neo-classical urban theory by arguing that planners are:

> ... engaged in practical work whose purpose is not to achieve full Pareto efficiency via remedial adjustments of the urban land market, but to resolve in political terms the disruptive effects and failures of that market in relation to the functional imperatives of commodity-producing society.

We can conclude, therefore, that despite its insights, the failure of welfare economics perspectives to allow for the structuring pressures which create change in planning represent fundamental problems in such attempts to explain the evolution of the activity.

Materialist perspectives

A common theme of materialist explanations for state activity is the support by the British post-war state for the process of capital accumulation. This support comes by providing social and economic infrastructure for capital accumulation and by legitimising the operation of that system (Cooke, b, 1983). Through the power of law, and expenditure financed by taxation, the state has some autonomy to operate outside of market criteria. This autonomy enables the state to run counter to market trends and conflict with individual capitals in order to ensure the overall capital accumulation process will not be disrupted by contradictions. This state intervention is, however, limited so that the fundamental capitalist nature of the economy will not be overridden. A persistent theoretical and empirical issue in materialist debate about the state has been the nature and extent of state autonomy from broader economic pressures.

Materialist perspectives on town planning have paralleled the development of materialist explanations of state activity. Within the early political economy explanations of the 1970s, town planning fulfilled functional and legitimatory roles in the process of land development (Castells, 1977; Harvey, 1973). Castells' work of the mid-1970s stressed the role of town planning in legitimising the urban development process through its guise of rationality, technical neutrality and apparent concern for the public interest (Castells, 1977, p. 76). The planning system was understood to exist in order '... to seem to be resolving social conflict equitably in a pluralist framework.' The planning system helped '... sustain a pluralist and participatory myth, especially at the local level ...' (Edwards, 1979, p. 23).

This approach underemphasised the functional role of town planning in the process of capitalist development (Cooke, 1983b, p. 144; Healey, 1983, p. 252), and other commentators explored the role of town planning in response to contradictions in the process of land development. The private ownership and control of land and the competitive orientation of private firms generate a range of contradictions, such as barriers to the development of land and the failure to provide collective infrastructure (Harvey, 1985; Scott, 1980). Town planning was seen to play a functional role in overcoming these contradictions. It organised and coordinated the provision of infrastructure with private development and facilitated the operation of the land market in order to increase economic efficiency and profitability.

These explanations of town planning provided significant insights into its operation by relating different town planning functions to the economic processes in which they operated. In doing this they revealed an implicit conflict over the allocation of resources underlying the apparent political consensus of the 1960s. In addition, they showed the limited power of town planning to challenge dominant economic processes. Finally, they revealed a tendency for planning strategies to be determined after fundamental directions of growth had been established. There were, however, significant shortcomings in these approaches, particularly the lack of attention paid to the form of town planning intervention and the methodological difficulties associated with structuralist materialist perspectives. There was a tendency for town planning explanations both to suffer from circular arguments and to place low significance on actual empirical events. As a result, the limited empirical research carried out within the political economy perspective tended to retreat into simplifications and broad generalisations despite stressing the need to 'ground the research in reality'. The low significance placed on empirical events meant:

> The discussion of class categories, of social movements, of the relation between the political and the economic seem to fall all too frequently into the traps of mechanistic theorising which can only be connected to actual experience in crude and often naive ways.
>
> (Healey, 1982, p. 193; see also Atkinson and Moon, 1994, p. 263)

From the end of the 1970s attempts were made to move away from these structuralist explanations in an attempt to understand more clearly the form and content of the state and town planning interventions. The 'dual-state' thesis proposed by Saunders (1979, 1986), for instance, sought to link economic interests to the ways in which state agencies operate and the levels of the state at which these activities are located. The great strengths of the Saunders thesis were in challenging functionalist interpretations of the local state as an agent of the national state and in developing the concept of different, corporatist or competitive, modes through which the state intervened in response to different types of economic interest (Healey, 1983, pp. 258–261).

Such perspectives still suffered from weaknesses associated with oversimplistic and mechanistic theorising. In addition, the relevance of such critical perspectives was challenged during the 1980s by the pressures facing planning practice and education (Hague, 1991). The overall result was to lead, in the latter half of the 1980s, to attempts to integrate agency and structural factors.

The 'structure and agency' perspective

In response to the weaknesses of the materialist approaches and the descriptive nature of organisational and ideological approaches, attempts were made in the late 1980s and early 1990s to integrate the various perspectives. These attempts, which were spurred by the work of Healey and Barret (1990), had two distinguishing features. First, they sought to:

> ... set the strategies, interest and actions of individuals and organisations within the context of broader social, economic and political processes.
>
> (Adams, 1994, p. 65)

As such they sought to connect:

> ... actor-based or institutional forms of analysis ... with relevant perspectives from neoclassical and Marxist economics.
>
> (Adams, 1994, p. 65)

Such perspectives, variously termed the 'structure and agency' or 'institutional' approach, recognise that the interests and actions of different actors in the town planning and property development process take place within the context of broader, structural, forces. They argue, however, that such interests and actions are:

> ... not automatically determined by such dominant social and economic forces. People can choose simply to accept and respond to powerful forces or instead, they can begin to challenge and transform them ... agency behaviour is diverse and always capable of challenging and transforming whatever constitutes the structural framework at any time.
>
> (Adams, 1994, pp. 67–68; see also Rydin, 1993, p. 74)

27

The second distinguishing feature was to relate change in town planning to the development process into which it intervened. This research on the political economy of the development process explored the complex processes through which land conversion took place, the role of different agents at various stages of the process and how changing macroeconomic conditions might drive the development process (Adams *et al.*, 1994; Ball, 1983; Barras, 1987, 1994; Barrett and Healey, 1985; Fraser, 1993; Harvey, 1985; Keogh, 1994). This has increased understanding of town planning through revealing the complex nature of its substantive concern, the process of land use change.

The 'structure and agency' perspective generates a number of insights into the operation of town planning most particularly by linking outcomes of planning activities to the economic, political and ideological context in which it operates (Rydin, 1993, p. 74). In particular, the perspective moved the understanding of town planning away from the 'overly abstract, overly idealist, and overly mechanistic' theorising of structuralist political economy interpretations (Healey, 1986, p. 106).

There remain, however, a number of important weaknesses associated with this perspective on change. In theoretical terms, the perspective has been criticised for its theoretical eclectism which, it is argued, means it contains irreconcilable conceptual elements (Hooper, 1992; Rydin, 1993, p. 73). Empirically, there are two main difficulties. First, difficulties arising from the complexity of the analysis. The range of the influences on specific outcomes means:

> The problem in analysis is 'keeping all the balls in the air' and allowing for: the dynamics of economic processes interrelation of actors; planners as mediators and a sectional interest group; planners as promoting change and being constrained in so doing; planning as structured by and involved in structuring social processes.
>
> (Rydin, 1993, p. 75)

Second, and related to the first of these difficulties, is a tendency for research to focus on the specificity of town planning interventions at the expense of identifying general patterns. A growing body of research has been conducted in this area, including the work of Adams *et al.* (1994) and Healey *et al.* (1992). Such empirical research contributes to the understanding of town planning by exploring the mechanisms by which economic forces are translated into planning strategies and planning activity. There remains a danger that such research focuses unduly on the specificity of change and this, in turn, generates problems in generalising from particular locations or eras.

Material pressures for change in town planning: the economy and the property development process

The range of perspectives discussed above provides insights into the operation and evolution of town planning. Each of the perspectives falls short of being able to offer a convincing explanation of change in town planning. The most recent developments in the institutional perspective appear to overcome many of the weaknesses by focusing on the interaction between 'structure' and 'agency'. Despite the potential of this perspective, studies tend to be focused on the specificity of change, and there is a need for a more general examination of the relationship between the economic context and town planning. A number of studies have implicitly linked town planning to the broader social and economic context with, for instance, Rydin (1993, p. 6) providing a 'Fairly rough and ready periodisation ...' in the relationships (see also Atkinson and Moon, 1993; Thornley, 1993), but there remains a need for a more systematic analysis of the relationships.

The remainder of this chapter provides such a systematic examination of the way town planning has been structured by the material context into which it intervenes. This examination is based on two central assumptions regarding the evolution of post-war British town planning. First, it is assumed that the institutional arrangements through which town planning has been carried out and the regulative nature of British town planning have remained essentially unchanged over the past 50 years. This assumption is based on the conclusions of Cherry (1994, p. 291) and others, that town planning:

> ... has continued to rest on the obligatory duty of local planning authorities to pre-pare development plans and to have them regularly reviewed, and to control public and private development against their basic provisions. Planning policies have come and gone, fashions and local preferences have varied and changing circumstances have necessitated revisions to the planning agenda. Yet continuities are more apparent than discontinuities; the system has been robust enough to withstand change and disruption.

The second assumption relates to the procedural nature of planning methodologies as discussed in Section 2.2 above. This emphasis on planning procedures means that although town planning is carried out to improve the, generally undefined, 'public interest', the relativity of town planning practice enables the introduction of marked changes in its substantive goals and scope.

Given these essential characteristics of post-war town planning, the regulative and procedural nature of town planning practice, it is necessary to identify dominant material pressures on the operation of town planning. There are two such pressures: first, the general processes of economic change and levels of economic performance which represent the material context within which town planning operates; second, the processes of land use and development which are the substantive concerns of town planning.

There is a wide range of materialist interpretations of the processes of capitalist development (see Aaronovitch and Smith, 1981; Cooke, 1983a; Harvey, 1982, 1985). The approach adopted here presumes that the drive to accumulate profits, through reducing costs and increasing markets, constitutes the core of economic activity and structures social and political change.

On this interpretation, accumulation is carried out through the uneven process involved in establishing, expanding and disintegrating dominant forms of accumulation, based upon particular processes of production, technologies and labour relations. These processes occur unevenly over time and space. The broadly alternating long phases in the expansion and contraction of economic growth have complex implications for different regions and localities, depending largely upon their industrial structure and the nature of prevailing dominant processes of production.

Attempts at identifying the driving force behind these different phases of economic activity are controversial (Massey, 1984; van Duijn, 1983). The process of uneven economic change can, however, be interpreted in terms of long waves of economic activity during each of which a related cluster of fundamental new technologies emerge. These new technologies, coupled with suitable social and organisational relations, can act as the driving force for the introduction and expansion of wholly new branches of industry (Barras, 1987; Johnston and Gardiner, 1991, pp. 2–4; Marshall, 1987; van Duijn, 1983). This expansion can lead to periods of sustained economic growth, the rate of which may vary depending on a combination of material, institutional and social factors. These include opportunities for new markets and investments and the quality, cost and availability of labour and raw materials. This growth continues until the markets become saturated, when innovation slows down and industries become less efficient. This leads to a period of structural recession which triggers a new wave of technical changes.

The process of capital accumulation and the competitive drive to create profits persistently gives rise to a series of general economic contradictions (Harvey, 1985; Massey, 1984; Scott, 1980). These include the continual restructuring of dominant processes of production to changing technologies and market opportunities, and the contradiction between short term capital accumulation and longer term capital reproduction. Capitalist economies also tend to fail in providing certain collective goods, services and infrastructure. Public sector expenditure arises largely in response to these contradictory processes. Public and private activity can, therefore, be seen as mutually dependent, with much of the cost of the private sector being socialised and both sectors being geared to the support of the accumulative process (Scott, 1988).

More specific contradictions relate to the process of land use and development. Integral to the consecutive long phases of economic activity are the uneven spatial, land use, property development and infrastructural processes of economic change. Each dominant round of new investment tends to be associated with particular spatial distributions of social and economic processes (Cooke, 1983; Hall and Markusen, 1985; Massey, 1984). Important aspects of these spatial variations in activity are the contradictions in the flexibility and mobility of capital and the immobility of productive capital and labour. Productive machinery, infrastructure and labour are relatively immobile. This means that the process of capital accumulation tends to proceed by establishing centres or areas of stable production and consumption, termed variously 'ensembles of production' (Scott, 1988) or 'spatial fixes' (Duncan *et al.*, 1988). As macroeconomic conditions change, the mobility of capital generates pressure both to deconstruct existing centres of production geared to previous dominant modes of production and restructure them to conditions more relevant to prevailing macroeconomic conditions. These pressures account for differential local economic performance and the competitive pressures between different localities.

The changing economic pressures and locational requirements of economic activity throughout long cycles are characterised 'by a distinctive pattern of building in terms of the type, location and physical characteristics of the buildings being produced' (Barras, 1987, p. 12). Property and infrastructural development tends to take place through cycles of activity, with a tendency for building activity and the production of capital goods to overshoot and undershoot demand due to the lagged response involved in the production of the built environment (Barras, 1987; van Duijn, 1983).

The long wave concept can be criticised for its inability to explain processes within long cycles or to account for the marked social, economic and institutional differences between long cycles. As stated by Marshall:

> Every long wave of capitalist development has entailed certain invariant features which are present in every historical phase. For example, they all involve short-term fluctuations, crisis tendencies and qualitative technological advances. ... But the nature and form of these factors vary markedly between each historical phase. There is no panhistorical theory of long waves capable of explaining the qualitative changes in their historical form.
>
> (Marshall, 1987, p. 226; see also Barras, 1994, p. 184)

Yet these are necessary limitations, due to the historical specificity of economic and social change. Long waves or phases can, as a result, provide essentially descriptive frameworks for investigating different processes of economic activity and levels of economic performance over time and space. In the next chapter the development of town planning in the post war period will be discussed in relation to the changing economic context.

Chapter 3

POST-WAR ECONOMIC DEVELOPMENT AND TOWN PLANNING INTERVENTION

Peter Hobbs

Post-war trends

Interpreting the activity

It is difficult to define economic and property development pressures for change unambiguously. This difficulty arises partly from the complexity of economic activity. In addition, what is referred to as 'economic' at any time is actually a set of social phenomena so that different economic indicators have different political, social and economic significance at different times and from different perspectives (Massey, 1984, p. 44).

Despite the acknowledged difficulties, it is clear that economic indicators relate to changing material pressures to which individuals respond (Aaronovitch and Smith, 1981; Saunders, 1986). Indeed, that political action is often based on incomplete theories and incorrect indicators merely demonstrates the strength of indicators in determining political action. For

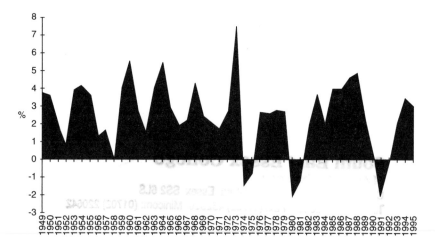

Fig. 3.1 Annual change in real GDP growth rate, 1945–1995

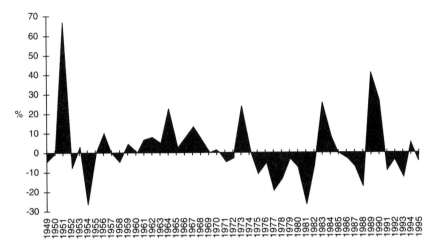

Fig. 3.2 Annual change in real government capital expenditure, 1945–1995

this reason, a number of indicators of economic and property development activity can be used as a basis for discussing the major trends and pressures during the post-war years.

The three indicators are the Gross Domestic Product (GDP), Government Capital Expenditure and New Orders for Development. The Gross Domestic Product, which measures the total value of final economic output, represents the level of economic activity in a given economy. The clear fluctuations in post-war British economic activity are revealed in Fig. 3.1, which shows annual change in the rate of growth of GDP. These fluctuations in GDP provide an important indicator of absolute prosperity and overall economic performance. A rise in GDP might materially benefit the general public in a number of ways. It might increase take-home pay or enable an increase in public expenditure on health, education or environmental improvements. Consequently, the growth rate of GDP provides an indicator of the material scope for government intervention. Of more direct significance has been the use of GDP as an input into policy making and its political importance in determining state strategies.

The second measure, that of Government Capital Expenditure, has been an important component of economic activity for two distinct reasons. Most fundamentally, such expenditure fulfils part of the broader role of the public sector in providing services which might otherwise not be produced by the market economy. Such development can be understood as either 'social' infrastructure (such as housing, education and recreation facilities) or 'productive' infrastructure (such as roads, rail and utilities which can serve to increase the productivity of the economy as a whole). Second, the government capital expenditure programme is shaped by its concern to ensure economic stability. The government capital expenditure programme is more responsive to change than government current expenditure as the latter,

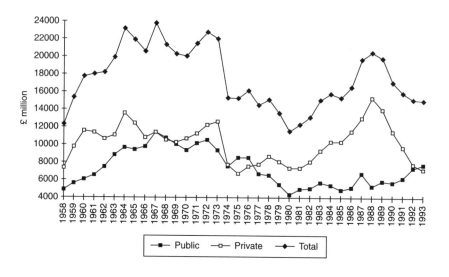

Fig. 3.3   Public and private new orders for development, real prices 1958–1993

which relates to salaries and contractual expenditure, can be difficult to vary over the short term. For this reason, the government capital expenditure programme is often used as a tool for macroeconomic policy. Post-war variations in government capital spending, presented in Fig. 3.2, could be expected to be an important influence on town planning, largely due to the potential role of planning in organising infrastructural investment.

The third measure, the level of new orders for development (Fig. 3.3), provides an indicator of secular trends and fluctuations in building activity. Although this indicator has only been produced since 1958, it reveals important differences in the composition of development activity, between the public and private sectors. It also provides a benchmark for more qualitative analysis of fluctuations in different types of development in different locations (Ball, 1983; Barras, 1987, 1994).

Table 3.1   Structural shifts in post-war UK economic performance

Period	GDP	Government Capital Expenditure
	Average annual growth (%)	
1949–1972	2.9	4.4
1972–1995	2.1	−0.9

Source: As for Figures 3.1 and 3.2.

Post-war economic pressures for change

The fifty year period between 1945–1995 can be divided into the period of structural economic growth from the late-1940s to the early-1970s and the period of low economic growth and restructuring from the early-1970s to the mid-1990s. The differences in the nature of economic and property development activity are revealed in the graphs presented above and the average annual rates of growth summarised in Table 3.1.

The marked differences in the rates of growth shown in Table 3.1 are based on a combination of international and domestic economic factors. The early period was one:

> ... in which the world economy enjoyed an unprecedented phase of expansion in the aftermath of the Second World War, fuelled by the explosive growth of a raft of new technologies and industries including electronics, oil and petrochemicals, pharmaceutical and vehicles ...
>
> (Barras, 1994, p. 187)

This contrasted with the period since the early 1970s during which there was:

> ... slower growth in the world economy, as the dynamics of the long postwar upswing finally ran out of steam. The industries which fuelled that expansion reached maturity, so that their potential for further technical progress and productivity gains diminished, halting the increase in investment and checking the rate of growth in output.
>
> (Barras, 1994, p. 187)

This structural shift in economic performance has important implications for the operation of town planning. However, superimposed on these structural changes have been short term cycles of economic activity, each of which has different characteristics (CSO, 1976, 1993, 1995a and b). These cycles, defined in Table 3.2, can provide the basis for a more detailed analysis of changes in industrial structure, technology, land use, the spatial organisation of the economy and macroeconomic policies which are embodied in the broadly distinct economic context of each cycle.

Table 3.2 Average percentage change in key economic and property indicators, 1945–1995

Period	GDP	Government Capital Expenditure
1949–51	3.1	20.1
1951–58	2.2	4.9
1958–63	3.0	3.2
1963–67	3.3	10.4
1967–72	2.6	2.3
1972–75	2.0	3.0
1975–81	1.0	−12.4
1981–85	2.1	−0.1
1985–92	2.2	3.3
1992–95	2.1	4.4

Source: As for Figures 3.1 and 3.2.

The years of the first cycle (1945–1951) were ones of physical and economic reconstruction following the Second World War, economic austerity, and heavy, if decreasing, public sector intervention. The immediate economic priority after the war lay with reconstructing the domestic non-military economy. This involved dismantling the military orientation of the economy and increasing industrial output in order to relieve the Balance of Payments deficit (Dow, 1970, 13–18). Public sector investment, which rose in the years immediately following the war, played a major role in physical infrastructure and housing provision and in increasing export-based production (Fig. 3.2) (Smyth, 1985). Property development continued to be largely public sector financed and organised.

The spatial organisation of state policies was, following the Barlow Report of 1940, central to the post-war economic reconstruction. The importance of such a spatial approach lay behind the large-scale state expenditure on the built environment (Ball, 1983, p. 220). It also lay behind the Treasury domination of regional policy and the new towns strategy. Regional policy, introduced under the 1945 Distribution of Industry Act, embodied a range of measures including the requirements for Industrial Development Certificates (IDCs) from the Board of Trade, the administrators of the policy, for the development of industrial plants over a certain size and incentives to locate in certain depressed 'development areas' (Hall, 1975, pp. 108–109).

During the second and third cycles (1951–1958), there was strong economic growth based upon the adaption of new technologies and the expansion of production (Fig. 3.1). Government capital expenditure was low and the average for the period would have been considerably lower but for a near 10% increase in such expenditure between 1951 and 1952 associated with the Korean War (Fig. 3.2). Development activity, the bulk of which was housing development (Barras, 1987, p. 11), was concentrated on existing centres and in the new towns designated in the 1940s.

Economic pressures were broadly similar in the fourth and fifth economic cycles (1958–1963 and 1963–1967). These years were characterised by major economic restructuring, strong economic growth and the widespread adoption of new technologies, with the state playing a major role in supporting the modernisation and rationalisation of industry, especially through infrastructure and property development. The cyclical and structural economic growth, as well as the growing spatial mobility of these years, lay behind the high and rising levels of public and private sector property development (Figs. 3.1–3.3).

The restructuring processes of rationalisation and modernisation in the face of new technologies and markets had distinct spatial implications and led to growing state involvement in economic change (Ball, 1983, pp. 249–251). New investment was carried out largely by multinational corporations which were less tied to local economic linkages. This locational mobility came at a time when the rationalisation of traditional industries provided a potential source of labour to compensate for the perceived absolute shortages of labour in the South East and West Midlands. Setting up in

Development Areas both eased pressure on wages and made it easier to employ different types of workforce (Massey, 1984, pp. 245–248). These years experienced the strongest attempts at economic planning since the immediate post-war years, with large-scale public spending and the adoption of modernisation strategies for the restructuring of industry.

The sixth (1967–1972) and seventh (1972–1975) cycles represented the crest of the long post-war boom. This was a period of continuing economic growth (Fig. 3.1) but growing uncertainty due to the stagnation of demand and the lack of international competitiveness in British industry. Structural weaknesses in the economy were concealed by the speculative economic and property market boom of 1972/3, but the recession of 1974/5 marked the end of the post-war boom (Fig. 3.1). The government did not respond immediately to these economic pressures, with government spending rising to its highest level over an economic cycle since the 1940s and revived attempts being made to develop corporate economic management.

The recession of 1974/5 led into a major economic slowdown and marked changes in macroeconomic policy during the eighth (1975–1981) cycle. The sharp end to the post-war boom was heralded by low and negative rates of growth and investment (Fig. 3.1), the massive loss of employment, particularly in manufacturing industry, the post-war slump in building and infrastructure provision (Fig. 3.3) and steady rises in unemployment. Many of the underlying economic problems at the time, such as the rise in inflation, falls in profitability and investment, and declines in international competitiveness were associated with the supply side of the economy (Aaronovitch and Smith, 1981, pp. 165–167). These changes in the nature of economic activity reduced the power of the government to control the economy through macroeconomic measures and lay behind the move away from Keynesian economic policies to focus on the supply side of the economy.

The severity of the recession at the start of the 1980s meant that the ninth cycle (1981–1985) was characterised by dramatic falls in investment, employment and growth in GDP, and an unprecedented rise in unemployment (Armstrong et al., 1985). The sharp rise in oil prices, the reductions in international demand and the rise of the British exchange rate were based on structural changes in economic activity. Although the economy came out of recession in 1982, the level of unemployment remained high and manufacturing investment and production low.

Prior to the end of the decade, the following cycle (1985–1992) was a period of strong growth based on favourable international conditions, the introduction of new technologies and the 'Lawson Boom' of 1987–1988 (Fig. 3.1). The expansionary North American economic strategy created a growing world market for the first time since the early-1970s. The introduction of new technologies, which involved the scrapping of obsolete, low productivity capital stock, the expansion of computing and new technology related industries and the application of new technology to established manufacturing industries, increased productivity and efficiency. North Sea oil provided the scope to reduce taxes and reduce the Balance of Payments pressure on domestic economic policies. These economic changes were associated with a changing ideological framework of economic management with the emerging dominant theme emphasising the advantages of market processes, the role of the private sector in generating wealth and the difficulties associated with a large public sector (Rydin, 1993, p. 60).

The economic growth of the late-1980s, which occurred unevenly between and within regions, led to unprecedented levels of private sector development activity (Fig. 3.3) (DTZ, 1994; Hall and Preston, 1988). These high levels of development were based on a combination of changing and rising levels of user demand and changes in the investment market (Barras, 1994; Keogh, 1993). The changes associated with the move towards 'flexible specialisation' production patterns generated new pressures on urban development, including:

> ... a more diversified pattern of development, more dispersed settlement, growth of the service sector and high technology firms, a new urban imagery linked to the individualised consumption patterns of the service class ...
>
> (Hague, 1991, p. 305)

Despite the growth of the late-1980s, the early-1990s experienced a severe and sustained economic and property market recession (Figs 3.1 and 3.3). The recession in the property market led to sharp falls in development activity, with the level of new starts in 1993 being 30% of the level at the peak in 1987, and the lowest level at least since the late-1950s (Fig. 3.3).

Despite the severity of the early-1990s recession, the economy made a strong recovery during the early years of the final cycle (1992–1995). This recovery was based initially on consumer spending and, more recently, on the strong growth in exports (CSO, 1994), which, in turn, was based upon the devaluation of the pound at the end of 1993.

The overview provided above demonstrates the marked differences in economic and property development activity since the 1950s. The most dramatic change relates to the structural shift in economic performance which occurred during the early-1970s. Overarching these structural shifts were the changes in technology, transportation and production patterns. This shift from 'Fordist' to 'post-Fordist' regimes generated pressures on urban development, with widespread decentralisation of economic activity and people from major conurbations. These pressures on the built environment were punctuated by three major waves of development activity, the first in the early 1960s, the second in the early-1970s and the third in the late-1970s.

Changes in the role of town planning

Interpreting changes in town planning

There are difficulties in measuring variations in the national town planning framework. The holistic nature of planning legislation and informal planning guidance, and the time lag in its production, complicate the measurement of how and when changes in the national framework are introduced. It is, however, possible to capture the essential changes in important dimensions of town planning which, together, can be taken to represent overall change in the activity.

The basic post-war British town planning framework, established under the 1947 Town and Country Planning Act, comprises legislation and national guidance for the control over land use change which is exercised largely at the level of local government. The central instruments through which this control is exercised are land use plans, development control and provisions for the taxation of development value. In order to capture the essence of the planning framework, its measurement can be based upon assessments of the instruments through which planning control is exercised, on four distinct dimensions.

The first dimension is town planning legislation and national guidance, as well as arguments and debates leading to the introduction of change in the framework. National legislation and guidance structure these instruments in terms of their purpose in land use control (for instance, the type of land use change subject to, and exempt from, planning control), the stringency of that control and the range of concerns in the exercise of that control. These aspects of the national framework can be interpreted to identify range and nature of planning concerns at any point in time. It is possible, however, to establish what is perceived to be relevant planning concerns at different periods in terms, for instance, of physical, economic, environmental or social issues, and the emphasis placed on the achievement of these different objectives.

The second dimension relates to the way in which town planning is carried out in practice. This relates to a range of issues including the content of local plans, the approach to development control and the ideology or spirit of town planning. These issues represent important indicators of the scope and nature of town planning concerns.

Third, the institutional arrangements through which town planning is carried out indicate the status and role of the activity. Issues here involve the degree to which town planning coordinates the activities of other statutory bodies, the degree of public participation and the relationship between local and national government.

The fourth dimension has, at times, represented a major component of the national framework for the control of land use and development, that of development value taxation (Lichfield and Darin-Drabkin, 1980; Reade, 1987). Development value taxation, based on the taxation of the gain accruing from the development of land, can be interpreted as, first, a tool to achieve more orderly development through dealing with the effects on land prices arising from planning control (Lin, 1987, pp. 40–43); second, a method of channelling investment to reduce land speculation, particularly in preventing the perceived diversion of investment from industry (Lin, 1987, pp. 45–48). The purposes for which development values are taxed, the level of the tax and its incidence can provide an indicator of the purpose and degree of planning intervention.

Key periods in post-war British town planning

On the basis of the four dimensions explained above, it is possible to identify a number of distinct periods in the town planning framework. These periods are summarised in Table 3.3 to show that the nature and emphasis of town planning has changed dramatically over the past 50 years.

As the quotation by Reade (1987) at the start of the chapter illustrates, town planning has pursued different goals in different ways throughout the latter half of the 20th century. In essence, four distinct types of town planning can be identified from Table 3.3. First, the 'architect/designer' approach that dominated during the late-1940s, when the scope of planning control concentrated on the physical and technical aspects of land use change. Second, the 'amenity/environmental' concerns of the 1950s and the early 1960s. Third, the broad and strategic 'functional/allocational' approaches that dominated during the 1960s and early 1970s. Fourth, the 'entrepreneurial' approaches of the late-1970s and the 1980s.

There are a range of factors that have combined to produce the distinctive nature of town planning in each of these periods. It is argued here, however, that the fundamental factor has been the material circumstances in which town planning has sought to intervene. For this reason, the following summary examines the relationship between dominant approaches to town planning and prevailing economic pressures.

During the first period (1945–1949) comprehensive town planning received widespread political support and contributed both to the physical and economic reconstruction, and the revival of post-war morale (Backwell and Dickens, 1978, pp. 7–8; Cullingworth, 1975, pp. 241–253; Greed, 1993, p. 117; Reade, 1987, pp. 50–51). Institutional arrangements meant that town planning was based on dominant, public sector, forces behind economic change. Yet town planning did not coordinate these public sector programmes as originally envisaged and, due to the limited scale of private development, the apparent stringency of the Development Charge represented lenient control over development (Healey *et al.*, 1988, p. 14). In practice, therefore, the main contribution of town planning came through the design and technical orchestration of the rebuilding programme.

The narrowing of planning concerns preceded the change of Government in 1951 and continued throughout the 1950s (1950–1959) (Glass, 1959). The tightening of control over development was based on growing affluence, infrastructural constraints and the reduced public sector economic role. This stringency did not, therefore, represent a challenge to economic growth with other changes, such as the abolition of the Development Charge, coming in response to growing private sector development.

During the third period (1960–1969), town planning concerns were broadened to cover the economic and social aspects of change (Greed, 1993, pp. 118–128). This shift in concerns paralleled the wider moves to indicative planning as the Government sought to encourage the scale of economic growth and organise large-scale infrastructural expenditure (Friend and Jessop, 1969). The formal broadening of town planning under the 1968 Town and Country Planning Act was introduced at a time of retreats from the indicative planning of the economy (Rees and Lambert, 1985, pp. 108–109).

This tendency to undermine broader town planning initiatives continued during the fourth period (1970–1975) when moves towards corporatist approaches in town planning associated with local government reorganisation were undermined by the 1974/5 recession (Ball, 1983, p. 245; Rees and Lambert, 1985, pp. 114–115). The abolition of taxation of development value in 1971 and measures to increase the supply of land paralleled monetary measures which fuelled the speculative property boom of the early 1970s. Development value taxation was only reintroduced after the peaking of the property boom.

During the fifth period (1976–1980) moves were made towards the narrowing of planning concerns. The pressures for this change in town planning came from moves in national economic strategies to free the supply side of the economy and reduce public expenditure. Both these changes came in response to structural economic changes and before both the recession of 1979–81 and the change in government in 1979.

The sixth period (1981–1989) was characterised by a growing 'entrepreneurial' approach to town planning. The narrowing and relaxation of planning concerns was spurred by the recession of the early 1980s, and ran in parallel with the economic strategies of deregulation for the remainder of the decade (Greed, 1993, pp. 136–137; Hague, 1991; Jones, 1989a; Thornley, 1993). The dismantling of a strategic approach to planning and the tendency to plan through development control and appeals was linked with increasing emphasis on competition and a reduced formal role for the public sector. This relaxation, competition and the ensuing fragmentation of approaches to town planning accommodated the pressures for more dispersed patterns of urban development and the uneven patterns of development that were occurring throughout the country.

The changes introduced during the final period (1990–1995) appeared to herald a new era in British town planning. These changes, and particularly the emphasis on sustainability, had links with the growing international concern over the depletion of resources and damage to the environment (Blowers, 1993; Marshall, 1994). The proposals to return to a more formal, plan-led, planning system had, however, been initiated earlier than the growing concerns over the environment. The period of the late-1980s saw considerable debate over the future direction and scope of British town planning (Brindley et al., 1989; Healey, 1989). A central concern within this debate was

Table 3.3 Key periods in post-war British town planning, 1945–1995

Era	Legislation & national guidance	Town planning practice	Institutional arrangements	Development value taxation
1945–1949 **The introduction of comprehensive town planning**	Creation of a national framework for the control of land use change through the 1947 Town and Country Planning Act.	Development Plan as the tool for coordinating public sector-led development. Scope of control based on physical, amenity and technical aspects of land use change.	Bulk of town planning carried out at local level, with strong national control over scope of concerns through the Development Plan public inquiry process.	Introduction of 100% Development Charge to remove speculation in the property market, and to enable the achievement of planning proposals.
1950–1959 **Downgrading and narrowing of town planning**	Relaxation of control early in the decade as indicated by the 1950 General Development Order, Circular 58/51 and the 1953 Town and Country Planning Act, followed by a narrowing and tightening of control over the physical aspects of change (Circular 42/55 and 1959 Town and Country Planning Act).	Narrowing of planning concerns to the physical and amenity aspects of land use change.	Increasingly localised and incremental strategies. Downgrading of status of town planning and reduced role in coordinating change.	Abolition of Development Charge by 1953 Town and Country Planning Act.
1960–1970 **The broadening of the scope of town planning**	Introduction of measures to accommodate and encourage economic growth, such as Circular 37/60, the revival of new town programme, the creation of the Location Offices Bureau, the introduction of Office Development Permits, the recommendations of the 1965 Planning Advisory Group, and the 1968 Town and Country Planning Act. The preparation of regional economic planning studies, and the creation of the Land Commission (1967) and the 'Overlord Ministry' of Local Government and Regional Planning (1969) as part of moves to indicative planning.	Broadening of planning concerns and adoption of organisational and rational planning techniques to include strategic public infrastructure and explicitly economic issues.	Increased functional roles and development of local autonomy within a clear hierarchical framework associated with coordination of infrastructure provision.	Return to taxation of development value through the 1964 Finance Act (introduced capital gains tax on land) and the 1965 Finance Act (introduced provisions for the taxation of development value). Introduction of the Betterment Levy in 1967.
1970–1975 **Contradictory changes in town planning**	Relaxation and downgrading of town planning as indicated by abolition of the Land Commission (1971) and measures to increase land supply (Circulars 9/70 and 102/72). Continued broadening of controls indicated by creation of the Department of the Environment in 1970, guidance on the early structure plans, and proposals of the 1974 White Paper 'Land' that led to the 1975 Community Land Act.	Increasing pragmatism indicated by the low number of structure and local plans commenced during these years and the flexible methodology used in the plan-making process.	Formal increase in local discretion in determining and implementing planning strategies through local government reorganisation and the proposals for the Community Land Scheme. In practice, however, reduced local control over strategic matters and the corporate approach envisaged for structure plans, and increasing national control (Local Plan Note 1/76).	Contradictory trends indicated in the strategy towards development value taxation, with abolition of the Betterment Levy in 1971, leaving betterment to be taxed at the capital gains rate.

Table 3.3 (contd.) Key periods in post-war British town planning, 1945–1995

Era	Legislation & national guidance	Town planning practice	Institutional arrangements	Development value taxation
1976–1980 **The downgrading of town planning**	Concern to relax control over development commenced from 1976 (1977 White Paper, Circular 71/77) and was accelerated with the 'bonfire of controls' announced in the 1979 White Paper. This relaxation of control was reinforced by various circulars (Circulars 9/80 and 22/80), the introduction of Enterprise Zones (1980) and measures contained in the 1980 Local Government and Planning Land Act.	Narrowing of planning concerns and undermining of strategic planning associated with a relaxation of control over land use change, and increased emphasis on market criteria.	Increased delegation of planning powers to local level but growing central control over policy content and growing use of *ad hoc* planning instruments and techniques (such as Local Plan Note 1/76 and the introduction of Urban Development Corporations and Enterprise Zones).	Introduction of Development Land Tax in 1976. Reduction in measures to tax development value (1980 Local Government and Planning Land Act).
1981–1989 **The restructuring of town planning towards more 'entrepreneurial' approaches**	Relaxation of control and increased emphasis on market criteria indicated by a range of measures and guidance notes (1981 General Development Order, 1985 White Paper 'Lifting the Burden', Circulars 23/81, 15/84 and 14/85, 1986 White Paper 'Building Business, ... not Barriers', 1986 Housing and Planning Act and 1987 Use Classes Order); suspending Industrial Development Certificates in 1982; introducing Simplified Planning Zones; establishing more Enterprise Zones; and maintaining high funding for an increasing number of UDCs.	Continued narrowing of planning concerns towards physical aspects of land use change and increasing informal awareness of market constraints. Growing fragmentation of town planning practice around the country, within the context of an emerging 'entrepreneurial' approach to planning to encourage private investment and economic development.	Town planning lost its strategic approach, became increasingly localised and operated alongside *ad hoc*, centrally controlled, initiatives for economic regeneration. Continued reduction of the scope for public participation.	Abolition of tax on development value in 1985, but growing use of planning gain agreements.
1990–1996 **Resurgence of plan-led environmental planning**	A major change in the approach towards town planning as indicated by the 1990 Town and Country Planning Act and the 1991 Planning and Compensation Act. These Acts provided a framework which heralded a return to plan-based planning, with greater emphasis on 'environmental' issues. Growing coherence in the strategy to encourage 'sustainable' development through a series of Planning Policy Guidance Notes (especially PPG6, PPG12 and PPG13).	A revitalisation of town planning practice associated with the preparation of local plans throughout the country and growing supra-state support for environmental strategies (European Commission and Agenda 21). Continuing emphasis on encouraging private sector development, but growing concern with the physical, environmental and 'sustainable' aspects of land use change.	Despite the return to plan-led planning central government sought to restrict the form and content of statutory plans to land use and development matters.	Formal recognition of scope for planning obligations through Circular 16/91, but reduced scope to extract such contributions due to the severity of the property recession.

Sources: Brindley et al., 1991; Cullingworth, 1975; Cullingworth and Nadin, 1994; Greed, 1993; Healey, 1988; Hebbert, 1977; Rydin, 1993; Ward, 1994

the dysfunctions associated with poor coordination of increasingly unregulated property development (British Property Federation, 1986; Healey, 1989; Jones, 1989a, p. 324; *The Planner*, 1988). It was these dysfunctions, combined with the severe economic and property market recessions of the early-1990s, that laid the basis for the return to a plan-led approach.

Understanding the relationships

The preceding discussion demonstrates that changes in the national planning framework have been shaped by the economic context in which it operates. This relationship exists at a number of different levels. At the broadest level, town planning has responded to post-war structural changes in the economy. During the period of strong economic growth from the late-1940s to the early-1970s, town planning fulfilled a number of roles, from articulating the reconstruction programme of the 1940s to helping organise and coordinate the growth of the 1960s. The roles of town planning altered during the period of low economic growth and restructuring of the 1970s to the mid-1990s, with a relaxation of control over the supply side of the economy followed by more proactive and entrepreneurial approaches during the 1980s and 1990s.

Town planning has also responded to short term fluctuations in economic activity, as demonstrated by the discussion in the previous section. A further feature appears to be the tendency for town planning controls to have fuelled, rather than dampened, cycles of development activity (Barras, 1994, p. 195). On the one hand, planning controls have been relaxed at times of high development activity. The 1947 provisions were geared to private development when the bulk of development in fact came from the public sector. The relaxation of planning controls fuelled the property booms of the early-1960s, the early and late-1970s and the late-1980s. On the other hand, controls and the major attempts at taxing development value (1947–1953, 1964–1971 and 1973–1984) might have arisen in response to dysfunctions in the process of land development, especially sharp rises in land and property prices. These financial provisions were, however, introduced after booms in development activity, and have never been really effective.

A further feature of the relationship is the lags in the formulation and introduction of town planning legislation in response to changing economic conditions. These lagged changes have meant that the basic legislative framework has been systematically out-of-step with economic pressures. Structural and institutional change in town planning has, as a result, been consistently undermined by changing economic conditions. Despite these structural lags, informal guidance and other forms of discretion have ensured that the town planning framework has rarely constrained economic growth. During periods of structural economic change, when town planning would be most likely to represent such a constraint, the formal framework has been restructured most rapidly. In the early-1950s, the financial provisions of the 1947

Town and Country Planning Act were removed to allow private sector development to proceed; in the early-1960s there was an abrupt relaxation of containment strategies so as to increase land supply in order to support economic growth; in the mid-1980s similar pressures to accommodate high levels of growth led to relaxed planning control. In periods of structural downturn the scope of town planning has been narrowed and the stringency of control relaxed so that the greater ostensible concern for the amenity and local aspects of change has concealed an actual reduction in control.

This restructuring of town planning to changing economic circumstances has been enabled by the emphasis on procedure in town planning practice. Whilst town planning is carried out to improve the generally undefined 'public interest', the procedural nature of planning methodologies and the relativity of town planning practice enable the introduction of marked changes in its substantive goals and scope.

Despite the responsiveness of town planning to prevailing economic pressures, there is a more fundamental dimension to this relationship. Specifically, at all stages during the post-war period, town planning has been constrained in its ability to shape economic change. This has obviously been the case during eras of economic recession, when town planning concerns have been narrowed and relaxed. It has also been the case at times of strong economic growth, such as the 1960s, or in periods of national reconstruction, such as the late-1940s. During such eras, town planning has appeared to possess a range of functional measures for the control of change. These functional measures have, in fact, been limited and poorly integrated with other economic strategies.

This fundamental constraint on town planning reflects the essential ideological role of the national town planning framework; that of supporting the varying pressures for economic change. Although the scope of the framework has varied in line with economic pressures, there have been fundamental limitations on the ability of town planning to shape land use change. These limitations are based on the difficulties of any political control over increasingly international economic pressures. As stated by Cullingworth (1994, p. 289):

> ... some of the most important underlying problems are well beyond any conceivable scope of 'planning': for example, much urban change has been due to global forces which are currently beyond any political control.
>
> (see also Hall *et al.*, 1993, pp. 20–21; Jones, 1989b, p. 324)

Such conclusions suggest that town planning interventions fulfil an ideological role in supporting and legitimising dominant processes of land use and economic change. The apparent openness of town planning to public pressures and the apparent determination of planning strategies in terms of their general benefits and costs create the impression that the process of land use change is controlled rationally and in the public interest. Similarly, the need for town planning to appear rational is the major reason for its continual restructuring in response to changing economic conditions. The relevance, and, therefore, rationality, of the town planning system is enhanced by its being alive to prevailing economic pressures.

Prospects for town planning

A particular configuration of economic, political and social forces came together in the 1930s and 1940s to produce the 1947 Town and Country Planning Act, and this Act has provided the post-war institutional framework for control over land use change. This chapter has demonstrated that, within this framework, the scope of town planning and the emphasis in its concerns has tended to be restructured in response to changing economic conditions. This process of restructuring has, in turn, been based on the basic institutional structure, and the procedural nature of town planning interventions.

It is with a recognition of the characteristics of town planning revealed during this chapter that future change in town planning should be examined. There has not been a straightforward relationship between town planning and economic change, and it is clearly not possible simply to read-off town planning from the prevailing economic context. However, an understanding of such material constraints should be a critical issue in writing any new agendas for town planning in the late-1990s and beyond. This is particularly important given the lag in the response of town planning to changed circumstances.

The lag in the response means there is an inherent danger of basing new planning agendas on prevailing circumstances. The danger is that any such agenda might follow contemporary issues which are undermined by changed circumstances. In this respect, it is good to see the healthy scepticism expressed in responses to the RTPI discussion document on the future of RTPI education (Hague, 1994; RTPI, 1993). These responses reveal a concern that the current focus on sustainability might lead planners to be '... lured by a fashionable and ill-defined concept ... ' (Hague, 1994, p. 20).

It is not possible in this chapter to set out the likely economic and property market context of the early years of the 21st century. Such forecasting is notoriously difficult, as evidence of the recent economic and property cycles demonstrates (Slater, 1995). Despite the difficulties, it is possible to generate insights into the likely nature of economic and land use change. For instance, an analysis of economic and property cycles over the past 30 years concludes that:

> ... building cycles are indeed inevitable, being the result of the uniquely long lags which cannot but separate an increase in demand from the supply response needed to satisfy the demand.
>
> (Barras, 1994, pp. 195–196)

Such conclusions mean it is possible to anticipate future cycles of property development. Specifically, Barras argues that the coming 10–15 years will be characterised first, by a small, investor-led, development cycle in the late-1990s (see also Barnett, 1994), followed by a more fundamental 'speculative boom' between 2005 and 2010.

These patterns in economic and land use change need to be understood in writing any new agenda for town planning. As it is, the relativity of the decision-making process means the structural determinants of town planning remain poorly understood. There might, therefore, be an argument for a more explicit assessment of the economic determinants of town planning objectives in general and of specific planning strategies in particular. In times of economic recession it might be argued that less resources could be allocated to environmental and social improvements. This does not imply that town planning should operate according to market criteria, as this would represent too narrow an interpretation of the 'economic'. It does suggest, however, that a more comprehensive, and explicit, assessment of prevailing social and economic conditions would improve understanding of the structural constraints on town planning interventions.

Chapter 4

REGENERATING CITIES AND MODES OF REGULATION

Nick Oatley

Planners and urban renewal

Town planners have always played a central role in the process of urban renewal and regeneration. The form and nature of their role has changed over time in response to a variety of pressures. Analysing this role has become problematic, particularly since the emergence of the debate on 'the inner city' during the late 1960s and 1970s. Stewart and Underwood (1994, p. 105) observed that the boundaries of the inner cities policy sector were unclear, which heightened the debate about the role of planners and planning in this area. They argued that whilst work on inner cities represented a significant area of planning practice there was much confusion over the tasks of describing, analysing and explaining the nature of the problem and much debate over the type of intervention proposed. In addition defining what 'planning' meant in this context was also problematic:

> ... planning for inner cities is not at first sight an activity of a particular type, undertaken by a particular institution, does not involve the guidance/regulation of particular classes of events, and is not undertaken by particular people who consider what they do to be planning. One might indeed argue that inner cities policy is so multi-faceted yet so opaque that it defies analysis. It is, however, precisely because it is like this – and resembles so much of the wide ranging but ill-defined planning initiatives of recent years – that it deserves attention.
>
> (Stewart and Underwood, 1994, p. 105)

Indeed, urban regeneration has been given much attention over the last fifteen years and there is a wide literature on the subject. Within this literature, one can identify a multitude of conceptual approaches to the analysis of changes in urban policy. It is only since the mid- to late-1980s that attempts have been made to locate evaluations of urban policy within theoretical perspectives that attempt to explain urban policy in relation to the political, economic and social processes that constitute society. For example, Lawless (1986, Preface) commented that one of the problems with the literature on urban policy has been 'that the immediate, the empirical, and the pragmatic have dominated the scene, to the detriment of the reflective and the theoretical. Intensive explorations of policy innovation are important, but they must not deflect us from attempts to locate developments within wider and often more illuminating insights.'

There are important examples of attempts to relate changes in urban policy more explicitly to economic, social and political processes (Cawson and Saunders, 1983; Cooke, 1983b; Duncan and Goodwin, 1988; Hobbs, 1992; Lawless, 1986; Rees and Lambert, 1985; Simmie, 1981). All of these works demonstrate the insights that can be gained by considering urban policy in this broader context. However, different theoretical approaches will lead to varying periodisations of change. Theories will differ in the importance that is attached to key themes, events or processes on which distinct periods of policy are based. The approach adopted in this chapter attempts to make sense of the changes in urban policy and the changing role of the planner in this sphere of activity by drawing on regulation theory. Regulation theory is concerned with the way the inbuilt tendencies towards contradiction and crisis within capitalism are managed through institutionalised structures of regulation as the basis for sustained economic growth. This approach effectively captures the broad complexity of changes in society by taking a long-term historical trajectory. By adopting a macroscopic conceptual framework it can be used to relate developments in urban policy and the changing role of planning to changes in economic, political and social processes. In particular it suggests that changes in urban policy are part of a complex process of societal change that can be understood in terms of a shift from a Fordist to a Post-Fordist regime of accumulation and associated mode of regulation.

It must be acknowledged that there is ongoing debate about this transition. In particular it is questioned whether the recent changes that have occurred in the regime of accumulation and associated mode of regulation can be characterised as new, coherent and distinct from the previous period. There are those who argue that current changes are still part of a transition and that the conditions for a coherent and durable mode of accumulation and regulation have not been met (Jessop, 1995).

The two conditions that would have to be met for a wholly new mode of regulation to be identified are 'first that it should resolve the contradictions and crisis tendencies of the Fordist mode of regulation and second that it should enable and promote sustained capital accumulation' (Goodwin, 1995, p. 12). There is little evidence to suggest that either of these conditions has been met with respect to the mode of regulation at the level of the nation state in Britain. The analysis in this chapter indicates that within the sphere of urban policy, recent changes have attempted to address the crisis tendencies of Fordist or Keynesian policy and institutional practices. However, in attempting to overcome one set of contradictions and crises another set has been produced. There is also evidence to suggest that with respect to the second condition there is no real sign that recent changes in urban policy are contributing to a more stabilised and sustainable process of capital accumulation.

This may suggest that current changes do not constitute the emergence of a new coherent mode of regulation but do, at least, constitute a transition away from Fordist practices. This chapter documents changes in urban policy since 1945, with particular emphasis on changes since the late-1970s, in the context of this transition in the mode of regulation away from Fordism.

Regulation theory and urban policy

Notions of 'Fordism' were first introduced by the work of French political economists such as Aglietta (1979) and Lipietz (1987). Regulation theorists argue that three broad stages in the development of capitalist societies can be identified. The first is a stage of 'competitive' regulation, which dates from the mid-nineteenth century to the 1920s. The second is characterised by a 'Fordist' phase, which covers the period from the 1930s to the early 1970s. The third phase is seen as a period of transition from 'Fordism' to 'Post-Fordism', which began in the 1970s. Regulation theorists start by analysing changes in the organisation of the economy then move on to consider developments in social and political structures. This work has recently been extended to account for changes in local government and the welfare state (Stoker, 1989, 1990; Cochrane, 1993; Geddes, 1988; Hoggett, 1987, 1990, 1991; Murray, 1989; Collinge, 1992; and Burrows and Loader, 1994). Attempts have also been made using regulation theory to explain recent changes in urban policy in both the United Kingdom and the USA (Gaffikin and Warf, 1993; Florida and Jonas, 1991). As Stoker (1990, p. 243) points out this approach is not intended to imply that economic conditions determine social and political processes, 'Rather there is a "certain correspondence" between economic, social and political structures in periods of stability and growth. Together these structures constitute a "regime of accumulation".'

Jessop (1994) has recently provided a very clear exposition of Fordism and Post-Fordism and has identified the implications for analysing the state and changes in the nature of economic and social policy regimes. Jessop (1994, p. 14) specifies the following four referents to analyse the modes of accumulation and modes of regulation known as Fordism and Post-Fordism:

1. The labour process.
2. An accumulation regime, i.e. a macroeconomic regime sustaining growth in capitalist production and consumption.
3. A social mode of economic regulation, i.e. an ensemble of norms, institutions, organisational forms, social networks, and patterns of conduct which sustain and 'guide' a given accumulation regime.
4. A mode of societalisation, i.e. a pattern of institutional integration and social cohesion which complements the dominant accumulation regime and its social mode of economic regulation and thereby secures the conditions for its dominance within the wider society.

In accordance with the above defining characteristics of a mode of accumulation, Jessop identifies four corresponding characteristics of the mode of regulation, which include the nature of the labour process within the state sector itself; the state sector's direct economic role in an accumulation regime; the state's wider role in the social mode of economic regulation linked to such a regime; and its role in securing the institutional integration and social cohesion of a particular social formation.

From this set of characteristics an ideal typical form of the Fordist and Post-Fordist state can be identified. In its ideal, abstracted form, the Fordist state is described as the 'Keynesian Welfare State' – which performs two distinctive functions in addition to the functions normally associated with a capitalist state of creating, maintaining or restoring the conditions for the expanded reproduction of capitalism. The first distinctive function of the Keynesian welfare state is to maintain full employment through demand management. The second function is to regulate collective bargaining so that it is compatible with policies to secure full employment, and to encourage more general levels of mass consumption to boost domestic demand and reinforce the Fordist mode of growth.

It is currently argued that a Post-Fordist regime in Britain has emerged to resolve the contradictions of Fordist accumulation and to address the crisis of the Fordist state. In Britain, there was a transitional period during the latter part of the 1970s in which the state initially intensified the policies associated with a Fordist state (continued attempts to promote full employment despite stagflationary tendencies and to maintain welfare commitments despite tendencies towards a fiscal crisis). Jessop (1994, p. 24) argues that what has gradually emerged 'is a structural transformation and fundamental strategic reorientation of the capitalist state.' Its distinctive functions are to strengthen the structural competitiveness of the national economy through neo-liberal economic measures and to subordinate social policy to the needs of labour market flexibility and/or the constraints of international competition. Jessop (1994, p. 24) observes that:

> In this sense it marks a clear break with the Keynesian welfare state as domestic full employment is de-prioritised in favour of international competitiveness and redistributive welfare rights take second place to a productivist re-ordering of social policy. In this sense its new functions would also seem to correspond to the emerging dynamic of global capitalism.

This theoretical framework is increasingly being adopted to explain the economic restructuring of Britain and the associated restructuring of the state and social policy. Cochrane (1993, p. 82) argues that the terms Fordism and Post-Fordism 'have almost entered the common sense of contemporary social sciences in ways which cut across customary disciplinary, theoretical and political allegiances. It is as if we all know that something important is going on and feel better if it can be labelled.' Useful insights have been gained from the application of this approach to changes in local government (Stoker, 1989, 1990; and Cochrane, 1993), and changes in the welfare state and social policy (Burrows and Loader, 1994). British urban policy is an area of state activity which has not been subjected to an analysis using this framework, except in a comparative study of current policy in Britain and the USA. The next section will attempt to use the regulation approach to develop an historical account of British urban regeneration policy.

Modes of regulation and urban policy

This section argues that in the sphere of urban policy, distinct changes have occurred that correspond to the broad stages in the accumulation process as described by regulation theory. Attention is focused on the Fordist (1930s–1970s) and Post-Fordist (1970s onwards) modes of accumulation and the modes of regulation that are associated with each period. Given that urban policy is a specific aspect of state intervention in general it is perhaps not surprising to find similar trends that have emerged in the restructuring of welfare state policy and local governance.

Urban policy during the period 1930s to the 1970s was almost exclusively concerned with welfarist issues: slum clearance, the provision of new housing through planned redevelopment and stimulation of the private building industry, the improvement of housing standards through rehabilitation and gradual renewal, and various policies directed at tackling poverty and urban decline. The dominant institutional approach was paternalistic, corporatist and managerialist. The approach to urban policy began to change during the late-1970s, and radical changes were introduced by the Conservative government during the 1980s. The emphasis shifted away from welfarist issues and came to be dominated by concerns about stimulating the economy and creating a culture of entrepreneurialism. This second phase of urban policy can be seen as part of a transitional regime that set about dismantling the conditions and structures of the Fordist mode of accumulation and creating the conditions for a new (Post-Fordist) regime of accumulation.

The institutional arrangements were dominated by privatism and a change in urban governance from a managerialist approach to an entrepreneurialist approach. Using the four referents identified by Jessop (1994) the distinct characteristics of the two modes of regulation can be presented (see Fig. 4.1).

These two broad periods of urban state intervention can be further broken down into four distinct phases of urban policy. During the period 1930s to 1968 the main urban problem was perceived as physical – a Victorian legacy of poor quality, decaying housing. Policy was directed at slum clearance and planned redevelopment. During the 1960s poverty and deprivation were 'rediscovered'. This led to a range of area-based experimental initiatives ostensibly designed to address the problem of social disadvantage. In 1979 these welfarist concerns gave way to the neo-liberal philosophy and concerns of the Conservative government, which stressed efficiency, wealth generation and competitiveness. This led to an emphasis in policy on property-led regeneration which prevailed until the effects of the property slump at the end of

Phases	1930s–1970s Fordist (Welfarist)	1970s–present Transitional or Post-Fordist (Entrepreneurial)
Labour process within the state	Monolithic state services based on professionally led hierarchical structures, characterised by corporate planning, bureaucratic paternalism, functionalism, uniformity and inflexibility	Introduction of Compulsory Competitive Tendering led to a contract culture. Leaner and flatter managerial structures. Decentralisation. Generic roles, team working, flexibility.
Direct economic role	Keynesian management to maintain levels of aggregate demand compatible with full employment.	Monetarist policies to control inflation and strengthen the structural competitiveness of the national economy.
Wider role – social mode of economic regulation	Public planning and the pursuit of redistribution and equity.	Deregulation and emphasis on the market to generate wealth and efficiency.
Institutional integration and social cohesion	Corporatist alliances involving central and local government, community and voluntary organisations and local industry. Local government seen as the natural agent of regeneration. Urban managerialism.	Centralisation of powers. Bypassing of local authorities. Shift in urban governance towards the private sector (urban entrepreneurialism). Creation of business elites and growth coalitions.

Fig. 4.1. Modes of Regulation: Ideal types

the 1980s undermined this approach. Government has since shifted its approach to the problems created by the restructuring of the economy by establishing a number of competitions for funding designed to encourage economic development. It has also established new integrated Government Offices in the Regions to oversee a unified Single Regeneration Budget (see Fig. 4.2).

1945–1979   Urban renewal, planned decentralisation and the emergence of the inner city crisis

After the Second World War the UK economy experienced a period of unprecedented growth based on the mass production of consumer goods by the motor vehicle and electrical appliance industries, and the retailing sector. During the long post-war boom (1951 to 1973) the economy experienced an average annual growth in Gross Domestic Product of 2.8%. Unemployment remained extremely low and policies aimed at sustaining full employment were an important part of the post-war political agenda. The emergence of a global economy and the commitment to Keynesian economic management by the British government supported conditions favourable for growth as

Characteristics	Keynesian (Welfarist)		Post-Keynesian (Efficiency, competitiveness)	
	Physical Redevelopment 1945–68	The Inner City Problem 1968–79	Entrepreneurialism 1979–1990	Competitive Policy 1990–?
Policy emphasis	Slum clearance and comprehensive redevelopment. Planned decentralisation.	Area based social welfare projects attempting to respond to economic, social and environmental problems resulting from structural decline of the economy.	Property-led regeneration. Reliance on partnerships to attract inward investment into the city.	Integrated initiatives attempting to link disadvantaged with mainstream economic opportunities. Competitive bidding for funding.
Policy initiatives	Slum clearance and planned production of housing via planned decentralisation – New Towns Act 1946 – Town and Country Planning Act 1947 – Housing subsidies	Area-based initiatives: – Urban Programme 1968 – General Improvement Areas 1969 – Community Development Projects 1969 – Housing Action Areas 1974 – Comprehensive Community Programmes 1974 – Enhanced Urban Programme 1978	Property-based, supply-side initiatives: – Enterprise Zones 1979 – Urban Development Corporations 1981 – Urban Development Grants 1982 – Derelict Land Grant 1983 – City Action Teams 1985 – Estate Action 1985 – Urban Regeneration Grants 1987 – City Grant 1988	Initiatives to improve the competitive advantage of localities: – City Challenge 1991 – Urban Partnership 1993 – City Pride 1994 – Regional Challenge 1994 – English Partnerships 1994 – Single Regeneration Budget 1994 – Challenge Funding for Local Authorities, Priority Projects 1996

Fig. 4.2   Features in the transition from a Keynesian to a Post-Keynesian form of British Urban Policy

public spending was used to iron out cyclical fluctuations in the economy. The 1951 Census recorded 1.8% of workers unemployed, rising to 2.8% in 1961 and 5.2% in 1971. In the early 1970s the economy began to falter. There was a severe recession that began in 1973/74.

The key to post-war urban policy was seen as planning – both for land use and for housing production. A vision emerged during the 1940s based on an active and mass consensus for planned intervention which overcame the political objections that had prevailed before the war. This vision was informed by a number of philosophies. The committees that reported during the 1940s (Barlow, 1940; Uthwatt, 1942; Scott, 1942; Dudley, 1944; Reith, 1946) and the regional strategies of Abercrombie were particularly influential. These influences informed the establishment of the Town and Country Planning Act 1947 and related legislation for New Towns, which was the first comprehensive system of development control and strategic/urban planning Britain had experienced.

Specific actions included the clearance of slums and the rebuilding programme, housing renewal and planned decentralisation. Keynesian principles of economic management were applied to the provision of housing with state-led slum clearance programmes and large numbers of rented properties provided by local authorities together with incentives to the private sector to stimulate the mass production of owner occupied housing. Thus, although the 'housing drive' was led by the public sector, Gibson and Langstaff (1982, p. 26) observe that 'in contrast with the fundamental reappraisal of many other sectors of the welfare state, the housing programme was quickly assembled and there was no attempt to introduce a comprehensive framework or socialise the means of housing production.' The approach here can be seen as an attempt to bring forward immediate plans for rebuilding with a firm commitment to create better housing in order to maintain civilian morale, whilst at the same time creating the conditions supportive for the mass production of housing by the private sector. The encouragement of owner occupation during this period was also intended to extend the ideology of the property owning democracy. In this way the accumulation regime and the social mode of economic regulation complemented the mode of societalisation. The encouragement of the property owning democracy did much to sustain the building industry and to secure the political support of the general public in the post-war period (Kennett, 1994).

However, there was a significant proportion of society who had missed out on the prosperity of the post-war boom. Social disparities were heightened towards the end of the 1960s. The inadequacy of policy which focused exclusively on the supply and quality of housing was exposed and new initiatives became necessary to address the worsening economic decline.

'Inner cities policy' represented a major break from the physical approach to urban problems. It emerged during a period of deepening recession and was influenced by the contemporary experience in the United States, where poverty and problems of racial tension were being addressed through area-based positive discrimination policies. A series of reports and official inquiries into diverse aspects of Britain's social conditions revealed high levels of poverty and social inequality. Pressure was also mounting due to increasing racial tension and the links between poverty and race.

The approach taken in Britain represented an attempt 'to come to terms with the failures of the Keynesian Welfare State and the breaking up of the social democratic consensus and settlement on which it was based' (Rees and Lambert, 1985, p. 127). In 1969 the Local Government Grants (Social Needs) Act was passed which invited local authorities to apply for funding to support projects in the fields of education, housing, health and welfare aimed at areas of 'special need', many of which would contain concentrations of black ethnic minorities. This was followed by other area-based experimental projects which were highly corporatist in their approach and based on managerialist modes of delivery, such as the designation of Educational Priority Areas, General Improvement Areas (housing), Comprehensive Community Programmes, Community Development Projects and Inner Area Studies (Lawless, 1979, 1981, 1986).

The economic crisis of the early 1970s led to a comprehensive review of urban policy which drew on the research from the area-based experimental projects. The 1977 White Paper which resulted (*Policy for the Inner Cities*) and the Inner Urban Areas Act (1978) which followed marked a watershed in urban policy. The White Paper argued that the problem of urban decline had to be understood in a wider context. In particular, urban problems were associated with long-term economic decline, the urban–rural shift and deindustrialisation and not with the social pathology of individuals or communities.

It is against this background of the breakdown of Fordism and the collapse of the post-war consensus, the introduction of practical monetarism by the Labour Party, and a realisation of the centrality of economic processes to the urban problem that the approach to urban policy taken by the Conservative Government under Thatcher in 1979 should be considered.

1979–1996   Reorientation of the state: the enterprise culture, property-led development and competitive urban policy

The recession of 1973/74 marked a turning point in the political and economic history of Britain. As Hobbs (1992, p. 231) observed 'the years from 1975 to 1981 represented a turning point in the role of the post-war British state, based on the collapse of the forces behind the "long boom" and the move towards a qualitatively new era of economic production.' Although elements of a monetarist economic policy were introduced by the Labour Government during 1974 to 1979, the advent of the Thatcher government introduced a radical new approach to urban policy based on a neo-liberal political ideology.

Stoker (1989, p. 154) argues that the Thatcher government provided a strategic political response to the breakdown of Fordism and involved an attempt to effect a radical transition from the crisis-ridden Fordist accumulation mode of growth and a flawed Keynesian welfare state to an effective post-Fordist regime and a neo-liberal variant of what Jessop (1994, p. 29) has called the 'Schumpterian workfare state'. This has pervaded all areas of state intervention. Jessop (1994, p. 30) describes how, in narrow economic terms, the neo-liberal strategy demands changes in the regulation or governance of both the public and private sectors:

> For the public sector, it involves privatisation, liberalisation and an imposition of commercial criteria in any residual state sector; for the private sector, it involves deregulation and a new legal and political framework to provide passive support for market solutions.

This was translated into attempts to demolish Fordist regulation of the wage relation through the promotion of 'hire and fire', flexi-time and flexi-wage labour markets combined with an attack on the power of the Trade Unions. Attempts were made to destroy the main forms of Keynesian Welfare State crisis management, with its commitment to full employment and social welfare, and to replace it with an enterprise culture sustained by a state-sponsored popular capitalism. The Conservative government was committed to the creation of self-regulating markets and the reorientation of economic and social policy to the perceived needs of the private sector. The general economic policies pursued during the early 1980s were strongly anti-interventionist and although attempting to strengthen the structural competitiveness of the economy, nevertheless, exacerbated the effects of recession.

Institutionally, the neo-liberal agenda sought to change the form of local governance away from urban managerialist approaches towards urban entrepreneurialism (Harvey, 1989; Deakin and Edwards, 1993). This involved the encouragement of business interests to set up business elites or growth coalitions to take Thatcherite enterprise into local communities. At a local level a range of quangos and voluntary bodies were established with strong private sector representation concerned with economic regeneration and welfare provision.

1979–1991   Property-led, market driven urban policy

In urban policy, the Government promoted three broad themes (Atkinson and Moon, 1993). The first of these consisted of changing the form of urban governance by bypassing or marginalising the role of local authorities and greatly enhancing the role of the private sector through partnerships. It soon became clear that the private sector would be called on to play a key role in urban regeneration. Pressure was exerted on the private sector to take a more active role. A series of private sector-led initiatives were launched such as British Urban Development (BUD), Business in the Community (BIC) and the

Pheonix Initiative. Learning the lessons from the USA it was also suggested that business could take on a leadership role to create growth coalitions.

A second theme that was pursued in urban policy was a reliance on property-led development. Again drawing on examples from the USA, emphasis was given to flagship projects, and boosterist or place marketing initiatives.

This approach was a response to industrial restructuring, the growth of the service sector and the emerging importance of global property markets. Although it depended on the operation of the market it was, nevertheless, supported heavily by state subsidies, grants, infrastructure investments and the relaxation of planning controls in order to improve the supply of land. Public–private partnerships were established to bring about developments and the Confederation of British Industry was clear on what was required from the public sector, suggesting that it should 'remove constraints, particularly on the planning front; provide the right physical environment through infrastructure development; help to overcome the confidence barrier by sharing some of the risks of investment.' As Gaffikin and Warf (1993, p. 79) observe, more often than not such partnerships amounted to little more than a thin excuse for privately led but publicly subsidised development.

In the same way that attempts were being made to restructure other areas of social policy to assist in the transformation of the economy, urban policy at this time was attempting to create the conditions for new forms of capital accumulation. As Tweedale (1988, p. 194) points out:

> the public sector is massively subsidising the private sector's efforts. ... redevelopment does not, therefore, represent an attempt to solve the inner city problem. Rather, it is an attempt to restructure the spatial form of the city in line with the restructuring of its economy, enabling new land uses to match the economic functions of the city.

The Government introduced a range of initiatives designed to promote these interests such as the Enterprise Zones, Urban Development Corporations, and the Urban Development and Urban Regeneration Grants (later combined under the City Grant). The Enterprise Zones, introduced in 1981, represented an experiment in deregulation as a means of unleashing investment in areas experiencing decline. Areas were designated in which companies would be exempt from the usual planning restrictions and eligible for tax relief and other public subsidies. Urban Development Corporations were introduced as a way of bypassing local authorities and to stimulate property investment. They were given extensive powers to control development within their designated areas and to acquire, assemble and dispose of land and other property. They were to achieve the regeneration of their areas through the leverage of private investment on the back of large public subsidies. Urban Development Corporations have been instrumental, perhaps more than any other initiative, in bringing about the restructuring of the spatial form of the city mentioned by Tweedale (1988) above. Further subsidies were available to property developers through the Urban Development and Urban Regeneration Grants. Local authorities were further bypassed when these were combined to form the City Grant in 1988, which enabled private developers to negotiate directly with central government.

The third strand in the Government's approach to urban policy was its emphasis on the role of small businesses. By the early 1980s new businesses were seen by the New Right as embodying all that was good about the free market. A number of initiatives were launched to encourage the setting up of small businesses. The tax system was altered to assist their formation and banks were advised to take a more supportive attitude to the needs of the small business person.

The Thatcher administration also inherited a number of initiatives which it reviewed and restructured to reflect its particular philosophy (Atkinson and Moon, 1994, pp. 111–138). The areas of regional policy, the Urban Programme, regeneration initiatives, and housing- and employment-related initiatives were all reviewed in line with the government's neo-liberal ideology. Generally this meant they were freed from local government control, exposed to competitive pressures, opened up to the private sector and targeted to specific areas. In terms of planning, Fainstein (1991) observed that during the 1980s planners became more directly involved in economic development. Considerations of market rationality and local competitiveness replaced comprehensiveness and equity as the primary criteria by which planning projects were judged. Long-term strategic planning and a concern with the environment competed with short-term concerns of job generation and more permissive planning regimes. Gaffikin and Warf (1993, p. 79) suggested that planning became more concerned with promoting development and less with regulating its aftermath.

By the mid- to late-1980s the range of urban initiatives were being criticised for their lack of co-ordination, disparate nature and confusing range of Ministerial responsibilities. The launch of Action for Cities (DOE, 1987) tried to address this problem by co-ordinating existing approaches, but in spite of this attempt the Audit Commission (1989, 1991, p. 4) observed, first in 1989 and then again in 1991, that 'urban policy was a patchwork quilt of complexity and idiosyncrasy' that was only loosely sewn together.

By 1989/90 the strategy of property-led regeneration, which had become a central feature of urban policy, began to falter in the wake of the stock market crash of 1989 and the slowdown in the property market. An evaluation of UDCs showed the difficulties encountered with an approach so heavily reliant on the property market. The poor economic climate, the slump in the property market and the high cost of money led to a decline in developer interest and commitment. The approach of UDCs depended too much on key sites and on investment by large developers and institutions. The recession also created a financial problem for many UDCs, which were unable to dispose of land bought at the height of the 1980s property boom (CLES, 1990, p. 56; Oatley, 1993).

Although the 1980s had led to an impressive amount of physical development it was apparent that the assumed 'trickle-down' of benefits had not occurred, the service jobs that had been created had not replaced those in manufacturing and social and spatial inequalities had accentuated. The approach adopted by the Conservative government as a conscious attempt to overcome the crisis of Fordism was failing. As riots flared in the outer estates of Cardiff, Bristol and Newcastle in the summer of 1991, threatening social cohesion in urban areas for the third time since 1979, it was apparent that an alternative approach was needed.

1991 to present (1996)   Competitive urban policy and local corporatism

A number of events and pressures combined to create a realignment of urban policy in the 1990s. The deepening of the economic recession and its effect on the land and property market together with an awareness of the selective impact of property-led initiatives prompted a re-evaluation of approaches to urban policy. Michael Heseltine's arrival back at the DoE in 1991 led to a review of the range of policy initiatives that were in operation, which led to the cessation of the Urban Programme and the establishment of a new competitive initiative, the City Challenge. Continued criticism of the fragmented nature of the government's urban policy led the Conservatives to make a manifesto commitment in 1992 to tackle this problem by creating integrated regional offices and a unified regeneration budget that brought together initiatives across a broad spectrum.

It was also claimed that this initiative would shift power from Whitehall to the regions, thereby delivering a 'new localism'. This was implemented in 1993 when the Secretary of State for the Environment (DoE, 1993b) announced a package of measures, primarily concerned with the organisation of government and the management of public expenditure designed to transform the machinery of policy planning and control. Central to these changes was the establishment of the Single Regeneration Budget (SRB) and Government Offices for the Regions.

The combined effect of these changes was to shift the emphasis of urban policy away from private sector, property-led regeneration towards what Stewart (1994, p. 11) describes as managerial localism, competitive localism and corporatist localism. Managerial localism is based on a renewed public/private sector managerialism embodied in the new financial and administrative arrangements of the integrated regional offices and the SRB. This purports to offer a coherence of planning and policy delivery which political and administrative structures organised on departmental lines failed to deliver. Competitive localism is characterised by a process of marketing and the presentation of bids prepared by localities for funding on a competitive basis to government (City Challenge, Rural Challenge, Regional Challenge), to the European Commission (Structural Funds) or to finance and development capital (City Pride and urban prospectuses). Corporatist localism reaffirms the government's commitment to remove urban policy from local government politics by changing the form of urban governance in which local elected politicians are distanced in the development of local regeneration strategies.

These changes represent the response of a political party struggling to address the social and economic problems in cities after seventeen years in office, confronted with ever-increasing pressures on the economy to compete internationally. In one sense they represent a continuation of themes that emerged in the 1980s (centralisation of powers, fiscal control, changes in urban governance) but they also represent a reorientation in terms of the institutional arrangements for regeneration with a return to corporatist approaches to the task of regeneration. City Challenge and the Single Regeneration Budget, in particular, encapsulate all the elements of this new approach.

City Challenge was launched by the (then) Environment Secretary Michael Heseltine in May 1991 as a new initiative to boost urban regeneration in England. It was heralded as a significant innovatory approach to urban regeneration and an example of the new institutional framework that was emerging in local governance. The initiative involved local authorities putting together plans for the redevelopment of neighbourhoods which they considered to be of critical importance to the regeneration of their area, in partnership with businesses, the community and the voluntary sector. These plans formed the basis of a bid to government for funding. The bids had to demonstrate effective local partnerships, targeted area-based regeneration strategies, and an integrated approach to the problems of economic decline and social deprivation. In the first round of bidding (1991/92) fifteen councils were invited to bid. Eleven bids were selected to receive £7.5 million per year for five years.

The second round (1992/93) was open to all 57 Urban Programme authorities, from which 20 bids were selected for funding. In 1993/94 City Challenge accounted for over a quarter of public expenditure in inner cities (Stewart, 1994), and over the six years 1991–1997 it will amount to over £1 billion of public expenditure.

In terms of policy since 1979, City Challenge (and the SRB which supersedes it) marked a shift away from the principles that informed Urban Development Corporations, Enterprise Zones, City Grants, and Training and Enterprise Councils. Burton and O'Toole (1993) have suggested that City Challenge embodies a shift away from the prime concerns of the 1980s viewed in terms of the three E's (efficiency, economy and effectiveness) towards an emphasis on the three C's (co-operation between regeneration initiatives and between organisations and groups, concentration of resources and competition between areas for a limited pool of resources). The initiative can also be seen as a response to some of the recent criticisms levelled at government urban policy.

For example, after twelve years of cut-backs and policies which have weakened the role of local authorities, City Challenge identifies a key (albeit enabling) role for local authorities in leading regeneration activities. In order to take on this enabling role local authorities have been encouraged to adopt more corporate practices and inter-agency working, to establish fast-track decision procedures and special sub-committees to expedite City Challenge matters, and to relinquish overall control to boards or trusts with representation from business, academia, the community and public agencies. In a DoE Press Release (DoE, 1992a) Michael Heseltine stated that the City Challenge was

> about the vision of the local authority and its ability to bring about the regeneration of its area. Above all it's about involving local people, with councils forging partnerships with community organisations, voluntary groups, and the private sector.

On the surface, this seems to be a radical departure from the anti-local authority rhetoric and emphasis on property-led regeneration activities that characterised urban policy in the 1980s. The local authority is back performing a pivotal role in partnership with other public agencies, the private sector, voluntary organisations and the non-statutory sector and the community.

The most important new dimension of City Challenge was the introduction of a controversial and highly politicised competitive bidding process which was intended to stimulate a fresh, innovatory approach to urban regeneration. Ministers felt that the long established Urban Programme had become too routine, lacked any cutting edge, and had failed to gain any significant degree of private sector and/or community involvement. Competitive bidding was seen as a way of promoting an entrepreneurial culture in local government and a way of producing bids which conformed to the government's objectives of creating innovative approaches to economic and social development and the establishment of partnerships which institutionalised the influence of a wider set of actors, most notably those in the private sector (Oatley and Lambert 1995).

Although City Challenge represents a new departure in British urban policy it also embodies some elements of continuity with previous policies. It shares many of the characteristics of the area-based initiatives of the late-1960s and 1970s including targeted strategies and the bending of main spending programmes, the concentration on Urban Priority Areas, an emphasis on community development projects, and the establishment of corporatist structures/alliances. However, beneath the surface similarity there is a different agenda for City Challenge. The Government saw the introduction of competition into the allocation of funds as a way of stimulating local authorities to adopt a different approach to their urban problems both in terms of the substance of their proposals and the process by which the proposals were produced. In this respect, City Challenge can be seen as a more subtle approach by central government to achieve its political aims for local government, namely, the continued dilution of local government powers and the increase in central government control together with the increased involvement of the private sector in local governance and the promotion of an enterprise culture via competitive bidding.

This new initiative embodies many characteristics of the transitional mode of regulation. The initiative attempts to formalise the role of the private sector in local policy making and whilst guidance has called for integrated approaches to economic, social and physical regeneration there has, nevertheless, been a continued emphasis on economic schemes designed to improve the competitive edge of cities. The initiative has also encouraged local authorities to operate differently, adopting different working practices, organisational forms and social networks. Although the initiative has been suspended after only two rounds many of the principles have been carried over into the newly established SRB.

The SRB was established in April 1994. It brought together under one budget 20 existing programmes for regeneration and economic development totalling £1.4 billion in 1994/95. The Government also created a new network of central government Integrated Regional Offices (now called simply Government Offices) to manage the new SRB and to provide a more comprehensive and accessible service (Fig. 4.3).

The creation of the ten Government Offices bringing together the functions of the Department of the Environment, the Department of Employment, the Home Office, the Department of Trade, the Department of Education and, in principle, the Department of Transport is intended to simplify the way government supports regeneration and to deliver an integrated approach to problems where local priorities are emphasised and where local needs rather than Departmental interests will be the prime consideration. John Gummer, Environment Secretary, announced that these 'sweeping measures' would 'shift power from Whitehall to local communities and make Government more responsive to local priorities' (DoE Press Release No 731, 4th November 1993).

During its first year (1994/95) the SRB operated through arrangements in place for existing programmes. However, the first of yearly competitive bidding, for the top-sliced and non-earmarked resources in the SRB (now called the Challenge Fund) began in April 1994. This first round of bidding, which concluded on September 7th 1994, resulted in 469 bids being submitted to Government Offices. Only 201 bids were successful. The cumulative bid for resources in year one was £367.54 m. The first year's allocation amounted to £125 m, resulting in 300% overbidding for the first year's resources. A second bidding round was launched in April 1995; £40 m will be available in 1996/97 with a further £200 m in 1997/98 (Mawson *et al.*, 1995, p. 50). The Regional Offices are responsible for considering the bids submitted and for making recommendations on their selected bids to Ministers.

Department of the Environment
Estate Action
Housing Action Trusts
City Challenge
Urban Programme
English Partnerships
Urban Development Corporations
Inner City Task Forces
City Action Teams

Employment Department
Programme Development Fund
Education Business Partnerships
Teacher Placement Service
Compacts/Inner City Compacts
Business Start-Up Scheme
Local Initiative Fund
TEC Challenge

Home Office
Safer Cities
Section 11 Grants (part targeted at 57 Urban Priority Areas)
Ethnic Minority Business Initiative

Department of Trade and Industry
Regional Enterprise Grants
English Estates

Department of Education
Grants for Educational Support and Training

Fig. 4.3   The Single Regeneration Budget – Constituent Programmes

The introduction of the SRB and Government Offices for the Regions can be seen as the most significant change in urban policy since the publication of the White Paper, *Policy for the Inner Cities* (DoE, 1977). The SRB is intended to encourage new approaches to deal with economic decline, social deprivation and social exclusion by providing flexible support for regeneration and economic development that is sensitive to local needs and priorities. The content of the bids demonstrates that the most prominent initiatives are aimed at encouraging sustainable economic growth and wealth by improving the competitiveness of the local economy, and enhancing the employment prospects, education and skills of local people. In a survey carried out by the University of Birmingham in conjunction with the University of Central England, economic growth and employment/education initiatives were listed as having the highest priority by 72% of respondents. Conversely only 5% prioritised ethnic minority projects and 12% housing. In this way the SRB continues the shift in urban policy focus away from social welfare concerns towards stimulating mainstream economic activity. The Government's recent decision to terminate the financial assistance available under the Urban Programme and through mechanisms such as Section 11 and the Safer Cities programme, together with the abandonment of the practice of allocating urban funding on the basis of targeting priority areas based on indicators of social and economic need, reinforces this trend and will significantly impact on the poorest areas in Britain.

The SRB and the new integrated Regional Offices represent a marked change in the institutional arrangements governing urban policy. The SRB carries forward the innovations of City Challenge, namely comprehensive multi-year regeneration programmes, local development partnerships, cross-departmental co-ordination within local authorities and inter-agency working. It also introduces integrated multi-departmental funding and Training and Enterprise Council/Local Authority/business leadership co-sponsorship. The new unified budget is intended to be flexible, enabling the transfer of funds from one budget to another. It is clear from the bidding guidance that economic regeneration is prioritised. The objective of regenerating deprived areas remains, but there is a new emphasis on improving the industrial competitiveness of firms and creating economic development initiatives that attempt to link the mainstream economy and deprived communities.

Stewart (1994, pp. 3–4) has observed that whilst the rhetoric of central government policy has stressed co-ordination, collaboration and partnership, the reality of much urban policy intervention, particularly during the 1990s, has, so far, been centralised, fragmented, and competitive. These trends are consistent with the 'hollowing out' of the nation state and the respecification of the roles and powers of central and local government observed by Jessop (1994) and Cochrane (1993). It has changed the nature of the activity of planning and shifted the priorities of local government. Local government has become less concerned with welfarist issues of social redistribution and the provision of public services and more involved with creating the conditions for economic competitiveness, attracting investment capital and the production of a favourable 'business climate'. Hoggett (1987) has even argued that the labour process within the welfare state and local government within that is beginning to mirror changes in the Post-Fordist modes of production, incorporating leaner, flatter managerial structures, decentralisation, generic roles, team working and flexibility. Much of this change has been brought about by the imperatives forced upon local authorities through the Compulsory Competitive Tendering legislation and bidding regimes for urban funding.

Conclusions

This chapter has attempted to apply regulation theory to the trends in urban policy. It has been suggested that urban policy as a specific form of regulation has shifted away from welfarist concerns towards entrepreneurialism and competitiveness. This shift corresponds to changes from a Fordist to a Post-Fordist mode of regulation. Although there is much dispute about the Post-

Fordist model of regulation (Cochrane, 1993, p. 89) it appears to capture what Hoggett (1990, p. 2) has described as 'the "deep structure" of the coming period.'

Through the current form of urban policy, the Government is attempting to respond to the pressures created by the globalisation of economic activity. The variety of competitive initiatives and the City Pride initiative have been designed primarily to create the conditions for the improved structural competitiveness of industry. The aim is to improve the competitive edge of cities and their regions in the European and international market place. Issues of social redistribution are secondary. This overt economic role of urban policy is to be implemented by institutional arrangements and labour processes within the state that are very different to those that characterised the period prior to the late-1970s. Within the context of increasing centralisation of powers and decision-making, initiatives such as City Challenge and the SRB adopt processes of corporatist localism (Stewart, 1994), which seek to involve a variety of local interests, particularly the private sector, in the development of local vision, priorities and bids for resources. As Stewart (1994, p. 12) observes: 'This approach to the management of inter-city competition and to the development of bids for regeneration resources seeks to further remove urban policy from the arena of overt and formal local politics. It establishes an arm's length process for the development of local regeneration strategies from which the majority of local elected politicians are distanced. The SRB, therefore, reinforces the tendencies evident within City Challenge to hive off urban regeneration from local authority mainstream debate, tendencies which Inner Cities policy has fed since the initiation of policy in 1977.'

These changes have also contributed to the pressures within local authorities to adopt new practices, including greater inter-departmental and inter-agency liaison, generic roles and team working, and fast track decision making. Very often the role of the planner in relation to the new urban policy initiatives has been central. The traditional role of the planner as a perceived mediator of interests, able to coordinate a range of professional inputs, and concerned with the formulation of area-based plans and strategies has meant that senior planners have found themselves coordinating the policy response of the local authority.

If this new approach to urban policy was intended as part of a transitional regime, to help overcome the current crisis of accumulation, just how successful has it been and how enduring is it likely to be? A Policy Studies Institute report on urban trends published in 1992 was unequivocal in its judgement, stating that: 'After 15 years and many new initiatives, surprisingly little has been achieved' (Wilmott and Hutchinson, 1992, p. 3). Robinson and Shaw (1994, p. 232) also claim that UK urban policy has failed: 'it has not reduced unemployment, cut crime, tackled homelessness or reduced poverty. It has not regenerated local economies or improved the quality of life for the majority of urban dwellers. ... In short, the inner cities (and conurbations as a whole) are now more dangerous, deprived and demoralised places than they were a decade ago.' Even the major study commissioned by the DoE on urban policy over the last 15 years is ambivalent about achievements (Robson, 1994).

It could be suggested that the poor performance of urban policy is a reflection of the poor performance of the government's attempt at economic management generally. For example, Jessop (1994, p. 29) has argued that Thatcherism has failed to resolve the interlinked structural crises of British capitalism and its state inherited from a flawed Fordist past, 'indeed, the Major government is now confronted with a more deep-seated structural economic crisis but has a much reduced and seriously weakened set of state capacities with which to address it.'

If this is the verdict so far, what alternatives have been suggested to deal with the intractable nature of the urban problem? There are almost as many alternative approaches as there are organisations concerned about urban policy. The Centre for Local Economic Strategies (1994) has recently published a wide ranging report on the need for new approaches to urban policy. In their view, urban policy ought to be based on the concept of active citizenship, involving a people-led, not a property-led approach. Local authorities should lead in developing city strategies drawing on new and more substantial resources for infrastructure projects. These resources should come from a revived local government finance system, a new national Urban Programme building on the achievements of the SRB, and a European Urban policy funded from the Structural funds. The report also deals with sustainable development but its suggestions here do not seem well integrated with the main policy recommendations. Others also advocate community economic development as an approach to urban policy (Association of Metropolitan Authorities, 1993; Colenutt and Cutten, 1994).

The Labour Party's ideas for a new urban policy are, in comparison with its ideas on other policy areas, well developed. The Labour Party instituted its own national inquiry into urban policy in 1993 under Keith Vaz MP. The results of the City 2020 inquiry, published recently for consultation, set out key priorities which involve strengthening local and regional economies, increasing economic opportunities for deprived areas, transforming urban environments into safer, greener, more healthy places to live and work, rebuilding neighbourhoods, enhancing the quality of life and ensuring that sustainable development takes place. This is to be achieved by following four key principles. First, a strategic approach which involves the integration of national policies and programmes with European regional, county and local programmes to ensure that the multi-faceted problems of social disadvantage are tackled in a holistic urban policy approach. Second, local authorities are to be strengthened and given a central role in urban regeneration. Third, harnessing the commitment, aspirations and talents of local people in promoting community economic development will play an important role in urban policy. Fourth, partnerships are to be encouraged. These principles are to be implemented in the context of a long-term, strategic framework, based on adequate resourcing distributed on the basis of need and public planning. There is to be a new Minister for Urban Affairs and new Civic Forums established.

Whilst Labour's approach to urban policy appears to be more concerned with achieving a balance between stable economic growth and redistributive goals, the pressures and constraints exerted on the British economy from global competition will set the limits to what can be achieved. In the short term existing practices are likely to be consolidated. However, as Jessop (1994) concludes, there can be various forms of the Post-Fordist state and various transitional routes from Fordist to Post-Fordist regimes. Geddes (1994, p. 174) argues that the apparent failure of current neo-liberal policies presents an opening for the development of 'new Post-Fordist economic practices, structures and industrial sectors, and the restructuring of old sectors, (which) require new institutional modes of regulation, including an active and innovative economic role for the public sector, both to achieve environmentally sustainable growth and to combat the strong tendencies towards a polarised society and labour market.' Given what is at stake, struggle over the determination of any future form of urban policy as a constituent element of a Post-Fordist mode of regulation is of crucial importance.

PART III

PLANNING FOR HOUSING

INTRODUCTION

This section consists of two chapters which extend the economic themes raised in Part II to the specific issue of housing provision. Housing constitutes around 70% of the development in any town or city, and is therefore a substantial component in any development plan or local planning document. House building is also a major component of the activities of the construction industry, and thus of the economy itself (CISC, 1994). In the 1960s over a third of housing consisted of council housing in the form of local authority provision, whereas, in contrast, nowadays over two thirds of housing is owner occupied. In 1995 the Minister for Local Government and Housing stated that 'councils will never build houses again' (quote from speech of David Curry, at the Association of District Councils' Annual Conference, July 1995). Instead emphasis is being put upon the role of housing associations in providing social housing, and attempts are being made to expand the private rented sector. In the light of this shift in emphasis, in the first chapter in this section by Stuart Farthing traces the development of 'social housing', and looks at the present day trend towards attempting to provide 'affordable housing' by means of housing association activity. Christine Lambert, in contrast, in the following chapter, looks at the private housing market and its uneasy relationship with town planning. In both these chapters, in addition to the emphasis upon economic issues, the reader will also find material of relevance to the wider policy debates about urban form, sustainability, and the social role of planning.

Chapter 5

PLANNING AND SOCIAL HOUSING PROVISION

Stuart Farthing

| Changing agendas |

There is no doubt that change has been an important theme in recent commentaries on planning in the 1970s and 1980s. The meaning, significance and causes of change however have been the subject of considerable debate. Two important gaps can be identified in this literature. First, much of the debate has been conducted at the level of central policy; it has been too 'top down' and concerned with the rhetoric of policy change rather than the practice of planning (i.e. the roles and relationships between actors in the development process). Second, whilst it has recognised the importance of economic change in affecting planning, it has not looked at the importance of change in different development sectors on the practice of planning.

A key area of change for any analysis of planning practice is housing development. Housing is the single most important land use in towns, and represents a very significant proportion of all planning applications for development dealt with by planners (Rydin, 1993). Changes in the nature of housing provision or of sectors of housing provision over time will therefore have an important impact on the nature of planning practice. What we have witnessed in the last 20 years is the decline of one structure of social housing provision (council housing) and the growing comparative dominance of a second (market-based, owner occupied housing). Since 1988 there has been the emergence of a new structure of social housing provision (affordable housing) based on housing association development but increasingly closely tied to the dominant market-led owner occupied sector discussed in the next chapter. This third structure of provision is seen by some as a 'residualised' sector for the poor in comparison with the wider social mix originally envisaged for the council housing sector after World War Two. It may also be a sector which is dependent in its current form on the support of a right wing government. That too may be short-lived.

The term 'social housing' as used here is taken to mean housing that is provided at a price which is not principally determined by the profit motive, is allocated according to some notion of housing need and is subject to considerable state regulation (see Ball *et al.*, 1988). The discussion in this chapter is therefore about the changing roles and relationships of planners in issues of social housing development. It gives an account of the emergence of the affordable housing sector and focuses specifically on the planning policy developments which have played a part in its emergence. It also discusses some of the implications of the new emphasis in Government advice on urban recycling for the viability of this new approach to providing social housing.

The involvement of planners in affordable housing is seen by some as representing a major change in the definition of planning, a break from the narrow land use and environmental focus of planning and its embrace of social considerations as part of policy, and in its practice, in terms of the relationships that are being and need to be forged between different actors in the development process. Some of the question raised by this development are:

- What led to the identification of the issue of affordability?
- What was the policy response to that problem?
- What have been the results in terms of the roles and relationships of planners in the development process?

Housing and planning policy in the post-war era

To assess the importance of the changes that are taking place in planning for housing, it is useful to know something about the history of planning for housing and in particular the setting up of the post-war planning system. The aim here is not to cover the ground in detail but to provide a context in which recent changes in planning for housing can be assessed. The history of planning for housing shows at one level some similarity with the market economic context for planning described in Chapters 2 and 3, but there are differences due to the fact that housing development and housing policy have operated through two distinct sets of institutional structures (or structures of provision (Ball, 1983)) in the post-war period. One structure, owner occupied housing provision, has been clearly market driven but the other, council housing, whilst still constrained by market forces and operating within a market economy, has been less sensitive to the market. These institutional relationships determine how the general trends of economic change are worked out in terms of the content of housing change and how the institutional structure itself is changed. On the other hand it is important to realise that some sources of housing change are located within the housing system and these play an independent role in generating problems, policy responses and institutional change.

To understand the role of planning in housing, we need to understand these forces and therefore the role of town planners in that institutional structure, but as Ball (1983, p. 193) has pointed out there has been until recently a great academic divide between studies of housing and studies of planning:

the planning literature tends to be concerned only with the spatial distribution of housing and the effect of planning policies on the land market, whereas housing studies tend to ignore spatial questions by focusing on state legislation and subsidies related to tenures and households.

This itself may be one effect of the structures of provision for housing creating a divide between the professions which were involved in planning and housing respectively. One feature of the growing closeness of the two is reflected in a growing literature on the links and relationships between planning and housing professionals. In the discussion below there is an attempt to relate planning practice to evolving housing policy issues. Land use planning is a set of instruments and practices which seek to regulate the use and development of land. Essentially, planning control has had three distinct aspects in relation to housing as a land use. First, it has sought to regulate the amount and location of land to be developed for housing. Second, it has sought to regulate the layout, density and form of housing. Third, it has sought to regulate the price at which land has been made available for housing. Of these the first has arguably been the most important and consistent theme in planning control and to which most attention is devoted in this chapter.

Housing policy objectives

The aim of national policy for housing since the Second World War has generally been expressed in a consistent way: 'a decent home for every family at a price within their means' (Government White Paper *A Fair Deal for Housing*, 1971, quoted in Hills and Mullings, 1990), though after 1979, the policy objective has been couched more in terms of the promotion of owner occupation. Housing policy, in the context of this broad aim and of a perceived housing shortage, was, for at least the first 25 years of the post-war period, concerned with the number of houses built each year. Labour and Conservative Governments vied with each other in the 'numbers game', in setting targets for annual completions and in achieving (or failing to achieve) those targets during their terms of office. The main role of the planning system in meeting this objective was to identify the amount and location of land needed to accommodate new building.

There were two main ways of providing housing. First, speculative housebuilders provided housing for owner occupation. This sector was of growing importance during the post-war period, as we shall see below, though the planning system was set up on the assumption that the private sector of development would play only a residual role in housing and other aspects of development. The development control system was intended to regulate and control this sector.

Second, there was council housing and new town development, initiated by the public sector, the former by local housing authorities, the latter by

New Town Development Corporations. This type of development was perceived to involve, as Hall (1993) put it, 'the close and virtually automatic union' of planning and development. This was to be the positive side of planning.

Whilst the main role of planning has been to identify the amount and location of land needed for residential development, it has also had direct impacts on the price paid for housing land and indirect effects through its effects on the land market. Chapter 3 has already looked at development value taxation in relation to key periods in British town planning. This is a subject of considerable complexity and debate and the discussion here is of the direct impacts. Under the 1947 Act and its associated financial regulations, the housing that was built by the public sector on land acquired in the period up to 1953 was built on cheap land, that is at prices reflecting 'existing use' value. The 1947 Act nationalised the right to develop land and landowners were to be compensated for lost development rights once and for all from a £300 m fund where they could show hardship. If land was developed privately for owner occupied housing, then a development charge of 100% of the increase in land value over existing use value would be paid by the landowner to the state. This was a severe disincentive to land sales and it was claimed that buyers were forced to pay the development charge twice over, once to the landowner and once to the state, in order to persuade owners to sell.

This system was scrapped in 1953 with the abolition of the development charge. However, under the 1954 Town and Country Planning Act, land sales through compulsory purchase to the public sector for housebuilding continued to be at existing use value but the price paid for land by private housebuilders was current market value. The explanation for this anomaly is probably the one put forward by Stephen Merrett (1979) that the scale of local authority housebuilding was greater than at any time in British history and that to introduce market values for land acquisition for this programme would have raised capital expenditure, increased rents and unleashed pressures for wage increases. It also has to be borne in mind that the political commitment to building 300,000 dwellings per annum was seen as being dependent on local authorities, which Macmillan, the Minister of Housing, saw in a pragmatic way as 'plannable instruments' (Donnison, 1967)

In 1959, to correct the perceived inequity between the sectors, full market value became the basis of compulsory purchase and land was acquired at the same cost in both sectors. Subsequent attempts in the 1960s and 1970s were made by Labour governments to tackle the land value question associated with the grant of planning permission but the measures were repealed by incoming Conservative governments before they had had much impact on the land market and they did not change the way local authorities acquired sites. For council housing land acquisition costs per dwelling rose from 2% to 3% of total capital costs in the early 1950s to a figure of 19% in 1975 (Merrett, 1979, p. 81).

Growing housing needs and demands

Initially at least in the post-war period it was expected that housing needs would be limited once war-time shortages had been overcome (Donnison, 1967). Population and housing needs were not expected to grow very rapidly and the task of the post-war planning system was to distribute or rather to redistribute an essentially static population within regions, decentralising the large conurbations, reducing densities and moving overspill population to new towns. But in practice, housing needs increased quite rapidly in the 1950s and early-1960s as both population and household formation grew. Coupled with the growth of the economy in favoured regions of South East England and the Midlands, there was unexpected pressure for urban development in and around the urban areas.

Hall (1994) concludes that it was inevitable that changes would be needed in the planning system and that the public sector alone would not have been able to adjust and cope with the increased demand for housing. He argues that the private sector would have had to play an increased role in any event. In practice the period of change coincided with a Conservative Government strongly committed to an increased role for private enterprise. Whilst the construction industry obtains business whether new building is promoted by the public sector through 'general needs' programmes or through private sector speculative development, the advantage of speculative development is that it gives an opportunity to make profit from both the construction and the land development processes. Merrett (1979) suggests that this may have been a factor in the Conservative government restricting the role of local authorities to slum clearance in 1956. The share of housing provided by the public sector in the form of council housing and housing in new towns fell from well over 80% in 1950 to a fluctuating level of between 40% and 50% of total output from the 1960s through to the end of the 1970s.

The planning system had, therefore, to find the land required by an expanded private sector. This land was sought in those suburban localities where containment policy as endorsed by central government through Green Belt policy (Circular, 1955) was trying to restrict development and where local political sentiment was strongly anti-development (Drewett, 1973). In practice, development leapfrogged the Green Belt and expansion took place in the towns and villages beyond it. Land was also required by the public sector but as Hall (1994) points out the big problem of the 1950s and early-1960s was that land was increasingly in short supply in the cities, where housing needs, slum clearance and the commitment to provide council housing were all most strongly felt. Hence the big 'planning battles' of the 1950s were around the development of council housing on large sites in the Green Belt. These were battles that the cities ultimately lost, forcing council housing development back into the cities.

Some important points follow from this history. First, the 1947 system was based on the production of development plans which were to show all the intended changes in land use over a period of 25 years. In practice, development plans have tended not to identify or allocate all the land that has been needed for housing development, because the unexpected growth of housing demand in the post-war period invalidated development plans, and because of the control of the local planning system in potential growth areas by politicians opposed to further growth. Hence much private sector housing land has been identified for development through development control decisions following planning applications from developers. By contrast, much of the public sector's demand for land has been met through planned land release, in new towns and expanded towns and in the redevelopment of inner city areas through slum clearance.

Second, the nature of the housing needs that are met by the new housing that is built has not in general been a concern to the planning system. The meeting of housing 'needs' has been a function of housing policy, through decisions on the type of housing constructed and through housing allocation policies for council housing, both areas in which local authorities had considerable discretion. 'Demand' has been met through the market process in the private sector.

Third, the type of land developed shows differences between the sectors. In general, the private sector has tended to develop mostly on greenfield or rural sites whilst the public sector has located in specific greenfield locations (under the new town and expanded town programme) or has been involved in recycling urban land, through particularly the redevelopment of inner city housing (see Best, 1981).

Finally, this pattern of development and division of responsibilities brought about distinctive and separate roles for planners and housing officers in local government. Planners have seen themselves (and have been seen) as having particular responsibilities and relationships with the private sector in housing supply and in assessing the overall requirements for housing. By contrast, housing officers have seen themselves as having responsibilities for council housing – the building, letting and management of that stock of dwellings – and meeting housing needs. Given the arguments above about the type of land developed, this division of professional responsibility had a geographical (urban–rural) dimension. In the rural areas planners were based in the county authorities whilst the few staff involved in housing work were at the local level (urban and rural district councils, municipal boroughs). Even in county boroughs, where collaboration was possible between planning and housing within a single purpose authority, collaboration was poor. As Donnison and Ungerson (1982) point out, housing functions were often not in a single department.

The restructuring of planning and the reshaping of housing policy

Despite the constant reshaping of planning over the post-war period revealed in Chapters 2 and 3, the period of the 1970s has been seen as one of 'crisis' for the planning system (Ambrose, 1986; Brindley *et al.*, 1989). Of all the products of post-war development and redevelopment, it was perhaps the high rise block of flats on a cleared inner city site (replacing the close-knit community of terraced housing) which was seen as symbolising the failure of planning and its ideology of modernisation of the city (paradoxically, given the arguments above about the respective roles of the housing and planning professions). Planners moved away from any vision of the city at all and became concerned instead with implementation or 'getting things done', which meant in practice working closely with the private sector.

Merrett (1979) says of the period from the late 1960s: 'there has probably been no other period in modern British history when the impact of broad macroeconomic trends on the sphere of housing have been starker or more powerful.' For this reason, therefore, it was also a period of transition for the housing system and housing policy though 'housing' factors too played a part (Williams, 1992, p. 160): 'Looking back over the 1970s it is clear that the decline in housebuilding and capital investment had already begun and that these were visible reflections of both the International Monetary Fund (IMF) imposed cuts and real uncertainty as to whether the public sector had reached its optimum size with housing needs largely met.' Given the crude surplus of dwellings over households, it was believed by the government that there was no longer a national housing problem, just a series of local difficulties.

But it would be wrong to date the questioning of the role of council housing to the 1970s. The inflation of construction and financing costs associated with the provision of new council housing in the 1960s led the government to reduce subsidy commitment to it, to encourage councils to raise rents of older housing to subsidise new construction and to introduce rent rebate schemes for the poor (Parker, 1967; Merrett, 1979). Through the 1980s, housing policy has been reshaped (Malpass, 1990) and the role of the planning system in meeting national housing policy objectives has been redefined. Planning is now concerned with planning for affordable housing.

Affordable housing

Identification of the problem

The problem of the lack of affordable housing needs to be seen in the context of the changes to British housing policy discussed above. The general aim of housing policy ('a decent home at a price within their means') which we have seen was espoused by governments in the post-war period, was replaced (or at least downplayed) in the 1980s with two main objectives: encouraging the growth of owner occupation and reducing and redefining the role of council housing. The 'Right to Buy' (RTB) policy implemented in 1980 made a significant contribution to both objectives by increasing sales of publicly owned stock through the grant of discounts to council tenants on the market prices of their houses. Williams (1992) suggests that about half the growth in owner occupation between 1979, when it stood at 54% of dwellings in the UK, to 67% in 1990 was due to this sales programme.

Local councils have not continued to build to replace the stock that has been lost through sales. The main factors here have been a shortage of capital funds, lack of subsidies and general government discouragement. Local authorities have seen the definition of their role in relation to housing change from one of the 'provision' of housing to an 'enabling role' in which they facilitate and support other agencies in providing housing (Bramley, 1993a). Over the period the number of dwellings built by local authorities has fallen from 79,009 in 1979 to 17,087 in 1989 and below 10,000 per annum in the 1990s. This has reduced the capacity of the sector to house new households though relets of properties have compensated to some degree.

One of the twin pillars of post-war housing policy – council housing – is certainly therefore in strong decline at least in terms of the provision of new housing. Efforts to distribute the stock which has not been sold under the RTB to private landlords and to the housing association sector have not so far been as effective as expected in eliminating the sector. Its role has also been redefined under the impact of sales. Sales have disproportionately been of the more attractive properties (houses) in the more attractive areas and have been bought by the better-off households within the sector. There has therefore been a 'residualisation' of the sector – a growing concentration of the poor, the unemployed and those dependent on state benefits in council housing (Forrest and Murie, 1988).

More households in the 1980s were therefore depending on the private owner occupied market for housing and there was a decline in the supply of new rented accommodation. Around the middle of the decade, there began to be quite serious concern about the shortage of rented housing. An independent inquiry into British housing (HRH The Duke of Edinburgh, 1985) suggested that this was a major problem and that private money ought to be brought into the social rented sector to help expand it.

Since more and (relatively) lower income households were expected to rely on the private market for housing, the costs to households of that housing became more important and their ability to pay those costs (affordability) also became more important. There is good evidence that the sector has been catering for lower income groups. Hills and Mullings (1990) show that in 1974 the average income of first-time buyers, as reported to building societies, was 30% higher than average male earnings but by 1987 it was only 7% higher. (See also Doling et al., 1986.)

Two factors which increased the salience of affordability were the changes in unemployment and in incomes in the 1980s. There were very large increases in unemployment in the recession of the early 1980s (Armstrong et al., 1985), which reduced incomes and effectively disbarred some households from seeking owner occupied housing. Perhaps more important, it caused considerable problems in terms of insecurity of tenure for those households who had bought and for whom the recession brought loss of first, second and subsequent household incomes (Doling *et al.*, 1986).

Unemployment remained high and continued to grow until 1986. Despite reductions in unemployment in the later-1980s, trends in income distribution have meant that the ability to pay for housing has been reduced for the lower paid. Research funded by the Joseph Rowntree Foundation (JRF, 1995a) shows that whereas between 1966 and 1977 all wages grew at much the same rate, after 1978 any benefits from economic growth were very unevenly distributed. Wages for the lowest paid have hardly changed, and by 1992 were lower in real terms than in 1975. Median wages grew by 35% while high wages grew by 50%. These effects of course are highlighted for those entering the labour market and hoping to set up independent households.

What however is 'affordability'? There is no doubt that the debate has led to considerable confusion. For individual households the amount they are prepared or able to pay for housing will depend on their incomes. The amount they have to pay to rent or buy housing of a given standard will reflect the operation of the housing system. Where the government judges that the costs to households are too high, it can either subsidise the cost to the household or the costs of production (or both). So 'affordability' concerns the relationship between the costs of renting or buying accommodation and the incomes of those who rent or buy. But it also includes some normative judgements about what households ought to pay out of their incomes to acquire housing of some minimum standard.

The starting point however is the cost of housing in relation to incomes. The cost of housing is unfortunately not unambiguous, as Hills and Mullings (1990) make clear. Different answers are obtained depending on which of property taxes, water charges, costs of repair and maintenance are included. How are the housing costs of owner occupiers to be measured and are they comparable with those of tenants? What recognition is made of the fact that an owner occupier is paying not just for the right to occupy accommodation but is also acquiring a capital asset that they will own once the debt is repaid? There is also the possibility of making capital gains from owner occupied housing, something which was of considerable debate in the 1980s, when house prices were rising rapidly. Concern in the 1990s has been over losses as house prices have fallen and increasing numbers of households have suffered from 'negative equity' (the price of the house they occupy being less than the loan raised to purchase it).

On top of this we need to decide whether we are interested in the costs before or after subsidies. Are we interested in gross rents or rents net of Housing Benefit receipts and in mortgage payments that include or exclude mortgage interest tax relief? If housing costs are rising it is possible that government subsidy may bear the cost through increased benefit payments or other subsidy. However, it is clear that from the 1970s through the 1980s, no matter how costs are measured, housing became 'significantly more expensive in relation to incomes' (Hills and Mullings, 1990, p. 201). This therefore means that government subsidies failed to address the rising costs of housing.

The reason for the increase in the costs of local authority housing to tenants has been attributed to reduction in general subsidy and increases in rents in the early 1980s (Cooper and Hopper, 1990) and reductions in the value of housing benefit, all of which can be seen as stemming directly from the policies of the Thatcher government to reduce the role of council housing and to encourage tenants to become owners through the RTB policy. For owner occupiers, the causes are rising real house prices over the period 1982–1989. Once again the government policy of encouraging owner occupation is in part implicated in the trend.

If the causes of the problem of rising housing costs are due in large measure to government policies, then the awareness of the problem has been shaped by the growth in indicators like the number of households in arrears with mortgages and households who were subject to repossession by building societies. Both grew very rapidly in the 1980s. But probably the most widely acknowledged indicator of the problem was the growth of homelessness. Official statistics show that households accepted as homeless by local authorities grew 100% between 1980 and 1990. Whilst the interpretation of the growth in homelessness is somewhat problematic (it is a flow rather than a stock measure, it excludes single people who have no roof over their heads, but includes others who are currently housed but who are threatened by homelessness) it has been very important in affecting public perceptions of the problems of access to housing.

Research sponsored by the Association of District Councils (ADC, 1987; Bramley, 1988) showed that on the basis of certain assumptions about incomes and mortgages, only about one third of households could afford to buy a three-bedroom house on the open market. This 'affordability gap' varied by region with only 16% of households in Greater London able to buy such a dwelling but even in the most favoured region – the North West – less than half of households (47%) could afford to buy. This research too was important in affecting the policy debate at the end of the 1980s.

The identification of the problem in the sense of government acknowledgement of the need to address the problem of the lack of affordable housing or housing for the poor came in 1987. The government indicated its desire to revive the private rented sector in a White Paper and to put housing associations at 'centre stage' of subsidised housing for rent (Langstaff, 1992):

> The Government believes that housing associations have a vitally important role to play in the revival of the independent rented sector. During recent years they have been almost alone in the independent rented sector in investing in rented housing and have played a key part in developing a new style of management and new forms of low cost home ownership. It will be important to build on this success and to develop it further.
>
> (DoE, 1987b, p. 12, *Housing: The Government's Proposals*, quoted in Langstaff, 1992; also see DoE, 1987c, *Land for Housing*)

Policy responses

By the mid-1980s it was recognised that the policy of increasing owner occupation alone would not meet the housing needs of all the population. Hostility to local government and to council housing ensured that the need for rented housing could not (for ideological reasons) be met by encouraging local authorities to expand their role in the building or provision of housing. Also for ideological reasons the revival of the private rented sector would be acceptable but there was an acknowledgement that in relation to private renting all that could be achieved was to stem the decline. The need for state support and subsidy for housing remained. Housing associations therefore became the agencies which would play this role.

In the 1980s, after a period of rapid expansion in the 1970s, housing associations had entered a period of what Langstaff (1992) has called 'benign neglect' in which their development programmes were cut but not eliminated, in which both the favourable subsidy system of the 1970s and the stable 'no risk' development regime were maintained. The 1988 Housing Act set out to change this environment but to allow for the expansion of the role of the housing association sector by a combination of increased public sector funding with a rising proportion of private funding. Though there was an unexpected 'hiccough' in expansion of the programme in the late-1980s (Randolph, 1993) there was rapid expansion in development in the early to mid-1990s (financial years 1990/1991 to 1994/1995).

Whilst the expansion of the housing association sector came from direct central government initiative, the changing role of the planning system in relation to the achievement of housing policy objectives originated from a mix of essentially local experiences and innovations in planning practice in both urban and rural areas. These initiatives, which central government initially sought to control and regulate but finally endorsed, involved the cooperation and collaboration of a range of public (local authorities, parish councils), private (housebuilders, land owners) and voluntary bodies (rural housing trusts and housing associations) working together to find solutions to the need for affordable housing in rural areas.

From the urban areas in the 1970s there were the initial experiments with 'planning gain' negotiations with developers (Herington, 1984). A whole range of 'community benefits' were sought by planners through the mechanism of an agreement under Section 52 of the Town and Country Planning Act 1971 (subsequently Section 106 agreements) with developers of private schemes. Finance and provision of land were negotiated for road improvements, public space, public access and facilities of various kinds. Housing played some part in these agreements (Byrne, 1989). In London, for example, there were agreements for some element of council housing in some private (re)development schemes. The practice of planning gain agreements spread in the 1980s and so did the practice of negotiating a proportion of low cost housing on private housing sites as a planning gain. But numbers overall were not large.

Research by Barlow and Chambers (1992) gives an insight into the origin of these policies, which were due to a mix of 'professional' and 'political' influences within local government and of political factors in the local area. They isolate four main groups of authorities involved in negotiating an element of low cost housing on private sites. In the first a proactive policy stance was led by planning officers (and sometimes officers from other departments) to find ways of providing affordable housing. Council members were brought in at a later stage and 'were simply presented with various policy options'. These authorities were most common in areas of rapid growth around London. In the second, the policy was politically driven with planning and housing officers translating the political objectives into policy. These were essentially London Boroughs. Interestingly they suggest that party political make-up here had no real effect on the evolution of policies. But political pressure resulting from local opposition to growth did have an effect and led to social housing being sought to reduce objections to new development. A third group of authorities were influenced by experience with 'exceptions' policy discussed below. The final group had had no clear policy but had responded in an *ad hoc* way to specific development proposals.

From rural areas particularly in the 1980s but starting with the Lake District National Park Planning Board in 1977 (Shucksmith, 1981), rural planning authorities experimented with 'local needs' and 'affordable' housing policies. In rural areas there was a particularly clear recognition of the problems of access to housing for low income households. Problems arose on both the supply and the demand side of rural housing markets (Lambert *et al.*, 1992). In rural areas there had always been a relatively low stock of local authority housing to meet housing need. This low stock was threatened by losses through the RTB policy. And as we have seen above local councils were unable to build new housing to replace the diminishing stock, whilst the housing association sector was very poorly represented in rural areas. The private rented sector, too, was in rapid decline in the 1980s due in part to agricultural restructuring and the continued decline in agricultural employment but also to the attraction for landlords of selling off rented housing for owner occupation. Overall the private rented sector declined more rapidly in rural areas in the 1980s than in the country as a whole.

Despite the perception of some 'loosening up' of the planning system in the 1980s in order to facilitate owner occupied housing development (as discussed by Lambert in the next chapter), the planning system was seen to remain very restrictive in those parts of the country with protective landscape designations (Green Belts, AONBs, Areas of Great Landscape Value, National Parks). This led to restrictions on the supply of housing in general but to the detriment particularly of the local low income population.

On the demand side trends in counter-urbanisation were well established (Herington, 1984). Population continued to grow in rural areas faster than in urban areas with particularly rapid growth in a belt of authorities on the edge of the South East region (Hall, 1988). Urban housing markets were spreading into rural areas, increasing competition for the available housing stock with local working class households in competition for housing with rich in-migrants (retirees, commuters from urban areas) and with potential second homes owners. In consequence there was a polarisation of the income distribution in rural areas. McLaughlin (1986), for example, showed that non-manual earnings were higher and manual earnings were lower in rural areas than in Great Britain as a whole.

According to CHICL and CPRE (1990) over 1,140,000 dwellings were built in the shire counties of England in the period 1981–1988 with particularly rapid growth in the southern regions of the country (East Anglia, South East and South West England) but this led observers to talk of a 'housing paradox': large numbers of houses being built at the same time as a growing problem of rural homelessness was being observed.

These trends led to the identification of the planning system as both a cause of the problems for low income households in rural areas but also therefore as a potential solution. There are three linked problems for low income households in rural areas: the lack of supply, the cost of housing and access to housing. The planning system was seen as a cause in the sense that it restricted land supply and new housing development in general in rural areas. Second, it was seen as a cause in that restrictive planning policies increased land values on those sites in rural areas that were released for development. Land value increases on the grant of planning permission in rural areas were particularly noticeable. Land in agricultural use was quoted at £700–£2000 per acre but at the height of the late-1980s boom the price for housing land was as high as £500,000 per acre (Clark, 1988). These high land values were seen as a major impediment to the provision of housing at a low cost 'affordable' to households on low incomes. The planning system was therefore a cause of the third problem – poor access to housing.

The planning system could potentially help resolve these problems by, first, releasing more land for housing development. Second, if land represents some 40% of the cost of providing a new house (Constable, 1988), then any reduction in land values engineered by using the planning system could make a major contribution to reducing the cost and therefore increasing the accessibility of housing to low income households. Third, the planning system might be made to restrict access to housing as it did, for example, in relation to housing for agricultural workers under Circular 24/75 *Housing Needs and Action*.

Early policy initiatives developed these last two ideas. The wholesale release of land in rural areas to permit more housing was unlikely to obtain widespread support from rural interests even if it was felt to be effective. 'Local needs' policies sought to retain tight control on the numbers of houses built but also aimed to restrict the occupancy of the housing to local people. By 1985, there were explicit local needs policies in 20 structure plans (Rogers, 1985). By restricting access to the housing it was hoped to restrict the market to local people with relatively low incomes. House prices and land values would therefore be reduced.

However as Bishop and Hooper (1991) point out, these policies led to conflict with the DoE, which through most of the 1980s was taking the view that such policies were not land based and were therefore outside the remit of development plans (as outlined in Circular 22/84 *Memorandum on Structure and Local Plans*). Nevertheless, research by the ACC (1989) shows that a number of local planning authorities had successfully used planning agreements or conditions to restrict occupancy to local people. The success of these policies in reducing costs and restricting access to local people is however not known, but Clark (1988) suggests that low valuations did not necessarily follow restrictions to locals only. Quoting an example in Kent, he says that the District Valuer had insisted that the market price is cut by only 20% and with land at the time (1988) at £500,000 per acre this resulted in a land value of £400,000 per acre, which is hardly more affordable.

Another local policy initiative – the 'exceptions' policy – associated particularly with New Forest District Council, which had a policy in its local plan as early as 1986, combined 'local needs' restrictions with policies to reduce land values more directly. Here the key to reducing land value and thus the cost of the housing to the final occupier was to grant permission for housing on sites that would not normally expect to get planning permission for housing – hence the term 'exception site'. These sites were typically on the periphery of villages. A landowner here might thus be inclined to sell the land because some development value could be obtained from the sale. On the other hand the land value would be substantially lower than open market value for residential planning permission and thus the housing constructed on the site would be more affordable to local people. Rural housing associations promoted by the Rural Housing Trust (formerly NACRT) have been involved in initiating these schemes in a number of areas. The restriction of the housing to local people only initially and in the long term is achieved through the mechanism of a planning agreement. The evidence of an evaluation of the schemes in operation in 1991 carried out for the Department of the Environment showed that though they reduced costs of housing significantly below market levels, the costs were not necessarily affordable to local households in need (Williams and Bell, 1992).

The significant turning point in the history of these initiatives and in the evolution of the role of the planning system in housing provision came with the endorsement of the 'exceptions' policy by the Secretary of State for the Environment in a written answer to a Parliamentary question in February 1989. The significance of the change is that it runs counter to the previous approach of the government as shown in Circulars 22/84 and 1/85 *The Use of Conditions in Planning Permissions*, and other advice on local needs policy (Bishop and Hooper, 1991). It recognises the importance of 'social issues' to land use planning, and the nature of the users of land rather than the use of land alone is established as a material planning consideration. The change of policy was also reflected in the advice given to planning authorities preparing development plans (PPG12 *Development Plans and Regional Planning Guidance*)

– they could include social issues in the preparation of policies – and in the advice on planning agreements and obligations, where the mix of uses in a development was highlighted as grounds for negotiating with developers (Circular 16/91, Planning and Compensation Act 1991: *Planning Obligations*).

The change of view on 'exceptions' policy in rural areas was incorporated into the related DoE Circular 7/91 *Planning and Affordable Housing* (and thereafter into a revised PPG3, *Housing*, in March 1992), which also promoted the policy of negotiating an element of affordable housing on private sites, sometimes known as a 'percentage' policy.

Circular 7/91 established that:

- the community's need for affordable housing was a material planning consideration;
- new housing developments of a substantial scale should include a reasonable mix of house types and sizes to cater for a range of housing needs;
- where there is a clear need for affordable housing that planners could indicate an overall target for affordable housing across the plan area, and on particular sites given evidence of need and site suitability;
- planners could seek to negotiate with developers for the provision of affordable housing on sites and could include policies in local plans indicating the intention to do so but the approach should be a flexible one and one that varied from site to site;
- policies could be incorporated in plans, but would need to establish what is meant by 'affordable' housing given the economics of the locality, and what measures would be taken to ensure the long-term reservation for those in housing need;
- planning agreements could be used to restrict the occupation of property to people in certain categories of need (provided the criteria are specified in the plan) but could not be used to impose restrictions on tenure, price or ownership.

There is a certain ambiguity and tension in this policy advice between the desire to deliver affordable housing and the desire to restrict the powers of the planning system to matters of land use, which reflects a legal interpretation of the ambit of the Town and Country Planning Acts. Hence whilst the Circular said that planners should not seek to restrict tenure or price it also said that the best way of achieving the benefit of affordable housing in perpetuity was through the involvement of housing associations or other social housing bodies.

There is also ambiguity, not to say confusion in the concept of affordable housing as further developed in government statements. Tim Yeo (1991, p. 2) for example drew a distinction between:

> on the one hand, 'social' or 'subsidised' housing, which is that provided by a social landlord, normally with public subsidy, and, on the other hand, 'affordable' or 'low cost' housing, which is any housing accessible to households who cannot afford to

buy in the open market ... Some of the need for affordable housing will be met by 'social' housing that receives public subsidy; some will be met through the provision of low cost housing in the market and the use, for example, of shared ownership arrangements.

The confusion arises here because the private market provides a range of housing, of different sizes and at different prices, and it is not clear that low cost housing provided in this way is to be counted as affordable or not. Similarly the notion of social housing given here is defined by the receipt of public subsidy yet shared ownership housing, which also receives public subsidy, is not counted as social housing and is described as being 'in the market'. The point I think here is that the government whilst conceding that some households will need rented and subsidised housing also wants as many as possible to become owner occupiers (with or without the aid of subsidy). These definitional problems have continued to be a problem for planners seeking to negotiate with developers. The latter have claimed that the housing they build is necessarily affordable.

Planning and social housing: with particular reference to housing associations

New roles and relationships for planners

Earlier in this chapter it was argued that the system that developed in the post-war period in planning for housing was one characterised by four main dimensions. It is now time to make a provisional assessment of whether the policy changes of the late-1980s and 1990s – the expansion of housing association development activity and the planning policy innovations – have produced a system which is significantly different from the one described earlier. Having done that, the section next assesses the impact of these changes on professional tasks and activities (research, policy formulation and implementation).

Before doing so, it has to be acknowledged that it may be premature to make these judgements in two senses. First, the changes are relatively recent. Housing association development activity under the new mixed (public/ private) funding regime only really achieved significantly expanded output levels in 1992/93. A Housing Corporation research study (Farthing *et al.*, 1996) showed that about half of the development activity over the period 1992/93–1994/95 took place on local authority land banks, land that in many cases was originally destined for council housing. The planning system was responsible for releasing only a small minority of housing association development sites through 'exception' site policies (4% of sites) and through 'percentage' sites (9% of sites). Part of the reason for this is the relatively recent endorsement of the new policy stance: 1989 in the case of the exception site policy and 1991 in the case of the percentage site policy. There has been a very rapid diffusion of policy adoption through the early-1990s. Farthing *et al.* (1996) conclude that housing association land development activities are in a period of transition from dependence on local authority land to privately owned and other public sector land. The current pattern therefore is heavily imprinted with traces of the declining council housing sector.

The second sense in which it may be premature to make judgements on the transition from one structure of provision to another is the possibility that the expansion of the housing association development programme and the change in planning policy may themselves be shortlived. The Approved Development Programme (ADP) for the housing association sector has been cut back quite substantially from the year 1995/96 onwards and the levels of construction actually achieved in the boom period 1992/93–1994/95 only returned the sector to the levels of activity achieved in the late 1970s (Walentowicz, 1991). The further development of the sector and of the role of the planning system will depend on the outcome of future elections. It might not be surprising to find a future Labour government committed to a revival of council housing in some form based on the spending of accumulated capital receipts from local authority sales of dwellings under the RTB policy and land sales.

Setting aside these considerations and accepting that we are witnessing a new phase of housing development, with both an owner occupied and a housing association sector, what changes can we observe from the previous system based on owner occupied and council housing? First, the mechanisms used to release land for owner occupied and council housing from the 1940s to the 1970s were, it will be remembered, distinct in that private sector development tended to take place in locations which were not identified in development plans whereas council housing development tended to be in areas allocated in plans. Under the emerging systems of provision in the 1990s, the planning mechanisms for affordable and owner occupied housing are reversed. Plans will show where housing will be permitted. The presumption will be that the majority of those sites will be for the owner occupied market. They will be less clear on where affordable housing will be located since provision will be negotiated on a site-by-site basis and much housing association development will be on small sites that the planning system has not traditionally been able to identify in development plans.

Second, whilst under the former system of planning for housing, housing needs were not a material planning consideration, now they are. Housing needs in a plan area can be used to justify the negotiation of some element of affordable housing with landowners and developers in the area.

Third, whilst historically there was a clear segregation between the location of owner occupied and council development, and distinctive patterns of land development with the owner occupied sector on greenfield sites and council housing typically on urban redevelopment sites, there is emerging a close relationship between the types of land developed for affordable and owner occupied housing, and the methods of provision are increasingly closely interconnected.

Finally, the distinct and separate roles for planners and housing officers in local government are being replaced by overlapping roles and responsibilities. A key theme is collaboration between a diverse range of organisations and interests. Dunmore (1992, p. 2) for example says: 'These changes have far-reaching implications for local authorities, housing associations, private landowners and developers. ... But they will also require much closer cooperation between local authority Housing and Planning departments and between local authorities and the private sector than has so far been the case. For such cooperation to be effective each side needs to understand the other's point of view and the constraints under which they operate.'

The urban–rural division of professional responsibilities of the 1950s through to the 1970s, when housing officers were concerned with new council housing development in the cities and planners were involved in private development in rural areas, has broken down. The impetus for new affordable housing provision has come from rural as much as from urban areas.

The conclusion of this analysis is, then, that the changes to the system of planning for affordable (housing association based) and owner occupied housing represents a substantial departure from the model which developed when council housing was the main means of delivering social housing. What, however, has been the impact of the changes on the professional activities of planners involved in planning for housing? Has it created a range of new tasks in planning for housing covering research and analysis, policy formulation and policy implementation? How are these tasks shared out in the more collaborative and corporate environment that is meant to characterise the new policy regime?

In research and analysis, in addition to the assessment of housing 'requirements' there is now also a need to assess 'affordability' in the local area and the need for affordable housing. The debate over land availability in the 1980s forced planners involved with housing issues to think increasingly about questions of demand and marketability of sites, despite criticisms of their ability or willingness to do so (e.g. Chiddick and Dobson, 1986; Blincoe, 1987), but the new system requires planners to assess in a more rigorous way the ability of local households to pay for housing and to identify the extent to which 'economic' factors are inhibiting the formation of new households in a locality. The fact that the housing market is a cyclical one means that these are analyses that need in principle to be constantly monitored and up-dated.

Recent research (Jackson et al., 1994; Farthing et al., 1996) has shown that the response by planning authorities has been mixed. Planning departments and planning officers have often played a leading role in parish surveys of housing needs in support of the release of an exception site in a village. In terms of the justification of percentage site policies, most authorities instead of undertaking new needs surveys and analysis are relying on the traditional Housing department measures of need – the housing waiting list and the numbers of homeless households. Many planning authorities view needs assessment as a legitimating device and place little weight on the figures that emerge from this process since total needs can be very large and in excess of both land release targets and the scale of likely resources for affordable housing provision. Housing research activity in local government is an area where housing departments and housing officers have taken the lead, responding to the very substantial change in role expected of them as local authorities have moved from being providers to enablers of housing.

It is clear that there has been growth in policy making activity since the endorsement of both the exception site and percentage site policies by the government in 1989 and 1991 respectively. By 1991 it was reported that three quarters of relevant authorities had adopted exception site policies (Williams and Bell, 1992) and by spring 1993 71% of local planning authorities had an affordable housing policy, an increase from only 18% in 1991 (Barlow et al., 1994). There is little evidence of planners and housing officers working together in multi-professional teams on these policy developments or on the preparation of local housing strategies. The status of the latter has increased in recent years as it has become one way in which the DoE judges the local authority's case for resources. What seems most typical is the sharing of information, for example on housing needs, with planners developing planning policies and housing officers developing local housing strategies.

New policy implementation challenges are experienced in promoting exception site and percentage site proposals. Cherrett (1993, p. 29) describes the pre-development process for exception sites as 'often a marathon involving landowners, local communities, housing associations and local housing and planning authorities in carrying out local needs surveys, site selection, planning negotiations, scheme design, and nomination procedures. All too often one of the hurdles creates delays or even abandonment of the proposal.' There are inherent conflicts in this process. Planners are often criticised for undermining proposals because the site is not acceptable on environmental grounds or because there are other more suitable sites available (Jackson et al., 1994; JRF Findings, 141, April 1995b). This problem of course is in one sense an inevitable part of the policy since any development will be an exception to normal planning policies.

Percentage sites also raise potential conflicts between housing departments and planning departments. Planning authorities have a long tradition of negotiating planning gains on new residential developments. Most authorities dealing with large sites negotiate highway contributions; open space, landscaping and play areas; the provision of sites for schools (and sometimes the buildings themselves); community buildings; health facilities; and shops and public houses (Farthing et al., 1993). Affordable housing is a new addition to this list. It may not always be seen as having the highest priority and hence the opportunity for land value subsidy of affordable housing may be lost. This has caused some frustration for housing officers (Jackson et al., 1994). As well as revealing the conflicts in provision, this also reveals the new importance of planners *vis-à-vis* housing officers in the provision of afford-able housing in local government. The contrast with the period when coun-cils built substantial numbers of dwellings could not be more marked.

Taken together, this evidence on the evolution of activities associated with the provision of affordable housing confirms the notion of overlapping roles and responsibilities for planning and housing officers and new patterns of corporate working. Research, analysis and policy development have become more important for housing officers, and planners are becoming increasingly important in the implementation of policy.

Two key themes emerge from the investigation of the new roles for plan-ning officers in relation to the implementation of affordable housing. The first is the need for flexibility in the face of a diversity of development situa-tions.

Planners need to work with the market to be sensitive to evolving housing market situations which offer scope for obtaining land and land value subsidy for housing association development. They also need to work with varying combinations of local interests – landowners, local residents, local enterprises – in different places as well as corporately with housing officers. Of course in many ways this is merely a restatement of what has long been said about plan-ning. Because planning departments have so few resources for implementa-tion, they need to work with other agencies, in particular the private sector (Moor, 1983), in order to ensure the implementation of plans. Nearly all policies therefore have to be the product of negotiation and compromise. Though the point is a general one, what is stressed by an investigation of planning for affordable housing is the importance of individual planning officers to the success of delivery.

A second and related theme is the importance of the local political environment within which planners are working. This will impact on the commitment of the local authority to housing (and other development) objectives and therefore the enthusiasm with which policies will be pursued. Affordable housing policies, as we have seen, emerged from local initiatives in the face of local housing problems. The current advice continues to give great discretion to local authorities and the existence of policies in the majority of authorities will be no guarantee of a great political will to pro-vide housing. Indeed there is evidence of growing resistance to housing development by local residents and environmental groups in many rural areas.

Prospects for affordable housing

There are doubts about the wisdom of relying increasingly on the planning system to provide affordable housing and there are undoubtedly tensions between planning policy objectives. A major challenge to planning for afford-able housing is the policy response to the environmental agenda and to the success of the Green Party in European elections in the late-1980s. Revised PPG3 *Housing*, issued in March 1992, made two important changes to previous advice. First, it said that there is to be an increased emphasis on reusing urban land, particularly derelict or under-used land, as a means of relieving pressure on the countryside. Second, it withdrew the 'special presumption' in favour of releasing land for housing development which was contained in DoE Circular 22/84 *Memorandum on Structure and Local Plans.*

The second guidance note PPG13 *Transport* (March 1994) has also placed the emphasis on reusing urban sites in pursuit of objectives to reduce the amount of travel and to encourage more environmentally friendly modes of travel (walking, cycling and public transport). It also appeared to rule out the possibility of free-standing settlements as a solution to housing needs unless they were to achieve an ultimate size of 10,000 dwellings. Together these two circulars can be seen as restating the longstanding principle of urban containment on which the planning system has been based.

The role of planners in relation to affordable housing is essentially two-fold: (i) identifying land on which social housing can be built; (ii) subsidising social housing through land values. The challenge of urban recycling is that it makes both tasks more difficult.

Despite the fact that much land developed during the 1980s was in urban areas or in previous urban use (Roger Tym Associates, 1987), identifying land in urban areas through formal policy documents has always been difficult (Humber, 1987). Landowners are more important in identifying these sites and landowners are responding to a mix of contextual and site factors. Hence land does become available but it is not always predictable by planners (Goodchild and Munton, 1985). The point here is that it is easier to estimate urban or windfall sites from past trends than from survey methods. Traditional methodologies for identifying land available for housing development work best where the task is to identify greenfield sites based on the current extent of the built up area. These do not work very easily within urban areas, where a more labour intensive, site by site investigation is required, which can be costly. Land ownership is also more difficult to establish on urban sites.

In terms of identifying a five year supply of land for housing development, therefore, planners have traditionally relied on the identification of large urban fringe sites for the major contribution, and the contribution of wind-fall sites (i.e. those from within urban areas) has been the subject of debate and disagreement with housebuilders in land availability studies. Advice in PPG3 puts some weight on the importance of sites of 'substantial scale' as making a contribution to social housing but sites in urban areas are typically smaller than those in urban fringe locations. Hence planners will need to adopt a more flexible definition of large sites and guidance may need to be rephrased to permit this. A major concern expressed by housebuilders is that the new urban emphasis of central policy advice will be used by planning authorities opposed to development of any kind to allocate urban sites in development plans which in practice cannot be developed profitably. Development will therefore be blocked.

Subsidising social housing, which is the second important role of planners in relation to the provision of social housing, depends on the size of the development gain to be extracted from converting from one land use to another. The size of the development gain is likely to be highest at the urban periphery. It will be lower in urban areas, reflecting higher existing use values but also the cost of redeveloping the site (clearance, site preparation etc.) (Roger Tym Associates, 1987; Humber, 1987).

Evidence provided by Farthing *et al.* (1996) in their study of housing association development activities in the period 1992/93–1994/95 confirms that the problems predicted for urban sites are borne out by recent experience. Land from 'percentage sites' is less likely in urban infill locations and more common on urban fringe sites or in large rural settlements. Though the levels of land value subsidy to development being negotiated through the planning system are small, a subsidy through a discount on land value is less likely on urban sites. Together these are factors that are contributing to a shift of housing association development activity away from urban infill sites towards urban fringe sites, a move which is in practice contrary to the objectives of urban recycling.

A major issue for affordable housing, therefore, concerns subsidy and its sources. If the subsidy for affordable housing is to come from land values then subsidy will depend on the working of the market in particular areas. To a large degree the buoyancy and success of the local economy is beyond the control of the planning system and this provides a constraint on the success of policies for affordable housing and a limit to the success of planners' new style of working. In general there will be greater opportunities to obtain land value subsidies in the south of the country than in the north, where land values are lower. A related question for this whole approach to provision concerns the numbers of dwellings that can be delivered through these mechanisms. As we have seen, very substantial efforts are needed by planners and other actors to make quite modest contributions to housing supply through exception site policies. Similar efforts are required in urban areas in a context in which the economics of development are less favourable and potential subsidy from land value is lower. All this needs to be seen in the context of a number of projections of social housing needs of over 100,000 dwellings per annum in the 1990s (National Housing Forum, 1989) and a social housing programme at half or less of that level (Annis, 1994).

Public subsidy in one form or another appears to be required. Goodlad (1993, p. 73) concludes that the planning-led approaches of the early 1990s 'do not provide a substitute for a dedicated programme of subsidised housing. ... and it is not yet clear that they can be a substitute for a programme of social housing.' The recent Joseph Rowntree Foundation Inquiry into Planning for Housing (JRF, 1994) came to a somewhat similar conclusion arguing that subsidies 'should for the most part be provided via general taxation.'

Conclusion

Turning to wider debates about policy change, a number of observations can be made on the story told here. First, the idea of a structure of provision (Ball, 1983) is a useful device for describing and helping to explain the interactions and relationships between actors and institutions in the provision of housing. Planners have played quite distinctive roles in the structure of provision associated with council housing (now in abeyance) and in the newly emerging structure of provision for affordable housing based around housing association development.

Second, it is clear that structures of provision change over time. They change in response to policy developments but there is an element of organisational and professional learning involved in the creation of a new structure of provision as new roles are created for social actors. From the point of view of planners in local government, they have moved from being insignificant players in council housing provision very much to centre stage in policy formulation and more particularly in implementation for affordable housing. The role of professionals can be crucial to the success of the approach, given the considerable discretion that local government has to implement such policies.

Third, affordable housing is a structure of provision which is locally diversified so that planners will be operating in somewhat different local institutional frameworks with a variety of actors and agencies and with varying commitments to affordable housing. The emphasis on urban recycling in recent policy advice reinforces this theme of diversity in terms of varying development opportunities and constraints.

Fourth, in terms of global changes, it is clear that the growth and decline of council housing in Britain is part of a process which is very similar to trends in social housing in other advanced capitalist countries and is a response to similar problems (Ball *et al.*, 1988; Forrest, 1991). In the post-war period, large-scale state support for social rented housing was a response to the economic and political problems caused by wartime dislocation of production and, in European countries, of the destruction of the built environment. It was also a response to the need for post-war economic growth and restructuring.

Subsequently, as the costs of construction have grown and therefore the subsidy needed to make housing affordable has also grown, all advanced capitalist countries have tried to redefine the role of social rented housing, to target it on low income households and to reduce overall levels of support for the sector. But since the late-1960s, the trends of employment and income change brought about by global economic restructuring and government responses to them have led to a reshaping of state support for housing. In the British context, Forrest and Murie (1986) have described the restructuring of tenure in the 1980s as a shift from 'collective welfare state provision concerned with the reproduction of labour power to individualised welfare state provision concerned with the maintenance of consumption in certain spheres. Previously the collective welfare state reflected the strength of organised labour and the necessity for its reproduction.' But the precise nature of the change in each country is in turn a response to the existing institutional framework in that country and the level of state involvement. In Britain, there are particular factors that facilitated the 'radical and visible restructuring of welfare provision' represented by council housing. First, council housing was a minority service so its modification had limited impact on others. Second, there has always been weak public support for council housing. Third, it was an easy target for cuts and offered attractive cash receipts in sales.

Finally, the changing role of planners in relation to providing land and subsidy to social housing also appears to be a change that is happening in those countries which have always had the strongest role for the market in housing provision (USA, Australia) (see Dawson and Walker, 1990) rather than those in Europe, where the commitment to social housing has been strongest.

Chapter 6

PLANNING FOR HOUSING: PROSPECTS FOR OWNER OCCUPIED HOUSING IN THE 1990s

Christine Lambert

The importance of housing

Housing is of intrinsic importance to us all. It is also typically the largest user of urban space, and a key function of land use planning is to allocate land for new housing development according to planned assessments of the need for housing, to coordinate these land allocations with supporting infrastructure, and to balance the goals of meeting housing needs with those of environmental protection and urban and landscape conservation. Planning therefore represents an important form of state intervention in a particularly important market.

In Britain governments during the post-war period have maintained a strong commitment to owner occupation. At some times in the period the construction of new social housing by local authorities has been considerable, but it has been argued that council housebuilding has since 1955, or thereabouts, been somewhat residual, confined to slum clearance, redevelopment and overspill (Merrett, 1979, p. 28). For much of the period private sector construction has dominated the production of new general needs housing, in Britain mainly produced by the speculative housebuilding industry (see Table 6.1 and Fig. 6.1). A range of public policies has been brought to bear to support the continued growth of owner occupation, including taxation and fiscal policy, state investment in infrastructure and land and planning policy. The predominant role of the private sector in the development of new housing means that planning has to rely mainly on responsive development control powers, waiting for private developers to put forward schemes, but tries to influence the form and pattern of new development through policies and land allocations in development plans. At various times in the past, measures have been taken to give the state a more positive role in assembling and supplying land for new development outside of the market mechanism, together with powers to tax the increase in the value of land consequent on the granting of planning permission. However these attempts have foundered due to administrative and political difficulties. Consequently, and especially since the mid-1970s, the public sector has abandoned an active

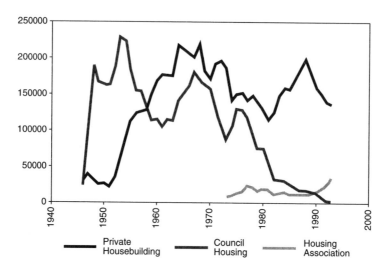

Fig. 6.1   Dwelling completions by tenure, 1946–1993

role in producing development and shifted to reliance on regulatory frameworks, and increasingly collaboration with the development industry in the design of policies (Healey, 1994).

A number of policy concerns permeate discussions of owner occupied housing. The British housing market has been distinguished by a high level of volatility with respect to both output levels and prices, and the damaging effects of volatility on both consumers and producers of new housing have attracted particular concern. The most recent period of housing market boom and slump, while illustrative of the sorts of problems price and output volatility can cause, has also presented a new set of problems (see Forrest and Murie, 1994). As prices rose from 1985 the concerns focused on the affordability of owner occupied housing and the extent to which many new households were required, or indeed encouraged, to borrow very large sums or were priced out of the housing market. High and rising prices, especially in the growth regions of the south of the country, were also implicated in problems of labour mobility and economic growth. The subsequent collapse of the housing market from 1989 has confirmed fears of the potential problems of over-extended borrowing, with growing problems of mortgage arrears and repossessions. Mobility is still restricted by the very flat market conditions and the new phenomenon of negative equity, and the output of new houses has declined dramatically. For the housebuilders, large stocks of unsold houses at the end of the boom and the discouragement to start new programmes have meant heavy company losses and high levels of unemployment in the construction sector.

In relation to planning, the issue of land supply for housebuilding has been perhaps the main policy concern and a major bone of contention between the private housebuilding industry, the planning authorities and

Table 6.1   Dwelling completions by tenure 1946–1993

Year	Private	LA	HA
1946	31,297	25,013	
1947	40,980	97,340	
1948	32,751	190,368	
1949	25,790	165,946	
1950	27,358	163,670	
1951	22,551	162,854	
1952	34,320	186,920	
1953	62,921	229,305	
1954	90,636	223,731	
1955	113,457	181,331	
1956	124,161	154,971	
1957	126,455	154,137	
1958	128,148	131,614	
1959	150,708	114,524	
1960	168,629	116,358	
1961	177,513	105,529	
1962	174,800	116,424	
1963	174,864	112,780	
1964	218,094	141,132	
1965	213,799	151,305	
1966	205,372	161,435	
1967	200,348	181,467	
1968	221,993	170,214	
1969	181,703	162,910	
1970	170,304	157,067	
1971	191,612	134,000	
1972	196,457	104,553	
1973	186,628	88,148	8,852
1974	140,865	103,279	9,920
1975	150,752	129,883	14,693
1976	152,181	129,202	15,770
1977	140,820	119,644	25,127
1978	149,021	96,196	22,771
1979	140,481	75,573	17,835
1980	128,406	76,597	21,097
1981	115,033	54,867	19.291
1982	125,416	33,244	13,137
1983	148,067	32,833	16,136
1984	159,492	31,699	16,613
1985	156,530	26,115	13,123
1986	170,565	21,548	12,531
1987	183,736	18,809	12,571
1988	199,485	19,002	12,764
1989	179,593	16,452	13,913
1990	159,034	15,609	16,779
1991	151,694	9,645	19,709
1992	139,962	4,085	25,640
1993	137,293	1,768	34,492

Private: Private housebuilding; LA: Council housing; HA: Housing association environmental pressure groups, especially in periods of housing market boom. The operation of the planning system and land supply links into the issue of housing output and house prices. The housebuilding industry has always maintained that planning through constraining housing output below that demanded in the market causes house prices to be higher than they otherwise would be, and the theme of planning and higher house prices is also pursued in some academic work (Evans, 1991). Other views are more circumspect, emphasising the dominant influence of the second-hand housing market and demand conditions in the wider economy in setting house prices. However the general view is that planning has done little to counteract the volatility of the housing market and in some respects may have exacerbated it.

Policy attention has also focused on the housebuilding industry itself and how its characteristics and its fortunes are affected by planning. It is argued by Ball (1983, 1988) that the response of the industry to market instability has been to adopt a mode of operation reliant on subcontracting, which gives flexibility and low overheads at the expense of technical backwardness, low skills and poor quality. Ball also argues that the high level of development profit (i.e. gains on land values) on new housing have been substituted for profits earned from efficient and high quality construction. Implicitly, the planning system, by restricting land supply, increases the likelihood of this happening. The industry may put too many resources into trying to work the planning system, and it may in some circumstances be tempted to defer development in the expectation of higher gains later.

This chapter addresses a number of these concerns. It begins with a brief historical overview of the growth of owner occupation and the production of new private sector housing. We then move on to an examination of planning and private sector housing development and the operational features of the housebuilding industry and its relations with the planning system. Towards the end of the chapter the emphasis switches to a more speculative discussion of the changed context in the housing market and in the planning framework in the 1990s, and how that may effect the housebuilding industry and what it supplies to consumers of new housing. The discussion is mainly concerned with the British experience of a relatively highly developed, but mainly regulatory, planning system and a predominantly speculative housebuilding industry, but towards the end draws in a limited way on experience in other European countries.

Planning and the growth of owner occupation

Mass owner occupation has its origins in the inter-war period, when the number of owner occupied dwellings grew from less than 10% of all dwellings to 32% in 1938[1]. Some of this growth is attributable to the transfer of previously privately rented houses into owner occupation, but the period was also one of substantial growth in the level of construction of new owner occupied housing. Despite the generally adverse economic climate of the time, speculative housebuilding was a particularly profitable activity. There was strong demand in regions where new manufacturing industry was developing (primarily the South East and the West Midlands), and as prices generally were falling, real wages rose for those in employment. Building costs were falling, and the crisis in agriculture meant that suburban land was relatively cheap. State regulation via planning was minimal and state investment in new transport infrastructure opened up areas on the fringes of large urban centres for new development. Consequently speculative housebuilding soared between 1928 and 1936, reaching almost 300,000 units built in 1936. This was the era when some of the largest contemporary construction companies became established as housebuilders. It was also the period when the ideology of home ownership as a way of incorporating sections of the working class into the dominant value system began to gain widespread currency in discussions of housing policy.

New housebuilding started to decline after 1936 and was brought to a halt at the beginning of the War. However, the widespread dislike of 1930s speculative development, which took the predominant form of low density, unplanned suburban development, helped to create the conditions for the introduction of planning controls in the post-war period.

The Town and Country Planning Act 1947, which introduced comprehensive planning controls and required local authorities to prepare development plans indicating the broad patterns of land use in their areas, represented an important new set of controls over the activities of private sector developers, motivated in part by the perceived need to regulate and structure urban growth in the aftermath of the inter-war housing boom. The Act also introduced a development charge equal to 100% of the increase in the value of land given planning permission, though this was shortlived and was abolished following the election of a Conservative government in 1951. The development charge was at the time implicated in the withholding of land from development, and despite the huge housing shortage of the post-war period the level of new private housebuilding was relatively low, falling to 23,000 in 1951. However, in the immediate post-war period, new construction activity was licensed, and local authority housebuilding was given priority. In 1951 the Conservative government took power with the promise of a major new housing programme to overcome the extreme post-war shortage, announcing an annual target of 300,000 new houses. Private sector completions rose steadily throughout the 1950s and early 1960s, reaching 200,000 in 1964. Planning controls continued but the development charge was abolished. Licensing was relaxed and eventually abolished in 1954 and the local authorities were urged to purchase land for resale to speculative developers in order to provide an adequate supply of sites.

Local authority housebuilding was also relatively high throughout the period, with the number of completions in 1953 and 1954 reaching the highest level in the history of British housing. However, quality was sometimes low, this being the era of the construction of large numbers of prefabricated dwellings, and from the late 1950s onwards subsidies were encouraging the growth of high rise construction. We might also note that the provision of development opportunities through large-scale public sector programmes facilitated the growth of a number of companies that subsequently became large volume housebuilders. The period therefore saw a substantial expansion of both owner occupied and local authority housebuilding. By 1964 almost a half of houses were in owner occupation and in excess of a quarter were rented from local authorities.

The Labour government which came to power in 1964 adopted a target for new housebuilding of 500,000 per annum, divided equally between the public and private sectors. There was a commitment to extending and broadening the base of owner occupation, and also pressure to improve housing standards, with the introduction of national building regulations and of the National Housebuilding Council's 10 year guarantee for new houses built by its members. The Labour government however failed to implement its private sector targets, due to a shortage of building society funds, and private sector starts fell initially. The Land Commision that was established in 1967 had wide powers to purchase land by agreement or compulsorily, funded from a betterment levy of 40% of the increase in the development value of land gaining planning permission, but in practice its achievements were meagre. Nevertheless there was a continued expansion in the growth of owner occupation, in the context of rising real incomes and secure employment prospects for most households, supported by changes in the taxation system that increased the fiscal advantages of owner occupation and lending initiatives to broaden the occupational base of the tenure. By the end of the decade a further housing market boom was beginning to build up and private sector completions reached 400,000 in 1969. In comparison with earlier booms, this one was distinguished by a very high level of house price inflation, followed by a spectacular collapse in 1974/75. Short term volatility of both demand and prices, largely in line with macroeconomic policy, has been a feature of the housing market ever since. While private sector housing output has fluctuated in line with short-term demand and price changes, the overall trend in levels of construction has been downward ever since (Table 6.1).

The early 1970s boom/slump gave rise to a major restructuring of the housebuilding industry with further consolidation of the role of large housebuilding companies. Ailing companies were taken over by others, which used the opportunity to penetrate new markets and regions. The crisis therefore speeded up the centralisation of the industry so that by the end of the decade around half of production was by a small number of volume producers.

The election of the Conservative government in 1979 saw a shift in housing policy away from the quantitative targets of the earlier post war years. The Conservatives' top priority was to bring about a change in the balance of tenures with policies to increase the home ownership proportion pursued vigorously on a number of fronts. These included the right to buy for tenants of local authority housing, large reductions in public expenditure on new rented housing and the eventual ending of construction by local authorities and the deregulation of mortgage finance, which had the effect of increasing the supply of credit together with a relaxation of lending criteria. The deregulationist agenda was extended to the planning system, which was urged not to inhibit the workings of the free market in land and property. The short surge in housebuilding activity in the mid-1980s, fuelled by credit availability and a brief period of low interest rates, was again followed by a spec-tacular slump in the context of much higher interest rates and a pro-longed recession from which the housing market has yet to emerge.

Planning and the housing market

Before going on to discuss planning and the production of new housing, it is worth stating briefly some of the particular features of the housing market and housing supply which distinguish this market from that of many other commodities. The important themes here are to do with uncertainty and expectations. As we have seen housebuilders in the British context face a market which is highly unstable. Changes in macroeconomic policy, particularly interest rates, lead to large fluctuations in demand over time. Housebuilding takes time and at the time a site is started there may be considerable uncertainty surrounding the likelihood and profitability of sales at the time, typically two years hence, when the houses will be ready. It would not be surprising if uncertainty about the future led to a hesitancy of supply. This leads on to the issue of expectations. A point stressed by a number of writers (Neutze, 1987; Bramley, 1989) is that of expectations about future house prices and land values. If, as has been the case in Britain in much of the last thirty years, the potential development value of land is likely to grow in real terms, then developers stand to gain by holding back on production. The more rapid the expected increase in values, the more it pays to hold on, leading to a perverse response of supply to price signals that development is profitable. This leads to the conclusion that in a competitive market system without any planning constraints there will still be constraints on the flow of land coming forward for development. Some draw the conclusion that by creating more certainty planning may well promote supply (Neutze, 1987).

Discussions of the impact of planning on the levels and patterns of new private housing in the post-war period generally emphasise two related aspects. The first is the pursuit of urban containment through devices such as green belts and other protective designations. The second is the issue of land supply constraints for new housebuilding. The first of these issues has been extensively discussed in the literature on the history of planning for housing in the post-war period, notably by Hall *et al.* (1973), and it is widely believed that containment is an objective that the planning system has pursued with some success, though Hall *et al.*, note more critically that the outcome has partly been the preservation of attractive rural environments for the few, at the expense of better housing opportunities for the many. However in many ways the history of the expansion of owner occupation in the period is also a history of suburbanisation, decentralisation and counter-urbanisation. An examination of changing population distributions in the period since 1950 shows the largest urban centres losing population consistently and the growth of population in smaller towns and in rural areas. New private sector housebuilding has until very recently been concentrated on greenfield sites on the edges of towns and cities, leapfrogging the Green Belts that were established around the major conurbations. It is perhaps therefore more accurate to speak of the planning system as having achieved a process of managed decentralisation together with the protection of valued areas of landscape and open space around large cities (Healey *et al.*, 1988).

The spatial expansion of owner occupation has been accompanied by growing conflict between housebuilders and planners over the issue of land availability. In fact the issue of land supply has a long history, with governments exhorting local authorities as far back as the 1960s to release additional land for new housebuilding. However, it is questionable whether planning has ever had the effect of restricting the total supply of land. The system has certainly tried to achieve a pattern of new development which is more efficient in relation to infrastructure expenditure and employment opportunities and less destructive of the rural environment, but the operation of the system in practice has always incorporated a high degree of flexibility. Much new residential development in the period up to the mid-1970s took place on so-called 'white land' released outside of the development plan process. From the end of the 1970s the advent of full structure plan coverage together with a confirmation of Green Belts has had the effect of restricting land supply in locations where market demand is most buoyant, but much of the research evidence confirms a picture of flexibility in the face of fluctuations in the market demand for housing.

As a result of controversy and lobbying, a number of studies of land availability and planning have been carried out (EIU, 1975; JURUE, 1977; DoE, 1980; Tym, 1990). These reveal a mixed picture with planning acting as a constraint on land supply in some places and at some times, but they also demonstrate the significance of other factors in constraining output, in particular uncertainties surrounding market demand and the behaviour of landowners and developers. Not all sites supplied through the planning system are developed, and for many of these the reasons for the non-implementation of planning consents are unclear (Tym, 1990). These findings underline the point that planners do not directly control the rate of development of land. The studies also demonstrate the flexibility of the system: a relatively large amount of development takes place on land that is not formally identified in plans and the release of such 'windfall' sites has been an important way of maintaining responsiveness to market demand. In the British context, plans have always been indicative and only one of the considerations taken into account in making development decisions. They could be outweighed by other considerations, notably central government policy. Central government intervention to override local policies of restraint became a much more common feature in the deregulationist 1980s.

While the planning framework throughout the post-war period is characterised by a good deal of flexibility, debates concerning the role of planning in constraining land supply were particularly heated in the 1980s. On the one hand, full structure plan coverage established more clearly areas of protection and restraint on the fringes of large cities and in large areas of high demand markets in the south of the country. The arrival of inner city policy from the late 1970s onwards gave added impetus to policies to concentrate new investment and development within urban areas, presenting more difficult and potentially less profitable development opportunities. The structure plan process itself also provided an arena for housebuilders in the most pressured regions to contest policies on the level and distribution of housing allocations. On the other hand, the neo-liberal rhetoric of the Conservative government emphasised the role of the market in meeting housing needs and the need for planning to be responsive to market pressures. Advice to local authorities stressed that the Government wished 'to encourage home ownership and to bring this within the reach of as many people as possible. The supply of new houses for sale is an essential part of this policy. ... it is essential that the planning system should cater effectively for the demand for private sector housing' (DoE Circular 15/84). Planning authorities were instructed to ensure a five year supply of land to meet forecast needs for new housebuilding, taking into account developers' own assessments of availability and the marketability of sites. The joint land studies that were advocated gave representatives of the housebuilding industry a formal role in the assessment of sites. Further advice discouraged planning authorities from intervening in decisions concerned with the detailed form and design of new development (DoE Circular 22/80 *Development Control: Policy and Practice*). Consequently the more consensual climate of the earlier post-war period was breaking down and central government intervened to push through a more relaxed regulatory regime, albeit on a selective basis. The most recent research evidence confirms that new housebuilding in the high demand areas of the south east substantially exceeded planning targets during the decade (JRF, 1994).

The intensity of the lobbying around the issue of land availability suggests, however, that the issue is of more than symbolic or political importance. An argument developed by Ball (1983) is that an important consequence of planning's role in determining the pattern of new housbuilding is its impact on the size and distribution of potential land development gains. Planning also creates a political framework through which conflicts between landowners, developers and anti-development pressure groups are fought out. The argument goes that planning is broadly beneficial to those landowners whose land is allocated for residential development and substantially improves their bargaining power with prospective developing purchasers. In this sense planning does raise the price of land to developers, though with a reduction of uncertainty and a securing of development gains on specific sites. This leads to the hypothesis that planning provides incentives to the speculative building industry to engage in land banking as a counter to the strengthened power of specific landowners, and to attempt to promote sites through the planning system in order to secure development gains for themselves. The vagueness of much planning policy provides additional incentives to pursue this sort of practice.

The housebuilders' complaints about land availability also need to be seen in the context of reductions in public expenditure to fund infrastructure and open up new locations for urban development, which began to impact in the period after 1975. As infrastructure expenditure is cut back then the locations where development is permissible are reduced. Alternatively, planning policy has attempted to load more of the cost of infrastructure onto the developers of new housing, which has the effect of reducing the development gain.

Planning and house prices

Whether planning, through restricting supply, pushes up house prices is another area of debate in the British context, albeit somewhat unresolved. This debate, rehearsed in Monk *et al.* (1991), goes something like this. On the one hand it is argued that house prices are determined by demand (demography, incomes, interest rates and the availability of credit), not supply, because new houses form only a tiny proportion of housing coming on the market in any time period. Because land values are a residual factor dependent on the expected selling price of a house, planning cannot be said to have an influence on the price of land. By contrast, a number of writers argue that restricting the total supply of land is bound to raise prices in the longer term. Evans (1988) uses a variety of indirect evidence to support this view and Cheshire and Sheppard (1989) contrast two cities which differ in their degree of planning restrictiveness to produce estimates of the amount of difference in house prices attributable to planning constraint. The latter work finds some evidence to support the view that planning does push up prices, but the effects are fairly modest, and removing constraints on land allocated for housing would lead primarily to large falls in density and increases in the built-up area.

A more systematic effort to determine the effect of planning on house production and house prices is represented in the work of Bramley (1993). This uses an econometric modelling approach to explore relationships between housing demand variables, planning policy variables and housebuilding output and house prices. This work confirms the picture of new housing supply as relatively unresponsive to changes in demand and price and also provides evidence that large additions to supply in particular localities have little impact on house prices, as local markets are very open. The release of land (as measured by planning permissions and completions) was not, however, strongly related to planning policies or targets either, reinforcing the point that it is developers who initiate development not local planning authorities. This leads to the conclusion that releasing large amounts of land through structure plans, even if it were politically practical, would not be a very effective way of increasing housing output or of reducing prices. More relaxed planning polices tend to be associated with lower densities and it could be that this masks price effects.

Planning and the housebuilding industry

At various points in the discussion we have made reference to the behaviour of developers as key actors in the supply of new housing. This section examines the structure and behaviour of the industry and how it relates to the planning system.

New owner occupied housing in Britain is primarily supplied by the speculative housebuilding industry, which generally controls all of the development functions involved in the land conversion process, and has to be concerned with land acquisition and land assembly, obtaining planning permission and marketing the final product. The volatility of the housing market, the long lead times involved in the production of new houses and the large amount of capital that needs to be invested in land and development prior to production makes the industry a relatively risky one.

As already described, the construction industry has undergone a long period of restructuring, so that a small number of large volume producers now dominate the supply of new houses. In 1992 there were more than 23,000 firms registered with the National House Building Council, but the top 32 companies supplied almost half of total production. This degree of concentration reflects a number of advantages of scale in a particularly risky market. As Ball (1983) points out, volume production allows the effects of market fluctuations to be minimised through a strategy of diversification of sites and house types. Other advantages include being able to achieve a higher turnover of capital, the ability to trim margins on individual schemes and consequently make higher bids for land than can be contemplated by smaller producers. Part of the restructuring of the industry also involves a diversification into industrial and commercial development activities and a degree of internationalisation.

Another response to risk and uncertainty has been the almost universal adoption of sub-contracting production as a way of achieving flexibility in the face of changing levels of demand. The system of sub-contracting may have advantages of cost and flexibility to the employing firm, but it has been argued (Ball, 1988) to have negative consequences in terms of the adequacy of training, shortages of skilled labour during market up-turns and a low level of technical innovation. The argument is that the system of sub-contracting removes incentives to improve the efficiency of production processes through investing in training or new techniques. The volume builders can to some extent pass on the costs of falling profits by squeezing the prices of sub-contracted labour, while for the smaller sub-contractors intense competition eliminates the possibility of such investment. One outcome of this may be problems of quality control and a poor quality product. A further result is an industry characterised by very poor working conditions and extreme instability in employment.

Two further factors are implicated in the low technical efficiency and lack of innovation in the industry. One is the volatility of profits, which have been shown to vary considerably in the short term (Barlow and King, 1992) and engender a certain conservatism. Hence, the widespread use of standard house types and the reluctance to innovate in design and production techniques. Another is the extent to which the industry relies on profit from land rather than profit from production. The strategies of individual companies with respect to forward land acquisition vary (Smyth, 1982), but for those which maintain longer term strategic land banks, the profit margin on each house may be substantially enhanced through the use of land with low historic value. Even companies which rely mainly on profit from volume production will benefit from inflationary gain during periods of high house price inflation as in the late eighties housing market boom.

The relationship between the housebuilding industry and the planning system has, as we have seen, been dominated by the issue of land supply. As well as the frequent complaint that planning fails to identify sufficient land (though the evidence above should make us cautious about the extent to which planning does effectively control the release of land), there is concern about the pattern and form of land release. Here the concerns involve the reliance in some regions on recycled urban land, where development costs are higher and the scope for profits are reduced, and the growing practice of very large scale land release in selected locations, which has the advantage of minimising political controversy and allowing the negotiation of large contributions to infrastructure and community facilities. The release of large sites, developed by consortia of volume builders, tends to exclude smaller and medium sized producers.

However, there is a large body of evidence that suggests that some housebuilding companies can exert considerable influence over the land release policies and decision making of planning authorities. Landowners and developers engage in sophisticated lobbying activities that seek to influence policy in general terms and to get their sites included in development plans. Lobbying extends beyond the formal stages of consultation on development plans and has been claimed to represent a degree of incorporation in the planning system (Short *et al.*, 1986; Farthing, 1996). Research in a number of localities suggests that developers package proposals for land release, including offers of supporting infrastructure and services, which are influential in determining the pattern of land release (Short *et al.*, 1986; Barlow, 1990; Lambert, 1991). At the level of development control, pre-application discussions are normal to test the acceptability of proposals and most of the large developers claim they can predict the outcome of outline applications fairly successfully. Again it is larger firms that are able to play the planning system most effectively, through land banking and the employment of specialist expertise to maximise the chances and improve the prediction of success in planning applications and negotiations.

To conclude this section we can say that the post-war period up to the mid-1970s represents a relatively stable period of growth in owner occupation and in levels of new housebuilding. Public policy with respect to economic and fiscal policy and public expenditure on infrastructure and social housing construction provided a broadly supportive environment, and planning operated to manage decentralisation and to conserve valued landscapes and open space in a relatively flexible way. From the mid-1970s these conditions were replaced by a more unstable environment. Housing market volatility, the negotiation of new planning frameworks and public expenditure reductions contributed to more difficult conditions for new housebuilding. Growing central–local conflict over the role of planning in relation to the market became a significant feature in the 1980s and a more deregulated environment was ushered in where housebuilders gained a degree of influence over the design of planning policy. Much of the research evidence of the 1980s suggests that the primary influence on levels and patterns of new housing development is the behaviour of the development industry, not planning. There is also little evidence that the house price effects of planning control are very large, though planning may exert more influence on the density of development. The housebuilding industry in the face of market uncertainty remains rather conservative and adopts a mode of organisation that emphasises flexibility rather than product innovation or quality. Land development gains have been a significant source of profit and provide incentives to put resources into influencing the planning system.

Planning and the housing market in the 1990s

There have been a number of significant changes in the planning policy framework in the period since 1990 which are likely to change the way in which the system affects new housing supply. In addition there are a number of contextual features of the housing market in the 1990s which will alter the conditions facing the housebuilding industry and may promote changes in the form of organisation and the nature of its products.

As a result of the Planning and Compensation Act 1991 all districts are now required to prepare a district-wide local plan, providing comprehensive plan coverage for the first time since 1968. The Act also gives added legislative force to the development plan by requiring that decisions on development should be made 'in accordance with the plan unless material considerations indicate otherwise'. Current advice emphasises the 'primacy' of the development plan (PPG12 *Development Plans and Regional Planning Guidance*). This shift to comprehensive plan coverage and primacy has a number of potential implications for the relationship between planning and the market. On the one hand plans which designate specific sites for development provide much more certainty, which should promote supply. In addition there should be fewer costly appeals against refusal of permission and economies in the provision of infrastructure. On the other hand, these changes may reduce the adaptive flexibility of the system in the face of market pressure to release more land during periods of high demand. It also places a higher premium on plans as a guide to decision making and provides additional incentives for landowners and developers to become involved in the process of plan preparation. Lobbying is likely to become more widespread and intense, with perhaps a greater emphasis on proposing an attractive package of community benefits.

The environmental agenda has also exerted a significant influence on planning and the system is increasingly used by environmental interests to promote a new set of environmental concerns to do with the use of non-renewable resources and pollution. While there may still be a good way to go in terms of understanding and operationalising the concept of 'sustainability' in development plans, the key issue that land use patterns are important determinants of travel patterns and energy consumption seems to be having an effect on the nature of government advice with respect to fringe urban development (see for example PPGs 3, 6, 13 *Housing, Major Retail Development,* and *Transport*). As far as new housing development is concerned, the guidance emphasises the recycling of urban land within built-up areas and the avoidance of large-scale peripheral development. Sustainability also may reinforce the case for more high density development, more durable products and better standards of energy efficiency in new housing. The 'green agenda' also provides the development industry with an increasingly well-organised and vocal set of anti-development pressure groups, who command considerable public sympathy.

A further factor that affects the relationship between planning and housebuilders concerns the linked issues of planning agreements for the provision of infrastructure and community facilities and the role of the planning system in promoting 'affordable housing'. Throughout the 1970s and 1980s, public expenditure constraints were forcing more of the cost of infrastructure and other services onto developers. While there have been periodic concerns about the legality and permissible scope of planning agreements, more recent legislation and advice suggests that the government is broadly sympathetic to approaches which 'internalise the costs it (development) imposes on the community' (Healey *et al.*, 1993a, p. 39) and potentially extend the range of admissible contributions. Contributions to the costs of infrastructure and other community facilities have sometimes been a focus of conflict between developers and planning authorities, but research (Barlow, 1990; Lambert, 1991) suggests this is not necessarily a major financial problem for developers who tend to reduce the price offered for land. There are nevertheless concerns about the uncertainty of requirements and the long negotiations surrounding the use of planning agreements, which may be resolved through the incorporation of more consistent policies in the new wave of local plans (Healey *et al.*, 1993b; Jones, 1989b).

Another significant feature of change is a new emphasis on the role of planning in enabling the provision of social housing, as discussed in the last chapter. Authorities are now encouraged to negotiate with developers seeking planning permission for market housing for inclusion of an element of affordable social housing, with free or subsidised land or completed units being made available to housing associations. This change further extends the range of 'planning gain' that authorities are allowed to seek. Recent research evidence suggests that the practice of negotiating social housing as part of market schemes will build up in the 1990s (Barlow, 1993). However, in relation to both contributions to infrastructure and community facilities and the provision of land for social housing, there may be an important geographical dimension. Schemes in the areas of the country where land values are much higher, and implicit subsidies therefore greater, offer far more scope to construct viable packages.

Housebuilding in Britain has currently to recover from a very severe recession under what is a less privileged fiscal regime. It will also face a more difficult demographic context in the 1990s as the number of new households forming in the younger age groups declines (Ermisch, 1990). We could add to this a view that owner occupation may be reaching saturation point, a view implicitly accepted by government in the new emphasis on rented housing in the 1988 Housing Act. Throughout the post-war period, the expansion of owner occupation has been sustained by secure and lifetime employment, rising real incomes, stable households, a stable financial context and housing as an asset that will increase in value. Many of these assumptions are currently being challenged. In the short term, experiences of house price falls, mortgage arrears, repossessions and negative equity may act to deter confidence and investment demand. The past experience of instability in the housing market may therefore be less of a feature of the 1990s. A future in which housing demand is less unstable and profitability less volatile has a number of implications for the housebuilding industry, including better prospects for developing longer term plans and less incentive to maintain flexibility through the system of sub-contracting.

The long-term trends to concentration in the housebuilding industry have already been noted. This has been accompanied by a strategy of diversification so that now the main firms are regional housebuilding subsidiaries of large corporations with wider interests in allied sectors such as civil engineering, and commercial and leisure developments. The advantages to large firms of being able to spread their risks across different sites in different areas, to finance the forward acquisition of land and to deploy resources to influence the planning system are unlikely to be undermined and may be reinforced. Large firms may also be better able to negotiate planning agreements for the provision of social housing and community facilities, for example by having the range of house types to offer or the ability to finance cross subsidies.

Demographic trends that signal a fall in the first-time buyer market will also have damaging consequences for those firms which have relied on volume production and high capital turnover in the cheaper end of the housing market. New household formation in the 1990s will be more diverse, reflecting relationship breakdown and the growing number of single person households across all age ranges. Some in these groups will have a low ability to enter or stay in owner occupation, depressing demand overall and further increasing the need for more social housing. Others may demand a more diverse product in terms of size, type and location. Elements of diversification for the housebuilding industry therefore include social housing, developed in partnership with local authorities and housing associations, which is already identified as a form of production insulated from the vagaries of the market. Opportunities for private builders to access subsidies through the Housing Corporation would further this trend.

While the profitability of housebuilding may be rather more stable in the future, the opportunities for large profits from the development gain in land values may be significantly less. The growing contribution that developers will be expected to make to both infrastructure and meeting social housing needs suggests that more of the profit will be creamed off through planning gain deals. With a plan-led system there may be little scope to exploit opportunities for high development profits on sites not identified for development. This implies also that planners will have to develop better awareness and skills in assessing likely levels of profitability in a sensitive fashion and that an ability to manage relationships successfully with the planning system will continue to be important to the ability of firms to operate successfully. If we accept the argument that land-related profit lessens the pressure on the industry to improve technical efficiency, then lower profits from this source may lead the industry to pay rather more attention to technical innovation, training and quality. The sustainability agenda would suggest that part of the quality improvement should include the durability and energy efficiency of new homes.

The evidence above would suggest that while planning has been identified as a significant constraint on housing output, this needs to be put in perspective. A more liberal planning regime would not eliminate the problems of an unresponsive supply side. The current trends are towards more planning rather than less. Perhaps more worrying is that planning for new housing is subject to a significant 'implementation gap' (Bramley, 1993), as planned targets for new housing do not seem to influence levels of either permissions or completions very strongly. Part of the problem here may lie in deficiencies in the process for assessing future needs and likely build rates. Planners may need to build in more emphasis on market demand and the likely contribution of windfall sites, as well as integrating the results of social housing needs estimates with those of generalised demographic forecasts.

The current changes to a greater reliance on site-specific local plans and the increased importance of 'affordable housing' needs in the planning system would appear to be a step in the right direction. However, the problem still remains that planning is essentially responsive to the decisions of private landowners and developers and solutions might therefore involve rather more positive intervention. Previous attempts in Britain at giving public authorities a larger role in the ownership and supply of development land have encountered serious political opposition leading to their abandonment after a relatively short period. Some other countries have been more successful here, including the Netherlands (Needham, 1992) and Sweden (Barlow and King, 1992), leading it is claimed to a cheaper and more stable supply of better quality dwellings. Public sector land banks, which operate in a limited way in some rural areas, and public–private partnership using inherited local authority land holdings as a more widespread mode of development, are, however, examples of this happening in practice in the British context.

The new emphasis on recycling land within urban areas may also require a degree of public intervention to deal with the relatively high development costs of such land. At a minimum, grant availability for land reclamation and preparation would need to be linked more effectively to development plan policies on land release. Research in 1994 on the capacity for more housing development within cities shows that substantial capacity does exist (Source: Llewelyn Davies Associates, 1994) but that the uncertainties and administrative complexities of the current grant regime are a significant deterrent.

Conclusion

This chapter has examined a number of themes about the relationship between planning, housebuilding and the housing market, drawing on recent experience in Britain and looking more speculatively to the future. What conclusions can be drawn from the research evidence and from these speculations?

The first key point is that the problem of an unstable and unresponsive housing supply would not be eliminated by an absence of planning or a much more liberal planning regime. There are inherent features of the housing market that account for instability and conservatism, and if it is desirable to create more certainty, then more rather than less planning may be desirable. This is not to say that the way the British planning system currently makes assessments of housing needs is perfect and should not be changed. Existing methods of forecasting housing needs rely on predominantly demographic forecasts with little attention to economic factors or market demand, and are subject to a high degree of political compromise. Assessments of the need for social housing use entirely different methods and are sometimes contrary to the results of the demographic models. There is scope to make these methods more sophisticated by bringing together demographic and economic factors and making political trade-offs more explicit. Better implementation of planning targets may ultimately require more direct intervention in the land market. Here the evidence from other European countries where public authorities have a role in the ownership of development land suggests that such systems generate a more stable supply at lower prices (Barlow and King, 1992).

Secondly, the housing market in the future may be less characterised by extreme volatility of output and prices, but with a new set of problems of quality, diversity and affordability. A more stable context with respect to production levels and profits should be helpful for both planners and the industry and may promote more considered long-term planning and more attention to the technical efficiency and the quality of production. Changes in practice with respect to planning agreements and social housing may reduce the scope for land development profit and housebuilders may find themselves increasingly competing on quality for more diversified markets. Given that a much higher percentage of new households may be unable to afford owner occupation, or may choose to rent rather than buy, then involvement in social housing schemes should be part of a diversification strategy. Again, it is difficult to see this happening on a large scale without some involvement by the public sector. Local authority land banks have been a significant resource during the past few years and have provided the basis for much new social housing or mixed tenure development, though local authority land is now much depleted. Social housing construction has also been an important source of business for housebuilders in the lean times of the early-1990s. One policy option is to provide local authorities with the resources to build up land banks in order to facilitate more social and mixed tenure development, something that may be attractive to a new Labour government.

Thirdly, we should note a potential contradiction between policies for sustainability that emphasise recycling urban land, and pressure on the housebuilding industry to meet the costs of social and community facilities and social housing. The higher cost of development within urban areas will not generate the kinds of surpluses required to fund substantial packages of planning gain. This suggests, again, either a greater role for the public sector in making such provision, or a more interventionist stance with respect to the urban land market.

1 For comprehensive discussions of the origins and growth of owner occupation see Merrett and Gray (1982), Ball (1983) and Ambrose (1994).

PART IV

PLANNING FOR SUSTAINABILITY

INTRODUCTION

This section comprises two chapters dealing with environmental issues but from somewhat different perspectives. In Chapter 7, Hugh Barton presents a concerned account of the relevance of 'sustainability' to town planning. He adopts, initially, a global environmental perspective, and then seeks to show how British town planning has, or has not, taken on board the principles espoused, with reference to governmental policy guidance documents. In Chapter 8, Derek Senior gives an account of minerals planning. 'Minerals' were previously identified by Barton as one of the key non-renewable global resources. However, minerals planning was always an integral component of traditional town planning, particularly in areas of the country where extractive industries were central to the economy. Indeed, colleagues and students from areas such as South Wales, Derbyshire, and Cornwall requested specifically that 'minerals planning' should be a component of this volume. Although the coal mining industry has declined, quarrying continues to be a controversial issue in many rural areas. Attempts to reincarnate unextinguished minerals planning permissions have generated great controversy. In the ensuing debates one can observe adherents of many of the different types of 'planning' policy identified in this book putting their views across, including traditional rural conservationists, new wave environmentalists, economic planning interests, and community action groups. Minerals planning does not operate in isolation but is influenced by policy shifts in the whole planning discourse.

Greater government commitment is reflected in improved legislation. Also the influence of EC policy and regulation is an overarching factor. The 1995 Environment Act (Ball and Bell, 1995; Lane and Peto, 1995), in theory, increases local authority powers to control pollution, for example from cars; strengthens recycling policy; and increases grants to conservation. Also it introduces new measures in respect of abandoned mines and contaminated land. The Act has introduced changes to the authorities responsible for control of the National Parks. It has strengthened control over all aspects of water resource control, flooding and pollution. Not least as a result of the Act, a National Environment Agency has been created. However, by 1996 many planners and environmentalists were questioning the efficacy and appropriateness of this legislation in the light of its apparent weakness so far. But the purpose of this section is not to deal with these changes in detail but rather to look at the global forces and policy factors which have brought about these changes.

Chapter 7

PLANNING FOR SUSTAINABLE DEVELOPMENT

Hugh Barton

Sustainable development

Politicians claim to aspire to it. Development plans claim to 'deliver it'. Developers argue at appeals that they will achieve it. The principle of 'sustainable development' is undoubtedly in fashion. But through overexposure and inaccurate use it is in danger of losing whatever resonance and motivating power it at first (back at the turn of the decade) possessed. It is easy to become cynical about it, dismissing it as the latest planning craze.

Yet to do so would be a profound mistake. Achieving sustainable development is the most fundamental goal of planning. Sadly, despite all the hype, it is a principle at present more honoured in the breach than the observance. The purpose of this chapter is to explain what it means, both at the level of international agreements and at the level of the UK government, then to explore the implications at the level of practical land use/transport decision making. The conclusion reached is that, far from being a passing fad, 'sustainable development' is an obligatory and inescapable goal of planning policy, and one that could give a coherent rationale for planning decisions. This is reflected to a small degree in the 1995 Environment Act, summarised in the introduction to this part of the book.

The first section gives a short historical perspective and stresses the key problems that have led to the emergence of sustainable development as a political priority.

The problem: unsustainability

Problems of unsustainablily are not new. On the contrary there is evidence of ecological disaster in relation to many early civilisations. Recent scholarship (Seymour and Girardet, 1986) points to an alarming picture of unsustainable land use practices in ancient Mesopotamia, Persia, Greece, the Roman Empire, as well as in the 'Modern' era, Spain (in its golden age), the Sahel, the upper Brahmaputra, the Murray–Darling Basin … . Recognition of unsustainable practices is also not new. Plato shows a real understanding of human ecology in this quote from *Critias*:

All other lands were surpassed by ours in goodness of soil, so that it was actually able at that period to support a large host which was exempt from the labours of hus-bandry ... . And, just as happens in small islands, what now remains compared with what then existed is like the skeleton of a sick man, all the fat and soft earth having wasted away, and only the bare framework of the land being left. But at that epoch the country was unimpaired, and for its mountains it had high arable hills, and in place of the swamps as they are now called, it contained plains full of rich soil; and it had much forest-land in its mountains, of which there are visible signs even to this day. Moreover, it was enriched by the yearly rains from Zeus, which were not lost to it, as now, by flowing from the bare land into the sea; but the soil it had was deep, and therein it received the water, storing it up in the retentive loamy soil; and by drawing off into the hollows from the heights the water that was there absorbed, it provided all the various districts with abundant supplies of springwater and streams, where shrines still remain even now, at the spots where the fountains formerly existed.

Such, then, was the natural condition of the rest of the country, and it was orna-mented as you would expect from genuine husbandmen who made husbandry their sole task, and possessed of most excellent land and a great abundance of water, and also, above the land, a climate of most happily tempered seasons.

(Plato, 5th century BC: 1929 trans. Bury)

Plato clearly understood the effect of deforestation on water retention, climate and soil fertility. Ironically, two and a half thousand years later, it is still these aspects of the environment that give cause for concern. Now, though, some of the issues are of global not just regional concern, reflecting the shift from basically agrarian societies to global industrialisation.

The current issues of global and regional ecology are well documented in official texts (see in particular DoE *et al.* (1994a) *Sustainable Development: The UK Strategy* and the Royal Commission on Environmental Pollution (1994)). Below they are summarised.

Global climate
- Increased likelihood of global warming and climate change as a result of high levels of greenhouse gas emission from fossil fuel burning and land use change (including deforestation and draining of bogs).
- As a direct result of the above, an unacceptable risk to low lying coastal cities and villages from rising sea levels as oceans expand and polar ice melts.

Biodiversity
- Progressive loss in the range and extent of wildlife habitats both at the world scale and within the UK specifically, due to the impact of develop-ment and human activity.
- As a result of the above, the endangering or total loss of rare/vulnerable species globally and within specific regions. The global 'gene-bank' is thus being impoverished.

Air quality

- Poor air quality, especially in urban areas, as a result of traffic and industry, leading to health problems – e.g. the increase in asthma.
- Atmospheric pollution on a wider scale, causing the problems of ozone depletion and acid rain.

Water

- In some areas: declining ground water levels, with consequent problems for water supply; increased run off, with consequent risk of flooding; water contamination in both urban and rural areas.

Earth

- In some areas: loss of soil through increased erosion rates; loss of nutrients and soil fertility; problems of land contamination/dereliction.

Minerals

- High rate of extraction of non-renewable mineral reserves and sterilisation of potential renewable sources.

The goal: sustainable development

The trends listed above cannot continue indefinitely without affecting the health of the biosphere and the ability of the Earth (or individual regions) to support human life and current life-styles. In some instances the biosphere is already badly degraded – for example the coalfield areas of Eastern Europe, and at a global level, the resilience of the ozone layer in the atmosphere.

'Sustainability' is about reaching a state where global ecosystems are capable of absorbing human impact without deterioration. For example, in relation to anthropogenic (i.e. human-caused) greenhouse gas emissions, the scientific consensus suggests that a reduction of 60% worldwide is necessary to avoid destabilising climate and oceans (Source: *The Intergovernmental Panel on Climate Change* (IPCC, 1990)). And at a more local level, the National Rivers Authority has recommended no further urban growth in parts of Kent because ground water levels and the quality of drinking water are threatened.

Put more simply, sustainability is about maintaining the health of the biosphere and husbanding key resources of air, water, land and minerals.

There are two valid perspectives on the significance of sustainability. One perspective is human-centred: we must be kind to the Earth so that the Earth is kind to us. The other is nature-centred: we must respect the Earth because the Earth and its creatures have as much right to exist as we. The former is sometimes referred to as 'pale green', while the latter is called 'deep green'. At one time these two orientations might have led to very different actions.

Now, however, there is widespread recognition that homo sapiens is not separate from nature, but an integral part of the natural world, so that the two views almost become one: the health of the Biosphere and the health of humanity are indivisible.

Whereas sustainability is about the ecosphere, 'sustainable development' is explicitly about the human condition, now and in the future. The current Secretary of State for the Environment, John Gummer, describes it prosaically as 'not cheating on our children'. The definition popularised by the Brundtland Commission (Brundtland, 1987) was:

> Development that meets the needs of today without compromising the ability of future generations to satisfy their needs.

In this context the notion of 'development' is broader than simply 'economic growth' or gross national product. Rather it implies improvement to:

- the quality of life, health and nutritional status
- equity in access to resources and services
- per capita income
- perceived quality of the human environment

Sustainable development is therefore about maintaining and enhancing the quality of human life – social, economic and environmental – while living within the carrying capacity of supporting ecosystems and the resource base (Barton *et al.*, 1995). Interpreting such a grand concept into practice is far from simple. It can be argued that in order for development to qualify as sustainable three criteria have to be satisfied:

- social: are human needs being met?
- environmental: are environmental limits respected?
- economic: is it viable?

To help explain what such criteria mean in practice, consider the case of a proposed out-of-town retail centre. While it clearly satisfies the economic test, it is doubtful or equivocal in relation to the social need criterion because, while car users benefit from extra retailing choice, non-car users do not, and the traditional town centre's viability and vitality may be threatened, further curtailing the options of those who rely on it or value it. In relation to environmental impact, the out-of-town centre generates extra car travel and induces higher car dependence, increasing energy use and exacerbating pollution levels. So on this analysis the proposal is not a 'sustainable development' and should be rejected. Conversely, the regeneration of the town centre probably satisfies the social and environmental criteria. The town centre's economic viability though may depend quite largely on refusal of the cheaper out-of-town option.

The environmental impacts may be more complex than the example above. For instance the location of housing development may affect energy use by at least 100%, and thus increase greenhouse emissions, pollute the air and denude fossil fuel reserves, while at the same time leading to the demand for extra road construction which might damage local habitats, increased noise levels and visual intrusion and require extra quarrying in sensitive landscapes.

The precautionary principle

The significance of environmental limits is not universally agreed. The suspicion is that they may be being exaggerated by specific interests. This is particularly so in relation to 'climate change'. The environmental lobby groups are arguing for quite draconian policy changes even though there is not as yet absolute proof that higher levels of CO_2 and other greenhouse gases in the atmosphere are actually forcing global warming. Doubts about our scientific understanding of the natural earth processes and 'feedback' mechanisms still exist. This doubting attitude is similar to that of industry and governments in the early 1980s over the significance of CFC emissions for the thinning of the ozone layer which protects Earth's surface from harmful ultraviolet rays. In that case action was eventually taken only when the evidence became overwhelming and irrefutable. If action had been taken earlier, when the evidence was strong but not overwhelming, then the risks to humanity of skin cancer could have been reduced. A similar 'precautionary principle', it can be argued, should apply to global warming. The evidence is strong but not conclusive. The risks are very great indeed. It behoves us to take action in good time to try to reduce the threat to future generations.

The Earth Summit and the National Sustainability Plan

In a sense the debate above is a little academic. The UK Government has accepted the precautionary principle and pledged itself to work towards 'sustainable development'. The historical context for this move and the sequence of official events and reports nationally and internationally is given in Fig. 7.1. The first major official step in this direction was the publication of the 1990 White Paper *This Common Inheritance* by the DoE when Chris Patten was Secretary of State (DoE, 1990). *This Common Inheritance* set out the problems of unsustainable development and committed the Government to do something (not very specific) about it. It was, in other words, strong on analysis but weak on action.

The event which galvanised the Government into greater dynamism was the so-called 'Earth Summit' in 1992. This was held in Rio de Janeiro under the auspices of the United Nations and involved most of world's nations, often with representatives at the highest level. Three important accords were signed up to by most governments at Rio, in relation to Biodiversity, Climate Change and Forests. The Summit has been lampooned by some environmentalists as nothing but an international talking shop. However, events since

Early 1900s	Ellen Swallow Richards, a MIT academic is credited with developing the concept and coining the word 'ecology'.
1962	saw the publication of *Silent Spring* by Rachael Carson which was on the leading edge of ecological awareness
1969	Photographs of the earth from the Apollo spacecraft gave us a consciousness of planet earth as an ecosystem.
1972	*Blueprint for Survival* (published by *The Ecologist* magazine)
1972	*The Limits to Growth* ('The Club of Rome') this was done in liaison with MIT academics. It was the first attempt to model global systems and suggest that resources could run out, if the course of events remained unchanged.
1972	**The UN Conference on the Human Environment**, Stockholm, (UN).
1976	**The UN Peoples Habitat Conference**, Vancouver with simultaneous events taking place around the world. The theme of this conference was that there should be involvement of local communities in the problems and design of settlements.
1980	*The World Conservation Strategy*, looked at the need to conserve species and habitats. (WWF).
1980	**The Brandt Commission** was concerned with the North South Divide. (Independent Commission on International Development Issues. ICID)
1983	*Our Common Crisis* this looked at the need for North/South co-operation for world recovery. (Independent Commission on International Development Issues ICID).
1987	*Our Common Future – The Brundtland Report.* (The World Commission on Environment and Development, WCED)
1988	Saw the UK response to *The Brundtland Report.*
1990	*This Common Inheritance* was the first comprehensive UK government White Paper on the environment.
1991	*Caring for the Earth, a Strategy for Sustainable Living* (IUCN, UNEP and WWF)
1992	*Towards Sustainability* this was the fifth environmental action programme published by the European Commission
1992	UK Government publishes a new Planning Policy Guidance Note 12, which requires land use planning to take account of global environmental concerns.
1992	The United Nations convened the UN Conference on the Environment and Development (UNICED), (The Earth Summit) and published Agenda 21, plus other conventions and strategy documents.
1993	DoE publishes the *Good Practice Guide on the Environmental Appraisal of Development Plans*
1993	DoE, Scottish Office and Local Government Management Board (LGMB) publish the Eco Management and Audit Scheme for local authorities.
1994	UK Central Government published four separate publications *Sustainable Development: the UK Strategy, Climate Change, Sustainable Forestry* and *Biodiversity.*
1994	Report of the Royal Commission on Environmental Pollution.
1992–95	DoE revises the whole range of planning policy guidance notes, reorientating them towards sustainable development

Fig 7.1 Chronology of the development of ideas for sustainable development (adapted from Simonen, 1995)

1992, at least in some parts of the world, give the lie to this. In time Rio may come to be seen as a turning point.

Following the Earth Summit, the UK Government has produced a national strategy for sustainable development, including special reports on climate change and biodiversity, that sets the context for planning policy (DoE *et al.*, 1994a, b and c). This strategy is paralleled by equivalent documents in other

EU states, all in the context of the EU's Fifth Action Programme on the Environment.

The UK strategy is very broad, covering issues of environmental protection, pollution, transport, energy, wildlife, waste and recycling as well as land use planning. Its main significance lies in the way it has extended concern for the environment out beyond the confines of the Department of the Environment. Other key government departments, such as Transport, Agriculture Fisheries and Food, and Trade and Industry, are drawn in as well. This is significant because issues such as energy policy (DTI) and transport (DoT) are central to sustainability.

Planning policy guidance

The principles advocated by the Strategy are also reflected in much more specific planning guidance. Most PPGs have been revised in the early 1990s to reflect the new agenda.

Most significant and widest ranging of them is PPG12: *Development Plans and Regional Planning Guidance* – produced in 1992. As well as instigating the plan-led development process (discussed elsewhere in this book) PPG12 instructs local authorities to incorporate the environment 'in the widest sense'. (For extracts from PPG12 see Fig. 7.2.)

The general principle:

Para 6.3   Local planning authorities should take account of the environment in the widest sense in plan preparation. They are familiar with the 'traditional' issues of Green Belt, concern for landscape quality and nature conservation, the built heritage and conservation areas. They are familiar too with pollution control planning for healthier cities. The challenge is to ensure that newer environmental concerns, such as global warming and the consumption of non-renewable resources, are also reflected in the analysis of policies that forms part of plan preparation.

Special emphasis on climatic change and its implications for land use/transport planning:

Para 6.11   At a global level, there are the implications of possible changes to our climate, and of the pervasive changes in human behaviour that may be needed to limit and adapt to global warming. So development plans need to address the implications for coastal defences, the siting of development in low-lying areas and freshwater and drainage systems. But they must also consider other policies that have the potential to reduce Britain's emissions of greenhouse gases. The Department will be issuing planning policy guidelines on renewable energy.

Para 6.12   One way in which development plan policies need to take account of energy conservation is in the location of new development. The full extent to which land use planning can contribute to global environmental objectives has yet to be explored in sufficient detail to permit the Government to offer definitive guidance. But it is clear that travel patterns influence CO_2 emmissions. In seeking to reduce such emissions, one aim would be to guide new developments to locations which reduce the need for car journeys and the distances driven, or which permit the choice of more energy-efficient public transport – without encouraging more or longer journeys – as well as cycling and walking, as alternatives to the private car. In the same vein, the provision of transport infrastructure will influence settlement and development patterns, and must therefore be taken into account in development plan preparation.

Fig. 7.2   Extracts from PPG12 (DoE, 1992b)

What is more, PPG12 requires local authorities to subject development plans to a systematic and explicit 'environmental appraisal'. The detailed guidance on appraisal, and the difficulties experienced by authorities which have so far embarked on appraisal, are explored in a later section.

PPG12 is non-specific in its policy requirements. Subsequent revisions to other PPGs have begun to put flesh on the bones and give some credence to the Government's claim that it is taking sustainable development seriously. There are, though, some interesting discrepancies in guidance. PPG13 on *Transport*, for example, gives welcome and challenging guidance on integrating commercial development with public transport planning, but PPG4 on *Industrial and Commercial Development*, and PPG6 on *Retail Development*, are relatively gutless by comparison.

Nevertheless the new generation of PPGs gives some hope that sustainability arguments will be given more weight both in the plan preparation/approval process and at planning appeals.

Inconsistency in government policy

While the DoE has been active in incorporating environmental criteria into its policy process, the same cannot be said of other government departments. This is particularly true in relation to the DoT and DTI, and can place local authorities in an invidious position. For example, in the case of transport, all the evidence published by the DoE points to the need to cut car reliance while boosting walking, cycling and public transport, in order to reduce congestion, danger and greenhouse gas emissions. Planning and transport authorities are therefore charged with devising plans that reduce the need to travel, and promote alternatives to the car. Many authorities have duly begun to do this, instituting traffic calming schemes, tighter parking controls, public transport priority measures, and so on. But they are greatly hampered by having little influence over privatised bus and rail companies, and no control at all over the biggest transport investor of all, the Department of Transport. So the local authorities can find themselves in a no win situation: unable to implement a sustainable transport strategy because of Government policy decisions, yet criticised by the Government and local people for failing to combat transport pollution and congestion. The Bristol area provides a relevant example. Avon County is trying to do all the right sustainable things, but the DoT is investing vastly more than Avon can afford in constructing the second Severn (road) crossing and widening the M4 and M5 motorways. These DoT investments will affect travel patterns and behaviour fundamentally and serve to undermine the Avon strategy.

In the field of energy the situation is little better. While on the one hand the DoE (and the Energy Efficiency Office which it contains) plans progressive and irreversible improvements in the building regulations so as to reduce heat loss from buildings, on the other hand the private oil, gas and electricity companies compete to sell more energy. There is no overall government body capable of ensuring the rational use of scarce fossil fuel resources, or able to co-ordinate a strategy of conservation, job creation and pollution reduction as advocated by environmental groups. The inevitable result is continuing fuel poverty (people unable to heat their homes), high levels of pollution and wasted resources.

The signs are not all bad, however. The momentum towards sustainable development has recently been given an extra fillip by the trenchant conclusions of the Royal Commission on Environmental Pollution (1994). The Commission recommends the setting of tougher pollution targets, national policy changes and the restructuring of the DoT to reflect altered priorities.

Interpreting sustainable development

The concept of sustainable development is so all-embracing that it is easy to think it is too vague to be interpreted into practice. This section therefore explores some specific principles which might give a sense of direction to planning decisions. These principles are derived from 'Sustainable Settlements' (Barton et al., 1995). A later section outlines processes for assessing whether policies are effective.

The principle of local self-sufficiency

The *Guide to Sustainable Settlements* argues that self-sufficiency is a key principle. The tension between achieving local self-sufficiency and recognising economic and functional interdependence is one reflected in planning ideas from Ebenezer Howard onwards. Howard stressed local provision of food, energy and services in and around small towns, but also the need for smaller settlements to be linked together by public transport into a 'social city' that offered high level services and a greater range of jobs.

Howard's balanced approach has sometimes been ignored by ecological utopians, who have promoted self-sufficiency at all costs. The 'Blueprint for Survival' for example (*The Ecologist* Jan 1972, see Goldsmith et al., 1972)) shows how it is possible on a technical level to achieve a decentralised pattern of development. The Blueprint aims to satisfy human needs locally, with local food production in small-holdings, and soil fertility maintained through the recycling of organic wastes from the settlement; renewable energy captured at the scale of the individual building (e.g. through solar heating) or through local biomass, wind and water schemes: water can be also captured locally (off roofs for example), locally treated and reused before being returned to the natural cycle; building materials can be quarried or grown locally, then reused again and again so as to reduce demand for virgin materials. Thus towns are designed on a human scale, where walking and cycling are the obvious means of movement, and a strong sense of community provides for material support and sociable patterns of behaviour. The people are linked by telecommunications to wider society, allowing them to participate in national or global economic and cultural activities. Energy efficient transport links the settlement to suppliers and communities, but the level of such contact is greatly reduced by comparison with today.

This seductive image has been influential both as a motivation for environmentalists and as a reason to denigrate the concept of self-sufficiency amongst cynics. It does not match up to reality. While it deals in technological possibilities, it does not deal with economic practicalities, in terms of the way in which employment or housing markets function. Nor does it provide the range of choices for social, leisure and retailing which people now expect. A small town does not, for example, offer a wide range of work opportunities, or of shops, or of cultural facilities like theatres, exhibitions and cinemas.

A realistic principle of self-sufficiency therefore stresses the importance of increasing local autonomy, while maintaining individual choice: self-sufficiency at the scale appropriate to social and economic needs.

A policy of increasing self-sufficiency is therefore appropriate at a wide range of scales, from the individual home or building up to a region, or the country as a whole.

> At every level the decision-maker should be attempting to maximise the level of autonomy of the ecosystem while enhancing its life-giving qualities. That means, in essence, reducing dependence on the wider environment for resources, and reducing the pollution of the wider environment by waste products . ...
>
> One way of approaching the problem of sustainable design is to see each development as an organism or mini eco-system in its own right. A home, or an estate, or a town is an eco-system in the sense that it provides the essential local habitat for humans, creating its own microclimatic condition, and should provide as far as possible for their comfort and sustenance. A settlement is like a living organism in that it has the capacity to reproduce or renew itself (both the people and the built environment); it ingests quantities of food, fuel, water, oxygen and other raw materials; it ejects quantities of waste fluids, solids and atmospheric emissions.
>
> (Barton *et al.*, 1995)

Each level treated as an ecosystem

Effective planning and design can substantially reduce these resource inputs and outputs, so that at each scale the impact on the broader environment is reduced. Thus, for example:

At the level of the individual building:

- energy use can be minimised by effective draught-proofing, insulation and heat retention in the walls and floors;
- solar gain can be maximised by facing the main rooms towards the south-west, south or south-east, and making windows on the south side larger;

- water from the roof can be collected for flushing the loo – thus greatly reducing demand for 'purified' water from the mains;
- organic waste from kitchen and garden can be recycled through a compost heap.

At the level of the neighbourhood:

- sewage can be treated by natural reed-bed pond systems that require no energy input and cost less to construct than conventional centralised systems;
- allotments can be provided close to homes, with community-based composting schemes;
- local shopping and neighbourhood facilities such as clubs, pubs, churches and primary schools can be clustered in locations that reduce the distance needed to walk or cycle;
- safe routes to school can be provided to encourage walking and cycling – direct and convenient, avoiding main roads, well supervised by residents;
- a local office centre or 'telecottage' can offer a full range of telecommunications and support services to encourage home/locality-based work.

At the level of town or city:

- energy can be supplied by a combined heat and power (CHP) plant which both satisfies local electricity demand and provides hot water for a district heating system serving all buildings;
- water and biofuels from the surrounding area (e.g. streams, wood) can be used to fuel the CHP plant;
- a wide range of jobs and services can be provided in locations that are well served by public transport and cycling/walking routes, reducing the proportion of motorized trips and the level of greenhouse emissions.

Energy decision making

The scale for dealing with inputs and outputs is conventionally defined by institutional and market factors. For example, in an era of multinational energy supply industries and centralised electricity production, the scale of energy decisions tends to be national or supra-national in scale and inputs and outputs dealt with by completely different agencies, to the cost of the environment. By contrast, the appropriate scale for decision-making needs to recognise not so much institutional/provider needs as those of users and consumers. In the case of energy for buildings, it is quite possible for users to seize the initiative by demanding greater energy-efficiency in buildings and appliances, and installing local (and preferably renewable) energy supply. Local authorities can facilitate this process by regulation (in plans and development briefs), by demonstration (in their own schemes) and by collaborative working (for example to promote efficient district heating projects).

Economically, such initiatives make sense. Capital investment in very energy-efficient new buildings, for example, can pay for itself in terms of reduced fuel bills. Some savings can be achieved with no extra capital at all: for example 10–20% savings through correct solar orientation of buildings. Such policies therefore can be written into development plans and should be backed by government as in line with its stated goal of promoting sustainable development (DoE *et al.*, 1994a).

The benefits of such increased local energy autonomy should be clear: households and businesses benefit from reduced costs and increased user control; the broader human environment benefits from less pollution and increased longevity of scarce fossil fuel reserves.

The appropriate scale for other aspects may be very different. For example in relation to employment, the most important scale may well be the commuting hinterland of a city. In relation to primary education, the scale could be that of the neighbourhood, defined by convenient walking distance. Awareness of technological innovation is also important. Recent advances (recovering old skills) in reed-bed technology make it possible to deal with waste water and sewage cheaply and locally rather than relying on expensive 'end-of-pipe' solutions which are damaging the water environment.

Greater self sufficiency at any particular level implies a move away from the monoculture ethos which has prevailed in recent times: providing local jobs and services suggests mixed use, not single use, developments; providing for local water treatment and greater biodiversity leads to a rich and varied pattern of open spaces rather than species-poor deserts of mowed grass.

The issue of choice

An awkward question for advocates of greater local self sufficiency is that of personal choice. It could be argued that the move to local provision will restrict people's freedom of action. The use of the car, in particular, might be restricted. If sustainability means living at higher densities to permit walking and district heating, then the freedom to choose a detached house with a big garden might be curtailed. This argument, though, can be turned on its head. Current trends in land use and transport are reinforcing the trend to increased car reliance and undermining the viability of public transport and the attractiveness of walking. The purpose of planning for sustainable development therefore, far from restricting choice, is to open up again the possibility of walking, cycling and public transport. It is to create opportunities for people to choose an environment friendly mode.

The principle of choice is fundamental to sustainability in other ways. For example the provision of a range of different kinds and sizes and tenures of housing in a neighbourhood increases both social choice and environmental sustainability, principally by allowing households the maximum opportunity to select locations that are convenient to them. Housing 'balance' in each area also helps to avoid peaks and troughs of demand for local facilities (especially in relation to age groups), and contributes to the local availability of a range of skills and professions, reducing the need to travel.

Social and environmental goals also go hand in hand in relation to quality of life and social equity. An energy-efficient house reduces fuel poverty and improves comfort, as well as cutting fuel use and pollution. Improving the local environment, reducing traffic and making walking more pleasant enhances health and aesthetic enjoyment as well as reducing emissions.

Sustaining local retail, educational and health facilities maintains convenient options for those without access to a car, as well tackling energy use. If such policies succeed in encouraging people back onto the streets, then there may also be benefits in terms of a greater feeling of security, safety and community.

Choice for users of the environment is one way of applying the precautionary principle. Planning policy should keep options open, both for current and future generations. While much recent development is based on satisfying one specific market niche, one mode of transport, one land use, a robust development would ensure good access by all modes, and flexible building design would permit use changes in the future if societal needs change.

Putting together these various social, environmental and commercial interests could add up to a very considerable constituency of support for sustainable development. As yet, though, conservative and NIMBY ('not in my back yard') attitudes often hold sway.

Assessing sustainability

If attitudes are to change, then it is essential that the rhetoric of sustainability is converted into recognition of practical ways forward. The environmental priorities need to inform decision-making from the outset, design solutions need to be tested to assess their efficiency, and diverse interests drawn into the debate. These are three of the aims of the new generation of environmental policy tools.

The intention of these tools is to ensure a systematic and comprehensive approach to decision-making. Various techniques are being actively promoted by the EU, the UK Government, and organisations such as the Local Government Management Board, English Nature and the Council for the Protection of Rural England. In this section we will look in turn at the 'environmental appraisal of development plans', environmental auditing and environmental management systems, then examine some of the concepts that are employed, such as critical environmental capital and environmental capacity.

Environmental appraisal

The environmental appraisal of development plans is a formal requirement in PPG12 *Development Plans and Regional Guidance*. Detailed guidance on

127

appraisal emerged in November 1993 (DoE, 1993b). The reason for appraisal is to ensure that development plans deliver sustainable development. The guidance adopts a pragmatic but comprehensive approach. It emphasises that the environment is not a 'bolt-on' extra, rather that appraisal of environmental impact should be integrated into the process of policy-making and subsequent implementation. This involves:

(i) setting the right agenda: incorporating sustainability objectives at the outset and ensuring that viable environment-friendly policy options reflecting best practice are examined;
(ii) monitoring progress: establishing an environment data-base that tells decision-makers what the current situation is and whether policies are moving in the right direction;
(iii) evaluating options systematically: assessing the impact of policies and proposals on all the important facets of environmental quality.

The guidance suggests that environmental policy-making should be 'explicit' and 'transparent', drawing other agencies and the general public into involvement. It should avoid complex technical procedures which exclude the non-experts from debate, rather it should aim to reveal key issues for political decision. The full range of issues recommended for consideration in the guidance is given in Fig. 7.3.

The DoE guidance may be criticised on several fronts. In the first place it is aimed only at local authority land use plans. It does not extend to other local authority policy documents, such as TPP's (Transport Policy and Programmes) or Water Plans, even though these clearly relate very closely to development plans. Neither does it extend to the government's own policies that have major impact on land use – most particularly the roads programme.

Another criticism is that the appraisal process deals fully with environmental issues, but barely at all with social and economic issues, with the possible result of an imbalance in decision-making. Conversely, there is nothing to stop local authorities choosing to give equality of treatment to these three aspects, and indeed some are aiming to do so.

The third criticism, voiced by many local authority planners, is that the guidance is too difficult and ambitious, especially for councillors to absorb, and requires a comprehensive database that is beyond any realistic budget. This is not entirely valid. The guidance is careful to suggest ways in which the essential ingredients of the process can be tackled without undue resource implications. It is probably true to suggest that the real reasons for inaction on the part of some local authorities are first, existing work commitments; second, resistance to new practice; third, potential political embarrassment. This final point is critical. Experience of environmental appraisal in practice suggests that it sometimes requires an embarrassing degree of consistency and honesty in decision-taking. Over questions such as the 'sustainability' of

Elements	Key Objectives for Local Authorities
A. *Global ecology*	
1. Atmosphere and Climate	Reduce CO_2 emissions: • reduce energy use in buildings • reduce energy use in transport • substitute renewables for fossil fuels Increase CO_2 absorption
2. Biodiversity	Conserve extent and variety of habitats Protect rare or vulnerable species
B. *Natural resources*	
3. Air	Maintain/enhance local air quality
4. Water	Improve quality of water courses and bodies Protect water supplies
5. Land	Maintain/enhance soil fertility Protect from erosion and contamination
6. Mineral and energy resources	Reduce consumption of non-renewables Protect potential for renewables
C. *Local human environment*	
7. Buildings	Availability and renewal of appropriate residential, social and commercial built space in convenient/accessible locations
8. Infrastructure	Provision and renewal of necessary/safe transport and service infrastructure
9. Open space	Provision/renewal and cleanliness of accessible and appropriate open space
10. Aesthetic quality	Enhance perceived environmental quality in terms of sight, sound, smell, touch and association
11. Cultural heritage	Safeguard archaeological remains, historic monuments, good architecture, attractive townscapes and landscapes

A version taken from Barton and Bruder, 1995, adapted from DoE, 1993b.

Fig. 7.3   Elements of environmental stock

the Green Belt, for example, councillors may prefer to fudge the issue rather than countenance public displeasure.

The environmental appraisal of development plans is a UK Government policy. It is also a particular expression of a concept that has wider currency in Europe and across the world – Strategic Environmental Appraisal (SEA). The EU is considering introducing a Directive which would make SEA of policies, plans and programmes obligatory not only for local authorities but for central governments as well. So while the UK, with 'appraisal', is in the vanguard of SEA at present, it may eventually have to adopt a more thorough-going approach to policy evaluation.

Environmental audits and indicators

The starting point for policy review is not only knowing where we want to go, but knowing where we are now. Environmental appraisal stressed the need, therefore, for environmental monitoring. At present few authorities have comprehensive monitoring procedures, and those that do have not always adopted them to monitor local impact on global concerns as well as on local concerns. There are two important elements: first, 'State of the Environment' (SOE) monitoring, which is concerned with the actual quality of the environment – for example water quality, air pollution, habitat construction; second, policy impact assessment, which is designed to assess whether a particular set of policies is working or not.

The SOE indicators, in particular, are of interest not just to the local authority but to the whole community. SOE monitoring can therefore involve, and indeed should involve, other agencies and local community groups. Information provided from a wide range of sources may be coordinated by the local authority on behalf of the wider community, and can then be a resource for not only environmentalists but developers as well, accessed through a computerised database system.

The SOE report forms an important part of environmental auditing. Environmental auditing encompasses not only the monitoring process but also the evaluation and review of policies and practices. The process of evaluation and review has recently been given specific form in the shape of 'Environmental Management and Audit Schemes' (EMAS). EMAS was originated by the EU for the commercial sector, but has now been adopted for use by UK local authorities (DoE/SS/LGMB, 1993). It requires the setting of environmental objectives and explicit systems for delivering those objectives and for assessing the effectiveness of the delivery. In common with other management systems, it has been criticised for being excessively procedural and bureaucratic (see Barton and Bruder, 1995), but it does ensure that environmental issues have a high profile in the training and job specifications of local authority workers.

There are problems with all these overlapping concepts and procedures. It is very easy to be confused, especially when different departments or individuals are associated with different procedures and are not working closely together. Nevertheless, there can be a close relationship. Figure 7.3 illustrates how the environmental appraisal of development plans, which is the key process for planners, can be seen as part of environmental auditing, sharing SOE monitoring with other aspects of policy assessment.

Environmental stock

In order for collaboration between different departments (and different environmental interests) to occur effectively, there has to be common ground in terms of the value put on environmental resources. The recognition of a useful list of key elements of environmental stock, reflecting Fig. 7.3, is a start.

The phrase 'environmental stock' (or 'capital') is itself significant. Some measures of wealth, such as GNP, or personal income, are measures of the flow of resources. But such flows may be actively exploiting the stock of key environmental resources. Thus the quarrying of non-renewable mineral resources, for example, appears in conventional economic balance sheets as a good, when actually it may represent a permanent loss of capital and result through its use in pollution of the atmosphere. It is therefore vital to set against the standard measures of flows an economy which values stock.

Some elements of stock, such as Sites of Special Scientific Interest (SSSIs), vulnerable coastal landscapes, or Grade 1 listed buildings, may be considered inviolate, justifying absolute protection. These elements are increasingly being grouped under the heading 'critical environmental stock'. Environmental agencies – such as English Nature, English Heritage, the CPRE and the NRA – are arguing that their particular interests should be reflected in a local authority map of critical environmental stock. The loss of specially valued wildlife habitats and historical townscapes raises justifiable public ire. In practice, exactly what is considered critical will vary from place to place in response to local values. For example in an intensely built up area with a paucity of open space every open space could be defined as 'critical', whereas in an area with plenty of open space this need not be the case.

Another category in common use is 'constant environmental stock'. This is appropriate where, rather than individual site resources being critical, it is the whole resource base which is of value, for example in relation to tree cover, or mineral reserves. In these cases it may be appropriate to replace or substitute resources, rather than necessarily safeguard individual sites. Total tree cover can be maintained, for example, by replacement planting when felling occurs. Equivalence of value is then important – perhaps in terms of wildlife potential and CO_2 absorption as well as landscape or timber value.

The concepts of capital and constant environmental stock tend to be associated with putting constraints on development. This is not always the case. In identifying the potential for sustainable development there are frequent situations where development should be positively favoured to make good use of spare capacity. One example of this would be derelict buildings or brownfield sites in urban areas. Another, perhaps less obvious, would be sites which are highly accessible to good public transport and local facilities. Development of such sites, in preference to others, can provide for more efficiency in the use of resources and reduction in pollution.

Taking these ideas of environmental stock together – the negative and positive factors – it is possible to define the environmental capacity of an area to accept increased population or human activity. There may be critical thresholds related to the capacity of the human-made stock of buildings and infrastructure, or to the impact on the natural stock of water resources or habitats, which define an appropriate level for development. Exceed the threshold and damage might occur, unless mitigated by effective planning and design.

Conclusion

The concepts of environmental thresholds and capacities are, however, awkward. There is a temptation to believe that it is possible to identify them scientifically, but that would be thoroughly misleading. While scientific knowledge informs the process, the key decisions are essentially about values: how much one aspect of the environment is valued as against another; how much economic growth to reduce unemployment is valued as against protection of the global environment. As always with planning, therefore, the decisions are political, involving the allocation of resources to different communities of interest. The role of the professional planner is therefore to inform the political decision making process as best she or he can, revealing viable options and their environmental (and other) implications, making sure the process is as transparent and open as is possible (Barton *et al.*, 1995, p. 18)

Implementing sustainable development will never be achieved by reliance on the local authority alone. Local authority powers are limited in relation to market interests and major governmental or utility agencies. Early in the chapter this point was illustrated in relation to energy and transport policy. The local authority therefore has to look for allies in the implementation process.

Recognising these problems, the Earth Summit agreed the 'Local Agenda 21' programme. LA21 assumes it is not only desirable but possible to achieve a high degree of collaborative action in a community by voluntary agreement. It recommends LA21 committees involving the public, private and voluntary sectors which could provide for a discussion of sustainability issues and work towards the production of an integrated plan. The UK Government is requiring every local area to produce such a plan by the end of 1996. The hope is that by involving different interests – e.g. the local Chamber of Commerce, utilities, environmental pressure groups and the local authority – insights will be shared and a coordinated strategy emerge. This is an immensely idealistic adventure. Yet it needs to be successful if the deep seated issues of unsustainability are to be addressed. It remains to be seen if government has the mettle to pursue it and its goal of sustainable development with the commitment that is necessary.

The role of town and country planning

In the context of the post-Rio environmental agenda and the new environmental planning mechanism, the role and scope of town and country planning has to change. The narrow view of planning – as concerned with land use plans and development control – is no longer adequate (if it ever was). Planners now have an obligation to consider all the key environmental resources – earth, water, air and atmosphere, energy resources – and work with others for their sustainability. The goal is an improving and sustainable quality of life, for this and later generations.

Bibliography

Official publications

Commission of the European Communities (1990) *Green Paper on the Urban Environment* (COM(90)218) Luxembourg.

Commission of the European Communities (1992) *The 5th Environmental Action Programme: Towards Sustainability* (COM(92)23) Brussels.

DoE (1990) *This Common Inheritance: Britain's Environmental Strategy.* London: HMSO. Command No. 1200.

DoE (1992a) NB: relates to another chapter.

DoE (1992b) *Planning Policy Guidance Note 12: Development Plans and Regional Planning Guidance.* London: HMSO.

DoE (1992c) *Land Use Planning Policy and Climate Change.* London: HMSO.

DoE (1993a) NB: relates to another chapter.

DoE (1993b) *Good Practice Guide on the Environmental Appraisal of Development Plans.* London: HMSO.

DoE/DoT (1993) *Reducing Transport Emissions Through Planning.* London: HMSO.

DoE/SS/LGMB (1993) *Guide to the Eco Management and Audit Scheme for UK Local Government.* London: HMSO. Command No. 2426.

DoE *et al.* (1994a) *Sustainable Development: The UK Strategy.* London: HMSO.

DoE *et al.* (1994b) *Climate Change: The UK Programme.* London: HMSO. Command No. 2427.

DoE *et al.* (1994c) *Biodiversity: The UK Action Plan.* London: HMSO. Command No. 2428.

IPCC (1990) *Climate Change: the IPCC Scientific Assessment,* Report prepared by the Intergovernmental Panel on Climate Change, Working Group 1, WMO/UNEP.

LGMB (Local Government Management Board) (1993) *Framework for Local Sustainability: a Response by the UK.* Luton: LGMB.

LGMB (1995) *Sustainability Indicators.* Luton: LGMB.

Royal Commission on Environmental Pollution (1994) *Report of the Commission.* London: HMSO.

Other texts

ACC (1991) *Towards a Sustainable Transport Policy.* London: Association of Metropolitan Authorities.

Barton H and N Bruder (1995) *Local Environmental Auditing.* London: Earthscan.

Barton H, G Davis and R Guise (1995) *Sustainable Settlements: a guide for planners, designers and developers.* Bristol: University of the West of England and Luton: LGMB.

Blowers A (ed.) (1993) *Planning for a Sustainable Environment: A Report by the Town & County Planning Association.* London: Earthscan with TCPA.

Breheny M (ed.) (1992) *Sustainable Development and Urban Form.* London: Pion.

County Planning Officers Society (1993) *Planning for Sustainability.* London: CPOS.

Elkin T and D McLaren (1991) *Reviving the City: Towards Sustainable Urban Development.* London: Friends of the Earth and Policy Studies Institute.

English Nature (1994) *Sustainability in Practice Issue 1: Planning for Environmental Sustainability.* Peterborough: English Nature.

Glasson J *et al.* (1994) *Introduction to Environmental Impact Assessment.* London: University College London.

Goldsmith *et al.* (1972) Blueprint for Survival, *The Ecologist,* January. Reprinted Harmondsworth: Penguin.

Gore A (1992) *Earth in the Balance: Forging a New Common Purpose.* London: Earthscan.

Houghton T (ed.). (1992) *Bristol Energy and Environment Plan.* Bristol: Bristol Energy Centre.

Howard E (1895) G*arden Cities of Tomorrow.* Reprinted 1974 London: Faber.

London Research Centre (1993) *London Energy Study: Energy Use and the Environment.* London: LRC.

Meadows D *et al.* (1972) *The Limits to Growth.* London: Earth Island.

Meadows DH, DL Meadows and J Randers (1992) B*eyond the Limits: Global Collapse or a Sustainable Future.* London: Earthscan.

Owens S (1986) *Energy, Planning and Urban Form.* London: Pion.

Owens S (1991) *Planning Settlements Naturally.* Chichester: Packard.

Plato (5th Century BC) *Critias,* Translation (1929) by Bury RG, London: Heinemann.

Seymour J and H Giradet (1986) *Far from Paradise: The Story of Man's Impact on the Environment.* London: BBC.

Simonen L (1995) *Agenda 21 Briefing Sheets.* Available from Lin Simonen, The Create Centre, Smeaton Road, Bristol BS1 6XN.

Theriral R *et al.* (1992) *Strategic Environmental Assessment.* London: Earthscan.

Whitelegg J (1993) *Transport for a Sustainable Future: The Case for Europe.* London: Belhaven.

World Commission on Environment and Development (1987) *Our Common Future* (The Brundtland Report). Oxford: Oxford University Press.

Chapter 8

MINERALS AND THE ENVIRONMENT

Derek Senior

Dilemmas

In 1974, the Duke of Edinburgh provided the introduction to a study of quarries and the landscape for the minerals industry (cf. Haywood, 1974). In this he suggested that there was no better illustration of the dilemma between conservation and the demands of an industrial urban society than the situation of the extractive industries. He commented that we needed the resources but we were naturally anxious about the damage done in their extraction. These issues, the environmental and economic aspects of mineral extraction, have remained on the agenda for many years, and problems and concerns remain today. The town planner is faced with these problems in many aspects of work; mineral planning is however different from other aspects of planning, and many of the differences stem from the inherent characteristics of minerals.

Definitions

Firstly, minerals provide the raw materials for construction, for industrial processes and some for essential energy. They thus underpin much of the country's economy, and have to be exploited to meet national need.

Secondly, minerals can only be extracted where they occur. With many kinds of development, planners and developers have a wide variety of locational choice. With minerals the scope for choice of location is strictly limited by their natural occurrence.

Thirdly, the extraction of minerals is a destructive process. Unlike development such as housing, office or recreational proposals, it is not a creative, end product activity.

This chapter will explore a number of issues which flow from these three key differences. These include the different planning rules set out by central government for minerals; the different kind of planning authority set up to deal with minerals planning; the different rule for development plan production; and the different regime for planning permissions and conditions. This will lead to a discussion of key mineral problems, including the relationship between the industry and the planners, and particular problems relating to superquarries, areas of special protection such as national parks, and the problems of sustainability when dealing with an extractive process. The setting for such discussions must be a review of the minerals industry in the UK.

Minerals in the UK

Mineral reserves are widespread across the country. Local building styles, for instance, reflect the local materials, and are very different in an area of clay from an area of limestone. The details of production figures and areas are published by the British Geological Survey in the *UK Minerals Yearbook* (annual). A wide ranging survey of individual minerals and sites can be found in Blunden (1982), which is still one of the best detailed reviews. It is convenient to classify minerals according to their end use, rather than their individual geology.

Minerals used for construction purposes make up the biggest production group, and ultimately, because of the amount of extraction, are likely to raise major environmental concerns. Minerals for aggregate use are the largest portion of the Construction group. The annual extraction of some 230 million tonnes of rock includes limestone, sandstone, sand and gravel, igneous rocks and marine dredgings. An important part of the group is brick clay providing over 3,000 million bricks each year. Cement and slate are other materials for construction. Every part of the country has some extraction for construction purposes but there are some heavy concentrations of the industry which give rise to particular concerns. It is important to note that aggregate demand and production responds to the cyclical ups and downs of the whole construction industry.

The second group of minerals are those used in industrial processes. These are much more localised in their occurrence, and whilst important to their

Table 8.1 Minerals production figures 1993

Aggregates of which:	Total	230 million tonnes
	Crushed rock	143 million tonnes
	Sand and gravel	87 million tonnes
Industrial rocks of which:	Various salts	5.7 million tonnes
	Silica sand	3.8 million tonnes
	China clay	2.5 million tonnes
	Potash	0.9 million tonnes
	Ball clay	0.8 million tonnes
Energy of which:	Deep-mined coal	53 million tonnes
	Opencast coal	17 million tonnes
	Onshore oil	4 million tonnes
Others including:	Peat	1.5 million m^3

respective industries, are less widespread across the country, and their total production figures are much smaller. The minerals here include china clay, ball clay, Fuller's earth, potash, gypsum, dolomite, fluorspar and salt.

A third group is the energy minerals, again less widespread than aggregates. This includes the deep-mined coal industry, now much reduced in size, the recently privatised opencast coal industry, and onshore oil and gas production.

Finally there is a group of metals such as iron, gold and lead, and other commodities such as peat. Table 8.1 gives an impression of the scale of mineral extraction in Britain in 1993.

This table from IBG data indicates the size of the problem of extraction for aggregates. Major extraction areas can also be identified. Crushed rock from limestone focuses on Derbyshire (16 mt (million tonnes)), Somerset (13 mt), North Yorkshire (8 mt) and Clwyd (7 mt). Over half the crushed rock from sand and gravel is extracted in the South East and East Midlands regions (including marine gravel). Crushed rock from igneous rocks is concentrated in Derbyshire and Leicestershire, and the Strathclyde and Highlands regions in Scotland.

The planning problems associated with the extraction of minerals are not solely related to the environmental concerns. The industry employs about 33,500 men and women. Much of this employment is located in rural areas where alternative employment is not easily found.

The role of central government

The governance and planning of minerals has followed a different route over the last 50 years from the main activity of town and country planning. This can be outlined through looking at the roles of central government and local government, the activities of development planning and control of minerals, the role of the minerals industry, and how these activities have evolved against a growing number of environmental concerns. Central government's role as legislator, adviser and researcher has been as important for mineral planning as for other parts of the British planning system. Long before the modern planning system, central government had introduced legislation in 1891 to control the impact of the extraction of brine from the underground salt fields of Cheshire. Since then there has been a slow but gradual increase in controls over the mineral industry. During the Second World War, central government granted a number of planning permissions for mineral extraction under Interim Development Orders, where the registration of the location, size, depth of workings etc., was omitted either because of the wartime emergencies or the lack of understanding of the impact of such permissions. These old permissions have come back to haunt the mineral planner over the following decades a century later.

The Town and Country Planning Act 1947 introduced powers for minerals which are similar to those for other uses – survey, land allocation, compulsory purchase power, granting of permissions and imposition of conditions. A flurry of activity in the 1950s included the issuing of general guidance on the control of minerals (known from the colour of its cover as the Green Book) (MHLG, 1951, 1960 *et seq.*), legislation to deal with Ironstone workings and a Restoration Fund, and legislation about subsidence from deep mined coal and about opencast coal operations (which updated wartime emergency regulations). The Green Book and its guidance was updated in 1961, and remained the key guidance for twenty years. Problems associated with mineral extraction from operational activity to abandonment and eventual dereliction were mentioned, but there is a general lack of power to ensure restoration or even top soil storage. When local government reform was finalised in 1972, minerals planning duties were given to the upper tier counties in both shire and metropolitan areas. By then, a widespread concern about operational problems with working quarries and long term dereliction of abandoned works led to central government setting up two important committees to investigate and advise on mineral problems. Central Government's role up to then was much criticised; evidence from a national park committee in 1973 suggested that: 'You get marvellous advice on supermarkets, motorways, everything, but nothing on minerals'.

The Stevens Committee (DoE, 1976a) reported on the wider issues of *Planning Control over Mineral Workings* and the Verney Committee (DoE, 1976b) looked at *Aggregates: The Way Ahead.* Already in 1972 through the Local Government Act of that year the powers for dealing with both the strategic and detailed planning of minerals had been given to the upper tier (county) authorities in England and Wales whilst most other detailed matters were given to the lower tier (district) authorities. After some considerable delay, key recommendations from Stevens and Verney were introduced by means of a new Minerals Act in 1981, which marked minerals planning out as a separate activity. New additional powers related to the restoration of sites, the aftercare of these restorations, and limitations on the duration of permissions. The legislation also accepted that since mineral workings lasted so long, it was necessary to review the current relevance of conditions imposed in the past on a regular basis.

Clearly this possible later revision of the conditions relating to a permission could involve compensation and unwanted expense for the planning authority. The strategic role of the counties, as mineral authorities in England, was strengthened when associated duties relating to waste disposal were given to the same authorities. For many years coal extraction had been a special case. A government sponsored study in 1979 (Flowers, 1981) recommended changes to the procedures for dealing with opencast coal which the Government accepted in revised legislation in 1984. From October 1984 planning applications from British Coal were drawn into the mainstream of development control and since then have been dealt with by the mineral planning authorities as with other mineral applications. Prior to 1984 both mineral authorities, and district planning authorities were merely consultees on applications made to the then Secretary of State for Energy, who granted authorisations to work coal by opencast methods, and which included planning consent.

In 1986, however, the concept of mineral planning being dealt with by a strategic authority in England was dented by the abolition of the metropolitan counties and the GLC. Mineral policies and details were to be incorporated within the newly announced Unitary Development Plans in the Metropolitan Districts and London Boroughs. However, later in 1986 a Green Paper on the future of Development Plans in the shire areas suggested that in addition to mandatory district-wide development plans, there should be mandatory mineral and waste local plans produced.

In 1988 the Department of the Environment introduced the Planning Policy Guidance Notes (PPGs) to replace and upgrade previous advice in circulars, and for minerals, the Green Book, focusing on national policy. Mineral planning was clearly marked out as a separate but related activity when a series of Mineral Planning Guidance Notes (MPGs) were produced. The six original notes have been extended to 14, and several have been revised in the 1990s (especially those on general issues, aggregates and opencast coal) to reflect aspects of environmental and sustainability concerns lacking in the more market-led thrust of the 1988 MPGs. At the same time in 1988, regulations concerning environmental assessment (EA) were introduced in Britain. This followed a European Directive on the issue in 1985, after long discussions and negotiations in the Community. Mineral extraction emerged as one of the list of projects which require a formal assessment of environmental consequences if the local planning authority considers it necessary.

New legislation, in 1991, required mineral planning authorities in the two tier planning system (and the National Park Authorities) to produce a minerals local plan for the whole of their areas, to complement the district-wide development Plan, and the Unitary Plans of the large conurbations. The DoE has in recent years commissioned a considerable amount of research on mineral topics, including a report on the environmental effects of surface mineral workings (DoE, March 1992). It is interesting to note how many of the chapter headings in the report reflect issues raised in the earlier Green Books. The intention is to describe 'good practice and bring it to the attention of mineral operators, planning authorities and communities affected.'

Proposals for local government reforms during the 1990s have led to changes for minerals in Wales (cf. Local Government Act (Wales) 1994). The 1994 legislation replaces all the former counties and districts with unitary authorities, smaller than the former counties, but larger than the former districts. Mineral planning duties fall to them. English reorganisation, which was steered by central government towards smaller unitary authorities, has moved during 1994 and 1995 to the retention of many of the County Councils, which will retain mineral duties. In other areas, mineral planning will be the responsibility of the new smaller unitary authorities. The privatisation of the deep-mined and opencast coal industry has brought a revision of legislation, which brings both industries to a similar position to the normal private mineral operator.

The minerals planning authorities

From the setting up of local planning authorities in 1947, most mineral resources were controlled by the County Planning Authorities. There were few minerals exploited within the jurisdiction of the urban areas of the County Boroughs, whose boundaries were often close around the built up areas. This was the position for some twenty five years. The Local Government reorganisation of 1972, which created the two-tier planning system, allocated minerals to the upper tier County Councils in England and Wales (and to the two special Planning Boards for the Peak District and the Lake District). This was done by defining minerals as a 'county matter'. It was one of the few matters of detailed planning and control allocated to the upper tier counties. Thus, whilst some 500 planning authorities were created for England and Wales, mineral planning was to be the duty of 56 mineral planning authorities. The justification was one of strategic overview. Ironically this logic did not extend to Scotland; mineral duties were given to the District Authorities.

These moves were strengthened by the Stevens Report in 1976 (DoE, 1976a) which stressed the specialist nature of minerals control and the associated specialist staff requirements. The Verney Report later in 1976 went further. In highlighting problems of continuity in aggregates supply for the South East of England (after the boom of the early 1970s), Verney confirmed the role of regional working parties which had been set up in some areas, and the government extended these to all areas, with a central coordinating committee. The working parties were an early attempt at informal coordinated regional planning, involving local mineral authorities, and representatives from both central government and the private mineral industry organisations. The key tasks of the groups were to assess and quantify planning constraints on aggregate production, and consider inter-regional flows of materials likely to be necessary to meet national demand.

Mineral planning authorities were strengthened in the 1980 legislation, which clarified many of the planning responsibilities of the two-tier system. Minerals planning was confirmed as a County matter, its scope extended, and in England the associated problems of waste disposal also became County matters.

In 1986, the abolition of the GLC in London, and the Metropolitan Counties, led to the minerals responsibility being transferred to the new unitary authorities in those areas. This increased the number of minerals authorities in England from 48 to 109, including some quite small authorities. However, the overall impact was slight as many of the Metropolitan

Authorities have few mineral resources; the major exceptions being the lime-stone and sand and gravel of Doncaster, and a number of other authorities with opencast coal reserves.

Local government reorganisation in Wales in 1994 has changed the special role of the mineral authority. English reorganisation will increase slightly the number of unitary authorities dealing with minerals, but most County Councils will remain as mineral authorities.

There are some concerns that because of the general unpopularity of mineral working, it will be increasingly difficult for the more local elected members of planning authorities to balance the environmental impact with national need for mineral resources. The local impact on employment may also make decision making at local level more difficult. The strategic concept of the mineral authority has been that with elected representation from a wider area, and with a wide geographical area within which to examine alter-native sites, a more balanced judgement can be made, both in plan making and on individual sites.

Development plans and minerals

Since the introduction of development plans in 1947, formal positive plan making for minerals has had a slow and uneven career.

The old style development plans of the 1947 Act required 'the inclusion on town and county maps, if applicable, of indications of land to be used for securing the winning and working of minerals, and any other particulars or proposals of importance. Whilst most authorities showed in development plans existing mineral workings and land for which mineral permission had been granted, only a few of them went further and showed land which the authority intended to reserve for future mineral workings' (Stevens, 1976). Their scale and format limited their real value.

With the introduction of new plan-making legislation in 1968 all County Structure Plans would contain policies for mineral exploitation and protec-tion. The well-rehearsed arguments between County and District about the level of detail which these plans should contain were less relevant to minerals since the County Councils were responsible for strategic planning and detailed control aspects. The Structure Plan having its key diagram without an Ordnance Survey base created some problems where mineral indications were made on such key diagrams. This has been discussed in the case of Cornwall (Roberts and Shaw, 1982).

The whole of England and Wales was covered by Structure Plan mineral policies by 1983, but there was no compulsion for Counties to produce a local mineral plan for their areas and practice varied markedly. A number of authorities used only Structure Plan policies as formal development plan vehi-cles; Hertfordshire and Norfolk rejected detailed mineral plans. North Yorkshire relied mainly on the Structure Plan but initiated a series of informal plans for selected areas of mineral interest. Another set of authorities decided to produce formal subject plans for a particular mineral for the whole county or for a particular area. For example, Nottinghamshire produced a study of sand and gravel (1984) and Tyne and Wear produced a Quarries Plan (1983). Cumbria and the Lake District Planning Board produced a joint mineral plan which excluded coal, and Cumbria produced a separate coal local plan. Other authorities produced mineral plans for all minerals for the whole of their areas – Buckinghamshire (1982), Berkshire (1984), and Hampshire (1987) are examples. Three mineral subject plans, which were at advanced stages when the Metropolitan Counties were abolished in 1986, were called in and approved by the DoE in 1989. Clearly this situation led to variation and disparity across the country in terms of what details were available to the industry and the public about likely mineral policies.

From 1986, the Unitary Plans of the Metropolitan areas were required to cover minerals in detail in Part II of their mandatory district wide plans. This was followed by the proposals of the green consultation paper on the Future of Development Plans in the rest of England and Wales, which recommended detailed Mineral Plans for all areas. This was included in the legislation in 1991, thus heralding a plan-led system for minerals as well as other development.

The approach to the preparation of these Mineral Plans highlights some further differences with other plan making. Mineral Planning Guidance says that policies should recognise that local, regional and national requirements for minerals be met. This raises many issues about who agrees these requirements, and how accurate are such figures. Secondly, the identification system within mineral plans is different to that of other development plans; areas identified can have varying degrees of specificity. 'At one end of the spectrum are sites which can be identified with a high degree of precision and where there is a strong accompanying presumption in favouring extraction, "preferred areas". At the other end of the spectrum are more broadly defined "areas of search" which provide a guide to the industry as to the broad areas where extraction might be permitted' (MPG1, 1988).

It is difficult to imagine the response to such a broad range of allocations when planners are dealing with housing or industry, or even shopping. The underlying reason for this range of allocations is a result of the varying knowledge of mineral resources in the plan area by the mineral authority, and occasionally also by the mineral industry. The detailed information on the quality of the mineral reserves tends to be in the hands of the minerals industry, and may be confidential, for instance, because of land ownership issues, or of competition. The 'control' which the mineral authorities' planners can exercise in such circumstances is much diminished. Some of the general and widespread 'areas of search' also cause considerable consternation amongst local people during public consultations on plans, because they appear to blight large areas of land. Interesting contrasts in mineral subject plan inquiries including claims to be 'reconciling the irreconcilable' have been examined (Everton and Hughes, 1987). Plan makers are also urged to take into account the high levels of capital investment involved in mineral exploitation, and the long lead-in times before full production. Government guidance also recommends that Mineral Plans provide sufficient stock of permitted reserves with planning permission in the form of land banks. These should ensure a rolling programme to secure continuous supply, even in the face of fluctuations in demand.

Mineral Plans are also required to include safeguarding policies for deposits of minerals of economic importance against other types of development which might sterilise the deposits. This links the mineral plan process with the land allocations and policies of district-wide plans for all other land uses.

Mineral plans are similarly required to have regard to environmentally important areas, and include policies to protect these areas from new development including minerals. This advice is balanced by the comment from central government that some mineral resources may not be available outside such sensitive areas. Clearly all the advice points to difficult yet balanced decisions in mineral planning.

Since 1991 the public and the minerals industry have had the opportunity to participate in detailed mineral plan making across the whole country, which was not widespread before that date. The recent record levels of interest and number of objections in some of the Metropolitan UDPs could presage similar interest in a nationwide series of public inquiries into mineral planning.

Development control and minerals

The need for a special form of control to deal with the unique nature of mineral operations has long been recognised. Gradually since 1947, stronger control has been imposed. The nature of mineral extraction as an ongoing destructive process in the landscape demands special consideration in the control process.

The Green Books of 1951 and 1960 (MHLG publications *The Control of Mineral Working*) indicated how complex was minerals control. Control in the case of minerals is about the ongoing operational activities of a site, which can go on for many years, as well as the overall impact and long-term restoration. Thus control can investigate the working programme and its phasing, depth of working, screening, and disposal of waste. It must also consider buildings, plant and machinery on site, and problems of dust, noise, smoke and fumes. Water problems are often encountered, and traffic and access roads are also essential considerations. Most of the issues raised in the 1960s have continued to be the basis of objections to mineral developments in the following thirty years.

The 1970s can be seen as a decade of pressure for more control powers over minerals to counter the problems outlined. The emergence of DoE statistics on derelict land resulting from mineral exploitation, and often site abandonment, strengthened the claim for more control (DoE, 1993c). The Stevens Report in 1976 contained firm recommendations for better and firmer environmental legislation on minerals in general, whilst the Flowers Report in 1981 complemented this with recommendations about the visual and land use impacts of deep-mined colliery spoil, and some harsh comments on opencast coal.

The pressures resulted in additional control powers from 1981. The Conservative administration brought in this legislation, responding to growing environmental awareness of the public, which contrasted with their insistence on market forces and non-intervention in other areas of planning. It was also well in advance of the general greening of Government policies later in the 1980s.

The complexity of major mineral applications is revealed by development control statistics (DoE, 1993c). In 1991/92 the mineral authorities dealt with some 300 major developments and 180 minor matters. While the DoE expects some 80% of planning applications to be decided within 8 weeks, the minerals position is different; of the major matters, only 4% were decided within 8 weeks, only 22% within 13 weeks, and three quarters took longer than 13 weeks. The DoE statistics on time calculations exclude those applications with environmental assessments. Clearly major mineral applications take time and implicitly those with environmental statements even longer.

Planning permissions for minerals include record numbers of conditions. The revised Green Book of 1961 included 49 examples of conditions and Leicestershire CC have, for instance, been known to impose over 100 conditions upon a mineral planning consent.

One key reason for this complexity is that the controls relate to much of the operational and day-to-day management of the workings. The long list of aspects to be covered recur in research reports for the DoE in the 1990s on environmental aspects mirroring many of the Green Paper concerns. Research indicates continuing problems with clarity about the exact area of working, the depth of working, and the direction and phasing of working. There will be concerns about blasting, vibration, noise, dust and odour. There will be concerns about surface and ground water, and pollution. There will be concerns about landscape impact, about traffic. There may be more localised issues concerning archaeology, wildlife or footpaths. There will certainly be interest in hours of working, and the operator's overall image.

In the overall assessment of schemes there will be concern about the life span of a working, the restoration scheme, storage of top soil and the possibility of continuous restoration. There will be discussions on what eventual after-use there may be.

Much of the work of the town planner in these circumstances is one of discussion, negotiation and damage limitation.

Restoration and aftercare have been improved both as a result of the response to the Stevens Report and a more responsible attitude by the minerals industry. Both the major employers' organisations, BACMI and SAGA, have regularly given awards to good examples of restoration, and so have some of the local authorities themselves.

In 1971 the DoE had estimated that at least 60,000 acres were derelict as a result of mineral workings, and more recent DoE surveys (DoE, 1972, 1982, 1988) make depressing reading despite the considerable investment in reclamation through derelict land grants. Clearly prevention is better than cure in these circumstances. Since 1981 Minerals Planning Authorities have imposed aftercare conditions requiring that restored land is planted, culti-vated, fertilised, watered, drained or otherwise treated for a specific period so as to bring it to a required standard of agriculture, forestry or amenity use. (See MPG2 listed at end of chapter.)

These additional powers did not solve the problem of permissions granted under Interim Development Orders prior to 1947. Responding to growing environmental concerns, legislation was introduced which required such per-missions to be registered with the Local Planning Authority by March 1992. If not registered a permission would cease to have effect. The permissions so registered were those where some working had taken place after 1948 and before 1979. The Local Planning Authorities then determined the area and terms of the permissions within three months, with a right of appeal to the Secretary of State. Development control was therefore to be strengthened on the old problem sites through the imposition of conditions for operational activity, and eventual restoration where relating to environmental and amen-ity aspects, without any need to pay compensation.

Permissions granted after 1947 often had inadequate conditions, and have been a cause of concern. The Environment Act 1995 contains provision for the review and update of old mineral permissions granted between 1948–1982 to protect the environment and amenity. This will strengthen restoration and aftercare provision.

Role of the private sector

The minerals industry is a powerful force. The town planner in the public sector working in the field of minerals can be seen as being at a disadvantage for a number of reasons.

The minerals industry invests large amounts of capital in mineral extrac-tion. Some parts of the industry are dominated by large national and interna-tional companies. Hanson plc, with a turnover in 1994 of £14 billion, owns Hanson Brick, which is Britain's largest producer, and also ARC, which is the second largest aggregate producer in the UK after Tarmac plc. Tarmac's list of sites reads like a who's who of quarries. There is, and has been, a plethora of small local and regional mineral operators.

The recommendations of Stevens and Verney led to an improved relation-ship between developers and planners. Discussions and joint working became much more common. The joint Regional Aggregates Working Parties, which were set up in 1970, brought Planning Authority, minerals industry and central government representatives together; this can be seen as analogous to the planning authorities' work with the National House Builders Federation in another area of planning.

Mineral planning guidance from central government specifically addressed the minerals industry. The guidance urged the industry to be continually aware of the need to make operations more environmentally acceptable, and the need for practices to command public confidence. It was also suggested that regular contact be kept with local groups and councils in order to build this confidence. This is quite common with many operations. The question arose and still arises for the local authorities as to whether they should be involved in such liaison if they are later to be involved in possible enforcement etc.

Many of the major mineral companies have developed a good reputation for operational and restoration activities. One of the problems for the town planner when working alongside the mineral industry is that the relationship can be seen to be too close by the general public and in particular by those objecting to specific applications. The planner, and the elected members making decisions, are often caught between the opposing factions of developer and objector.

Recent advice from DoE research indicates strong pressure for the mineral companies to introduce and use self-auditing and self-regulating procedures. The industry is urged elsewhere to develop operational codes of practice. The positive approach to self-regulation is shown in a recent CBI publication, which includes details of environmental codes of practice from several operator associations and an environmental charter from the minerals industry (CBI, 1994).

The future for aggregates production

The problem of aggregates production, especially for the South East of England, was highlighted by Verney some twenty years ago. The key problem is not one of lack of reserves in the sense of no materials. It is a problem of further reserves being in particularly sensitive areas, whether close to special landscape designations, or close to residential areas.

Verney suggested a number of possible developments. These included more rail facilities for transporting aggregates, further investigation of marine dredging, alternative materials in the construction industry, underground workings and possible superquarries with sea transport.

Revised MPG6 (1994) takes forward most of these proposals. Marine dredged aggregates are expected to produce some 4% of supply up to year 2006. This activity is not subject to normal planning control, but a special regime is operated by DoE for licences. There are a number of environmental concerns which are taken into account in this process.

Coastal superquarries are normally those which can produce 5 mt p.a. with reserves of 150 mt. One quarry has been established at Glensanda (Loch Linnhe), Scotland. Research has focused on sites around Scotland, Norway and Northern Spain. A current proposal is at Lingara Bay on South Harris in the Outer Hebrides. The long distance transportation issue for such sources clashes with the concept of sustainability, which could be seen to minimise transport/energy use.

Planning guidance on aggregates (MPG6) encourages extended use of secondary and recycled material. This includes waste from collieries, china clay works, slate works and power stations, and other slags. Further use of demolition and construction waste and asphalt removed from roads is encouraged. Much of the progress in the area will depend upon close cooperation between the users of materials and the providers. An important issue is the specification of particular standards for materials for a particular job. Whilst there is a need to avoid sub-standard material, research indicates that some margins in the standards could be excessive, and lead to high grade materials being wasted.

Aggregates in the 1990s are used for the following purposes:

- new roads 24%
- new housing 20%
- other public 13%
- private commercial 12%
- private industrial 11%
- repairs and maintenance 16%

The cuts in the new road programme in the mid 1990s could have a significant impact by reducing demand. This could however be balanced by an increase in road maintenance use unless overall traffic falls. Similarly, there may be pent-up demand for housing, other industrial building and general maintenance as a result of the recession in the construction industry of the early 1990s. The overall reduction in demand envisaged in revised guidance in 1994 may only be a temporary respite.

Some of the benefits

The full range of building materials available in the various corners of England have been fully explored (Clifton-Taylor, 1987). This ranges from limestones and sandstones through to marble, flint and brick. Much of the value of our rich historic built environment is a reflection of the variety of local building materials before the age of rail transport. Some have been saddened by the demise of dependence on local materials (Hoskins, 1955). Others have exploited great grandeur from a richer array of minerals transported from far afield. Scott's use of materials in the St Pancras Hotel in the 1870s exemplifies this; salmon pink bricks from Nottinghamshire, honey coloured stone from Ancaster in Lincolnshire, red sandstone from Mansfield and different limestones from Devon and Connemara. By the end of the twentieth century a rich variety of materials continues to be produced by the minerals industry for construction purposes. Local materials, however, remain important in the conservation of many towns and villages.

Mineral workings have produced other benefits. The restoration of various mineral sites has led to new landforms which have provided new land uses. Whilst DoE surveys (1988) have shown that the bulk of mineral workings are restored to agriculture (59%), sizeable areas have been developed as amenity areas (28%). In addition, built development covers 9%, and forestry some 4%.

Some of the more well known restorations such as Thorpe Leisure Park in Surrey and Holmepierrepoint in Nottinghamshire are merely the tip of an iceberg of water recreation and conservation facilities which have emerged from good mineral restoration. Opencast coaling has eventually resulted in large water recreation resources near to Sheffield and Wakefield, where the local authorities have worked closely with the operators to provide good positive benefits from the mineral activity.

Opencast coal activity has often been associated with the inclusive restoration of surface dereliction. It has been a basic plank of planning policy that extraction may well be allowed where such environmental benefit can be exploited. One of the largest opencast schemes is at Merthyr Tydfil, where amongst other land use benefits, the former Dowlais iron works is being removed by the scheme. Such reclamation work during coal excavation reduces the profitability of the scheme and there are fears that the 1995 privatisation of the coal industry will reduce such examples in future.

Many mineral excavations have provided major landfill sites for waste deposits. These have provided valuable resources. It has often been suggested that the void created by mineral extraction has been more valuable for tipping than the value of the material extracted. Clearly infill is the only solution to restoration of voids created if level surface uses, such as agriculture and forestry, are being considered. From the local public's view, this form of restoration may extend the time when environmental problems occur at a site from traffic, and other activities.

Minerals and sensitive areas

Twenty years ago (DoE Circular 4/76) Planning Authorities were told that whilst mineral applications in National Parks had to be treated on their merits, they should be subject to 'most rigorous' examination. This included the consideration of national need, environmental impact, alternative supplies, local economic impact and public interest. Such pressures have been particularly felt in the Peak District and Yorkshire Dales National Parks, but other National Parks and Areas of Outstanding Natural Beauty are affected by local mineral problems.

Friends of the Earth commissioned a study of Slate Quarrying in the Lake District (Friends of the Earth, 1988). The report suggested fewer quarries, with closures and compensation being paid. The report contrasted the 233 jobs in slate workings with 25,000 in the tourist industry, and favoured protecting the greater number. This was supported by the fact that most of the slate quarried was not for local or even national need but for export.

The balancing act of economic and environmental factors in sensitive areas has moved in favour of conservation in recent years. In 1995, draft mineral guidance looked specifically at nationally recognised sensitive areas and recommended that 'major developments should not take place in these areas, save in exceptional circumstances'. The criteria of the 1976 Circular (DoE Circular 4/76) are repeated, but overall any permissions would need to be shown to be in the public interest. Other sensitive areas without national recognition are to be offered a lesser degree of protection. Elsewhere in the guidance, it is suggested that extensions to existing mineral sites may be preferable to new greenfield sites in many, but not all cases. This, taken with local economic considerations, persuaded the Yorkshire Dales National Park Committee in 1995 to allow an extension by deepening at Swinden Quarry south west of Grassington after long discussions and earlier refusals. Other National Park Authorities, such as the Peak National Park, have tried to put very restrictive policy into development plans, but have been constrained by intervention from the DoE.

Minerals and sustainability

The dominance of the concept of sustainability has grown both in academic works, in inter-government agreements and policy guidance in the last decade. It is difficult to bring the traditional concept of sustainability to the process of mineral extraction, in that it is of itself a destructive process. Different criteria have to be introduced. The Government has attempted to spell these out in the revisions to MPG1 and MPG6. The overall thrust is to seek to use less raw material by the encouragement of the use of alternative materials, especially recycled materials. Secondly there is the concept of using high quality materials only where essential. Thirdly there is the continuing concept of good management of extraction sites during operations, followed by suitable restoration and after-use when extraction is completed.

The concept of minimising transport costs and impacts is clearly central to sustainability. The location of mineral resources and the growing interest in superquarries in remote places clashes with some elements of this transport issue. However, longer journeys by sea or by rail would be likely to fit into a wider definition of protecting the overall environment. The problems relating to some of these issues may not be in the hands of either mineral operator (as supplier) or local planning authority (as regulator) but in the hands of the consumer of minerals, primarily through the specifications required by the general construction industry (Bate, 1994). The public in general may also have their part to play as consumers, especially in the case of such materials as peat for garden use, but also a growing awareness that future mineral exploitation for cheap materials will have growing environmental impacts. Minimising these will be a major task for local authority mineral planners and for the various arms of the mineral industry. Public pressure and awareness will no doubt keep mineral issues at the forefront of the environmental debate.

References

Anfield J (1988) The role of the planner in national parks, *The Planner*, Vol. 74, No. 1, January.

Bate R. (1994) Paper at RTPI Yorkshire Branch Minerals Seminar Wakefield.

Blunden J (1975) *Mineral Resources of Britain*. London: Hutchinson.

British Geological Survey (1994 and annual) *UK Minerals 1993*. London: BGS.

CBI (1994) *Living with Minerals*. London: Confederation of British Industry.

Circular 4/76 Report of the National Parks Policies Review Committee.

Clifton-Taylor, A (1987) *Patterns of English Buildings*. London: Faber and Faber.

Commission on Energy and the Environment (1981) *Coal and the Environment*. London: HMSO.

DoE (1972, 1982, 1988) *Survey of Derelict Land*. London: HMSO.

DoE (1976a) *Planning Control Over Mineral Working* (Stevens Report). London: HMSO.

DoE (1976b) *Aggregates: The Way Ahead* (Verney Report). London: HMSO.

DoE (1986) *The Future of Development Plans*. London: HMSO, Green Paper.

DoE (1989) *Environmental Assessment: A Guide to Procedures*. London: HMSO.

DoE (1991) *Environmental Effects of Surface Mineral Workings*. London: HMSO.

DoE (1993 a and b) NB: these relate to other chapters.

DoE (1993c) *Development Control Statistics: England, 1991/92*. London: HMSO.

Everton AR and DJ Hughes (1987) Minerals subject plans in action, *Journal of Planning and Environmental Law*, March: pp. 174–184.

Flowers Report (1981) *Coal and the Environment*. London: HMSO.

Friends of the Earth (1988) *Slate Quarrying in the Lake District*. London: FOE.

Haywood SM (1974) *Quarries and the Landscape*. London: BQSF.

Hoskins, J (1955) *Making of the English Landscape*. London: Hodder & Stoughton.

MHLG (Ministry of Housing and Local Government) (1951 and 1960) *The Control of Mineral Working* (the 'Green Books'). London: HMSO.

Roberts P and T Shaw (1982) *Mineral Resources in Regional and Strategic Planning*. Aldershot: Gower.

Minerals Planning Guidance:

MPG1 1988 (Revised 1995) *General Conditions and the Development Plan System.*

MPG2 1988 *Applications, Permissions and Conditions.*

MPG3 1994 *Coal Mining and Colliery Spoil Disposal.*

MPG4 1988 *Review of Mineral Working Sites.*

MPG5 1989 *Minerals Planning and General Development Order.*

MPG6 1994 *Guidelines for Aggregates Provision in England.*

MPG7 1989 *The Reclamation of Minerals Workings.*

MPG8 *Planning and Compensation Act 1991: Interim Development Order Permissions – Statutory Provisions and Procedures.*

MPG9 *Planning and Compensation Act 1991: Interim Development Order Permissions – Conditions.*

MPG10 *Raw Materials for the Cement Industry.*

MPG11 *Noise at Surface Workings.*

MPG12 *Disused Mine Openings.*

MPG13 *Guidelines for Peat.*

MPG14 *Review of Mineral Planning Permission.*

PART V

PLANNING FOR CITY CENTRES OR DECENTRALISATION

INTRODUCTION

This section comprises two contrasting chapters which relate to the future of town centres, retailing, and therefore the quality of urban life. Firstly Geoff Walker looks at the debates and issues centring on the advantages and disadvantages of out-of-town shopping development. Retail store decentralisation has been one of the significant forces in reshaping the traditional structure of urban form in recent years. Such motor car dependent development hardly contributes to creating sustainable urban environments, whilst socially, relocation disadvantages the carless and residents in traditional districts who have seen their local shops rendered uneconomic by this change. But economically, such development creates investment and jobs in an area. Significantly town planners have lacked the statutory power to limit such development. Indeed in some cases local planning authorities have welcomed such change as a means of reducing town centre congestion and car parking problems, and were apparently oblivious to negative knock-on effects. In contrast, whilst Geoff Walker concentrates on city-wide, macro-level issues, in the second chapter Kimberly Paumier takes a more detailed, micro-level approach to city centre problems. But she is not a town planner, rather a city centre manager, although it may be argued that she is performing an important role which town planners should have undertaken long ago, and which is effectively 'planning' in all but name. She looks at ways of making central areas both more culturally vibrant and economically viable, and thus is contributing towards creating sustainability.

Chapter 9

RETAILING DEVELOPMENT: IN TOWN OR OUT OF TOWN?

Geoff Walker

Urban spatial change

The spatial structure of our towns and cities is constantly changing. We tend to perceive the developed urban fabric of these areas as being permanent, but the balance and disposition of different land users is certainly not so. Certain land use components – the major ones like housing for example which dominate this structure – tend to change only at the margins, usually because they become more extensive (as in the case of housing) or sometimes because they contract (as in the case of primary and manufacturing industry in many of our industrial towns and cities). Others are more fluid so that the spatial pattern changes discernibly and sometimes over a period of only a decade or two. Retailing is probably the major example of the latter. Here, following a period after World War Two which saw little change in the overall patterns of retail land use, either in urban or in rural areas, the 1970s onwards have witnessed major changes. These changes in the spatial pattern of retail activity have been variously represented as a major frontal assault on established principles and values of public policy (as expressed by land use planning policy); a capitulation to the pressures or powers of market forces; a divisive force which has further disadvantaged those already disadvantaged residents of town or city; a force leading to the unnecessary further use of energy and creation of pollution as a result of increased journeys by motor car; or, a major benefit to shoppers in terms of choice, price and convenience.

The changes have been driven by a complex combination of factors. Not least among these are socio-economic forces which influence the way in which we go about our daily lives – values, levels of prosperity, aspirations to greater mobility etc. The other important factors, in the particular context of retailing, are the aspirations of the community as consumers seeking convenience, choice and value for money; the dynamics of the retail industry seeking essentially to increase profits; and finally, public policy in the shape of the land use planning system, seeking to intervene in the process of change in the interests of the community as a whole. Retail development and in particular the tension between the traditional town or city centre location and the new out-of-centre one, has become a major issue. This chapter identifies the major elements which make it such an issue. It traces its emergence as an issue; outlines the development of the public policy response to retail change over the last 20 years or so; and finally it looks to the future by means of a number of emerging issues.

Definitions

It is useful, at an early stage, to define certain things which are referred to on a number of occasions within the chapter.

- *In-town* is used to refer to locations which, although within an urban area are not necessarily within the recognised centre or centres of that area. They are, in other words, out-of-centre.
- *Out-of-town* is the 'generic' term which has come into popular use in this field to refer to any retail development which is not within the town centre as traditionally recognised. More accurate would be its use in connection with retail development which is physically outside a defined urban area.
- *Town centre (or city centre)* is the traditional retail heart of an urban area, providing a broad range of shops and other facilities which fulfil a function as a focus for both the community and public transport.
- *Retail hierarchy* is the range of shopping centres within a particular area (usually County or larger) expressed in terms of their size and importance with few centres at the 'top' and many at the 'bottom' e.g. Regional/City Centre, sub-regional centre, major town/district centre, district/local centre. The basis of almost all development plan retail policy.
- *Vital and viable town centres.* Twin concepts which are central to current public policy concern for the future of traditional town centres, 'vitality' refers to 'life' as measured in terms of pedestrian volumes, shop vacancy rates, retailer representation and demand, general diversity of uses and quality of environment. 'Viability' refers to the ability to attract and retain commercial investment and relates to such factors as confidence, retail competition and the dynamism of the local economy.
- *Convenience goods* are food and drink and other items forming part of everyday domestic shopping.
- *Durable goods* are those non-food items, generally of much higher unit value, such as electrical white goods, furniture, carpets and DIY materials, purchased much less frequently.
- *Supermarket.* A single level, self-service food store with between 5000 and 25,000 sq. ft (500–2500 sq. m) of sales area (i.e. that used for the selling and display of goods), often with its own car park.
- *Superstore.* A single level, self-service store with dedicated car parking, selling mainly convenience goods, but some durable goods as well with at least

25,000 sq. ft (2500 sq. m) of sales area. Storage and other space can often add up to as much again to give the gross floorspace, often referred to as the GLA or gross lettable area. The average size of superstores has been increasing so that 30,000 sq. ft and more is now not uncommon. Amongst the largest of more recent examples are the Savacentres (Sainsbury), some of which have reached 100,000 sq. ft in sales area. There are now estimated to be 1500 superstores in Britain.

- *Hypermarket.* A term now less used than when it was first introduced in Britain in the 1970s (e.g. by Carrefour), used to describe a superstore with a sales area of at least 50,000 sq. ft (5000 sq. m) with a large dedicated car park and usually free-standing. The term has always enjoyed much wider popular usage in mainland Europe, where it is frequently used to describe what by British definition would rank only as a superstore. One of our largest is in fact one of the earliest – the Asda store at Cribbs Causeway, Bristol, which opened in 1976 as Carrefour, with a retail sales area of 90,000 sq. ft and an overall (gross) area of 170,000 sq. ft.

- *Regional shopping centre (RSC).* A purpose built, fully enclosed complex containing a wide range of shops and other facilities, including leisure, with dedicated parking space for many thousands of cars. Always free-standing, in town or out-of-town, with at least 500,000 sq. ft of retail sales area. Of the four largest examples to date in Britain each has a total sales area in excess of 1 million sq. ft.

- *Retail warehouse.* A single-level store with dedicated parking space, usually in an out-of-centre location with at least 10,000 sq. ft of sales area and selling durable goods such as electrical goods and appliances, carpets, furniture and DIY items. Many early examples were adapted light industrial or warehouse buildings on industrial estates. There are now estimated to be more than 2000 individual units of this kind in Britain.

- *Retail warehouse park.* An agglomeration of at least three retail warehouses. Early examples were simply small groups of second generation, purpose-built retail warehouses sharing a site and often common road access off a major urban route. Later examples have more integrated site layouts and design with shared parking and circulation space and proper landscaping. The first park opened in 1982 and it is now reckoned that there are some 250 of them in Britain.

Relevant texts

This chapter concentrates on the major issues associated with retail change, past and future, with particular reference to spatial considerations and land use planning policy. As such it does not pretend to cover every facet of retail development. It may therefore be helpful to the reader to briefly review the range of reasonably up-to-date texts which do, collectively, cover the ground.

Some of these have been used as sources for material presented in this chapter, as noted appropriately in the text.

Looking first at what might be termed the retail planning 'textbooks' – *Planning for Shops* by Keith Thomas (Estates Gazette/Leaf Coppin, 1990) takes the reader concisely through just about every aspect of retail development in the UK in the space of some 80 pages; *Retailing – Shopping, Society, Space* by Larry O'Brien and Frank Harris (David Fulton Publishers, 1991) represents a comprehensive treatment of retailing as an industry, a force shaping social attitudes and contemporary culture and as a force for change in townscape terms; *Retail Change – Contemporary Issues* by Rosemary Bromley and Colin Thomas (UCL Press, 1993) deals comprehensively with the social, economic and environmental contexts of retail change in the UK, Europe and North America since the 1970s. It looks at the land use planning implications of retail change and at social issues such as the 'disadvantaged consumer', working conditions, shopping as leisure and the 'greening' of shopping; *The Retail Development Process – Location, Property and Planning* by Clifford Guy (Routledge, 1994) is by far the most comprehensive work to date on the processes behind different types of retail development. These processes are related to the land use planning system, property development and finance.

In another category are to be found a number of commissioned and other 'professional' studies which represent useful sources, for example – *Planning for Shopping into the 21st Century*, the report of the RTPI Retail Planning Working Party 1988, provides a good overview of trends, issues and policy responses up to the mid-1980s; *Change in the Retail Environment* by Elizabeth Howard and Ross Davies (OXIRM/Longman, 1988) looks at change from a geographical perspective and the ways in which the retail industry has responded locationally; *The Effects of Major Out of Town Retail Development* by BDP Planning and OXIRM (HMSO, 1992) is a substantial 'literature review' produced for the DoE, containing both evaluation and prescription, which has had a major influence on central government thinking on retail policy (as seen in the 1993 revision of PPG6); and finally, *Shopping Centres and Their Future* by the House of Commons Environment Committee (HMSO, 1994), seen by many as a 'landmark' document in the evolution of central government retail policy with its growing emphasis on the 'vital and viable' town/city centre.

Three different perspectives

Understanding of the issues associated with retail development requires an appreciation of the markedly different perspectives applied to the process. A three-way grouping of these is illustrated in Fig. 9.1. The community is the 'consumer', but not only of retail goods. It is also the consumer or recipient

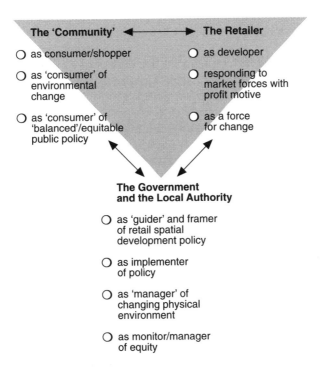

The 'Community' ←——→ The Retailer

○ as consumer/shopper

○ as 'consumer' of environmental change

○ as 'consumer' of 'balanced'/equitable public policy

○ as developer

○ responding to market forces with profit motive

○ as a force for change

The Government and the Local Authority

○ as 'guider' and framer of retail spatial development policy

○ as implementer of policy

○ as 'manager' of changing physical environment

○ as monitor/manager of equity

Fig. 9.1 Retailing development: three different perspectives

of environmental change, which it may seek to influence or resist, and the consumer of attempts to introduce and implement balanced and equitable public policy, e.g. equal shopping opportunities for all. The retail industry is very big business and one of the most dynamic sectors of the British economy. In 1992 it contributed 14.1% of the nation's GDP and retailing and distribution employed 9.2% of the workforce (House of Commons Environment Committee, 1994, p. XIII). Between 1955 and 1985 the volume of retail sales in Britain doubled, whilst the value of these sales increased twelve-fold (Thomas, 1990, p. 2). In 1971 there were just 21 superstores; by the end of 1994 there were some 1500. This massive industry can be seen as developer responding to market forces and as a major force for change both in what it produces in the environment and as an opinion former in its own right. An industry in such a powerful position can exercise considerable political influence. At the third corner of the triangle is the public policy mechanism in the shape of central and local government. Many would say that it has the most difficult task of the three – seeking to manage change in the physical environment in the interests of equity and doing this by the essentially crude means of land use policy. Retailing development is, in essence, a response to the interplay between such perspectives.

Retail development – 'in-town'

Until the 1970s, retail development in Britain was not a major issue, because it was not associated with significant locational change. The development plans supported the *status quo* as far as retail location was concerned. Shops continued to be largely where they had been for centuries – within the centres of our towns and cities and, on a much smaller scale, within villages and suburbs of the larger urban areas. Britain's retail industry saw its market response as being best met within those traditional locations. The changes made, in response to rapidly growing consumer spending power seeking 'up-to-date' shops selling a growing range of convenience and durable goods, involved redevelopment within these traditional locations.

From the 1950s onwards, central area redevelopment, with retailing and commercial office space as the main components, typified retail change. Initially this took fairly modest forms in most towns – the purpose-built shopping mall, open to the elements, together with piecemeal refurbishments of individual retail sites. In a number of larger towns and cities, particularly those embarking upon major rebuilding programmes following bomb damage, more ambitious schemes emerged. Until the early 1960s the work was carried out either by retailers themselves or by large specialist developers who often retained ownership of their centres. By the late 1960s this process was being further fuelled by massive injections of capital by big institutional property developers – mainly the pension funds and insurance companies. By international standards, the extent of ownership of retail property by the institutions which fund its development is high in Britain.

If the rise in 'consumer power' and the institutional investment provided the fuel, the land and supporting infrastructure were both provided by local authorities. Councils wished to retain, or if possible enhance, the status of their retail centres, and planning policy and other mechanisms were geared to this purpose. They were, for example, instrumental in the process of assembling land for town centre retail schemes. Some of these schemes, representing 'planned' retail development (Guy, 1994, p. 107), were individually very large, especially the fully enclosed multi-unit complexes, such as the Arndale Centres developed by Town & City Properties. The one in Manchester has almost 1.2 million square feet of gross retail space. Guy (1994, p. 107) notes the important distinction between 'planned' and unplanned retail space. Town and city centres still have a huge legacy of unplanned retail space. Quite what the total amount is is hard to define, but he has estimated that even up to the late 1980s, 80–85% of the total retail space in England remained in unplanned forms.

Town centre retail development reached a peak in 1976, during which year just over 8 million square feet of new floorspace was completed or scheduled (figures by Hillier Parker Research; see occasional Paper 8, Brian Raggett, 1992). However, at about this time the further growth of such new retail development decreased sharply when the commercial property market collapsed.

This form of retail development did not however have parallels in those other parts of the world whose trends in retailing are typically said to influence those in Britain. In North America at this time, the process of decentralisation was underway with an increasing proportion of new retail development taking place in 'cheaper' out-of-centre locations, often by speculative developers and within a much freer planning regime. In mainland Europe, in countries such as France, Germany and the Netherlands, town centre redevelopment with a high retail content was rare at this time and most new retail schemes appeared in out-of-centre or even out-of-town locations, typically at road communications nodes. Carrefour is French for crossroads!

If the mid-1970s represented a peak in town centre retail development never since exceeded and a level of total new retail development in Britain which was not to be surpassed until the late-1980s, they also heralded the arrival of out-of-town, decentralised development. Although the overall scale of such development has never to date exceeded that in town centres in any one year (Hillier Parker Research, 1992, *op. cit.*) the share of new development taking place in out-of-centre locations in our towns and cities began to become significant in the late-1970s and early 1980s. The phenomenon which was to challenge much of the conventional wisdom of development plan policy and become such a major issue had arrived.

Retailing moves – out-of-town

Out-of-centre retail development (popularly referred to as 'out-of-town') was part of a process of suburbanisation and counter-urbanisation which is generally acknowledged to have begun in Britain in the mid-1960s. As the foci of commercial and employment activity changed, most notably in terms of decentralisation from the traditional urban core or CBD, so did the spatial pattern of retail activity. This so-called 'spatial transformation' (Bromley and Thomas, 1993, *op. cit.*, Chapter 1) has gone hand-in-hand with organisational changes within the industry such as the concentration of capital (fewer but larger retail outlets and growing market share for a few big companies) and the introduction of new technology. (Electronic point of sale information or 'EPOS' computer-based systems for ordering up goods from a few very large warehouses for example.)

Collectively, these changes have been dramatic – the so-called 'retail revolution' – but it is those associated with new patterns of land use which are the concern of this chapter. The retail industry began to see its desire to meet growing consumer need in terms of relatively cheap and easy-to-develop out-of-centre sites with the space for ground-level development, plenty of free parking and good road access for both customers and the delivery of stock. It is generally acknowledged that it was Russell Schiller who first articulated what was happening in terms of distinct 'waves of retail decentralisation' (Schiller R, 'Retail Decentralisation – the coming of the third wave', *The Planner*, Vol. 72, 1986, pp. 113–115) and it is useful to look at the move out-of-town firstly in these terms.

First wave – late-1960s to early-1970s

The development of out-of-centre and even out-of-town sites of the first free-standing superstores and hypermarkets – the former by Sainsbury, Tesco and others, the latter pioneered by a new entrant to the British retail scene, Carrefour.

Second wave – late-1970s to mid-1980s

The arrival of the retail warehouse selling durable goods – typically electrical white goods, carpets, furniture and DIY products – as basic 'no frills' single storey buildings typically located on industrial estates. DIY has since become the most important of the group with the biggest players including B&Q, Texas, Do-It-All and Great Mills. For the other product areas, the main names have been Comet and Currys (electrical goods), Allied Carpets and MFI (self-assembly furniture). These developments were both purpose-built premises and, particularly in the early years, adapted standard light industrial or ware-house buildings.

Third wave – mid-1980s to early-1990s

The move outwards of the larger High Street players in comparison goods retailing, such as Boots (Children's World), Habitat, and latterly Marks & Spencer, which made the decision to go for out-of-centre developments in 1984 and had 12 'edge-of-town' stores trading by early 1994 (*Marks & Spencer Magazine*, Spring 1994). Some of these outlets were also teamed up with major convenience goods stores, notably those of Tesco and Sainsbury, and were joined in some locations by new players such as Toys 'R' Us from the USA. This 'third wave' saw the development adjacent to motorways and other major routes of small clusters of comparison outlets providing something of the range and choice traditionally the preserve of the town centre.

Out-of-town regional shopping centres

Also part of this wave, though in many senses a distinct retail phenomenon in its own right, has been the Regional Shopping Centre, one of the most high-profile elements of Britain's retail revolution. Although the arrival of the

Regional Shopping Centre in Britain dates from the second half of the 1980s, the concept had first challenged the planning systems some 20 years earlier. In 1964 an RSC with a million square feet of retail floorspace was proposed at Haydock in Lancashire but refused on appeal in 1965 on the grounds of its likely adverse impact on existing town centres in the region. In 1970 a 900,000 sq. ft scheme was proposed at Cribbs Causeway, about 6 miles to the north of Bristol City Centre on the edge of the greater Bristol urban area and close to the intersection of the M4 and M5 motorways. Like Haydock, this was a very 'strategic' location. It too was rejected on appeal in 1972. Meanwhile the only slightly less massive Brent Cross Centre at Hendon in north-west London had been approved in 1970 because it appeared to 'fill a gap' in the then current shopping hierarchy of this part of the capital. Brent Cross (790,000 sq. ft) opened in 1977 and though not out-of-town as such, was certainly a non-traditional out-of-centre location and is generally considered to be Britain's first Regional Shopping Centre (Guy, 1994, p. 171).

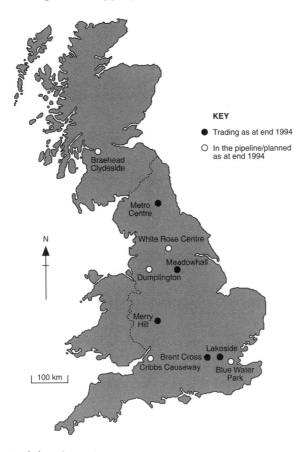

Fig. 9.2 Regional shopping centres

Table 9.1   Regional shopping centres

Centre	Location	Gross floorspace (sq. ft)	Date opened
Completed:			
Brent Cross	N W London	790,000	1977
Metro Centre	Gateshead	1,630,000[1]	1986
Merry Hill Centre	Dudley, W Midlands	1,390,000[2]	1989
Lakeside	Thurrock, Essex	1,310,000	1990
Meadowhall	Don Valley, Nr. Sheffield	1,031,000	1990
In the pipeline:			
White Rose	Leeds	650,000	Allowed on appeal
Cheshire Oaks	Chester	623,000	Approved 1990
Blue Water Park	Dartford, Kent	1,500,000	Approved 1990
Cribbs Causeway	Avon	700,000[3]	Allowed on appeal 1991
Awaiting decision:			
Trafford Centre	Dumplington, Greater Manchester	667,000	Subject to ruling in the High Court 1994
Braehead Park	Govan, Clydeside	475,000	Application called in Sept 1994

Notes: [1] 1,360,000 sq. ft on opening
[2] Application submitted for a 650,000 sq. ft extension, Oct 1994
[3] Work on site starting Spring 1995

The first RSC associated with the third wave of retail decentralisation in Britain was the Metro Centre in Gateshead on Tyneside, which opened in 1986, and by the end of 1990 there were three others each with a gross retail floorspace of over a million square feet. However, the significance of the RSC as a retail innovation has been reduced by the fact that many more such schemes that were proposed at the time never materialised. It is generally accepted that between 1986 and 1988 over 50 were proposed which in total amounted to over 50 million sq. ft of new retail space – almost as much as was completed in all new shopping schemes in the 10 years up to 1986 (BDP/OXIRM, 1992, pp. 26–28). RSCs could thus have made a massive impact on the spatial pattern of retailing in Britain. What did materialise is illustrated in Table 9.1, which shows the picture as at the end of 1994 in terms of schemes completed (just over 6 million sq. ft in total, including Brent Cross), 'in the pipeline' and awaiting decision. Fig. 9.2 shows the location of these schemes.

Fourth wave – late-1980s to mid-1990s

The period since the late-1980s has seen the emergence of a fourth wave – the development of the Retail Warehouse Park. In the six years up to 1988, 90 such parks were opened, whilst by the early 1990s there were around 250 (BDP/OXIRM, 1992, p. 23). The earliest examples of these parks were simply small groups of second generation purpose-built retail warehouses, generally on edge-of-town sites. Later examples, with greater involvement by the local planning authorities, were more sophisticated, with shared parking and circulation space and proper landscaping schemes. Just as the out-of-centre convenience superstores of the big players – Sainsbury, Tesco, Asda etc. – have become a prominent and distinctive feature of the urban scene virtually everywhere in Britain, so too are the groups of 'big coloured sheds' – the Retail Warehouse Parks.

It may be too soon to positively identify a fifth wave, but the durable goods Factory Outlet Centre is emerging as a further form of decentralisation. The factory shop, of which there are estimated to be at least 1400 scattered around Britain, sells manufacturers' products direct to the public – usually discounted or other lines not otherwise available in traditional 'High Street' outlets. What is significant from a land use policy point of view is the movement towards grouping such shops into centres. The concept originated in the USA in the 1970s, but is quite recent in Britain. As at mid-1994 there were two centres trading – at Hornsea in Humberside and Street in Somerset – a further handful were either under construction or had planning consent, whilst there were proposals for at least a dozen others. Many of these are in out-of-town locations and the largest has 140,000 sq. ft of retail floorspace (Booton C, *Planning*, **1079**, 29 July 1994, pp. 8–9).

Major retail decentralisation case study

The example of Cribbs Causeway on the northern edge of the Greater Bristol urban area near the intersection of the M4 and M5 motorways illustrates the process whereby, almost in spite of development plan policy, development representing successive waves of retail decentralisation has taken place. The site of one of Britain's first hypermarkets, Carrefour, which opened in 1976, Cribbs Causeway is a prime example of a 'strategic retail location' (see Fig. 9.3). It sits on one of the most accessible locations (by road) in the Bristol/Bath city region – an area coterminous with, until its abolition in April 1996, the County of Avon with a population of just under 1 million – and on the northern edge of the Greater Bristol urban area which itself has a population of 750,000. Within less than a hour's driving time, across the nearby Severn Estuary, are two of the major urban areas of South Wales, Newport and Cardiff. At the time of writing, the local (District) planning authority with responsibility for Cribbs Causeway is Northavon, not the City of Bristol, the northern boundary of which lies a kilometre or so to the south, with Filton Airfield occupying the strip in between. As of April 1996, Northavon will become part of the new unitary authority of South Gloucestershire, whilst Avon, the strategic County Planning Authority for the area since 1974, will disappear. Work on site to construct the £100 million, 700,000 sq. ft Regional Shopping Centre on over 30 ha, started in Spring 1995, with a planned Autumn 1997 opening date.

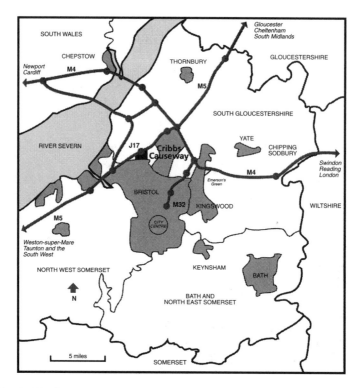

Fig. 9.3   Cribbs Causeway regional shopping centre

The background to this scheme is a 25-year-long planning saga involving three public inquiries, the first in 1972 (which has already been referred to), the second in 1987 and the third at the end of 1989. Throughout the process the issue of the extent to which such a development would adversely affect Broadmead, Bristol's main shopping centre, remained a critical one, as did the fact that major retail development at Cribbs Causeway has never formed part of the Avon County Structure Plan retail hierarchy.

In November 1991 Secretary of State Michael Heseltine announced his support for the Inspector's recommendation to allow the development 'to extend the existing retail park' and to create a 'regional shopping centre with associated leisure facilities and car parking' at Cribbs Causeway. No evidence was found that this would harm the existing centre at Broadmead and there were no grounds for a refusal due to highways or public transport access. He found ample potential retail expenditure in the area to support a fully redeveloped Broadmead and the Cribbs Causeway Centre. At the same time (and in a sadly rare example of co-ordination in strategic decision making!), the Secretary of State refused permission for the potentially competing retail scheme at Emersons's Green some six miles to the east. In July 1993 final planning permission was granted by Northavon, whilst in March 1994

John Lewis announced that it was to move out of its Bristol City Centre (Broadmead) store in favour of a unit twice as big in the Cribbs Causeway Centre. The desired package of anchor units (Marks & Spencer, BHS, Boots and John Lewis) was thus in place.

Retail development as an issue and the planning policy response

Having looked briefly at post-World War Two town centre developments and at the 'waves' which have characterised the moves out-of-town, we now turn to a chronological examination of the development of retail planning policy. We have seen that until the mid-1970s the development aspirations of the retail companies themselves, the expectations of the consumer and the land use planning policy framework provided by both local authorities and central government were more or less in harmony: retail location was not an issue. We have also seen that by this time, however, there were powerful forces of spatial and economic change which were soon to see the decentralisation of retailing and other commercial activities. The 1960s had witnessed a growing concern about the implications of ever-outward urban growth. Population projections at the time suggested that major growth was in prospect over at least the next two decades – especially so in Central and Southern England – and land use planning policy at the strategic level became preoccupied with appropriate measures to accommodate this growth.

At the same time, the mid/late-1960s were to see a radical change both in the development plan system, as recommended by the report of the Planning Advisory Group in 1965, and in the structure of local government – from April 1974 onwards in England and Wales and 1975 in Scotland. To what extent these changes either facilitated or hampered the process of activity decentralisation, and within this the spatial transformation of our retail structure, is not clear. To begin with it is perhaps helpful to think in terms of our three perspectives – the retail industry, the community as consumer, and central and local government (the planning system).

It is clear that by the mid-1970s, the retail industry in Britain was looking towards major innovation. Returns on the energies expended over the previous two decades in town and city centre retail schemes were diminishing or at least not increasing at rates hitherto enjoyed. New retail developments on non-traditional out-of-centre or even out-of-town sites offered the opportunity to introduce new formats, with more space, on easier sites. Furthermore, the ideas had already been tested out both in North America and in mainland Europe where, as we have seen, heavy retail investment in town centre schemes had not been the tradition.

The community as consumer continued to enjoy growing spending power which it was using to seek out a bigger and better range of both convenience and durable goods. It also began more and more to value choice and comparison: the process of seeking out best value for money. Coupled with this,

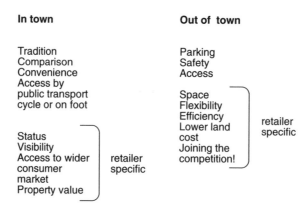

Fig. 9.4   Retailing development: in town and out of town: a comparison of advantages

and probably even more significant, was the growing personal mobility of the shopper. Increasing car ownership (in 1950 there were 2.5 million private cars in Britain, by 1961 there were 6 million and by 1985, 16.5 million, with 62 per cent of households owning a car), together with an ever expanding high speed road system, made it possible to contemplate shopping trips – from one side of an urban area to another or from one town to another – which hitherto would have been unthinkable. The 'shopping basket on wheels' liberated the consumer from reliance on the nearest local shop or town centre, whilst domestic refrigerators and later freezers enabled the same mobile consumer to purchase larger quantities of food at less frequent intervals. At the same time, increasing traffic congestion and parking problems were beginning to act as a deterrent to town centre shopping trips for those with motor car mobility. The 'comparison of advantages' as between traditional town centre retailing and that out of town has been well documented elsewhere. The advantages for the shopper and the retailer are summarised in Fig. 9.4.

Central and local government both entered the 1970s singularly unprepared for all this! It seems that the North American experience and the 'signals' which it contained were either not fully taken on board or ignored as largely irrelevant, whilst contemporary mainland European experience was poorly documented. In essence, the response in terms of land use planning policy was to go on the defensive, to assert the importance of maintaining existing 'retail hierarchies', and present innovative retail formats as a threat to this (Elizabeth Mills, *Recent Developments in Retailing and Urban Planning*, PRAG (Planning Research Advisory Group) Technical Paper 3, December 1974).

The mid-1970s found the (new) local planning authorities, most notably the County Councils, working on their first structure plans, acknowledging growing pressures for retail change, both from the retail industry and from the consumer, but failing to fully appreciate the implications. Authorities sought to channel new development into existing shopping areas, notably in town and city centres. Out-of-centre retailing was seen largely in terms of its possible future role in relieving pressure on existing town centres (Mills, 1974, p. 87).

Whether or not local planning authorities at this time were as blinkered to the need to respond to retail change as this implies is perhaps debatable. What is clear, however, is that this was a hostile policy environment for a retail industry seeking change in the spatial distribution of its activities. Proposals for new out-of-centre developments were invariably refused planning permission, either because they did not fit in with the existing shopping hierarchy of the area and posed the threat of adverse impacts on existing town centres, or because they were regarded as premature. In the many planning appeals which resulted, planning authorities had great difficulty in proving assertions of unacceptable impact, because of the lack of central government guidance on appropriate methods of doing this and the lack of adequate data on retail activity and relationships. Central government had no choice about whether or not to become involved! Within the first three years of the 1970s, the Secretary of State had been called upon to make decisions in respect of some 20 major out-of-town retail proposals in England following either an appeal or call-in (Mills, 1974, Appendix 2, based on data from the DoE, produced by PRAG (Planning Advisory Group)). The approach taken by the government was to take each case entirely on its own merits. The outcome – a growing list of retail schemes opposed by the local planning authorities but allowed on appeal.

Steps had, however, already been taken to assemble hard evidence on retail trends and their implications as a basis for framing comprehensive government policy. Generally cited as being of critical importance in this respect is the report published by the National Economic Development Office (NEDO) in 1971 (NEDO, *The Future Pattern of Shopping*, HMSO, 1971).

The NEDO report provided an overview of changes in the structure of retailing and went on to offer guidance as to what needed to be taken into account in future planning policy. The report noted the growing pressure for new retail developments in non-central locations, but at the same time concluded that there was likely to be little change in the basic framework of the British retail system over the next 20 years. The central shopping areas of large towns were unlikely to lose their importance, it asserted. Its recommendations were rather more perceptive however! Among these were the need to better recognise the implications of rising car ownership, the need to press on with the pedestrianisation of more shopping areas, the need to plan (in future) over wide enough areas to allow co-ordination of policy between different local authorities – a plea for strategic retail planning of a kind which the pre-1974 local government structure made well nigh impossible. Finally, and perhaps most significantly in the context of this present chapter, the report identified a need to formulate policy to control pressures for new developments in non-central locations. It suggested that the DoE should 'lay down guidelines stating criteria for their acceptability … ' (NEDO, 1971, *op. cit.*, p. 6).

The government's response to this was Development Control Policy Note (DCPN) 13 *Out of Town Shops and Shopping Centres* published in 1972 (DCPNs were the forerunners of today's PPGs). They provided guidance on development control matters and set out current government policy on the subject in question. The Circulars which were usually issued with them were the means by which central government formally drew the attention of interested parties, particularly local authorities, to the content of the notes. (DoE Circular 17/72 accompanied DCPN 13.)

Its policy thrust was that the development of new convenience shopping facilities in suburban areas should be encouraged, that comparison shopping should remain concentrated in town centres, that isolated new facilities in 'greenfield' locations should generally be resisted, that all parties involved should guard against the over-provision of facilities, and that the maintenance of existing town and district shopping centres should always be a high priority (DCPN 13, 1972, *op. cit.*, para 6).

The other important provisions set out in DCPN 13 were the requirements that County Planning Authorities should carry out studies of shopping provision in their areas (if necessary jointly with other authorities) as part of their structure plan work and that planning authorities should inform the Secretary of State of 'all applications for planning permission for stores or shopping centres of 50,000 square feet or more outside existing city, town or district centres' (DoE Circular 17/72, 1972, *op. cit.*, para 6).

The stage thus appeared to be set for a national policy stance against retail innovations seeking out-of-town sites. The consolidation and development of the advice was slow, however. DCPN 14, *Warehouses, Wholesale Cash and Carry etc.*, was issued in 1974, whilst in 1977 came *Large New Stores*, a response to the growing edge-of-town superstore push by the big players and also referred to rather confusingly as DCPN 13. In 1978 the Scottish Development Department issued *The Location of Major Shopping Development* in its National Planning Guidelines series.

Almost 10 years then passed before the appearance of further substantial government advice on retail policy. This period – the mid-1970s to the mid-1980s – saw a marked slowing down in the rate of new retail development overall, but there was significant out-of-centre development which was equated especially with the first two waves of retail decentralisation referred to earlier. By mid-1986, out-of-centre schemes accounted for 2.8 million square feet under construction, with a further 6.3 million square feet with planning permission and another 16.2 million square feet proposed. After 1986, things really began to take off with quite massive increases in both out-of-centre retail generally and retail warehouse park schemes in particular in the pipeline (RTPI, 1988, *op. cit.*, p. 6). However, town centre retail development remained more important overall with 8.2 million square feet under construction as at mid-1986 (*ibid.*, p. 6).

The retail industry's challenge to the initial public policy stance can thus be seen to have had considerable success. The 10-year policy development gap was used to good effect as was the fact that the new development plan policies, in the shape of the first round structure plans, were a long time in the making and in getting central government approval.

Large-scale growth and public policy consolidation

The last half of the 1980s saw a dramatic upsurge in the scale of new retail development, both town centre based and, increasing in importance as a proportion, out-of-town based. In 1985 just over 2 million sq. ft of new retail space was either completed or scheduled in Britain. By 1987 this figure had risen to almost 9 million sq. ft and by 1990 to nearly 15 million sq. ft (Hillier Parker Research/Brian Raggett, 1992, op. cit.). The 1990 figure included some 3 million sq. ft of out-of-town development and a further 6 million sq. ft in retail warehouse parks, much of which was also out-of-centre.

This rise in activity was in part an almost inevitable outcome of the relative quietness of the period from the mid-1970s to the mid-1980s. Pressure for change had built up awaiting new market confidence and was attributed mainly to the expansion of multiple retailing in the comparison goods sector, where growth in consumer expenditure was most marked. Retail warehouses received a boost as a result of significant increases in home ownership whilst, as we have seen earlier, the third wave of decentralisation was taking place with major new developments by the larger retailers including Marks & Spencer. This rise in activity was also associated with the emergence of the Regional Shopping Centres.

On the planning policy front, this period was essentially one of consolidation. The local planning authorities had by now more or less finished the task of fleshing out their retail development policies, at least as far as the structure plans were concerned, and were thus in a better position to challenge proposals which were outside the established retail hierarchy of their areas. Central government began to elaborate on its criteria for constraint and caution in the handling of retail change. It did this however within the context of the deregulation of the development environment and burden lifting which had become such a central plank of the Conservative administration's philosophy for the 1980s. The result was a certain ambivalence in government policy.

The years 1984–88 saw a spate of new central government policy advice. Circular 22/84, *Memorandum on Structure and Local Plans*, marked the start of this, at least for England and Wales. Included in it were references to the need for broad guidance on floorspace provisions; the need to take account of new trends in retailing, especially moves away from existing centres; the need to take account of the impact of new developments on existing centres and the need to take account of access to shops for all sections of the population. There was also a warning not to seek to regulate competition between retailers 'nor to stifle the evolution of new forms of retail provision' (Circular 22/84,

DoE/Welsh Office 43/84, 1984, para 4.22). There was plenty here about what local planning authorities should have been doing, but little guidance as to how to do it! In July 1985 the then Secretary of State, Patrick Jenkin, issued a statement in reply to a Parliamentary Question about government policy in relation to applications for large new retail developments. The statement confirmed that the advice contained in DCPN 13 still stood and that Circular 22/84 still represented current policy. More significantly, however, the statement reasserted that commercial competition as such was not a land use planning consideration, so that, in this sense, the effects of a major new scheme on existing retailers was not a relevant planning matter. At the same time, it suggested that local planning authorities might have to intervene if the 'vitality and viability' of a nearby town centre as a whole was under serious threat. Thus officially emerged the concept of 'vitality and viability of the town centre' which has been part of central government retail policy ever since.

DoE Circular 21/86, *Policy on Major Retail Developments* (Welsh Office 58/86), introduced the Shopping Development Direction whereby local planning authorities were required to notify the Secretary of State of any proposals for retail development with a gross floorspace of 250,000 sq. ft or more, who would then have the opportunity to call-in the application for his own decision. This provision was born out of government concern at the steadily increasing size of new out-of-centre retail proposals. The 1986 Direction was up-dated to substantially the same purpose in the *Town and Country Planning (Shopping Development) (England and Wales) Direction* of September 1993. This formed an Annex to the 1993 version of PPG6. The same year also saw the publication of further Scottish central government guidelines on the location of major retail developments (*National Planning Guidelines, 1986: Location of Major Retail Development*, Scottish Office).

Planning policy guidance on retail development

PPG6 Major retail development

Central government policy was consolidated in January 1988 with the publication, jointly by the DoE and Welsh Office, of PPG6 *Major Retail Development (Planning Policy Guidance Note 6: Major Retail Development*, DoE/Welsh Office, HMSO, January 1988). This was one of the first in a series of Planning Policy Guidance Notes introduced in England and Wales in an effort to better communicate government policy in a number of 'strategic' subject areas. PPG6 replaced DCPNs 13 and 14 as well as the retail policy section of Circular 22/84 (43/84) and included, as an Annex, the 1986 Shopping Development Direction. In PPG6, statements of general policy were prefaced by references to the importance of retailing and its dynamism to the economy, to the need to accept new forms of development as well as encouraging the modernisation and improvement of existing town centres, to changing spatial patterns and consumer shopping habits, including greater mobility, to the marked trend in some types of retailing towards a smaller number of larger shops, to the continuing importance of the small and specialist shop and to the fact that important sections of the community would continue to rely upon public transport or walking in order to gain access to shops.

In terms of policy, the Guidance advised care in the consideration of new retail developments, including the matter of their potential impact, but at the same time, local planning authorities were advised not to set floorspace limits either overall or in terms of specific localities. Authorities were also warned off attempting sophisticated impact studies and seeking to intervene in matters of commercial competition or 'attempting to regulate volume changes in supply and demand for retail services' (*ibid.*, para 10). What the local planning authorities could do, however, was to intervene where significant development posed a threat to existing town centres, whose future diversity and activity had to be maintained if they were to retain their vitality. Likewise they could intervene positively in the process of town centre improvement and in supporting large new convenience stores and retail warehouses, particularly if these stores and warehouses made good use of derelict or 'neglected' sites within urban areas to bring about environmental improvement and new local employment. The clearest policy advice concerned major retail developments having no place in the Green Belt or generally in open countryside. Even here however, the door to developers was left slightly open by a reference to possible special circumstances in which such developments outside urban areas might be acceptable.

As indicated earlier, PPG6 and its policy build-up coincided with a period of major new retail development activity. This activity was putting the planning system under great pressure, but it is now generally recognised that the Guidance did not provide the necessary clarification of government intent which was then so needed (BDP Planning/OXIRM, 1992, *op. cit.*, p. 112). For local planning authorities, there was no real guidance on either 'significant impact' or on the meaning of the concepts of town centre 'vitality' and 'viability'. In addition, many had already in their development plans begun to work with the kind of floorspace limits which were suddenly ruled as unacceptable. Only in certain areas (for Green Belt proposals and general town centre promotion) did the Guidance provide any meaningful support for their development plan policies and development control decisions. The retail industry welcomed the consolidation of the government's policy framework, but at the same time still had no clear picture of the extent to which many of the encouraging statements, e.g. about the importance of the industry and the need to accommodate innovation and change, actually squared up with the policies of the local planning authorities.

A changing context post-PPG6

PPG6 was the main thrust of central government retail land use policy put in place as a response to the hectic retail development activity of the mid-1980s characterised by high profile challenges by the industry to local planning authority intervention seeking in particular to limit the extent of out-of-centre development. No sooner had the advice become operative, however, when Britain experienced another economic downturn. The end of the decade saw a sharp decline in consumer confidence which affected retail spending especially on durable goods.

There was no immediate downturn in new retail development however. The retail sector remained characteristically less vulnerable than other areas of commercial development, but more importantly, the plans and investment decisions made earlier in the 1980s were still working their way through as new completions. The year 1990 actually saw an all-time peak in completions or schemes scheduled, with town centre development at a level equal to that seen in the early-1970s. New speciality retailing was flourishing in many town centres with a move towards more sympathetic character schemes than hitherto seen. The end of the 1980s also saw considerable refurbishment activity in town centres, which often involved modest increases in retail floorspace. Out-of-centre development, notably in the convenience goods sector, also reached a post-war peak in 1990 with new superstore openings, mainly by the big five retail companies (Sainsbury, Tesco, Argyll (Safeway), Asda and Gateway), running at around 50 per year. The years 1989 and 1990 also saw record levels of new retail warehouse floorspace completions, mostly in out-of-centre locations.

The downturn in retail development activity when it did come was sharp however. The years 1991 to 1993 saw massive drops in all sectors, which probably had little directly to do with either PPG6 or the policies of the local planning authorities. The economic downturn was due to a number of factors, among them a rise in interest rates, and a drop in consumer confidence (it was the first time in post-war years that consumer expenditure on comparison goods ceased to rise). Among the land use related factors behind the retail development downturn were increases in land costs for out-of-centre locations and overstretched company development programmes which could not be sustained. There was also the onset of market saturation in some major urban areas – too many new superstores chasing a finite level of convenience goods expenditure. The pressure on the planning system for out-of-centre development was relieved not least because, as we have already seen, the threat of the Regional Shopping Centres largely failed to materialise and really quite suddenly the general thrust of public sector retail policy became more pro-active and changed to focus on the town centre. The town centre and its future became a serious concern of central government as well as of the local authorities, leading to a revised PPG6.

Retail policy 're-invents' the town centre

Town centres have always been seen as the cornerstone of the retail hierarchy by local planning authorities. Their role has never been seriously questioned in development plans and the view has been reflected in the pro-active stance taken to town and city centre change referred to earlier in this chapter. Most commentators would probably see the publication of the draft revised PPG6 in October 1992 as marking the fundamental 'conversion' of central government to this view also. The original (1988) Guidance *Major Retail Development* became *Town Centres and Retail Developments*.

The revision of the Guidance took its lead from the results of a DoE commissioned study of the effects of major out-of-town retail development (BDP Planning/OXIRM, 1992, *op. cit.*). This was a wide ranging piece of work, but its most important conclusion in this context was 'that town and city centres must command much more local authority attention and commitment than had been the case in recent years' (*ibid.*, para 10.50, p. 158).

The new PPG6 *Town Centres and Retail Developments* was published in July 1993 (*PPG6 (Revised): Town Centres and Retail Developments*, DoE/Welsh Office, HMSO, July 1993; revised again 1995). Concern for the well-being of the town and city centre as a retail location was a fundamental plank of this revision. The Guidance elaborated on the concept of 'vitality and viability', suggested the role that town centre management could play in its promotion, emphasised the significance of traditional shopping locations, including town centres, in maintaining a spatial development pattern which minimised the need to travel and promoted transport choice, and encouraged local authorities to devise positive and realistic policies for town centres. But it was not all about town centres: a wider context was also accepted. The guidance stressed that a suitable balance had to be struck between town centre and out-of-centre retail facilities, taking account of factors such as accessibility and effective competition to the benefit of consumers. It stated that the fundamental approach to retail development and the nature of public policy intervention had not changed and it was emphasised that the planning system should continue to facilitate competition between different types of shopping provision, by avoiding unnecessary regulation of development. The guidance also stressed that local planning authorities should not refuse permission for new retail development outside a town centre unless there was clear evidence that the result would be to undermine the vitality and viability of that centre.

The months immediately following the publication of the revised PPG, which might have been expected to see greater clarity as to government policy as far as the main actors were concerned, actually saw just the opposite! Firstly there was a widespread belief that there was now to be a ban on all further out-of-centre shopping development and secondly there was confusion over the issue of demonstrable harm to the vitality and viability of a nearby town centre. A sequence of speeches and Ministerial statements, including that by Tony Baldry in November 1993 launching the results of the Merry Hill Impact Study and others by Environment Secretary John Gummer, added to, rather than reduced, the confusion (House of Commons Environment Committee, Fourth Report, *Shopping Centres and Their Future*, Volume 1, HMSO, October 1994, paras 20–23).

1994: Changes in the economy

Sequence of change

1994 saw signs of an up turn in the British economy. Consumer confidence gradually increased once again and within the retail industry there was a combination of consolidation and investment reappraisal by several of the major players and strong growth by some of the smaller and newer ones. Tesco, for example, completed a major strategic reassessment involving, amongst other things, downward revaluation of its property and land bank assets, a reduction in its development programme, a move towards the development of smaller superstores in market town locations rather than the major urban areas, a return to the town centre in the shape of the Tesco Metro format and a greater emphasis on refurbishment and extensions to existing stores rather than the opening of new ones. The strong growth was seen in areas such as the factory shop (as we have seen earlier) and grocery discounting, where companies such as Kwik Save, Netto and Aldi continued to thrive within the major urban areas. Here, their relatively small outlets, opened at modest cost in new or converted premises and in locations which generally represented little threat to development plan policies, continued to flourish serving the less affluent, less mobile consumer (Jonathan Reynolds of OXIRM speaking at RTPI South West Branch Conference on Retailing, October 1994).

1994 also saw the publication of a range of reports and policy statements. Individually, each had important things to say about retail land use, whilst collectively they signified a 'change of context' which could yet turn out to be as dramatic as that which saw retailing move out of town in the 1970s.

- January   Secretary of State for the Environment *et al., Sustainable Development – The UK Strategy,* CM 2426, HMSO
- March   DoE/Dept of Transport, Planning Policy Guidance Note PPG13 *Transport*
- May   DoE, Urban and Economic Development Group (URBED) *et al., Vital and Viable Town Centres: Meeting the Challenge,* HMSO
- July   DoE, *Quality in Town and Country, A Discussion Document,* HMSO
- October   Cmd Paper No. 2674, *Transport and the Environment,* Eighteenth Report of the Royal Commission on Environmental Pollution, HMSO

    House of Commons Environment Committee, Fourth Report, *Shopping Centres and Their Future,* Volume 1, HMSO.

The UK strategy for sustainable development

(Re: Secretary of State for the Environment *et al., Sustainable Development –The UK Strategy,* CM 2426, HMSO, January 1994.) This was the nation's first prescriptive response to the obligations entered into at the 1992 Rio Earth

Summit. It looked at the relationship between energy use, transportation and land use patterns, raising the issue of the sustainability or otherwise of the changing spatial pattern of retailing since the 1970s.

Planning Policy Guidance Note 13: Transport

(Re: DoE/Dept of Transport, *Planning Policy Guidance Note PPG13: Transport*, HMSO, March 1994.) This is generally agreed to have marked a sea change in central government thinking on the relationship between land use and transport. Far more strategic than the 1988 PPG13, *Highway Considerations in Development Control*, which it replaced, it took the principles of sustainable development as a basis for new guidance on how local authorities should integrate transport and land use planning. The underlying aims were to reduce growth in the length and number of motorised journeys, to encourage alternative means of travel which have less environmental impact, and to reduce reliance on the private car. Such aims are not consistent with the decentralisation of retailing and its reliance upon the motor car and the guidance called for future shopping development to be in existing centres which are more likely to offer a choice of access, particularly for those without the use of a private car. If suitable central sites for large retail development were not available, convenient and accessible edge-of-town sites should be identified. The guidance went on to say that the sporadic siting of comparison goods outlets outside existing centres or along road corridors should be avoided (*ibid.*, Introduction and paras 3.9, 3.10).

Vital and Viable Town Centres: Meeting the Challenge

(Re: DoE, Urban and Economic Development Group (URBED) *et al.*, *Vital and Viable Town Centres: Meeting the Challenge*, HMSO, May 1994.) This was the outcome of work begun around the time of publication of the revised PPG6. It put practical flesh on the bones of the guidance with respect to the future promotion of town centres. It looked at some alternative shopping futures and policy responses; how to assess vitality and viability including town centre 'health checks', action plans and strategies, and examples of emerging 'good practice' within different types of town.

Quality in Town and Country

(Re: *Quality in Town and Country: A Discussion Document*, DoE, July 1994.) This was an innovative DoE discussion document linking, for the first time in such a form, the physical quality of the environment, principles of sustainable development, land use policy, and transport. Three of the ten chapters included references to towns and city centres, with one of these taking vitality and viability as its main theme (*ibid.*, Ch. 3, pp. 8–9).

Transport and the Environment

(Re: Cmd Paper No. 2674, *Transport and the Environment*, Eighteenth Report of the Royal Commission on Environmental Pollution, HMSO, October 1994.) This, produced by the Royal Commission on Environmental Pollution, looked in some detail at our transport systems, their effect on the environment and the potential impact of continuing with existing policies. It then went on to look at the kinds of policy action needed to achieve sustainable transport as a long-term aim within a total of 110 different recommendations! The Commission identified a number of areas where current transport philosophy conflicted with the principles of sustainability, such as using up finite resources of fossil fuel and other materials. Even more telling as far as retail decentralisation is concerned, however, was the concern that patterns of land use were being promoted which depended for their operation on transport systems which were not sustainable.

Shopping Centres and Their Future

(Re: House of Commons Environment Committee, Fourth Report, *Shopping Centres and Their Future*, HMSO, 19 October 1994.) This contained the outcome of the House of Commons Environment Committee's rapid yet searching investigation into the context of and policy for retail development in England. It considered over 100 written submissions, and oral evidence from 27 different organisations, including the Departments of the Environment and Transport. It also took study tours to a range of new shopping developments and traditional town centres in England, France and Germany.

The Committee saw 1994 as an opportune time to review retail planning policies given the recent revisions to the PPGs on shopping and transport and the imperative to find more sustainable land use policies. It welcomed the government's more cautious stance on out-of-centre retail development, but was concerned about some of the results of the hitherto more *laissez-faire* approach. It presented some 40 different recommendations and conclusions, but among the more important in the context of this chapter were a call for clearer and more consistent policy guidance, so that retailers, planning authorities and the development industry could each operate more efficiently and effectively. A ban on further out-of-centre development was not advocated (despite widespread popular interpretation to this effect!) but the 'sequential test', whereby permissions should not be given for a new retail proposal outside a town or city (centre) if there was a suitable site within or close to the centre, was advocated by Ministers. The Committee called for proper impact studies in cases where damage to existing centres was suspected and, related to this, the development of a nationally consistent set of retail data. Overall, a dual approach was advocated: 'initiatives to make existing town and district centres attractive and viable places in which to shop', complemented by 'more sensitive planning controls on new retail development' (*ibid.*, pp. xiii–xviii, Preface and Summary of Recommendations and Conclusions).

Conclusions and future issues

It is as yet too early to assess the full impact of 1994 on retail land use policy, but one outcome will almost certainly be an increased level of public sector intervention in the process of retail change. As we have already seen, central government in particular has, since 1992, been moving towards a more interventionist model. An approach with the emphasis on *laissez faire* has given way to one of much clearer support for local planning authorities in their pursuit of development plan policies seeking as far as possible to maintain traditional retail hierarchies. The hand of the development plan has also been strengthened as a result of the 1991 Planning and Compensation Act, Section 26 of which states that planning decisions should accord with the development plan unless material considerations indicate otherwise. A very firm line has now been taken on Regional Shopping Centres and the onus is shifting onto the retail developer to prove that a proposed new scheme would not cause harm to existing centres. Finally, to complement all this on the pro-active side of things, positive guidance and support has now emerged on promoting the future vitality and viability of existing town centres. As part of a raft of techniques and approaches now coming forward in this area integrated town centre management is rapidly gaining currency, based in part on experience in the USA. This particular approach is considered in detail in the next chapter.

This chapter has looked at retail development as a major spatial issue. We have seen evidence of the dynamic nature of the retail industry – the start, in the 1970s, of the move out of town, then the desire for larger and larger new schemes, culminating in the emergence of the Regional Shopping Centre and followed, more recently, by a shift of emphasis, in part back to locations within or near town centres, but more significantly towards development within the smaller market towns. At first, the public policy realm was ill-prepared to deal with this, but as we have seen, it has gradually moved from a reactive to a much more pro-active position. But the fact remains that it has an unenviable position with the triangle of interests. The planning system, both at central and local government levels, faces the same challenges as it always has, but with the added environmental dimension of the sustainability imperative.

In the words of the House of Commons Environment Committee these challenges are:

- how to be sufficiently flexible to deal with the needs of different types of shopping;
- how to be sufficiently flexible to deal with different areas which may have different levels of shopping provision;
- how to be sufficiently strong to control inappropriate development which would harm existing centres;

- how to make town centres more attractive;
- and how to be consistent in the implementation of government policy between local authorities, Planning Inspectors and the DoE.

    (House of Commons Environment Committee, 1994, *op. cit.*, para 17, p. xix)

Also see Regional Planning Guidance (RPG) details in Appendix.

Chapter 10

CITY CENTRE MANAGEMENT

Kimberly Paumier

Civilisation and the city

Throughout civilisation, city and town centres have played important roles as meeting places for people, a place where people of all backgrounds can come together to exchange information and ideas and goods and services.

While the city historically was primarily a place of commerce and exchange, the city today has taken on an important role as a centre for arts, leisure and culture. Urban life provides an outlet for individual expression and a tolerance of diverse cultures and lifestyles. The city is therefore by nature dynamic and evolving, and at the cutting edge of change within society. Because of these forces, it is also a place where competing needs and interests are expressed, and where diverse sectors of the community strive to have their needs met.

With the rise of out-of-town shopping centres as well as a decrease in the number of holidays taken within the UK, the vitality of many city and town centres is under increasing threat. In a 1994 study undertaken by URBED and the Department of the Environment, only 6% of all town and city centres studied were considered 'vibrant'.

Purpose of city centre management

It is within the context of enhancing the vitality of city and town centres, and balancing competing needs and interests, that the position of City or Town Centre Manager was established in Great Britain. In the late 1980s, two leading retailers, Boots and Marks & Spencer, took the lead in promoting the development of this new role. By 1994, there were over 100 town and city centre managers around the country.

While the position varies greatly within each town or city, a common purpose is to improve the quality of the experience for all users of the city centre, which typically include residents, office workers and visitors/tourists. As these needs often conflict, the role of the City Centre Manager is to create partnerships around key issues and identify solutions to problems in order to meet the needs of these sectors. Depending on the particular issue, this will often involve a dialogue with community residents, retailers, police, city council (members and officers), county council (members and officers), business representatives and civic societies/special interest groups. It is also not uncommon for different departments within a Local Authority to have conflicting aims and objectives. Through dialogue, it is possible to develop an agreed purpose and direction to achieve the optimum result.

Structure of city centre management

In towns and cities around the country, the concept of city centre management is often initiated through a dialogue between the public and private sectors. There is often an agreement for joint funding of the post, with a wide range of businesses including retailers and property investors involved. The City Centre Manager typically will report to a committee which includes representatives from the public, private and voluntary sectors.

Creating a strategy

As each city centre faces unique challenges, one of the first tasks of the City Centre Manager is to identify the key players and actors in the city, often referred to as stakeholders. These individuals are likely to be aware of the most pressing issues in the city centre. Through discussions with a wide cross-section of the community, it is possible to obtain a comprehensive view of the nature and extent of the issues facing the city. This can then lead to the development of a strategy and action plan, often in the form of a city centre audit. An audit could include an SWOT (strengths, weaknesses, opportunities, threats) analysis, identification of key issues and possible solutions, and a proposed action plan (based on short-, medium- and long-term objectives).

It is important that this audit serve as a collective agreement by the stakeholders as to the key issues and the way forward. This can be achieved by circulating a draft document and receiving comments back from as many individuals as possible. This is an important part of the process, since it creates a firm foundation for future partnerships. Without a consensus on the issues, the role of City Centre Manager becomes more difficult, as divergent groups will make competing and conflicting demands on the City Centre Manager.

Greater consensus can be achieved by asking stakeholders to prioritise a list of defined issues. It is important that the list balances the need for immediate short-term wins (to help to establish the credibility of the post), with the longer term issues which can threaten the overall vitality of a town or city.

The specific background and experience of the City Centre Manager will also influence the proposed work programme. For example, if the City Centre Manager has a background related to property there may be a stronger focus on property-related issues, relative to management or marketing objectives. The work programme will also be guided by work already being undertaken by other local authority departments and by identifying areas where gaps exist in the provision of services.

Once priorities are established, it is important that there is sufficient flexibility in the programme to take advantage of opportunities as they arise. For example, if one of the priorities is to improve transport infrastructure and money becomes available, this objective would then become an immediate priority.

Components of a city centre management programme

While the specific components of the Management Programme will vary according to each city's priorities, there are a number of components which are typically found in any strategy. They can be broadly described as follows:

- Consensus building/empowering organisations
- Management issues
- Development issues
- Developing a city identity

Consensus building and empowering organisations

Because different public and private sector organisations, as well as different departments within the public sector, have divergent goals and responsibilities, it is difficult to establish a consensus regarding priorities. Without a consensus the result is often a fragmented approach and a reacting to, rather than responding to, challenges based on a well-thought-through strategy. By contrast, a forward looking vision for the future, which is shared by all major stakeholders, can become a powerful mechanism for enabling change to occur.

A measure which has frequently been used to achieve consensus is carefully planned symposia or sessions usually lasting one or more days, where stakeholders from the public and private sectors can meet to discuss priorities and develop a coordinated strategy on a way forward.

In 1988, Birmingham held a two-day session to develop a vision for its city centre. The result was the creation of specific quarters of activity, changes to the road network to improve pedestrian movement, a new public space, and an increase in public art. A further symposium held a year and a half later resulted in a design study to create planning briefs for major sites.

While this approach can often seem slow and cumbersome, there are untold benefits achieved through breaking down barriers and prejudices and agreeing common goals and purposes for a city centre. In many cities there are significant barriers to communication between businesses and the local authorities, as well as between city and county officials, paid officers and elected members, and between residents and other groups. These prejudices can have an undermining and harmful impact on the ability to achieve mutually beneficial results.

It is important that the person leading a consensus event is knowledgeable about city centre issues, is experienced in leading groups and is not one of the stakeholders (who would have their own agenda). The group ideally does not comprise more than 30 people but includes a balance of public, private and voluntary sector representation.

The outcome of a successful consensus event is likely to include agreed decisions and outcomes, as well as improved working relationships and greater cooperation among individuals.

The City Centre Manager can play an important role in helping the private sector to focus on critical issues and improve its organisational capacity. In Bath, the Chamber of Commerce was encouraged to establish a retail committee to deal with a number of issues involving promotions and security. Major businesses were also encouraged to meet in order to establish a strategic view of the city's future.

In Cardiff, a strategic document was produced which identified clearly defined outcomes to be achieved. This provided a framework for decision making by all organisations and stakeholders, including investors, banks and the Welsh Development Agency (WDA). The prospectus was created by a core team comprising the City Council and the WDA, followed by in-depth consultation with all public and private sector bodies.

Management issues

Management issues within a city centre can range from improved 'housekeeping', such as street cleaning and refuse collection, to strategic issues such as transport policies and improved visitor management.

Street cleaning and refuse collection

The cleanliness of city streets is one of the most visible measures of how well a city is caring for itself, and the public will tend to measure the quality of the city centre based on how well litter and refuse is collected. It is therefore important to achieve a high standard.

In Nottingham, the position of Urban Ranger was created to deal with day-to-day maintenance issues including the removal of flyposting and graffiti. Because the Urban Ranger is visible to the public, it has helped to increase the sense that the city is concerned with its upkeep, thereby engendering greater civic pride.

The Tidy Britain Group, a voluntary organisation established to promote higher standards of cleanliness, is very active in most cities working in partnership with the Local Authority. This organisation can assist in creating new initiatives for improvements to both street cleaning and refuse collection. In Bath, the City Centre Manager's Office has worked closely with the City Council and Tidy Britain Group to ensure that refuse is picked up from the main shopping area by 10 a.m. daily.

Transport and car parking

Due to the increasing level of car ownership and car usage, transport is frequently identified as the most important issue facing a city centre. An RICS survey found that traffic and parking were considered the two most important issues by Town and City Centre Managers. The viability of town and city centres in the future will likely depend on the ease with which visitors can arrive and park at their destination, as well as enjoy a quality pedestrianised environment without the hazards and conflicts associated with moving vehicles. With increasing competition from out-of-town centres, which have good road infrastructure and free parking, if customers' needs are not met, they are likely to 'shop with their feet' to the detriment of town and city centres.

One of the difficulties in dealing with transport and parking is that issues often fall within the jurisdiction of more than one statutory authority, with the result that conflicting policies are in place regarding parking and transport. The City Centre Manager can play a role in identifying and encouraging immediate short-term improvements as well as facilitating a dialogue regarding longer term strategic goals and objectives.

There are also extremely diverse demands for parking and transport made by retailers, environmentalists and the local authority. Retailers want inexpensive parking close to their establishments, environmentalists will often want parking and transport eliminated from the city centre, while the Local Authority, if it owns the parking garages, will want to maximise revenue. Another conflict which often arises is the patrolling, ticketing and towing away of vehicles, which can have a negative impact on the tourist and visitor trade.

While there is generally a benefit in removing unnecessary traffic from the city centre (i.e. through traffic), it is important to ensure that road closures do not have detrimental effects on other parts of the city. In each of these issues the City Centre Manager can encourage improved communication and facilitate a dialogue.

Pedestrianisation is often an area of discussion and debate, with many cities in the process of pedestrianising large portions of their city centres. The decision whether to pedestrianise, or which areas to pedestrianise, needs to be made carefully and with a significant amount of public consultation. For retail areas which are already vibrant and healthy, this can reduce congestion and significantly improve the visitor experience. Issues which need to be addressed before pedestrianisation is undertaken include:

1. Maintaining access for goods vehicles to retail shops and other premises, possibly during restricted hours;
2. maintaining access for the disabled;
3. considering the benefits of providing access for vehicles in the evenings in some pedestrianised areas to encourage evening activity and ensure greater safety on the streets.

On peripheral streets, where retailing activity is marginal, it is important to carefully weigh the decision to pedestrianise. If a street has few pedestrians, it may be detrimental to commercial trade if vehicular movement is eliminated. The decision to pedestrianise should therefore be based on whether there is a need for additional space for pedestrians to move comfortably.

Parking is a critical factor to a city's viability. There is often a conflict between the desire of shoppers and retailers for affordable and accessible parking, while recognising the constraint of limited road infrastructure and increasing congestion from car usage.

Park & Ride, a system of parking at peripheral locations with frequent public transport into the city centre, can significantly reduce the number of cars in the city centre. While Park & Ride can be of benefit to shoppers, it is particularly important to encourage its use by office workers who occupy space on a daily basis. This will then free space for casual shoppers and short stay visitors, who may be less willing to visit if adequate parking is not provided.

To meet the needs of visitors and shoppers who are unwilling to leave their cars at outlying, peripheral locations, car parks can be provided which are not necessarily in the city centre but within walking distance (Park & Walk). This can reduce traffic in the city centre while allowing people to have immediate access to their cars.

There are a number of different systems for paying for car parking. With car parks, there are advantages in payment on exit schemes, as opposed to Pay & Display. With Pay & Display, customers must decide in advance how long they plan to stay, which can result in their visit being curtailed. It also encourages theft from vehicles as cars clearly display how long their owners will be away. Car parks which limit a visitor's stay to 2–3 hours can reduce the length of stay and the amount of money spent in the city centre. In relation to on-street parking, a Pay & Display system has significant advantages over a card parking system, since a card parking system requires visitors to locate a shop which sells cards and frequently limits the length of stay.

It is important that visitors are able to locate long-term car parking easily, including the location and number of spaces in car parks. In some cities, electronic signs at the entrance to the city centre identify how many spaces are available in each car park as well as direct people to the location of the nearest car park with spaces available. In Nottingham, radio announcements inform visitors of the location of parking spaces in the city centre.

The quality and safety of car parks are equally important to attracting visitors, particularly as the majority of shoppers are women and safety is a

Plate 10.1   Entrance signs to Baden Baden in Germany, which clearly indicate the location of parking and other attractions in the city

prime area of concern. Measures to improve car parks include installing quality lighting, clearly identifying levels (by colour and forms or shapes), providing planting and greenery, and installing closed circuit television cameras (CCTV).

Visitor management

Visitor management is an important element of any city centre strategy or action plan, particularly for cities where visitors are an important component of the economy. These measures can result in the average visit being lengthened as well as the economic viability of certain areas of the city being enhanced. While visitors may find the main shopping area where the majority of national retailers are located, they can become discouraged if the shops look identical to those in any other city. By improving the quality of streets where small unique independent shops are located, a more interesting and diverse mix of retail shops can be provided for residents and visitors to enjoy, as well as new businesses supported.

Signposting can help to indicate the location of visitor attractions. One form of signposting, known as town trails, can facilitate this process by providing a route through the city (either with signposts or paving stones) which visitors can follow. A brochure can be made available as well which provides further information on each point of interest.

Another method of encouraging visitor movement is to establish and promote an area for particular types of activity, thereby creating a cluster of uses.

Plate 10.2   Finger posts indicating the location for visitors of major attractions (Bath)

For example, an antiques area can be enhanced by providing quality signage at the entrances to that area. An evening entertainment area can be established by encouraging the development of restaurants, cafes, theatre, clubs and quality physical spaces, such as fountains and sculptures. The creation of clusters helps to establish a critical mass of activity, which in turn generates greater visitor numbers.

One of the most important aspects of visitor management is to ensure that good quality public conveniences are available, including toilets and baby changing facilities. These facilities should ideally be located within close proximity to where the majority of people are located, to minimise any inconvenience to the visitor.

Access for the disabled

Cities are actively identifying how they can better meet the needs of disabled people. This often includes improved pavement access, as well as access into retail shops, public toilets and parking facilities. Wheelchairs or motorised vehicles provided in the city centre, often referred to as shop mobility, allow disabled people greater mobility in the city. The percentage of the population who will benefit from such schemes is expected to increase as the population grows older.

Customer care

The importance of customer care programmes is growing as people's expectations increase for good quality service and with the realisation that cities need to maintain their competitive edge. A coordinated approach to customer care is necessary to ensure that all available resources, including those available at nearby colleges and universities, are utilised. The Investors in People programme designed by the Department of Trade and Industry provides a benchmark of good practice, ensuring that training is geared to a company's objectives and that staff are competent to meet those objectives. The National Vocational Qualifications (NVQ) Level 3 provides a qualification to a national standard in retail management and customer care, allowing individuals to obtain a qualification which reflects their prior learning.

Security issues

Issues related to security are some of the most serious facing retailers, with the retail sector losing over £1 billion annually from theft, burglary, and ram raiding.

Measures which have been established to act as a deterrent include:

- holding seminars for retailers where specialist expertise is provided on controlling theft and burglary;
- developing closed circuit television (CCTV), a system of cameras installed throughout the city centre to monitor activity on the street;
- developing a two-way telephone link system between retailers (to alert retailers and police to shoplifting threats);
- providing physical barriers (i.e. street furniture, bollards etc.) in front of vulnerable retail shops or at the entrance to pedestrianised streets;
- creating a dedicated city centre police team, which is available on the street to deal with issues as they arise.

Street entertainment

Street entertainment can increase the liveliness and enjoyment of the city centre and enhance the visitor experience. While it can be a major asset to a city, it is necessary to manage conflicts between street entertainers and residents and office workers. In Bath, a Buskers' Code of Practice was created

Plate 10.3 A busker performs in a public square bringing life and activity to the city

in consultation with entertainers and the police in order to minimise these conflicts. The code stipulates hours of operation (i.e. not after 10 p.m. in the evening), requires buskers to move location every hour, and prohibits amplified music and drums. This has proven effective in assisting the police and local authorities in regulating street activity.

Environmental issues

Many cities have extensive programmes to encourage improved environmental practices such as energy conservation and recycling programmes. Increasing traffic congestion can create serious air pollution problems which affect the health of those living and working in the city as well as the restoration of buildings. The City Centre Manager can give encouragement and support to these schemes.

Begging issues

Begging can be a volatile and emotive issue, with people expressing strong views for and against allowing begging in the city centre. For cities which depend on tourism, begging can have a negative impact on the city's image. Aggressive begging (defined as harassing or threatening behaviour) requires active involvement on the part of the police.

A pro-active measure which has been found to reduce begging, and which has been implemented throughout most of the UK, is the development of the *Big Issue,* a newspaper sold by the homeless. This has been shown to provide a small income for vendors, reduce the number of people begging and assist in increasing the self-esteem and self-worth of those selling the magazine. It is hoped that other similar types of initiatives could be established to help homeless people who might otherwise beg.

City centre development

Physical improvements and new developments which are strategically placed are important to the viability of a city centre and require a strategic approach. Two areas of particular significance are:

- quality urban design and public spaces;
- encouraging development activity.

Urban design and public spaces

Public spaces in cities can be a focal point for activity and a meeting place for people. They deserve a high degree of consideration in determining how people use these spaces and the unique contribution each space can make to the city centre. For example, public spaces can reflect the life of the city through fountains, sculptures and other forms of public art. They can also provide a means for the public to contribute their ideas and take greater ownership of the city.

Often physical improvements are undertaken in a piecemeal fashion, without a strategic plan identifying which spaces will have the greatest influence on people's enjoyment of the city centre as well as the potential for future investment. Public money spent on physical spaces should be leveraged to create the maximum output in terms of new investment and jobs.

The City Centre Manager can act as a catalyst in coordinating people and resources, bringing together such diverse professionals as conservationists, urban designers and property experts and engineering services, and assisting in creating a comprehensive approach to the city's physical development. A coordinated approach can then be established on the future development of public spaces, street furniture (seating, litter bins etc.) and paving policies. The result can be increased investment in the city, including new

Plate 10.4 An example of quality improvements to the physical environment (Horsham)

developments such as offices and housing, as well as the sponsorship of amenities and public art by the private sector.

In Reading, three urban design schemes were undertaken on a partnership basis, with the private sector contributing both funding and ideas. These improvements have significantly upgraded the quality of the physical environment, resulting in increased investment in the area. In Maidstone, Market Buildings Street was repaved in York stone and the yellow lines removed. Within weeks, owners of adjacent shops had repainted their buildings and opened a number of street cafes, enhancing the cafe culture.

Development activity

The city is a prime generator of economic activity, and efforts undertaken by various council departments including the City Centre Manager can act as a catalyst in encouraging this activity to occur. By understanding market forces and commercial trends and working closely with property developers, investors and estate agents, it is possible to identify and promote development opportunities. The key sectors of development activity in a city centre are: retail, office, residential, hotel and conference facilities, and attractions.

Retail

Retail is one of the primary activities found in most cities. In a 1994 study completed by URBED, the diversity of shops and services was considered the

Plate 10.5 A new retail infill development with outdoor cafe and square (Bath)

most important factor in a city's health by 96% of respondents. The retail mix in cities and towns will vary according to the city's catchment area, proximity to other towns and cities and the total number of office workers and visitors.

Retail in historic cities and resort towns can serve as an attraction and leisure pursuit for the visitors. It is therefore important that small independent shops are encouraged which add character and uniqueness to the area.

For cities which serve as regional shopping destinations, the purpose of the visit is more often based on comparison shopping, with the diversity of retail shops and department stores playing a critical role in the success of the shopping area. Regional centres are likely to be affected by the development of out-of-town shopping centres, which typically offer a wide merchandise mix with relative ease of transport and parking, in a well-managed, climate-controlled environment.

For smaller towns which have a food store as their main anchor, the primary motivation for visiting will be food shopping, with smaller purchases made at adjacent shops. The viability of these towns is particularly vulnerable to competition from out-of-town food stores.

Office development

The office sector is an important source of employment for a city, as well as providing additional spending on retail and other services. To encourage the development of new office space or refurbishment of existing space, it is necessary to identify gaps in the type of office space required. For example, although there may appear to be a sufficient amount of vacant office space, the location, quality and size of the space may inhibit businesses relocation. Increasing technological requirements of businesses mean that smart new office developments need to be built. Increasing competition from out-of-town office developments which provide free parking and easy access may require cities to improve their competitive advantage, through grants, free parking or Park & Ride provision for employees.

Residential

Housing within a city centre can help to sustain a broad mix of daytime and evening activity, including restaurants and night life. It can also have the impact of reducing crime levels by ensuring that there are more people with eyes on the street.

Although there are significant benefits to encouraging housing in the city centre, there are sometimes conflicts which need to be resolved. Although the city centre may be a convenient location, noise generated by daytime busking and evening entertainment can sometimes be incompatible with residential use, particularly for the elderly. It is also important to ensure that there is sufficient parking to meet the needs of residents. To encourage the development of second and third storey space for residential use, the government introduced the programme 'Living over the Shop', which provides grants and advice to property owners. Although this programme has proven successful, one difficulty in converting space is often the need to reduce valuable retail frontage to create separate entrances.

Hotel and conference facilities

Hotels and other conference facilities encourage business and visitor spending in the city centre. Larger hotels often have their own facilities which can attract conferences, banquets and corporate meetings. In some cities large purpose-built facilities are being created. Although they are not financially profitable without the support of other commercial developments, they can generate additional revenue for a city including filling bed spaces.

Attractions

Visitor attractions often include museums and galleries, but can also be libraries and sports facilities. There tends to be a high rate of failure of new attractions. For this reason it is important to establish what new attractions will be most important to ensure the attraction has a specific niche market, with good management and financial backing underpinned by a detailed feasibility study. If new attractions are strategically located in relation to other developments, it is possible to affect visitor flow through the city centre, enhance visitor experience and potentially encourage new development to take place.

Developing a city's identity

A city needs a positive identity and image. It is all too easy for the local press in particular to publicise only the bad news and fail to mention the positive initiatives which may be underway. The City Centre Manager, in conjunction with other public and private sector groups, can help to change the way a city views itself through a concerted marketing and public relations effort and public events and festivals. The result of these efforts can be felt in terms of greater civic responsibility, increased investment, and a greater willingness and ability to tackle difficult problems as they arise.

By actively promoting a strong relationship with the local media (newspapers, radio, television), the City Centre Manager will often be quoted for stories and issues related to the city centre. This is an ideal opportunity to start to initiate a more positive image of the city. Likewise, the City Centre Manager may be aware of good news stories from within the Council that have not been recognised and can ensure that they are brought to the attention of the press. In Bath, the key facts were compiled into a brochure about what made the city an ideal place to live, work, and visit in order to better enable those who promote the city to become more aware of the city's assets.

A campaign can be developed which helps to define the image and qualities of the area. An example is the slogan 'Glasgow Miles Better', which can be seen to have dramatically changed the image of that city. Bath has established several campaigns, one entitled 'Bath Means Business' to attract new businesses, and a 'World Class Service in World Heritage City' to promote customer service levels.

Festivals and other public events can have an important impact on developing civic pride and community spirit. This is particularly important in cities where there are a large number of tourists and a relatively small local population.

It is equally important that residents take an active role in the organising and developing of events and festivals, in order to help build the sense of ownership. A well-known American authority on festivals, Prof J Mark Schuster, has been quoted as saying:

> Festivals must be part of the shared life of the community. Participation must be encouraged if not expected, and citizens must be actively involved in creating, conducting and maintaining the festival. If those who attend are primarily observers or

consumers, a golden opportunity will have been missed. For those wishing to redevelop or indeed establish the 'civil society' that can be fostered in the best of our cities, they must pay attention to the rise of the new urban festival.

The City of Leeds has been very effective in developing an events strategy with the focus on allowing for the cultural and economic renewal of the public realm. These events have included installing over nine miles of Christmas lights, with shops staying open late each night during the Christmas season, and a Valentine's Fair (one of the largest in Europe), which runs for one week with activity each night from 6 p.m. until midnight.

Components of many festivals include a carnival procession, arts and crafts stalls, music and dance entertainment, street parties and evening activities. In some cities, festivals have developed into a sense of tradition, despite not being in existence for any length of time. It is important that festivals be organised in a manner by which they have some degree of autonomy from the local authority and yet maintain a close relationship, in order to ensure that issues are resolved rapidly and without extensive bureaucratic procedures.

Conclusion

In many ways, the City Centre Manager is called upon to be a jack of all trades. It is important to have an understanding of commercial interests as well as an ability to relate to the politics of working with a local authority. The ability to plan effectively and carry out those plans is equally important in order to achieve results. It is important that while identifying the long-term goals and objectives, there is a focus on immediate wins which give some credibility to the position early on.

In addition to undertaking specific initiatives, the City Centre Manager should be seen as a catalyst and initiator. There is great potential within the position to help create important links between the public, private, and voluntary sectors, and to play a pivotal role in public relations and in working with the media. If successful, it can assist the community to take a more active role in the future of the city.

There are a number of Local Authorities which are considering widening the role of City Centre Manager to take on responsibility for all city centre management issues, including street cleaning and refuse collection. The City of Coventry is considering the development of a city centre partnership company which would be responsible for all aspects of management, development and commercial activity. In the United States, many cities have adopted what are known as Business Improvement Districts. Within these areas, properties are assessed and charged a fee, which is used for the general maintenance and upkeep of the district.

The Association of Town Centre Managers (ATCM), established in 1991, creates a forum for discussion and debate on city centre issues, with membership including retailers, transport and urban planning professionals, and

Local Authority members. Through this organisation, and continuing evolution of the management of cities, the role of City Centre Management will be likely to evolve over time to reflect the changing needs of cities and towns throughout the country.

Bath – a case study

As one of the few cities in the world to receive UNESCO status as a world heritage site, Bath is a city with ties to the Roman era as well as the largest concentration of Georgian architecture in the world.

The City Centre Manager post was established in Bath in April 1993. Because the City is considered vital, there was a tendency towards complacency and therefore a reluctance to change, with some ideas having difficulty coming to fruition. In a city such as Bath there is a need to ensure that the architectural quality of the past is preserved, whilst also allowing for new ideas and innovations to be pursued.

One of the first tasks undertaken by the City Centre Manager was a 30-page audit of the City Centre, which included a SWOT analysis, and an in-depth assessment of specific areas including management issues, arts and entertainment, retail leasing, physical improvements, and development issues. Over 100 individuals were consulted, and it was reviewed by councillors, City Council officers and members of the private and voluntary sectors.

The City Centre Steering Group then prioritised a list of 25 issues from the audit. The first three issues in order of priority were (1) consensus building, (2) improved security and (3) providing public conveniences. Other issues which were considered particularly important were begging, retail vacancies, and transportation.

In the first year of operation, the City Centre Manager's office focused on several issues which had received negative national and local press coverage. The first of these was begging. After discussions with people who were begging on the streets, the City Centre Manager contacted the *Big Issue* newspaper in London. After several meetings, The *Big Issue* began to be sold in Bath, initially working out of the City Centre Manager's office. The *Big Issue* has since moved office, and now employs four full-time people and has 25 vendors operating in Bath. This initiative has been seen to significantly reduce the amount of begging in the city centre.

The most important area identified by the Steering Committee was achieving consensus on the major issues in the city centre. Two consensus events were held with 30 individuals representing the public, private, and voluntary sectors attending. At the first event, city centre issues were generally addressed, and the reasons for begging were discussed in detail. The result was the creation of a dedicated city centre police force, which has dramatically reduced the number and extent of problems in the city centre. During the second consensus event, issues related to public spaces, transport, and economic development and tourism were discussed. One of the results of these two events was a greater sense of partnership and dialogue between the public and private sectors, which has had a positive impact on many other aspects of the city.

Retail vacancies were also seen as a major issue, particularly as it was regularly reported in the national press. A retail study was commissioned as a joint public/private sector venture and undertaken by the University of Bath business programme. The results of the study indicated that the city's vacancy rate was well below the national average (8.5% compared with 12.5% nationally). It also highlighted the fact that small independent retailers had suffered most during the recession, as a result of not having the financial underpinning more common in larger national chains. Many of the conclusions reached from this study are now in the process of being implemented.

Other initiatives undertaken include improvements to the railway station (an important gateway to the city centre), a security seminar for retailers, an outdoor cafe, a brochure outlining the 'good news about Bath as a place to live, work, and visit', a public forum on urban spaces, creating a screen to televise events during the European Youth Olympics to be held in Bath, improving refuse collection, improving the quality of street trading and enhancing areas with a predominance of independent retailers.

While the City Centre initiative is less than two years old, it has provided an important link between the public, private, and voluntary sectors and helped to create a stronger and more vibrant City Centre, reflecting the needs of the entire community more fully.

References

DoE and the Urban and Economic Development Group (May 1994), *Vital and Viable Town Centres: Meeting the Challenge.* London: HMSO.

Manchester (1994) Papers Presented to a Conference on The Night-time Economy, Manchester: Published by Manchester Institute for Popular Culture Publishing, The Manchester Metropolitan University, Cavendish Building, Cavendish Street, Manchester M15 6BX, including 'The Evening Economy of Cities', by J. Montgomery, and 'Two Urban Festivals: La Merce and First Night', by M. Schuster.

Montgomery, J (1994) The Evening Economy of Cities, *Town and Country Planning,* Vol. 63, No. 11. pp. 302–307.

Paumier, C (1990) *Designing a Successful Downtown.* Washington DC: The Urban Land Institute.

Shaw, M (ed.) (1994) *Caring for Our Towns and Cities.* London: Boots the Chemist and Civic Trust Regeneration Unit.

WDS (1994) Are Town Centres Managing?, *Broadsheet 12.* London: Women's Design Service.

Also 'ideas' from John Montgomery and Mark Schuster.

PART VI

CHANGING AGENDAS AND AGENCIES

INTRODUCTION

In the last section the questions of future directions in planning policy, and related to this, the chances of actually achieving implementation, are reconsidered. In seeking to shift the agenda of town planning towards greater emphasis being put upon social, economic and environmental policies, planners must be cognisant of the limitations, or opportunities, presented by the legal and governmental context. Therefore in Chapter 11 Tracey Merrett illustrates the boundaries of planning power and effective policy attainment drawing on examples of current planning appeal decisions, with particular attention to the chances of achieving planning gain, and secondly of imposing environmental policies on developers which forward the cause of sustainability. In respect of the latter she sees European Union legislation as an important factor. In the following chapter, David Ludlow gives an overview of the implications of European 'planning' Directives, governmental agencies, and regulations for British town planners. In the final chapter the editor seeks to draw together what appear to be the common themes and objectives expressed by contributors to the book. In this chapter it is argued that the key to attaining both sustainability and economic and functional viability in our cities is to develop a well-planned, positive transportation strategy, combining both public and private transport modes. Linked to this there must be a reformatting of land use patterns and urban form, greater attention to the needs of all sectors of urban society, and stronger governmental guidance and support.

Chapter 11

POLICY FRONTIERS AND PLANNING APPEALS

Tracey Merrett

| Conflicts between planners and developers |

This chapter discusses the conflict between the Government's efforts to enforce planning policy to control development and developers trying to manipulate planning policy and case law to achieve the maximum development possible. This conflict between the controller and their tools of control, and the enthusiastic challenger to those controls through the judicial process has been highlighted in recent times in three main areas. First, the concept of development plan pre-eminence; second, the ambit and use of planning gain; and third, the controls and restrictions placed on development by environmental concerns.

The Planning and Compensation Act 1991 introduced many changes to the planning system, particularly the increased emphasis on the importance of the development plan in the decision making process. The presumption in favour of development in accordance with the Development Plan unless material considerations indicate otherwise was introduced by Section 54A of the Town and Country Planning Act 1990 (the 1990 Act). Regard should be had to the development plan so far as it is material, and for it to be material it must be relevant, up-to-date and in accordance with national policy. This new presumption was an attempt to move away from speculative development, which the Government felt prevailed in the 1980s.

Following the introduction of planning obligations by Section 106 of the 1990 Act, there has been a spate of case law which highlights the conflict between the desires of the Government to limit planning gain and the wishes of Planning Authorities and developers to obtain as much planning gain as possible.

Another overwhelming trend is the need to pay increased attention to the environmental implications of development both in local plan creation and in determining planning applications. The European Union is constantly creating new legislation which gradually filters through to our national statute book. The importance of environmental issues in planning matters can be seen both in recent case law and in government policy.

Plan-led development v. speculative development

Origins of the current agenda

The emphasis on the development plan and the introduction of Section 54A of the 1990 Act arise from a combination of factors. One of these is the recession, which has given local authorities time to reflect and consider what kind of development has been permitted on appeal in their areas. It has also allowed the Government to review the development which had taken place as a result of a market-led development industry and what impact that has had on town centres in strategic planning terms.

Despite the fact that most Government policy aims to centralise matters and weaken the role of local government, in this area the government has given more power to local authorities in the determination of the regional plan, structure plan, local plan and the determination of applications and appeals.

Analysis of current issues

Section 54A requires that where a planning application is to be determined regard must be had to the development plan (provided it is relevant) together with other material considerations. The determination should be made in accordance with that plan unless material considerations indicate otherwise. The Development Plan will be relevant only where it has policies that are material to the development in question and is up-to-date.

This changes the previous legislation, which contained a presumption in favour of development. There is now a presumption in favour of development which is in accordance with a relevant and up to date development plan. David Keene QC in Canterbury City Council *ex parte* Springimage comments,

> There could be no doubt that it increased the importance of the statutory Development Plan in the decision making process.

The consequence of the main caveat being 'unless material considerations indicate otherwise' has been an increase in case law to determine what is a material consideration. In order to establish this we must look at the guidance in Planning Policy Guidance Note 1 (PPG1) and relevant case law. Paragraph 23 of PPG1 states that material considerations must fairly and reasonably relate to the application (R. v. Westminster City Council *ex parte* Monahan) and they must be related to the purpose of planning legislation and be genuine planning considerations.

In the case of Bolton Metropolitan Borough Council v. SOSE a decision issued by the Secretary of State failed to take into account material considerations and it did not explain why he had done this or why the eventual decision had been made. In this case the advantages of the development had decreased during the time between the end of the inquiry and the time at which the decision letter was written. The material considerations that the inspector has to consider are policies and facts which exist at the time of making the decision not those prevailing at the time of the end of the inquiry. As a result of this it was held that he had failed to have regard to material considerations in relation to the retail impact of the scheme and had thereby come to a wrong decision, and his decision was quashed. This shows not only the importance of taking into account each material consideration but also the time at which material considerations are judged to be relevant.

Many decisions have been challenged on the basis that applications have not been determined in accordance with the development plan pursuant to Section 54A of the Town and Country Planning Act 1990.

For example, in the case of Newham London Borough Council v. SOSE the High Court refused to quash an inspector's decision for failing to cite Section 54A. The principle of looking at the decision letter as a whole was upheld and in this case it was decided that the inspector had determined the application in accordance with the Development Plan.

The Planning and Compensation Act 1991 aimed to streamline the Development Plan process. This has resulted in the Secretary of State taking a lesser role in approving structure plans. In the case of Structure Plans, District Plans and Unitary Development Plans the Secretary of State for the Environment now only has 'call in' powers and all these plans are determined locally.

The importance of the Development Plan as a result of S.54A and the fact that it is drafted by the Local Authority and approved by it has had an impact on the way in which planning applications are pursued. All clients are now urged to be vigilant in monitoring the process of Local Plans in their area. Planning advisors stress the importance of assessing the impact of the draft Local Plan on land ownership, and making representations relating to the Local Plan within the short time allowed.

The Pelham Homes case challenged the decision of a Local Planning Authority in rejecting recommendations made by the local plan inspector. Its facts give an example of the delay involved in the current system. The Authority resolved that in the event that their proposed modifications to the Local Plan had been objected to and not withdrawn it would make preparation for a further Local Plan Inquiry. At a later date, it resolved not to call for a further inquiry to be held, despite the fact there were still several objections outstanding. The Court held that the earlier resolution had given rise to a legitimate expectation that there would be a further inquiry, and that the objectors should have been consulted before the authority reversed the decision. This shows both the willingness of the public to challenge the decisions of local authorities who reject recommendations by Local Plan inspectors and the need to ensure that there has been compliance with the proper procedures for the adoption of the Local Plan.

The impact of the approval of Local Plans at a local level has meant that the private sector's interests can be completely ignored in the creation of plan policies. Under the new system for Structure Plan approval by County Councils themselves, any criticisms of the plan by the Department of the Environment have to be aired by the Department itself appearing at the Examination In Public and giving evidence. The County Council still has the ability to reject the advice of the Structure Plan Panel, which chairs the Examination In Public. The resources of the Department of the Environment are inevitably limited, and although there is an ability for the Secretary of State for the Environment to call in the Structure Plan, this does not happen frequently. The reality of Examinations In Public under this new system has unfortunately shown that the County Council becoming judge and jury in the determination of Structure Plan policies has had a negative impact on the fairness and width of debate. There is no right to appear at an Examination In Public; the list of participants is drawn up by the County Council. This can also lead to an imbalance in the evidence put before the Structure Plan Panel. The Examinations In Public into Structure Plans which have been carried out under the new rules have all resulted in objectors criticising the outcome and in one case requesting the Department of The Environment to call in the Structure Plan.

PPG1 *General Policy and Principles* discusses the Development Plan and its place in the determination of a planning application. It stresses that if an applicant wishes to pursue a development which is clearly in contravention of the Development Plan he will have to show good reason to demonstrate why the plan should not be followed.

Appeal decisions by the Secretary of State for the Environment and the Inspectorate illustrate a marked reluctance on the part of the Department of the Environment to determine applications for large-scale development in advance of the formal development plan review process. There is a formal ability to reject applications on the basis of prematurity; this requires there to be a consultation draft of the Local Plan (PPG1, para 33) and is subject to other caveats. The idea that determination of an application for development would pre-empt consideration of the scale of development and locational issues through the Development Plan process has been used as a reason to refuse many development proposals. If all major developments in the area are expected to be discussed at the local plan hearing, the length and complexity of the Local Plan process will be changed considerably.

The 1991 Act has also removed the requirement for a consultation draft of the Development Plan to be prepared and therefore the first draft which the public may see will be the deposit draft, to which there is a short period of six weeks for objections to be made, followed by a discussion of those objections at the Local Plan Inquiry.

Local government reorganisation has also caused new problems which will arise as a result of the new plan-led system. The transitional provisions which have been produced by the government are unclear as to what would be the status of the Local Plan Inquiry were it to be partly heard within the life of a District Council soon to become a Unitary Authority. The result of this has been that where District Councils have been in the process of preparing a new Local Plan, their Local Plan Inquiry has been frozen until the effective date of reorganisation so that the inquiry may be heard fully under the control of the new authority. Many County Councils facing abolition which are proceeding towards Structure Plan alterations are also abandoning the work they are currently undertaking although some of the changes may well appear in the new Unitary Developments Plans.

Plan-led development

It is apparent that the changes brought in to emphasise the importance of plan-led development have had a major impact on the way in which development proposals are pursued through the planning system and on the way in which Local Plan Inquiries and Structure Plan Inquiries have been conducted. The increase in importance of representations at these inquiries will lead to an increase in the number of people appearing and hence the length and cost. This has already had severe financial implications for local and central government. Suggestions such as limiting the time for making representations at inquiries have not yet been adopted but it is clear that there cannot be an unlimited opportunity for everyone to make objections and representations at length.

The Planning Inspectorate in 1994 issued a draft paper entitled *The Efficient and Effective Use of Time in Planning Inquiries and the Role of Cross Examination*. The aim of this was to criticise diplomatically advocates who cross examine on irrelevant subjects as well as for too long and others who cross examine too aggressively.

Time available to participants at Local Plan Inquiries is constantly being reduced. The normal procedure is for one participant to give an estimate of time to the programme officer and for him to fit that participant in. The practice is that representations are restricted to a much shorter length of time than has been reasonably estimated. When they carry on to another day participants are either required to put their representations in writing or it is suggested that the inquiry will have to resume specially to hear those particular representations on a separate occasion. This can be detrimental to the presentation of most cases which are best presented as a whole.

The danger is that the increased importance of Local Plan Inquiries may lead to a situation where the opportunity of the participant to present his case properly is severely damaged. The enhancement of the importance of Local Plans together with the inability to make proper representations at Local Plan Inquiries will lead to a large amount of dissatisfaction.

This makes a farce of the aim to streamline and speed up the Local Plan System which, in order for it to become pertinent under Section 54A, has to be relevant, and in order to be relevant, must be up to date. If the Local Plan Inquiry process takes so long then the final product will not be as up to date as it should be. The Department of the Environment has published its intentions to revise its Code of Practice on Local Plan Inquiries. The aim is to speed up the process and prevent local authorities from being dissuaded from revising their development plans. It also wants to increase the consultation period. This appears to contradict its first aim.

The impact of the uncertainty relating to local government reorganisation on the flow of Structure and Local Plan review will be delay and disruption. This must result in increased costs and uncertainty for all those concerned with Local Plan Inquiries.

The other implication of S.54A of the 1990 Act is the search to find material considerations which indicate otherwise. A string of case law has manifested the need to show compelling reasons why the Development Plan should not be followed. Although there has been a shift in the way in which planning applications are determined, cynics might argue that for developers with large amounts of money to justify material considerations, the change has not been so great. The largest area of debate over what is a material consideration has arisen in determining what planning gain can be taken into account in the determination of a planning application.

Planning gain: law v. policy

Analysis of current issues

The questions of significance which have been the subject of great debate in the Courts recently are as follows:

1. What is a legal planning obligation (legality)?
2. What planning gain may be taken into account as a material consideration in granting planning consent (materiality)?
3. If it is material what weight should be given to it?

1. LEGALITY

To determine the legality of a Planning Obligation it has to be studied independently from the planning permission itself. When determining whether the gain offered is a material consideration the permission and the Planning Obligation will be considered together. In assessing legality the first step is to look at Section 106 of the Town and Country Planning Act 1990 (the 1990 Act). Section 106 of the 1990 Act was amended by the Planning and Compensation Act 1991 and Planning Agreements have now been replaced by Planning Obligations. The main change was to allow a unilateral Obligation to be entered into. The idea of this was to address problems which had been met by developers on occasions where the Local Planning

Authority refused to negotiate or complete an Agreement. Now landowners can bind their land or make offers of benefits unilaterally.

The legality of a Planning Obligation therefore rests primarily upon the provisions of Section 106 itself as interpreted by the Courts together with requirements for it to be reasonable and for a planning purpose. The Obligation may:

(a) restrict the development or use of the land in any specified way;
(b) require specified operations or activities to be carried out in, on, under, or over the land;
(c) require the land to be used in any specified way; or
(d) require a sum or sums to be paid to the authority on a specified date or dates periodically.

The rest of the section sets out other requirements which the Obligation must meet in order to be legal. There are also general principles and case law which state that a Planning Obligation must be related to planning purposes and not be unreasonable in the Wednesbury sense.

It is worth questioning why unilateral undertakings should be subject to the Wednesbury test if the landowner is willing to enter into an undertaking to offer benefits? Why apply the Wednesbury test, which was essentially to control the abuse of powers by administrative authorities? This is totally different to an individual exercising his right under Section 106 to offer some benefit, or agree to be bound by some Obligation.

An offer of £1 million to a Local Authority for the preservation of listed buildings could be legal, if it meets the test of S.106, it is related to planning purposes i.e. the preservation of listed buildings and is not Wednesbury unreasonable.

The second question to be asked is what elements of planning gain in the Planning Obligation meeting the previous test of legality have to be taken into account as material in considering the related planning application?

2. MATERIALITY

The case of Stringer v. Minister of Housing and Local Government established the general principle in relation to material considerations that in order for any consideration to be material it must relate to the use and development of land. In deciding in each particular case whether something is material, you have to look at the circumstances of that particular case. This has generated a large amount of case law.

Looking at the Planning Obligation in our example, if the planning application was for a motorway service area ten miles away and totally unconnected, would it still meet the test of being a material consideration and be a matter which therefore should be taken into account in the decision making process?

Pursuant to Section 70 (2) 'in dealing with such an application the authority shall have regard to the provisions of the development plan, so far as material to the application, and to any other material considerations.' When determining whether something is material to a planning application you not only look at the application itself but also at the development plan.

The impact of Section 54A has meant that the development plan must always be considered as a material consideration in the decision making process and therefore should a policy exist which says 'any applications for motorway service areas within this district must be accompanied by a contribution to the Local Authority for the preservation of listed buildings,' this would then have additional weight as a material consideration by virtue of Section 54A, giving greater importance to local policy rather than national policy. The weighting in S.54A is subject to a proviso – unless material considerations indicate otherwise. Where the Secretary of State is the decision maker he may decide that the Planning Obligation is legal, that the planning gain is material and because of S.54A it is more material, but he can override that because his circular is a material consideration which indicates otherwise, overriding the emphasis on the development plan in S.54A.

The conflict between local and national policy was an underlying problem discussed in the Tesco case. This case concerned an offer by Tesco to pay the full cost of a new link road near to its proposed store. The highways figures show that this was a traffic measure to address an existing traffic problem and the new store would generate less than 10% of the traffic on the new road in excess of development which was already permitted. It was argued that this payment was not sufficiently related to the development in scale and kind as required by paragraph 9 of Annex B to Circular 16/91.

The Secretary of State refused consent and said that the gain was not necessary to enable the development to go ahead and it was not fairly and reasonably related in scale to the development. If he was wrong to make this decision and he should take the offer into consideration, he would only consider the part of the offer which related to the traffic generation as a result of the development and partial funding would be so limited that it would not change his decision.

Tesco appealed to the House of Lords on the basis that the offer of funding was a material consideration and that the Secretary of State had failed to have regard to it.

The court held that the Secretary of State did treat the funding of the road as material and he had carried out a weighting exercise to establish what weight to give it.

A Planning Obligation which had no connection with the proposed development plainly would not be a material consideration, unless it was set out in the Development Plan as a requirement as in our example. If there is some connection, then regard must be had to the planning gain offered in the Planning Obligation.

The judgement also confirmed that it was a matter for the Courts to decide what was a material consideration and if the decision maker failed to take into consideration a material consideration then his decision could not stand.

The decision maker once having decided a matter to be material/relevant can decide how much weight to give it. The weighting is not for the Courts to challenge unless it is Wednesbury unreasonable.

Lord Hoffman supported the principle that there can be a material consideration which should be given no weight by the Planning Authority. He said: 'Provided that the planning authority has regard to all material considerations, it is at liberty (provided that it does not lapse into Wednesbury irrationality) to give them whatever weight the planning authority thinks fit or no weight at all,' and 'if the decision to give that consideration no weight is based on rational planning grounds, then the planning authority is entitled to ignore it.'

Planning Authorities wondering how they should quantify the amount of planning gain to be required in connection with development can look at the case of South Northamptonshire District Council.

The South Northamptonshire case concerned the requirement for developers to fund the provision of infrastructure which would be necessitated by the proposed development. South Northamptonshire District Council made it part of their Local Plan that the funding of the Towcester by-pass was secured by contributions of a fixed sum, or the gift of land, or a levy of between 11.15% and 20% of the uplift in value of the land after the grant of consent.

This policy was challenged by Crest in the Court of Appeal and it was upheld as a valid Local Plan policy. This case addressed Crest's criticisms that the percentage formula was not based upon the cost of provision of the infrastructure nor did the formula make any sufficient connection between the individual development in terms of scale and any specific community benefit. The Court of Appeal however fully upheld the Local Authority's plan and stated that it believed that the Council was operating in a *bone fide* manner and that it was not necessary to show a complete match between the money required as planning gain and what is necessary to pay for the infrastructure. It accepted that there were a number of variables, e.g. the cost of the works and the economy in general, and therefore condoned the establishment of a formula to calculate the relevant level of planning gain. The question therefore of how much planning gain is material does not have to be calculated with great precision.

3. WEIGHT

Once you have established that a consideration is material or relevant to the determination of a planning application it is for the decision maker to decide, and not the Court, what weight should be attributed to that material consideration. This brings into focus the two-tiered system of decision making. If the Planning Authority is the decision maker it will put more emphasis on the development plan but if it is the Secretary of State then he will emphasise the Circulars. In cases where the Development Plan has policies requiring planning gain the developer will make corresponding offers; however, these may be reduced or withdrawn if the local authority refuses the application and the developer appeals.

A developer in assessing how much planning gain to offer will always consider in which tier the decision will be made. If there is a possibility of a grant of consent by the Planning Authority then the planning gain will be more generous than if the application will be determined by the Secretary of State. The Secretary of State will view the gain differently and will not have the same bias towards the planning gain as the Planning Authority.

The decision maker making his decision is entitled to have regard to policy in Circulars when determining the weight he attaches to different material considerations. Lord Hoffman said: 'If there is one principle of planning law more firmly settled than any other, it is that matters of planning judgment are within the exclusive province of the local planning authority or the Secretary of State.'

The references in Circular 16/91 paragraphs B.5, B.7 and B.8 to the need for Planning Obligations to be necessary mean that Planning Obligations should not be given weight if planning consent could soundly be granted without them. Lord Hoffman said: 'The criteria in Circular 16/91 are entirely appropriate to be applied by the Secretary of State as part of his assessment of the planning merits of the application. But they are quite unsuited to application by the Courts.'

This policy test is not a matter of law and is one which is not usually found in local plans because it would reduce the amount of benefits which could be taken into account.

The public policy angle is that planning consent should not be bought or sold. This was stated in the City of Bradford case by Lloyd L.J. and has been reinforced since by Steyn L.J. in the Tesco (Court of Appeal) case, where he expressed reservations that a recent decision (the Plymouth case) came perilously close to emasculating the principle that planning permission may not be bought and sold.

Perceived conflict

The perceived conflict between law and policy arose because the two sets of tests, one set for the materiality of planning gain and the other test set out in Circular 16/91, which exists to assist the decision maker in establishing what weight to attribute to material planning gain, were compared as though they were tests determining the same issue. There is no conflict between these tests. They are in fact two different levels of tests relating to two different decisions. They are complementary tests.

The only conflict which remains is a political conflict in the way in which applications will be handled. A two-tier system exists whereby in negotiations between a developer and a Local Planning Authority the main concern will be that the Planning Obligation is legal and that is it material to the planning application. Once these tests have been met and provided no immaterial considerations are taken into account; neither the Obligation nor the permission will be open to challenge.

If however the determination of planning application is made by the Secretary of State he is more likely to take into account the guidance given in DoE Circular 16/91 to determine what weight should be attributed to the relevant Planning Obligation.

The concern which exists is that the system of negotiating planning gain is not a particularly public one, although the eventual agreement can be obtained and the committee resolution should be public. The public in general may not be aware of what is being offered by the Planning Authority and by the developer respectively. Once consent has been granted it is very difficult, if a Local Authority can show that the Planning Obligation is legal and material to the application, to challenge or test the amount of weight that the Local Authority gave to the Planning Obligation.

In a situation similar to the Tesco case, where a large amount of gain has been offered but only a small amount of it is material, there is no redress to the public if they feel that a large immaterial element of planning gain has swayed the Local Authority's decision, unless they can prove that the decision in its entirety is unreasonable in the Wednesbury sense.

As Lord Hoffman said in the Tesco case: 'The reluctance of the English Courts to enter into questions of planning judgment means that they cannot intervene in cases in which there is sufficient connection between the development and a planning obligation to make it a material consideration but the obligation appears disproportionate to the external costs of the development.'

There is a need for the Secretary of State to police planning gain policies in development plans because there is no other way of controlling planning gain accepted at a local level.

The Court is the final judge of what is a material consideration under Section 70 (2) of the 1990 Act. The question of what weight is to be given to it is a matter of judgement for the decision maker and there is very little opportunity for challenge.

In considering planning gain we are not practically concerned with law and legal rules but with the operation of a political process. Planning is not devoid of politics, it is fundamentally political; this can be seen by the way in which the two-tier process operates and how each sees the public interests being served.

If there is a two-tier system of decision making then there will always be a conflict between the interventionist views of Planning Authorities trying to maximise planning gain and the more libertarian approach of the Secretary of State, who does not think so much pressure should be placed on developers.

The two tiers, not surprisingly, have radically different views of what planning controls can be used to achieve.

Environmentally aware planning

Sources of the agenda

Concerns about environmental matters in relation to development originate from the European Union. There is also growing public awareness and public concern relating to environmental matters. This has been fuelled by the availability of environmental information, which has recently been enabled by the Environmental Information Regulations 1992 and EEC Council Directive 90/3813.

It will be familiar to all planners that nearly all government policy documents in the last two years have made reference to environmental concerns, for example PPG23 *Planning and Pollution Control* and PPG9 *Nature Conservation.*

The concept of sustainability has also been an issue which is very much to the fore in planning circles. Planning Policy Guidance Notes 6 and 13 pay lip service to this phrase. However, most people are unaware of its true meaning.

The rejection of contaminated land registers, which attracted much publicity, has been followed by the Government's document *Paying for our Past* (March 1994). This recommends that land be cleaned up to a level which is suitable for its future use, as opposed to the Dutch ethos of cleaning up as much as possible so that the land will be suitable for any future use. This approach has now been encompassed in the 1995 Environment Act as the appropriate level of clean-up.

Analysis of the current situation

EUROPEAN-DRIVEN POLICY AND LEGISLATION

Regulations and directions issued by the European Union have resulted in additional controls being placed upon developers in the UK. For example the introduction of Environmental Impact Assessments and controls on birds and habitats by Directives have impacted greatly upon the UK's planning legislation.

The EC Directive No 79/409 *Conservation of Wild Birds* and the EC Directive No 92/43 *Conservation of Natural Habitats and of Wild Fauna and Flora* have both been implemented at the national level to some extent. The Habitats Directive and the Wild Birds Directive were implemented in The Conservation (Natural Habitats etc.) Regulations 1994 (SI 1994/276) and the Wild Birds Directive was also implemented by the Wildlife and Countryside Act 1981 and the Wildlife and Countryside (Amendment) Act 1985. PPG9 *Nature Conservation* also gives guidance on these issues.

The habitats regulations identify special protection areas which conserve the habitat of the species listed in Annex 1 of the Birds Directive. There is also the concept of Natura 2000, which is the European network of Special

Areas of Conservation, and Special Protection Areas under the Wild Birds Directive, provided for by Article 3(i) of the Habitats Directive.

The Habitats Regulations relate to the protection of wild animals and wild birds, and also give a list of European protected species of plants. If sites are identified as of community importance or as Special Areas of Conservation then another layer of controls will apply to restrict development.

Another Directive which has affected development projects is EC Directive No. 85/337 *The Assessment of the Effect of Certain Public and Private Projects on the Environment.*

This Directive has been implemented by the Town and Country Planning (Assessment of Environmental Effects) Regulations 1988, which came into force on 15 July 1988.

The Planning and Compensation Act 1991 gave the Secretary of State power to enlarge the classes of development for which an Environmental Assessment may be required.

The ambit of the regulations was expanded in April 1994 to include privately financed toll roads amongst other types of developments.

The regulations distinguish between two schedules of projects: Schedule 1, where an assessment is mandatory e.g. privately financed toll road schemes and Schedule 2 projects, where assessment is required only if the project would give rise to significant effects by virtue of factors such as its nature, size or location.

THE OVERLAP BETWEEN PLANNING AND ENVIRONMENTAL REGIMES

The aim of the planning system is to control the use and development of land; the aim of the Environmental Protection System is the improved control of pollution. There is an inevitable overlap between the planning system and environmental regulation, and no clear dividing line can be drawn. For example, where a chimney stack is needed for environmental purposes the higher the better, but for planning purposes, i.e. visual impact, the lower the better. How should conflicts of this type be dealt with and what is the interface between planning and environmental law?

This question was dealt with by the Government in PPG23: *Planning and Pollution Control,* which sets out the guidelines for the relationship between the two systems. PPG23 states that there are often issues which are relevant to an application for an authorisation or licence under the environmental regime which are also material considerations to be considered in the determination of a planning application. The weight to be given to these issues depends on the scope of the pollution control system in every case.

PPG23 states three main aims: to encourage consultation, to prevent duplication of controls, and to prevent any conflict of interest between planning authorities and environmental regulatory bodies.

The Environment Agency is the main regulatory body which combines the services of the National Rivers Authority, Her Majesty's Inspectorate of

Pollution and the Waste Regulation Authority. District Councils still maintain the regulatory function for air pollution caused by certain processes in that area.

PPG23 makes it clear that Councils should use their respective control systems to achieve their respective aims. This means that where they have controls systems relating to waste management, air pollution and planning, they should not use powers in relation to air pollution to achieve a planning aim and *vice versa*. The PPG identifies matters outside the remit of the planning authority; for instance it must not give any weight to matters that have no land use implications and can be controlled by environmental regulatory bodies. The assumption of the planning authority should be that pollution controls will be properly implemented when considering pollution matters. The guide also identifies matters appropriate for planners rather than pollution control bodies, for example the control of new development near to polluting industry.

Matters relating to pollution control should ultimately be dealt with by the environmental regulatory bodies and planning should focus on whether development is acceptable, rather than the control of environmental processes carried out on land or substances stored on land.

PPG23 also gives planning authorities a responsibility for setting out criteria in Development Plans by which applications for potentially polluting development can be determined.

The guidance identifies six main material considerations, which are:

1. need and availability of land, taking into account surrounding land uses;
2. impact on amenity from pollution, design of site and visual impact;
3. sensitivity of area, e.g., high quality agricultural land;
4. identify any environmental benefits;
5. impact on road and other transport networks and on the surrounding environment;
6. condition of site and potential for remediation.

Where a Planning Authority identifies a risk of environmental incident, the guide advises that it should rely on the advice of the pollution control authority. Where the consequences of an incident have been considered and are unacceptable to the Planning Authority and cannot be overcome by planning controls, the Planning Authority may have to refuse consent. If this happens, however, the Planning Authority has to show the land use planning reasons which have led it to its decision. These reasons must not be matters which could have been resolved by environmental controls.

An example of where the risk of environmental incident resulted in a refusal of planning consent is the case of Envirocor Waste Holdings v. SOSE. This case concerned a planning application for a waste transfer facility near to a factory manufacturing cocoa products. The fear of incident was the risk of malodorous emissions prejudicing the operation of the food processing plant. The inspector dismissed the appeal: he considered the risk of harm to the cocoa factory represented an overriding objection to the proposal. The applicants appealed against this decision to the High Court. It was decided that there had been no evidence that a tainting incident would definitely occur as the Inspector had suggested, and he had made no effort to estimate the likely frequency of a tainting incident. The Court did not understand the inspector's conclusions that malodorous emissions would adversely affect the food processing plant. In this case the inspector's fear of possible incident was not backed up by evidence and his thought process was not properly set out in his decision letter and therefore the decision was overturned.

The publication of PPG23 was delayed pending the determination of a case which highlighted the conflict and overlap between planning and environmental controls. The case was Gateshead Metropolitan Borough Council v. SOSE: the rationale in this case was that planning permission for a development which would also require environmental consent should not be refused purely on pollution grounds unless the environmental consent would clearly be refused. If, however, issues were outstanding which should properly be decided by Her Majesty's Inspectorate of Pollution (HMIP) on an application for an authorisation and which were not sufficient to warrant a refusal of environmental consents, then consent should not be refused on environmental grounds.

The facts of the case were that Northumbrian Water applied for planning permission to build a chemical waste incinerator in Gateshead. An environmental authorisation was required from HMIP, planning permission was applied for and refused. Northumbrian Water appealed against refusal of planning permission and the matter went to inquiry. The Inspector recommended refusal on environmental grounds because of the impact of discharges into the air on air quality and the environment generally. The Secretary of State, however, ignored his inspector's recommendations and granted permission.

In his decision letter he explained: 'While the planning system alone must determine the location of facilities of this kind, taking account of the provisions of the development plan and of the material considerations, the Secretary of State considers that it is not the role of the planning system to duplicate controls under the Environmental Protection Act 1990. Whilst it is necessary to take account of the impact of potential emissions on neighbouring land uses when considering whether or not to grant permission, control of those emissions should be regulated by HMIP.'

It was concluded that environmental controls were sufficient to deal with the emissions from the plant and the risk of harm to human health as a result of those emissions. Gateshead Metropolitan Borough Council applied to the High Court to quash the Secretary of State's decision and their application was refused; they then appealed to the Court of Appeal.

The overlap between the two systems was recognised and condoned in the Gateshead decision, where the deputy judge said: 'Where two statutory controls overlap, it is not helpful, in my view, to try to define where one control ends and another begins in terms of some abstract principle. If one does so, there is a very real danger that one loses sight of the obligation to consider each case on its individual merits.' He then cautioned: 'Lest this judgment be misinterpreted, I stress that this decision is not carte blanche for applicants for planning permission to seek to ignore the pollution implications of their proposed development and say leave it all to the Environmental Protection Act.'

The Court decided that the pollution of the atmosphere is a material consideration in determining a planning application. However, the environmental regime which exists under the Environmental Protection Act 1990 to prevent or mitigate this is also a material consideration. It was decided that only if it is clear that HMIP would refuse an authorisation that the Secretary of State could refuse the planning consent on environmental grounds. In the present case the inspector had been addressing such issues as what discharges would be acceptable, and whether the integrated pollution control regime under the Environmental Protection Act 1990 could control them. These questions are within the competence and jurisdiction of HMIP and therefore the Secretary of State was right to say these were matters which should properly be dealt with by HMIP. It was made quite clear that the grant of planning consent should not inhibit HMIP from refusing the grant of an authorisation if it decides that is the proper decision.

The Gateshead case concerned an outline planning application and PPG23 makes it quite clear that outline applications are not acceptable if the risk of pollution is significant. The conclusion is therefore that the Local Planning Authority can consider the potential for pollution of a development but only so far as it impacts on the current and future use of the land.

PPG23 and Gateshead leave us with the situation where there are two distinct situations, one where pollution problems can be overcome and permission should be granted, and one where evidence states that pollution problems cannot be overcome because the environmental problems are too great and planning permission should be refused. This means that Local Planning Authorities will be considering the potential for a pollution incident and the general potential pollution problems of a development. However, they should be liaising with the Environment Agency or the respective bodies and relying on their advice as to whether the potential problems are controllable or not. This in no way gives a clear cut guide and creates a system of overlapping forums for the control of development.

OTHER ENVIRONMENTAL CONSTRAINTS ON DEVELOPMENT

Other Government policies intended to control development driven by environmental problems are the National Rivers Authority Groundwater Protection Zones, PPG24 *Planning and Noise*, PPG13 on *Transport*, PPG20 *Coastal Planning*, PPG9 *Nature Conservation*, PPG22 on *Renewable Energy* and PPG6 *Town Centres and Retail Development*. It is clear that environmental concerns will increasingly constrain the implementation of development proposals and carry an increasing importance in the determination of planning applications. Some of these individual environmental policies reflect the Government's commitment to the overall strategy of sustainable development.

SUSTAINABLE DEVELOPMENT

The aim of sustainable development is to provide a balance between economic growth, development and environmental resource protection.

What is sustainable development?The document *Our Common Future* 1987 which was the report of the Brundtland Commission states that sustainable development means:

Development that meets the needs of the present without comprising the ability of future generations to meet their own needs.

In June 1994 the Government published its first annual energy report, where it stated that sustainability does not imply that all renewable resources must be permanently preserved.

This will inevitably impact on the planning system and a policy document was produced in 1994 called *Sustainable Development: the UK Strategy*. An example which it gives of its effect on development proposals is a development which would have an impact on the need for water. It encourages the regeneration of urban land and buildings and derelict or contaminated land and it recognises the role of the planning system in achieving the aims of sustainable development.

Clause 4 of the new Environment Bill which came out in December 1994 requires the Environment Agency to work towards achieving sustainable development. In order to implement this in 1995, the Department of the Environment released a draft of its guidance to the Environment Agency on how it is expected to contribute to sustainable development.

The emerging policy from central government shows evidence of its Sustainable Development Strategy to reduce the need to travel. PPG13 on transport addresses this issue. It states: 'By planning land use and transport together in ways which enable people to carry out their everyday activities with less need to travel, local planning authorities can reduce reliance on the private car and make a significant contribution to the environmental goals set out in the Government's Sustainable Development Strategy.'

The Trunk Road Review Programme, published in March 1994, forecasts a doubling of traffic growth by the year 2025. In line with its sustainable development policy on transport, the Government cannot address this need through continued road building.

The success of the objective stated in PPG13 to reduce car travel is largely dependent on improvements to public transport systems. It remains to be seen whether sufficient Government funding will be made available to enable these improvements to be made.

Sustainable development policies will encourage the consolidation of development within city centres; they will bring about a change in parking policies to discourage private car travel and will restrict sprawling development even where there is no Green Belt. Sustainable development policies will also encourage the redevelopment of contaminated land.

CONTAMINATED LAND

The clean-up of contaminated land is now to be on a suitable-for-use basis and guidance has been issued as to standards for certain specified after uses. Draft guidance was issued in May 1995 setting out criteria to determine whether land is contaminated within the definition of Part IIA of the Environmental Protection Act 1990. This is the first time in 20 years that any Government has given any indication of what levels of contamination are suitable or acceptable for certain uses. Prior to this the development industry has been struggling along with a patchwork of European and American guidelines, and there have been no consistent clean-up levels across the country.

The suitable-for-use approach is designed to put remediation standards at a level which will enable cost-effective solutions to be implemented. It is hoped that the approach will ease the cost of remediation, encourage the redevelopment of brown land and help relieve the pressure on greenfield sites. The danger perhaps is that owners will seek the easy option with the lowest level of clean-up needed and cause a glut of car parks, which have the lowest clean-up requirements.

There are new powers under the Environment Act 1995 for Local Authorities to issue remediation notices. The general rules follow the 'polluter pays' principle but they also pose new potential liabilities for owners and occupiers of land if the polluter cannot be found. There are powers to carry out remediation works in default by local authorities. However, this does not take into account the reality of Local Authority funding and the cash flow consequences of carrying out remediation works and then seeking to recover costs from the owner. In practice it is doubtful whether Local Authorities will be able to afford to do this, except in the most serious cases.

The Environment Bill has already been weakened as it passes through Parliament as a result of representations by industrial and financial interests. The definition of contaminated land is land which appears to the local authorities to be in such a condition because of substances in, on or under it which are seen to be causing, or pose a serious risk of causing, harm or pollution of controlled waters. The amendments mean that land will be treated as contaminated where significant harm is being caused or there is a significant possibility of such harm being caused.

Local Authorities are given a duty to identify contaminated sites and there will not be public registers of sites where the Local Authority has taken action under the Act, containing details of what has been done. The main tool for the clean-up of contaminated sites will be the issue of remediation notices by Local Authorities. It is interesting to note that a cost–benefit exercise is recommended. If it would be unreasonable to require clean-up because the cost is disproportionate to the seriousness of the harm or pollution, then a remediation notice will not be issued.

Conclusion

It is fundamentally important that in making decisions regarding development there is a balance between environmental protection and economic growth.

The UK strategy on sustainable development shows how the planning system can play a large part in the government's strategy for improving the environment. The planning system has always been the tool for balancing the interests of the private sector in seeking to maximise development and the requirements of the public sector to protect the amenity of their area and the environment generally. Now with the presumption in favour of the Development Plan together with all the economic material considerations planning will pay an even greater role in ensuring that development is carried out in a sustainable fashion. Sustainable development is not a purely negative concept. It is about growth, but growth in an environmentally friendly way. Bearing in mind the decision regarding planning gain in the Tesco case and the increase in the importance of the Development Plan, it can be expected that an increasing number of Development Plan policies will emerge requiring environmental benefits and mitigating factors to be provided as part of development itself.

The way forward

When considering the impact of these trends in planning law and policy, one sees an increasing importance attached to Development Plan policies and consequentially an ever-increasing importance in challenging and making representations to Local Plans at Inquiry. It also enhances the role of the Government in policing the progress of development plans, as the policies which appear in Local Development Plans will carry so much weight and determine development in the area to such a great degree.

This is particularly important when looking at both the control of speculative development and the changes which have recently occurred in planning gain law. It is more than clear that there is confusion, and a dichotomy of opinions which exist at different levels of decision making about what is appropriate planning gain. The development plan can sanction planning gain which would not pass the more stringent tests applied by DoE Circular 16/91.

Table 11.1 List of cases referred to in Chapter 11

Bolton Metropolitan Borough Council v. SOSE CA [1994] 2 PLR 42

City of Bradford Metropolitan Council v. Secretary of State for the Environment [1986] 53 P & CR 55

Envirocor Waste Holdings v. Secretary of State for the Environment and Others [1995] EGCS 60

Gateshead Metropolitan Borough Council v. Secretary of State for the Environment and Northumbrian Water Group Plc [1994] JPL 138

Newham London Borough Council v. Secretary of State for the Environment [1995] EGCS 6

Pelham Homes Limited v. Secretary of State for the Environment [1994] JPL B 122

R. v. Canterbury City Council ex parte Springimage [1994] JPL 427

R. v. ex parte Plymouth and South Devon Co-operative Society Limited [1993] 67 P & CR 78

R. v. Westminster City Council ex parte Monahan [1989] 2 All ER 74

R. v. South Northamptonshire District Council ex parte Crest Homes Plc [1994] 3 PLR 47

Stringer v. Minister of Housing and Local Government [1971] 1 All ER 65

Tesco Stores Limited v. Secretary of State for the Environment and Others [1995] 2 All ER 636

Tesco Stores Limited v. Secretary of State for the Environment and West Oxfordshire District Council and Another 68 P & CR 219 Court of Appeal

When considering the protection of the environment, a large amount of policy has emerged over the last two years to try and marry the development of land with environmental protection towards an aim of sustainable development. This means that there is again a role for central government to play in policing local development plans to ensure that these aims are achieved. It will be interesting to see what changes the government does suggest to the local plan system to make the local plan system more effective, economic and speedy as this is now such a critical part of the planning system.

Chapter 12

URBAN PLANNING IN A PAN-EUROPEAN CONTEXT

David Ludlow

Europe and the profession

This chapter focuses on the various ways in which the European Commission as a supra-national governmental agency is exerting an increasing influence upon the evolution of town planning within the European Union (CEC, 1991a; RTPI, 1995). At present there is no single locus of this influence, as policy and legislation supported by funding actions are emerging from many of the Directorates-General of the Commission, of which there are 24. Two are of major importance for planning, Environment, Nuclear Safety and Civil Protection (DG XI) and Regional Policy (DG XVI). Many others have at least some involvement in planning, including Employment, Industrial Relations and Social Affairs (DG V), Agriculture (DG VI), Transport (DG VII), Energy (DG XVII) and Tourism (DG XXIII).

These EU Directorates-General have an impact on land use and development, whether it be through financial support for development and infrastructure (Baldock and Wenning, 1990), legislation on the environment (Collins, 1991), or by facilitating and encouraging innovation and the transfer of experience between Member States (Cecchini, 1988). It is necessary, therefore, to identify and assess the influence and significance of a number of individual strands in order to specify the totality and magnitude of the Commission's influence.

However, the principal focus of this chapter is upon the urban and environmental dimensions of Community policy and legislation and other initiatives. It aims to provide an overview of a highly dynamic situation and to relate this wherever appropriate to the specifics of the UK planning context. This focus excludes consideration of both the rural and regional dimensions and the other areas of the Commission's activities, referred to above, which impinge upon land use planning. This conscious selection is justified on the basis that the urban dimension, although in many respects embryonic in nature, is nonetheless the focus of policy and legislation which at present most closely addresses issues of relevance to the UK planning profession.

In addition, a number of important matters affecting land use directly or indirectly have been omitted from consideration including, for instance, employment legislation; social issues including ethnic relations, crime and law and order; and demographic trends including changes in the Community's age structure and the effects of immigration. These matters are excluded from the chapter on the basis that their prime effects would be felt more indirectly, with less effect on the day-to-day operation of planning legislation and the planning system. However, in a later Volume which will be related more specifically to Social Planning these issues will be discussed within a more appropriate context.

A full understanding of the competence and rationale and indeed substance of intervention by the European Commission in the development of policy and legislation which impinges upon the practice of town planning requires a knowledge of the evolution of the European Union, the nature of its institutions and decision-making processes and the political context of the Commission which is well beyond the scope of this section. It is intended therefore to wrest from this historical, organisational and political milieu the principal characteristics of the Community's institutions whilst reflecting on a significant debate within the Commission regarding the responsibilities for planning issues between the Commission and Member States and on the extent to which intervention by the Commission is legitimate in the context of subsidiarity (Ware and Miller, 1991) .

As a starting point it is interesting to reflect briefly on some evidence of the perceptions of the UK planning community of the impact of Europe on the profession. In November 1992 the RTPI commissioned Professor H W E Davies of the University of Reading to undertake a study (Davies, 1994) with the following terms of reference:

> to consider the activities of the European Community and their likely impact on town and country planning in Europe with particular reference to the UK. The impacts of particular interest are on planning legislation, planning policy priorities, planning practice and professional activities, and professional training. Recommendations should be made on appropriate action to the Institute.

In the introduction to the study Robin Thompson stated:

> This study exploded one myth before it began. There has been widespread lament about the indifference of planners to the European context – an alleged compound of arrogance and insularity. However, returns of the author's initial questionnaire provided some substantial evidence of a growing awareness of the European dimension amongst planners.

A postal survey of local planning authorities in this country referred to by Robin Thompson provided information about the level of awareness about the EU amongst local planning authorities, and showed that two-thirds of the respondents had read at least one major Community report with land use implications, and about half were directly supported by the EU, chiefly through Regional Policy funding (Council of Europe, 1989; Garner and Brafells, 1986; Steer, Davies and Gleave Ltd, 1989). A smaller number were actively engaged in a wide variety of pilot projects or networks with cities and regions in the rest of Europe.

Most significantly, nearly half of the local planning authorities responding to the survey expected to see a substantial increase in the impact of EU policy on land use planning in the next five years, chiefly through stricter environmental policies, but also including economic development and links with other countries.

The Reading report (Davies, 1994) concluded that what the Community is doing, and the ways in which it is developing, will affect planning and property development in Britain (Punter, 1991), as it will affect planning in every other Member State of the Community, through:

- its direct and indirect impact on planning policies and legislation at the national, regional and local levels;
- and in the constraints which it may impose;
- but more significantly, in the opportunities which it will open up for the development of planning practice.

The report also concludes that any impact by the Community on land use planning will take place within the existing framework of the operation of the planning system and the changes which it faces, in terms of policies and practice as well as local government reorganisation. It is also clear that the potential impact will be influenced by the understanding by the UK planning community of the opportunities presented by, and by active participation in, the development of a pan-European planning perspective.

An essential prerequisite of this understanding is a basic knowledge of the role of the EU and its institutions, as well as awareness of the key issues identified with the development of the urban system in the European Community. These issues form the focus of the next two sections.

The European Community, its institutions and planning

The European Economic Community, as it was originally known, was created in 1957 by the Treaty of Rome (CEC, 1957), the original Member States being France, Germany, Italy, Belgium, the Netherlands, and Luxembourg. The United Kingdom, Denmark and Ireland joined in 1973, Greece in 1981, Spain and Portugal in 1986, and Austria, Sweden and Finland in 1995.

The Community's principal institutions are as follows (Lasok, 1991):

- *Council of Ministers*: the prime decision-taking body in the European Community, acting on proposals made to it formally by the Commission. It comprises ministers from each of the fifteen Member States with the chairmanship rotating every six months amongst the fifteen. Its membership varies according to the matters under discussion, whether it be, for instance, regional policy or the environment. Depending on which policies are under consideration, it may act by majority decision, by a qualified majority decision, or by unanimous vote of all fifteen Member States. The European Council is the meeting of the heads of state or prime ministers.

- *European Commission*: based in Brussels, is the permanent executive of the EU, with sole responsibility for initiating proposals to the Council and for overseeing the implementation of all of the EU's policies and programmes. It functions through 24 Directorates-General. The Commission has to consult, and is advised by, an Economic and Social Committee on all relevant matters.
- *European Court of Justice*: interprets and rules on legal questions raised by the Treaties and EU legislation.
- *European Parliament*: consists of 626 elected members from the fifteen Member States, although under the Treaty on European Union (CEC, 1992c) its oversight of Community legislation has increased to some extent. Its role is to debate all matters of EU policy, to question the Council and the Commission, and to supervise the budget.

The Community operates through a variety of instruments and mechanisms established under the Treaty of Rome (CEC, 1957), as amended, including powers in respect of:

- *Legislation*: passed either in the form of:
  Regulation – has a general application and is 'binding in its entirety and directly applicable in all Member States' (art. 189, Treaty of Rome).
  Directive – is 'binding in its entirety upon those to whom it is addressed' (art. 189, Treaty of Rome). Member States have to pass into national legislation, with some discretion as to how and when this might be done.
  Recommendations or Opinions – 'shall have no binding force' (art. 189, Treaty of Rome). Issued about matters of EU policy which however are not binding, but more in the nature of an encouragement to act.
  Decision – is 'binding in its entirety upon those to whom it is addressed' (art. 189, Treaty of Rome). This is an atypical instrument, principally used in relation to external accords (such as international Conventions and Protocols).
- *Communication*: sets out a Commission action plan and may contain proposals for legislation.
- *Green Paper*: sets out the Commission's policy orientation, as a basis for receiving reactions from Member States and interested parties.
- *White Paper*: sets out the concrete actions to be introduced into the Commission work programme.
- *Funds*: allocated for programmes such as the Common Agricultural Policy and Regional Policy.
- *Research*: including studies and sponsorship of other forms of action such as pilot projects in order to assist in the development of policy.

The relationship between the Community and a Member State, however, is not a simple hierarchical one, but rather an interactive one, in the form of a dialogue between sovereign bodies. So in addition to a policy or regulation being initiated by the EU, initiatives also originate from Member States. In the field of environmental planning, for example, Directive 79/409 (see European Union Controls section after Bibliography), on the conservation of wild birds, is based largely on British legislation, pioneered by the influence of the RSPB.

The Maastricht Treaty on European Union (CEC, 1992c) further amends the Treaty of Rome. It takes the process a stage further towards full economic and political union. Article 130s of the Treaty provided the first explicit, formal mention of town and country planning by setting minimum standards rather than ensuring common action. In amplification of the EU's environmental objectives, the Article states that:

> the Council, acting unanimously on a proposal from the Commission and after consulting the European Parliament and the Economic and Social Committee, shall adopt ... measures concerning town and country planning, land use with the exception of waste management and measure of a general nature, and management of water resources.

However, the article is subject to several qualifications:

- Article 130t states that any such measures 'shall not prevent Member States from maintaining or introducing more stringent protective measures', and
- the article is subject to the unanimity rule, that all fifteen ministers must agree.

EU competence in this field should also be considered in the principle of subsidiarity. Subsidiarity is defined in Article 3b of the Treaty on European Union. It states that the EU shall take action:

> only if and in so far as the objectives of the proposed action cannot be sufficiently achieved by the Member States and can therefore, by reason of the scale or effects of the proposed action, be better achieved by the Community.

The meaning of subsidiarity was further clarified when a set of Guidelines on when and how the principle should be applied was issued by the European Council at Edinburgh in December 1992. The Guidelines lay down the tests to be used and the procedures to be followed as an integral part of establishing that any proposals for action by the Commission do conform to the principle of subsidiarity.

The matter is complex, especially where as in the case of planning, the competence for action is shared between the Community and Member States. But, in essence, the EU can act only where it is explicitly given the power to do so by the Treaties and any such action shall not go beyond what is necessary to achieve the objectives of the Treaties. Furthermore, the Commission is required to present an annual report to the European Council and the European Parliament on the application of the Treaty in respect of subsidiarity.

The guiding principle for town planning elaborated by Laurens Jan Brinkhorst, Director-General for the Environment (Brinkhorst, 1991) in the context of 'the need to protect the environment of the EU as a whole, not just of individual Member States', is that the EU should intervene only where any required action would transcend the frontiers of Member States, or could be undertaken more efficiently by the EU than by Member States acting separately. The principle is therefore one of partnership in which it is left to the local and national levels to put together the most appropriate combination of instruments designed to achieve well-defined and transparent objectives fixed at the Community level. The choice of action is therefore left to the local or national level, within an overall framework set by the EU.

Within the focus identified for this chapter two areas of EU responsibility are of particular relevance to land use and planning. They are:

- environmental policies and programmes (DG XI) (Haigh,1987)
- urban policy (responsibility of several DGs).

Given the focus of this chapter on the urban dimension the next section considers the substantive issues identified with the urban dimension at the pan-European level.

Characteristics of the European urban system

Recent changes in the European urban system have been assessed in depth in the study *Urbanisation and the Function of Cities in the European Community* (Dawson, 1991). The share of Europe's population living in all settlements defined as urban continues to increase, with the largest cities continuing to house a very significant proportion of the population. Over two thirds of West Europeans now live in urban areas with populations exceeding 300,000, and in individual Member States the share of urban residents in the total population ranges from 65 to 90 per cent.

Overall, the EU is the most highly urbanised region in the world with 79% of its population living in urban areas: a close network of cities with more than 10,000 inhabitants as compared with around 1,000 urban agglomerations of the same size in both the USA and Japan. In the EU, 169 cities have more than 200,000 inhabitants and 32 more than 1 million accounting together for 56% of the total European urban population. Small and medium-size cities are of particular importance for the EU's spatial organisation since 44% of the urban population lives in agglomerations of 10,000 to 200,000 inhabitants.

However, urbanisation patterns have not been consistent across space and time. Different patterns of urbanisation are the result of differences in countries' economic and social development. Southern European cities have been growing faster while northern cities have reached stabilisation. In particular, the largest European cities have experienced an alternate cycle of growth and decline in the form of population expansion and suburbanisation and finally de-urbanisation in favour of smaller and medium-size cities.

Urbanisation patterns have followed important changes in the economic structure in the last few decades. Since the late sixties, most large cities and the core of metropolitan areas have been rapidly de-industrialised. At the same time on the periphery of large metropolitan areas there has been an accelerated process of tertiarisation and the attraction of dynamic firms and international services. These trends reflect the shift in countries' structural changes from traditional industries towards knowledge-based manufacturing industries and services. As a consequence of these changes large metropolitan areas and cities have developed problem areas characterised by high levels of spatially concentrated unemployment, poverty, and urban dereliction, accompanied by severe social and environmental problems.

These social and environmental impacts of economic restructuring upon various European cities reflect a number of important factors such as their size, regional location, and economic base (Ambiente Italia, 1994). Urban decline has affected primarily cities dependent on heavy industries and port functions rather than cities whose economy is based on favoured sectors such as research and development in manufacturing and services. The most important factors influencing these impacts are the function that cities perform and their adaptability to change.

The success or failure of cities to adapt as economic restructuring and unification proceed depends in many ways upon the cities themselves, and in particular upon visionary political leadership and sound management. It may be argued that the emergence of the entrepreneurial city is likely to be characterised by strong civic leadership and by the establishment of effective local partnerships between the public, private and voluntary sectors (SAUS, 1991).

The European Commission Expert Group on the Urban Environment (ECEG, 1994) suggests that the sustainable city will initially share many of the organisational attributes of the entrepreneurial city. However, it argues that 'the environmental quality of the sustainable city will be substantially better, and there will be a stronger focus on reducing the use of resources, waste minimisation, equity and social welfare. Cities perceived as sustainable will in future come to be seen as attractive locations for investment as well as pleasant places in which to live and work.'

A comprehensive review of the state of the built and natural environment in European cities is provided in the Urban Environment chapter of *Europe's Environment: The Dobris Assessment* (European Environment Agency, 1995; and compare OECD, 1990). The chapter analyses the quality of the physical environment in 51 European cities using data on 20 indicators, focusing on urban patterns (population, land use cover, areas of dereliction and urban renewal and urban mobility), urban flows (water consumption and waste, energy, transport of goods, waste production, treatment and disposal, and recycling) and urban environmental quality (air and water quality, noise, traffic safety, housing conditions, accessibility to green space and wildlife quality). Five key problems are identified – air quality, noise, traffic, housing quality, and the extent of, and variable access to, green areas and open space.

The Dobris Assessment in many ways complements the analysis of economic and social trends, for the links between urbanisation and economic change and environmental conditions are firmly established. Different patterns and stages of economic development generate different kinds of environmental problem and distribute them unequally both within and between cities. The European Commission Expert Group on the Urban Environment (ECEG, 1994) indicates that in areas of both growth and decline the development and re-development of buildings and infrastructure have direct impacts upon natural ecosystems. Congestion, pollution from traffic, stress and noise have major consequences for health, and, more generally, for the quality of life. Furthermore the increasing degradation of the urban environment increases pressures of cities on natural resources. Environmental problems from local to global level often originate in cities. The degradation of the urban environment accelerates particulary in periods of rapid change. Both urban growth and decline have caused increased pressure on the urban environment.

It is apparent from the above brief analysis of the evolution and characteristics of European cities that a major challenge concerns their capacity to reverse interdependent economic, social and environmental trends. The next section examines the various ways in which the EU is addressing these issues in respect of environmental policy and legislation.

EU environmental policy action programmes

The Treaty of Rome (1957), which first established the Community as a trading bloc, made no specific mention of the environment. EU environmental laws initially had to develop within a framework designed to encourage the free trade of goods and services within the Community. It was not until 1987 that important Treaty changes introduced by the Single European Act (CEC, 1987b) gave the EU's environmental policy explicit legal backing for the first time (Brinkhorst, 1991).

Prior to 1987 the context for EU environmental policy was principally defined by the growing recognition that the very economic success of the EU was generating adverse environmental consequences including pollution of water and damage to wildlife caused by intensive agriculture; poor air quality in cities caused by exhaust gases from ever-denser road traffic; and damage to the global environment resulting from releases of carbon dioxide or CFCs into the upper atmosphere, all of which might act to constrain further economic growth.

Critically it was clear that environmental problems of this nature do not conform with national frontiers and that pan-European cooperation would be required to ameliorate these problems and safeguard continued economic growth. Following a declaration by the EU's Heads of State and Government in October 1972, the earliest manifestation of an EU environmental policy came in 1973, with the publication of the First Action

Programme on the Environment (CEC, 1973). Subsequently there have been four such Programmes (CEC, 1977; 1983; 1987a; 1992a).

Environmental Action Programmes effectively have two main purposes: first to identify specific proposals for legislation that the Commission intends to put forward over subsequent years, and second to provide an opportunity to develop new concepts in environmental policy and identify new directions for the future. The Action Programmes provide a policy framework, but unlike items of Community legislation, they cannot be regarded as constituting Community policy. This is because, although the Council of Ministers will adopt a resolution on the Action Programme to approve its 'general approach', the Council does not commit itself to every point of detail. Each item will subsequently be decided on its merits after the Commission has made a formal proposal to the Council.

The First Action Programme provided a general statement of the objectives and principles of a Community environmental policy and set out the actions that the Commission proposed based around three organising principles:

- that the polluter should pay
- that prevention is better than cure
- that all EU decision making should take into account environmental effects

The Second (CEC, 1977) and Third (CEC, 1983) Action Programmes both increased the emphasis upon preventative measures and by 1987 some 200 items of environmental legislation had been agreed under either Article 100 of the Treaty of Rome (on the approximation of laws affecting the functioning of the Common Market), or under the 'catch- all' Article 235. However, the lack of a clear legal base for the Community's environmental policy was evident and criticised in several Member States, particularly in Germany, and by the UK House of Lords' Select Committee on the European Community.

A second rationale for the development of a common approach to environmental problems by the European Community and the legal basis of environment policy emerged from the recognition that fair competition between member states and the free movement of goods throughout the EU's Single Market required common environmental standards to keep the 'playing field' level. As the development of the internal market progressed, it became more apparent that harmonisation of environmental standards was an important element in securing fair competition, and that the Community had a role in ensuring that standards were set at a high level of protection.

As a consequence important changes to the Treaty of Rome came into effect through the Single European Act (1987), including a new Environment Title (Articles 130r, s and t) which for the first time gave an explicit legal underpinning to the Community's environmental policy.

The environmental objectives set out in Article 130r(1) were framed:

- to preserve, protect and improve the quality of the environment
- to contribute towards protecting human health
- to ensure a prudent and rational utilisation of natural resources

These objectives were very broad, enabling the Commission to propose legislation for new environmental target areas. Consequently EU environment policy expanded from pollution control (water, waste, air, noise, and the control of harmful substances like chemicals) to cover the environmental standards of traded products; the protection of wildlife habitats and countryside matters; the assessment of the environmental impact of major development projects; and freedom of access to environmental information.

The Act also added the important new principle that environmental protection requirements shall be a component of the Community's other policies (amendment to Article 130r (Lasok, 1991)), so strengthening the power of the Commission's Environmental Directorate in monitoring policies developed elsewhere in the Commission.

The Single European Act (1987) preceded the Fourth Action Programme on the Environment (CEC, 1987a). The Action Programme incorporated the 'integrative principle' of amended Article 130r (Lasok, 1991) as one of four underlying principles stressing the need to integrate environmental policies more fully with other EU sectoral policies, e.g. environmental goals incorporated into ERDF grants. The introduction in the UK of 'integrated pollution control' in Part I of the Environmental Protection Act is a reflection of this approach, and the Commission itself is now preparing proposals for 'integrated permitting' for industrial plants. The Fourth Environmental Action Programme also identified the need for the use of 'economic instruments' as an alternative or additional method to legislative regulation for securing environmental protection.

The 1990 Dublin Summit marked a further significant advance for EC environmental policy with the adoption of the declaration *The Environmental Imperative*, which set out guidelines based on the principles of sustainable development.

The remainder of this chapter examines the emergence of sustainability as a key concept underlying EU urban environmental policy and action.

Sustainable development – policy dimension

'Sustainable development' was defined by the Brundtland Report (WCED, 1987) as 'development which meets the needs of the present without compromising the ability of future generations to meet their own needs.' This principle is now enshrined within EU environmental policy by the Maastricht Treaty on European Union 1992. At Maastricht EU Member States formally accepted for the first time that 'sustainable and non-inflationary growth respecting the environment' should be one of the EU's principal objectives. Similarly Article 3 of the common provisions of the Treaty refers to 'economic and social progress which is balanced and sustainable.'

Overall these changes represent important shifts in the ethos of the Community away from the pursuit of economic growth regardless of its environmental consequences. Now, environmental protection is placed on an equal footing in the Treaty with economic concerns, symbolising a significant step towards the 'greening' of the EU Treaty.

These shifts in policy focus are reflected in *Towards Sustainability* (CEC, 1992a), which sets out the basis of the EU Fifth Action Programme of policy and action in relation to the environment and sustainable development. The programme extends over the period to 2000 with a mid-term review in 1995. The Fifth Action Programme addresses continuing concerns within the Community for the impact of the Single Market on natural resources and the environment (including built environment); global concerns about climate change, deforestation, energy crises; underdevelopment and economic and political change in central and eastern Europe. The programme also addresses the objectives introduced by the new Treaty on European Union (Maastricht) for the promotion of sustainable growth.

One important ingredient of sustainability is the integration of environmental concerns into other public policies and economic activities (DoE, 1994). This concept is emphasised in both the Maastricht Treaty and the Fifth Environment Action Programme. The latter underlines the need to integrate environmental considerations 'into the formulation and implementation of economic and sectoral policies, in the decisions of public authorities, in the conduct and development of production processes, and in industrial behaviour and choice.'

The explicit recognition of the urban dimension of EU policies has developed as a further facet of the broadening of EU environmental policy in parallel with the incorporation of the sustainability principle (EC, 1994); indeed the two are increasingly interwoven in EU policy. It is clearly significant that the Fifth Action Programme specifically identifies integrated sectoral and spatial policy as one of the seven instruments, other than legislation being utilised to secure sustainability objectives. Directorate-General XI, as the policy Directorate responsible for the generation of much EU environmental policy and coordinator of the LIFE Programme, implementing the Fifth Action Programme, clearly has a pivotal policy implementation role in this regard.

The recent work programme of the Directorate has in large measure focused on the implementation of concepts identified in the Green Paper on the Urban Environment (SAUS, 1991), in which the theme of the development of sustainable urban policy frameworks has occupied a prominent position. Specific studies arising out of the Green Paper have already been published by the Directorate including, for example, *Villes sans Voitures*, which examines the ways in which cities can function when cars are given a lower priority.

The Green Paper on the Urban Environment in 1990 established the rationale and called for detailed consideration of the urban environment in EU policies. The Green Paper marked an important step forward in linking environmental sustainability and the quality of urban life. It discussed the key role of cities as the home of an increasing proportion of Europe's population and as the organising units of economic, social, cultural and political life.

Subsequently, the establishment of the Expert Group on the Urban Environment by the European Commission in 1991, following the publication of the Green Paper via the Council of Ministers resolution on the Green Paper (CEC, 1991c), offered the opportunity to explore the urban dimension of EU environmental policy and to advise on how the Commission could contribute to the improvement of the urban environment. The Group composed of national representatives and independent experts has a broad remit, set out in the Council of Ministers resolution on the Green Paper, as follows:

- to consider how future town and land use planning strategies can incorporate environmental objectives;
- to advise how the Commission could develop the urban environment dimension within Community environment policy; and
- to consider how the Community could further contribute to the improvement of the urban environment.

In 1993 the Expert Group launched the European Sustainable Cities Project with principal aims as follows:

- to contribute to the development of thinking about sustainability in European urban settings;
- to foster a wide exchange of experience;
- to disseminate best practice about sustainability at local level; and, in the longer term,
- to formulate recommendations to influence at European Union, Member State, regional and local level, as called for in the Council resolution of 1991.

European sustainable cities project

The European Sustainable Cities Project is based upon a challenging experiment (Ludlow, 1995) in pan-European networking (EURONET) which links over 40 urban environment experts from the fifteen Member States. A further 30 experts are involved in the Expert Group, including representatives from relevant Directorates-General of the European Commission and a range of international organisations with an interest in urban issues, including the Council of Europe, the Council of European Municipalities and Regions (CEMR), Eurocities, the European Academy for the Urban Environment, the European Foundation for Improvement of Living and Working Conditions, the International Council for Local Environmental Initiatives (ICLEI), the OECD, the United Towns Organisation (UTO) and the World Health Organisation (WHO).

The first output of the work of the Urban Environment Expert Group is the report on European Sustainable Cities (ECEG, 1994). The report explores the prospects for sustainability in urban settlements of different scales, from urban regions to small towns. However, the main focus is on cities, in line with the Green Paper on the Urban Environment.

The report reiterates the conclusions identified elsewhere that despite a growing raft of legislation, directives and regulations, European cities continue to face economic and social problems and environmental degradation. The report argues that new ways of managing the urban environment need to be found so that European cities can both solve local problems and contribute to regional and global sustainability. The report argues as follows:

> The challenge of urban sustainability is to solve both the problems experienced within cities and the problems caused by cities, recognising that cities themselves provide many potential solutions. City managers must seek to meet the social and economic needs of urban residents while respecting local, regional and global natural systems, solving problems locally where possible, rather than shifting them to other spatial locations or passing them on to the future.

The report is aimed at a wide audience. For whilst elected representatives in cities, city managers/administrators and urban environment professionals have key roles to play in urban management for sustainability, successful progress depends upon the active involvement of local communities and the creation of partnerships with the private and voluntary sectors within the context of a strong and supportive government framework at all levels. Political leadership and commitment are critical if progress is to be made.

Sustainable development is identified as a much broader concept than environmental protection. It has economic and social as well as environmental dimensions, and embraces notions of equity between people in the present and between generations. It implies that further development should take place only as long as it is within the carrying capacity of natural and man-made systems.

An important argument derived from these principles is that sustainable development must be planned for and that market forces alone cannot achieve the integration of environmental, social and economic concerns. The report therefore seeks to provide a framework within which innovative approaches to the planning of sustainability can be explored. In this respect the report aims to identify a set of ecological, social, economic and organisational principles and tools for urban management which may be applied in a variety of European urban settings and which can be used selectively as cities move towards sustainability.

As such the Sustainable Cities Project has both an institutional and a policy focus. It is concerned with the capacity of local governments to deliver sustainability. The local authority planner is therefore well placed to participate in the development and formulation of multi-levelled corporate strategies for the sustainable management of the local environment. Such action aims to reinforce and complement global initiatives.

The report strongly advocates the development of city-wide management strategies for sustainability, although in recognition of the need for transition in urban management the report considers the application of this approach to a range of key policy areas with the intention of facilitating integration across the policy areas. Urban economy, land use planning and mobility and access form the core of the policy areas selected as priorities in the first report.

Many of the principles and mechanisms for sustainability are already present in land use planning systems. However, further tools may be needed. The report identifies the need for greater prioritisation of environmental issues in planning policy, advocates strategic environmental assessment of policies and plans, reviews the use of indicators in land use planning and places strong emphasis on public participation in formulating policies and proposals.

Overall, integrating urban environment and land use planning implies that a narrow land use focus is no longer appropriate. Indeed the report considers that there is an identifiable shift amongst land use planning professionals towards more environmental analyses. The solutions advocated are seen as applicable in all urban settings, for example, in historic city centres, suburbs and new settlements.

The recommendations for policy, practice and research which emerge from this first stage of the Sustainable Cities Project concern:

- further integration of the economic, social and environmental dimensions of sustainability across all policy sectors at European Union, Member State, and regional and local government levels;
- improved capacity for managing urban areas for sustainability;
- greater coherence of policy and action, so that the development of sustainability at local level is not undermined by decisions and actions by Member State governments and the EU;
- measures to avoid wasteful duplication of work and to enhance the productive exchange of experience; and
- both the enhanced application of existing policies, programmes and mechanisms and, where necessary, the development of new ones.

In general, all governmental and public agencies are urged to apply the principles and tools for policy integration although particular recommendations are addressed to the EU, national governments, regional and local government as follows:

- Those addressed to the EU and Member States focus principally on the establishment of more supportive policy frameworks within which cities can innovate; on the provision of funding and support for city projects and for networking so as to encourage the development and sharing of good practice for sustainability; and on the provision of guidance on particular tools (such as the extension of environmental appraisal to sustainability appraisal). New initiatives for urban policy at European level are welcomed, and national governments with explicit urban policies are urged to build sustainability goals and mechanisms into their programmes. In general, action for sustainable cities is seen as in line with Agenda 21 (cf. UNA, 1994), to which all levels of government are urged to respond.
- Member States are encouraged to work towards an adequate structure of regional and local government in urban regions. Often there is a gap between functional and administrative structures, with negative impacts for

environmental protection, land use planning and transport planning. In many European urban regions there is a need to establish metropolitan governments with a strong planning competence at the strategic level. It is recommended that, in the longer term, cities are given increased freedom to experiment and to devise and implement their own policies and actions for sustainable development.

- At local level, municipal governments are urged to develop city-wide strategic approaches, applying the principles and tools outlined in the report. This in turn requires enlightened political leadership, the establishment of cross-sectoral management structures, and the employment of appropriate specialist staff. Partnership approaches are particularly encouraged, and these have implications for awareness and commitment, not only for city managers but also for local business and communities. The effective involvement of local businesses in both the formulation and implementation of policies for the urban economy, land use and transport planning is seen as essential if progress towards sustainability is to be achieved.

Overall, the European Sustainable Cities report envisages the sustainable city in process terms. It highlights policy mechanisms as well as policy content. Both emphases are significant when it comes to the transfer of good practice from one locality to another.

Within the Expert Group on the Urban Environment, thinking about cities has undergone a reappraisal with a return to a view of the city as a complex system requiring a set of tools which can be applied in a range of settings. Although the system is complex, it is appropriate to seek simple and elegant solutions, especially solutions which solve more than one problem at a time, or several solutions that can be used in combination.

The suggested approach includes, for example:

- the synthesis of old and new ideas;
- encouraging interdisciplinary working, team work, shared responsibility and networking;
- recognising the importance of changing attitudes and lifestyles;
- not ruling any particular methods in or out on ideological criteria, but instead, within framework of shared goals, being prepared to experiment with a diversity of approaches in a spirit of openness; and
- a commitment to conscious planning and management to achieve the social, environmental and economic qualities desired for European cities.

The sustainable city process is about creativity and change. It is about the substance of policy as well as policy methods. It challenges the legitimacy of traditional governmental responses and seeks new institutional capacities and relationships. The notion of sustainability is dynamic and evolving and will change over time as understanding of the local and global environment becomes more sophisticated and shared. This report and its conclusions represent a 'last conversation' in a dynamic process, to be refined and consolidated as the Sustainable Cities Project progresses.

Indeed the future agenda for European sustainable cities is now focused on further policy areas which have formed the basis of the second report and include:

- Social Sustainable Systems – Lifestyle/Culture
- Quality of the Built Environment – Heritage/Tourism
- Technical Management of Cities – Energy/Waste/Resources
- Holistic Urban Management – Institutional Mechanisms and Management Tools
- Urban Rehabilitation – Renewal/Derelict Land Reclamation

Clearly the legal and organisational basis for urban environmental action varies between Member States, in part reflecting differences in the responsibilities assigned to different tiers of local government. In addition, cities differ in their geographical circumstances. This report does not suggest blanket solutions for all cities. Instead it advocates the provision of supportive frameworks within which cities can explore innovative approaches appropriate to their local circumstances, capitalising on traditions of local democracy, good management and professional expertise.

Whatever their responsibilities and competencies, local governments throughout Europe, through the many and varied roles which they perform, are now in a strong position to advance the goals of sustainability:

- As a direct or indirect service provider, regulator, leader by example, community informer, advocate, adviser, partner, mobiliser of community resources, initiator of dialogue and debate, the local authority is ideally placed to formulate a multi-levelled corporate strategy for the sustainable management of the local environment. Such action reinforces and complements global initiatives.
- Since the goal of sustainable development involves significant choices between conflicting objectives and major change in the way of life of communities, it cannot merely be imposed from above. It must be built by, through and with the commitment of local communities. Individual routes to sustainable development must be worked out at local level.
- The local authority's role should be as manager of the local environment, committed to ensuring that the linear flow of natural resources into wastes and pollutants is transformed into the circular, self-adjusting flow of an ecosystem (Local Government Management Board, 1992).

Sustainable development – legislative dimension

DGXI is continuing to fund studies contributing to the development and flow of themes from the Green Paper, as outlined above, but the Commission has now agreed that the Green Paper will not, contrary to previous expectations, proceed to the White Paper stage, which would have secured a legislative programme. Tensions exist, identified in the context of the subsidiarity debate, which raise doubts regarding the extent to which policy formulation can be extended into legislation.

At present the principal legislative initiative in support of sustainability objectives, with specific and widespread implications for the planning process, is the *Proposal for a Directive on the Environmental Assessment of Policies, Plans and Programmes* (CEC, 1991b), and the subsequent *Proposal for a Directive on the Environmental Assessment of Actions Approved During the Planning Process* (CEC, 1992b).

The draft Directives propose three objectives for the extension of EA (Environmental Assessment):

- the attainment of the Community's environmental objectives;
- to assist in the attainment of the single internal market by removing disparities in environmental legislation which may create unfavourable competitive conditions;
- to help to ensure that new developments are sustainable within the ecological and global context.

The draft Directives are viewed as separate from Directive 85/337/EEC dealing with EA (CEC, 1985). Although neither document has so far been adopted by the Commission for transmission to the European Parliament and Council, the content of the proposed Directives is nevertheless an important indication of official thought on this subject.

The first draft Directive (CEC, 1991b) notes that when Directive 85/337/EEC on Environmental Assessment (see section on European Union Control after the bibliography) was adopted it was considered as only the first stage in the development of a comprehensive assessment system, and that the general principle of assessment should be of great value in decision-making processes concerning policies, programmes and plans, including regional development programmes, economic programmes and land use plans. Thus the gradual extension of the field of application of the assessment of environmental effects would be considered in the light of experience with the Directive and other developments.

EA for projects is seen as having inherent limitations:

- prior assessments often take place too late in the planning process to ensure that the environmental implications of all relevant alternatives (both technological and locational) are adequately assessed and taken into account in decision making;
- cumulative and synergistic impacts associated with multiple developments envisaged in policies, plans and programmes often cannot be adequately assessed and taken into account within authorization procedures for individual projects;
- some policies, plans and programmes give rise to significant environmental impacts by changing practices (e.g. farming practices) without entailing investment in major projects subject to environmental assessment.

In relation to the above the benefits seen for the extension of the EA as proposed are seen as:

- assessment of the environmental implications of alternatives to the chosen option at earlier stages in the planning process opens up the possibility of adopting an alternative which is environmentally and/or economically superior but which could not have been realistically considered at the later stage of project EA;
- cumulative and synergistic impacts associated with multiple developments can be more readily identified, and mitigated more effectively and economically if the assessment takes place at a sufficiently early stage in the planning process and at a sufficient scale of aggregate activity;
- the land use planning and development control process can be improved if environmental assessment is systematically integrated into land use planning as well as into the development control stage;
- by focusing assessments on those stages and impacts that are most appropriate it is possible to simplify and streamline the assessments to be undertaken at other stages in the process including the project assessment stage;
- the extension of the assessment system enables the impacts of measures within policies, plans and programmes to be assessed and so reduces the distortions within the Single Market due to differences in development and land use planning processes between Member States.

The timetable for publication of the planned EA Directive is less certain as consultations within the European Commission have not been finalised yet, although it may be adopted during the second half of 1996. Consequently the draft Directives identified above remain the most completely developed statements on what constitutes an environmental appraisal of plans and how this might be regulated.

Sustainable development – funding actions

The prominent role of the European Commission in addressing the policy and legislative dimensions of urban sustainability is complemented by its funding actions. The urban sustainability dimension is mentioned or directly targeted for financial support by a number of EU programmes aimed at achieving sustainable development through, for example, promoting integrated management models (e.g. LIFE) urban energy and transport efficiency (e.g. THERMIE), telecommunications (e.g. RACE II) and advanced information technologies (ESPRIT), and social cohesion (e.g. POVERTY III).

In addition, the Community's regional policies make explicit reference to urban communities as part of the criteria for Objective 2 eligibility in the Structural Funds regulations as revised in 1993. Objective 2 areas are those in industrial decline and are predominantly urban areas. Several cities also receive Community support through Objective 1 status. Beyond mainstream initiatives, increased support by the Commission is being targeted at new integrated and innovative approaches. About 100 million ECU has been spent on 32 urban pilot projects under Article 10 of the European Regional Development Fund (ERDF) regulation. A new Community Initiative concerning urban areas (URBAN) was also launched in March 1994 to achieve effective coordination and improve the capability of cities to benefit from EU actions in the period 1994–99. The initiative, with funding of 600 million ECU, is already contributing to economic, social and environmental objectives by improving the infrastructure and the environment in selected urban areas throughout Europe.

Conclusion

The numerous initiatives outlined show increasing attention by the EU to the role of cities in achieving transition to a new development model based on urban sustainability, as specified in the EU White Paper on Growth, Competitiveness and Employment (CEC, 1994). It is evident that the sectoral approach to policy making is inadequate to the task of dealing with the complex and interlinked nature of urban problems and to take full advantage of the capacity of cities to create synergies. British planning theorists have long recognised the linked, interdependent nature of urban issues, but have lacked legislative powers to act upon their insights into planning practice. However, EU measures and policies have begun to exert a tremendous influence upon British town planning (DoE, 1989), which will increase with growing European integration, and have challenged traditional images of what 'planning' is 'meant' to be about. Further EU actions are widening the urban policy agenda to include environmental and social issues, alongside physical and economic considerations and are providing the legislative funding and implementation environments necessary to create a new, sustainable Europe.

Chapter 13

RECONCILING THEORY AND PRACTICE

Clara Greed

Conflicts and commonalities

In this final chapter the aim is to reflect upon the preoccupations and agendas of town planning, as illustrated in the book, and to consider its likely future emphasis. This chapter is written by the editor, and, in order to encourage debate, the account does not just constitute a conclusion to the contributions, but also includes the editor's own observations on the situation (linking back to earlier Volumes and her other work on the professional culture of planning, such as Greed (1994a and b)), in places taking the role of Devil's Advocate to stimulate debate. Most contributors imply that British town planning must inevitably be concerned with sustainability to a greater extent than previously. Therefore one key theme in this chapter will be to consider what effect the sustainability agenda is actually having on reshaping the town planning discourse, and thus the other 'plannings'. As has been demonstrated, each contributor, including the editor, holds somewhat different views on the priorities and solutions to the 'urban problem', reflecting the range of views found within the planning profession itself, which is by no means a unitary group. Some planners are quite cynical about, and untouched by, the current 'hype' about sustainability. This is because so many of the issues now 'clothed' within the jargon of the green movement are not 'new' but long-standing planning matters for which there are no instant total solutions, because they need to be tackled by a subtle combination of long-term physical, social, economic and environmental planning strategies. However, the sustainability agenda is valuable in giving a new perspective on old issues, in inspiring a new generation to take an interest in town planning, and as a means to achieving more effective statutory planning control. As suggested in Chapter 1, it is hoped that readers adopted a critical and analytical approach to reading the book, and as a result can develop further their own informed views on the urban situation and solutions. As stated in Volume I, there is no one right answer in town planning; it all depends on who you are and what you want to achieve and for whom.

In discussing the different 'plannings', especially environmental planning, it is important to distinguish between currently fashionable sentiments, theories and 'buzz words', which form the planning discourse for those planners and/or academics who are on the 'conference circuit'; and policy issues which are recognised by practitioners operating the statutory framework of development plan and development control systems within local authority planning departments. Arguably the former (theory) generally informs the latter (practice): but typically there is a considerable cultural gap and time-lag between the two agendas, which Hobbs, attributed, in part, to the effects of cyclic economic processes. It has been argued – although some would hotly dispute it – that the green movement could only arise at a time of economic prosperity among people who had the leisure to reflect upon their situation, although the poor might be the ones more likely to experience the effects of environmental crisis (Tucker, 1978). One must also consider the nature of existing power structures in society. The situation is further complicated, especially for students and newcomers to the subject, by the fact that many 'planning' issues are popular media topics nowadays, such as the 'greenhouse effect', or the Newbury Bypass, and therefore are 'obviously' assumed by the general public to be part of (if not the fault of) town planning, when in fact the statutory planning system has limited powers in these areas even after the passing of the 1995 Environment Act.

The new agenda of sustainability appears to coexist somewhat uneasily with extant economic, social and physical planning agendas, creating potential conflicts, and new dualisms (see end of Chapter 1 for list of dualisms). For example, to use alliteration, Walker and Paumier, in the retail-related chapters, stress the economic and social importance of 'vital and viable' cities, whereas Ludlow in discussing pan-European planning objectives talks of 'villes sans voitures' (towns without cars). Whether, in practical terms, within the constraints of existing urban structures, it is possible to create a functioning city which is both vital, viable, and sans voitures is the great question. It is one matter to pedestrianise a few city centre streets; it is quite another to 'de-car' a vast sprawling suburbanised city, where a large proportion of the population (and thus the economy) is dependent on the car to get to work, shops and schools, and where public transport is minimal. The viability of the location of modern, decentralised commercial, industrial, and residential development is highly dependent upon the con-tinuation of the complex road systems, and motorway networks which serve them. Seeking to introduce negative controls on the use of this transport infrastructure, in the name of sustainability, before providing alternatives, including providing adequate, reliable, and frequent public transport, would have a detrimental effect on the functioning of the economy, and create major social restrictions on the way people live their lives. Such attitudes have been described in the press as 'environmental crassness' (*Planning Week*, 27.7.95, p. 4). Therefore this chapter will not only highlight the likely conflicts between the new sustainability agenda and other 'plannings' but also discuss the chances of integrating environmentally motivated planning with economic, physical and social planning, in order to find a way forward, based on positive, sensitive, long-term strategies rather than quick fix solutions.

It would seem at present that this conflict has not been entirely acknowledged, let alone resolved. Alarmingly, in considering the sanity of the town planning profession, it appears that some planners possess the facility 'to hold at least two conflicting views at once' (a sign of madness) without appearing to realise this is the case. Perhaps this state of mind is a reflection of the compartmentalised nature of planning education, and of narrow professional perspectives and practice specialisation. More positively, it might be argued that there are 'planners' who are aware of, and trying to reconcile, the conflicting relationships and clashing agendas found within the contemporary professional arena. Indeed, as Hobbs suggests in Chapter 2, town planning might be on the brink of a major transformation, or, at least, of a major 'rethink' as to what constitutes 'town planning', and what components and instruments should be kept within, what John Allinson (in Volume 2) described as the planner's toolkit. Perhaps the key to resolving conflict is to transcend established compartmentalisations, and dualistic divisions which demarcate the different 'plannings', and the very nature of British town planning (as a result of over 100 years of legislation and conventional wisdom), and to restructure town planning around current, pressing policy issues and problems. But, to be realistic, to achieve change one must work pragmatically within the existing statutory frameworks, but one can also seek to lay down new ways of thinking, and of organising the constituent parts of the discourse for the future development of more effective urban governance (cf. Healey, 1989). From the chapter on the European Union, new approaches to planning appear imminent.

The dimensions of planning

For convenience it was decided to structure the last chapter around a discussion of the different types of 'plannings' as expressed with the four following categories (compare with the division adopted in Chapter 1 of market, state, people and environment):

- Economic
- Environmental
- Physical
- Social

The first two, economic and environmental planning, have been strongly represented by chapter contributions, and reflect the red/green (economic/ environmental) axis or dualism, which was identified in Chapter 1. This may be seen as a fault line along which town planning will eventually tear itself apart, or it may be seen as a resoluble, 'solvable' dualism, or dynamic antithesis, which will, through a process of synthesis, bring forth a stronger, richer, and more relevant form of town planning, as economic planning becomes more environmentally concerned (or vice versa). However the environmental and economic dimensions may be seen as but two of the tent-pegs which hold the 'four-square' structure of town planning down to the ground. (There is a long history of conceptualising the 2, 3, 4 or more reference points of planning, for example, cf. Geddes, 1915 (reprinted 1968); Doxiades, 1968; Greed, 1994b.) Indeed it is incomplete, and dangerous, to deal with these two components in isolation from other key factors, as arguably 'everything is linked to everything else' in town planning (Greed, 1993, p. 126). Therefore two of the other major components of the town planning agenda are also discussed in this chapter, namely the physical and the social.

Classic questions

As may be seen from the various chapters some of the contributors would take a more determinist view than the editor and argue that the economic aspect is primary in shaping other components and not just one factor among others of equal weight. From this position it might be argued by some that addressing, for example, physical, social or environmental issues, without taking into account underlying economic forces and power structures, is an incomplete approach. The physical component, although unnamed, has in fact been an integral component of much of the book, being evident particularly in the chapters on planning for housing, and in the accounts of the changing pattern of urban form and retail decentralisation. It is for the reader to decide which factors are primary determinants and which are of secondary importance. Do economic factors 'determine' everything else? Or do physical, social, cultural, political, and environmental factors 'feed back' and 'reshape' the economic and political base of society? This is one of the classic questions that must be addressed in assessing the efficacy of physical town planning policy (as originally raised in Volume I of this series). The social component has not been given specific chapter coverage in this volume, although it forms an important component of both Volumes I and II in this series. Alternative arguments about the power of the social aspects of planning, and debates about the power of the cultural values held by urban decision makers in shaping urban space and society, are discussed in other works by C. Greed (1994b, and in a forthcoming book specifically on *Social Planning*). However, as will be explained, every aspect of planning policy is likely to have social implications, for better or worse, whether or not these are recognised or considered by the policy makers themselves, and some contributors have already highlighted this fact in their chapters.

Each of these types of planning will now be discussed in the above order. Since 'economic planning' has already been the subject of two chapters of its own, the first of which dealt thoroughly with changing agendas, and it has also been a key theme in the chapters on housing policy, the section on economic planning will consist of an introduction to the whole in which the current political context of planning will be highlighted. This is a primary consideration in understanding the extent to which 'planning', as a form of state intervention in the market and in society, is likely to be condoned, and thus its form, priorities, and degree of power and success. This section will also provide the opportunity for some lateral thinking on the nature of 'economics' itself, and on what is considered to 'count' in assessing economic performance within our culture. As to the environmental dimension, the challenge which the theory (way of seeing the world) of 'sustainability' presents to town planners has been discussed by Hugh Barton, whilst Derek Senior's chapter has sought to relate the broad concepts to specific planning practice in relation to minerals planning. Both Tracey Merrett's and David Ludlow's chapters have also demonstrated the increasing influence of European legislation in determining the attention which British town planners should give to environmental matters in making planning decisions. In this section the extent to which this new environmental agenda is actually affecting mainstream planning practice is taken further, as manifest in governmental policy guidance and in development control. This section illustrates the gap between theory and practice alluded to earlier in this chapter, and highlights likely conflicts, commonalities, and, at least, linkages with the four other planning agendas.

As to physical planning, traditionally British town planning theory and practice have been centred upon seeking to solve urban problems by physical policy solutions, such as land use zoning, clearance and relocation, density control, and new town development (cf. Greed, 1993, Chapter 6). As indicated in Chapter 1, some would see this strategy as doomed, as it is dealing with the end product – the built environment, and not the forces which determine the nature of its development in the first place (cf. Massey, 1984), that is it should be dealing with cause rather than effect. Equally there are dangers in seeking to implement economic or social planning policy without reference to the likely effects on the built environment, particularly in respect of inner city regeneration policies as highlighted by Nick Oatley. As has been seen from the various chapters, economic, environmental and social conditions are strongly constrained by the spatial location of different land uses (and vice versa), especially in the cases of housing (as discussed by Stuart Farthing and Christine Lambert) and retail development (as discussed by Geoff Walker and Kimberly Paumier).

Planning law is still strongly orientated towards controlling land use and development, so much so that attempts to impose wider social, economic, or environmental controls have often been deemed *ultra vires*, that is 'not a land use matter' (see Greed, 1993, pp. 236–239). In Britain the scope and nature of planning have always been ambiguous. Strictly speaking it is concerned with 'land use planning'. In respect of achieving wider policy objectives through the development plan system, it is stated in PPG12 *Development Plans and Regional Guidance*, 1992, that the unitary (new) development plan system provides local authorities with positive opportunities to reassess the needs of their areas, resolve conflicting demands, consider new ideas and bring forward appropriate solutions. However, as discussed in Volume II the parameters of what is acceptable are somewhat limited, constrained by tradition, case law, and the attitudes prevalent within the subculture of the planning profession. Any imposition of 'conditions' on planning permissions in the development control process must be for a genuine planning reason (Morgan and Nott, 1988, p. 139). The use of 'planning gain' (agreements to get additional social and environmental provision from the developer) can be utilised in some instances (under Section 106 of the 1990 Town and Country Planning Act, and Sections 106 A and B of the 1991 Planning and Compensation Act (Greed, 1995, p. 84), provided these benefits are seen as relating directly to the development of the site in question, as discussed by Tracey Merrett in the legal chapter.

Many of the 'clashes' between the different 'plannings', especially between physical and environmental planning – often manifest in debates about car parking restrictions and road pricing – were reflected in the discussion of retail development provided by Geoff Walker. In his chapter, many traditional, geographical, urban planning issues were incorporated into the discussion, or even taken as given, such as the question of the optimum location of different land uses, hierarchies of centres, the structure of urban form, and the interrelationship between transportation policy and town planning. Likewise the question of city centre management, discussed by Kimberly Paumier, inevitably included consideration of transport issues, such as access, car parking, street management, and the likelihood of car-based retail decentralisation undermining and blighting traditional town centres. Transportation policy has emerged as a major factor in shaping urban form, determining the viability of developments, and facilitating people's access to facilities. Therefore in discussing the physical dimensions of planning, emphasis will be put upon transportation planning. Again this does not exist in a vacuum separate from the other 'plannings' (although some highways engineers appear to imagine it does!). Current transportation policy may be seen as a barometer of the relative 'strength' of the different 'planning' agendas, reflecting pressures and influences from economic, environmental, physical, and increasingly social planning agendas.

In the final section social planning is discussed briefly. It is important to remember the truism that 'planning is for people', and that 'people' are not a unitary group but have different experiences of the built environment, and different levels of satisfaction with planning policy, according to their class, age, gender, race, disability, cultural and lifestyle characteristics; and whether they have a car or not. In the past, as illustrated in earlier chapters, social planning may have been seen as an adjunct to economic planning, centred upon 'public' matters such as employment and housing provision (albeit very important issues). But nowadays the scope of 'the social aspects of planning' has broadened enormously to include a consideration of what have often been perceived as the more 'private' realm: matters of women's 'different' experience of the city, childcare needs, the demands of ethnic minority groups, and the increasing problems that would-be public transport users, especially the elderly, encounter in cities where the distribution of land uses and facilities is predominantly designed for car drivers.

Again, there seems to be an enormous gap between 'what is written' and 'what is built' in this field, as, for example, there is now a very extensive literature on the need to make cities more accessible to all so-called minority groups. Apart from an occasional ramp or dropped curb there is very little evidence of structural change in the way cities are planned in terms of land use interrelationships, and the creation of an overall accessible urban form. The reasons for this have been explored by the editor elsewhere (Greed, 1994b). Briefly, in the case of dealing with urban social issues and problems, especially in the case of equal opportunities matters, it was found that cultural rather than purely economic considerations came into play in determining policy priorities. The vexed question of the interrelationship between sustainability and 'women and planning' issues (that is the green/gender dualism) will be touched upon. Some see the two as surprisingly similar in agenda and mutually supportive, whereas others see 'sustainability' as nothing but another gender-biased planning conspiracy aimed at taking attention away from the needs of the majority of the population: women.

Economic planning

As can be seen from Chapters 2, 3, 4, and 5 economic planning remains an important component of the planning panoply, but its objectives have shifted somewhat over the years. In the past, under Labour governments, especially in the 1960s, economic planning was shaped by a more 'socialist' agenda, concerned with replacing the market by a planned economy in order to achieve a more efficent economy, scientific and technological modernisation, growth, and the allocation and distribution of scarce resources in a more equitable manner (Pimlott, 1992, p. 274). Also under past Conservative governments, which operated more within an ethos of consensus politics, it was recognised that there was a need for state intervention, and for the town planner to set out the pitch, in terms of providing a development plan for urban growth, and related infrastructural development. The planner took on the role of the umpire introducing an element of control and order in the world of property development, within the context of a somewhat paternalistic political culture in which it was accepted as natural that there should be a mixed economy and state intervention. Also the state acted as a developer itself, with both Conservative and Labour governments playing the 'numbers game' building more council houses than each other, and being involved, respectively, in expanded town, and new town development. If one reads some of the standard post-war town planning textbooks (such as Keeble, 1969 and earlier editions) it appears that the authors simply took it for granted that there will be large-scale government-directed development, and it does not seem to have crossed their mind that town planning, as they knew it, might be proved a short-lived phenomenon. Nor did they envisage the dismantling of the Welfare State and a betrayal of the trust that ordinary citizens had placed in a quasi-socialist 'planned' society which would care for its people from 'cradle-to-grave'.

From the late 1970s when the Conservative Government came to power much of this changed fundamentally. Great emphasis was put ostensibly upon cutting back the powers of the state, and related bureaucracy, and encouraging free enterprise and small firms, in order to achieve growth and national prosperity, particularly during the Thatcher years (Thatcher, 1993). The Major administration has also stressed the importance of 'self-help' and personal endeavour rather than state intervention, or welfarism, as a means of achieving equality and a classless society. However, as illustrated in Chapters 3–5 there was in fact a great deal of 'planning' going on in all but name. Also, much of what was presented as the achievement of private enterprise was, arguably, heavily subsidised by public sector money, and enabled by governmental bodies. However, there was also some apparent concern for continuing to use governmental measures to create greater equality in deprived areas, such as the inner city. But the emphasis was now put upon this being achieved through encouraging private sector investment to generate job creation, rather than through direct financial support for deprived urban populations through social welfare and public sector housebuilding measures.

Throughout the last fifty years the goal of economic wellbeing, as aided and abetted by town planning policy, has traditionally been equated with economic growth as measured by industrial production, employment figures, and retail consumption figures: regardless of the impact on the environment, the health of the nation, and the effect on social structures, as these factors simply did not count in the calculations. What 'counts' in economics has long been of concern to 'women and planning' groups (as well as environmentalists), because much of women's work has often been left out of the calculations because it is not paid employment. For example, it might be more sustainable to produce food, clothes, and household wares for the family at home than to buy them ready-made from shops, but under the current system their economic value is calculated as nil. These issues are summarised from an international perspective in a most readable format by Steinem (1994) in a paper *Revaluing Economics*. Indeed as Hugh Barton has indicated in his chapter, economic policies based on the extraction and exploitation of non-renewable resources, and upon a growth in retail markets based upon short-life, non-recyclable, consumer goods, and convenience foods, which in turn create vast amounts of non-biodegradable refuse, are fundamentally in opposition to sustainability objectives. Nick Oatley has commented on the relationship between the new sustainability agenda and traditional economic planning goals, and concludes the two do not go well together (Chapter 4). Indeed many consider there is a need for a fundamental reconceptualisation of 'economics' and not least of the way in which GNP and 'growth' are measured relative to sustainability indicators.

One must ask if concepts of urban regeneration, and related policies (such as the Single Regeneration Budget, Enterprise Zones, City Challenge, Urban Development Corporations etc.), which are essentially 'property-led' (that is they are dependent upon private developers and businesses investing and building in deprived areas) as against 'environment-led' (that is concerned with achieving sustainable urban settlement policies), are appropriate any more. Interestingly, current Labour Party policy projects such as the 'City 2020' studies referred to by Oatley do appear a little 'greener' than Conservative equivalents, but it is not clear how, in practice, economic and sustainabilty goals might be linked to national economic policy. Clearly urban economic policy, and thus town planning, to be meaningful, has to be set against the wider national and international economic context. Perhaps in the past, when the public sector was much stronger, some planners imagined that if they pretended the private sector property market did not exist, it would go away and not bother them. In contrast nowadays within a more market-led economy, both public and private sector town planners must give more attention to property market analysis. As town planners' powers have declined, or at least been redirected, and they have less control over urban development, it is vital to 'capture' the hearts and minds of the private sector decision makers to achieve urban change. But, what are the chances of 'sustainability' issues being taken on board by private sector market interests? It would seem that many advertisers, in respect of consumer goods, find it worthwhile to stress the 'green' merits of their products. Also in respect of individual developments, 'green buildings' may be seen as having a prestige value, in the same way that refurbished listed buildings for commercial use (as against 'modern' high rise offices) were sought after when urban conservation first became fashionable. Clearly such choices are not purely based on economic considerations but factors of culture, education, and lifestyle 'image' come into play too.

However, it is one thing to make an individual 'green' building a marketable commodity, it is quite another to seek to green economics, and the urban economy. The book *New Times* (Hall and Jacques, 1989) sought to address some of these issues previously, as in the chapter 'Green Times' (by Fred Steward, 1989). This remains an unresolved issue, which nevertheless is having to be tackled by inner city planners, some of whom are arguably running ahead of governmental policy, and creating their own sustainable economic agenda and solving the problems as they go along. Incidentally this approach is often linked to an equal opportunities agenda too and related to encouraging minority groups, including women, to establish 'starter' green businesses, particularly in London boroughs as a continuation of early GLEB (Greater London Enterprise Board) pioneer initiatives, and for communities themselves to get involved in making bids for the Single Regeneration Budget for their area (WDS, 1995a). Admittedly this is small scale, but perhaps the start of a signficant trend, which provides a role model of how the economic and sustainability agendas might be linked. If one peruses

Development Plan policy statement documents written in the 1990s (such as the new Unitary Development Plan documents produced by London boroughs and metropolitan authorities) one will find evidence that planners are trying to integrate this aspect into policy documents.

Government initiatives such as City Pride (referred to by Nick Oatley and currently being developed in London, Manchester and Birmingham) are also encouraging a more comprehensive, 'city wide' view of strategic planning which transcends mere town planning and seeks to develop a total vision for the future covering economic, spatial, social and environmental considerations (*Estates Times*, London Review, 28.7.95, pp. 5–6). For example, in the case of London five priority policy areas have been identified, which are business growth, raising skills, improving transport, housing and environmental quality. Likewise the revised RPG3 (Regional Planning Guidance) *Strategic Guidance for London Planning Authorities* of 1995 provides a more unified approach. However, both City Pride and RPG policy are, arguably, advisory rather than executive in capacity, and the need for their creation may be seen as the result of a gap at the regional, or supra-urban, level of strategic planning for London and the South East. It would seem reasonable that a fusion of environmental and economic planning strategies might be best achieved at the regional planning level if this were reincarnated.

In conclusion, for those who believe that economic base is a major determinant of the nature of all other human activity including town planning, the current situation is likely to be seen as a major brake on achieving sustainability. Without increasing and extending town planning powers further into the realms of economic activity and policy little can be achieved, but the likelihood of this happening at present is low. But perhaps in the long-term future 'planning' will inevitably develop in this direction, but with quite a different agenda than the present. For those who believe (in these post-structuralist, post-modern, post-Fordist times) that it is not a one-way system in which everything is determined by economics, but that the economic 'structure' can be influenced and even altered by changing the nature of the 'superstructure' (to use Marxian jargon), that is by changing cultural beliefs and social values, and by reshaping the nature of the built environment through town planning policy, there is still much to be done.

Environmental planning

Hugh Barton's chapter has already 'proved' to the reader the undeniable importance of environmental planning and of making sustainability an important priority within town planning. Adopting a narrow physical perspective upon statutory town planning, without giving consideration to wider ecological issues which might lead to eco-disaster and the demise of Planet Earth, is rather like 'rearranging the deckchairs on the Titanic'. (Significantly, this phase has been more used in the past to decry inner city planning policy which emphasised the social and physical aspects without looking at the underlying economic restraints.) But the adoption of the sustainability agenda is not automatic, but somewhat fraught, because of the lack of strong governmental support, and the potential clash of agendas with other equally worthy types of 'planning'. Also the suspicions held by many members of the public as to what it will mean for them, if car restrictions are introduced, is a key political factor, anecdotally expressed in comments such as 'we don't want to wait for hours at some draughty bus stop trying to get to work' or 'I can't be expected to carry home a week's supply of food from Sainsbury on the handlebars of a bicycle, and hold down a full-time job as well.' The environmental agenda has got a somewhat negative image among many hard-pressed suburban commuters, trying to get to work, to get their children to school, to do the week's shopping, for whom time is also a non-renewable resource, as they seek to get through all their home and work roles and duties. Likewise suggestions that town planners themselves should travel by bicycle or public transport, rather than by car, has caused some private sector planning consultants to argue that this would take much longer and that they would have no choice but to pass the cost of the time lost in such travel on to their clients. The economic costs of sustainability are likely to be high, as measured by current monetary values, although the environmental benefits would be equally great. There is, undoubtedly, a need to undertake major structural change in the nature of urban form, rather than 'blaming the individual', who is often not a free agent. There is a need, fundamentally, to restructure location patterns, vastly to improve public transport provision, and to create more compact city form.

In the following section a range of government documents will be considered to gauge the extent to which sustainability policy is getting into the fabric of town planning, by means of perusing recent urban policy statements, including PPGs. To recap, according to the Town and Country Planning Association (Blowers, 1993) sustainability policy has four objectives: to conserve stock of natural assets, to avoid damaging the regenerative capacity of ecosystems; to achieve greater social equality; and to avoid imposing risks and costs on future generations (Greed, 1993, p. 182). One might argue that town planners are already, and have always been, concerned with environmental issues, as discussed in Volume I (Greed, 1993, p. 182). Within traditional 'town and country planning' there has been an emphasis upon 'protecting' the countryside from the town, and generally upon a somewhat protectionist mentality, in which 'countryside' and for that matter 'farmers' were seen as 'blameless'. The protection of the countryside, like so many other British planning objectives, has been instrumentalised by means of the designation of special spatial zones, and land use areas, such as National Parks and Green Belts, rather than been manifest in a concern for global ecological issues (Shoard, 1980). The uneasy relationship between traditional rural planning and modern environmental planning has not been pursued in this Volume because the book has centred upon urban issues, but certainly this is another area of contradiction which the reader might choose to investigate further. For example, the development of power alliances between 'shire tories' and relatively left-wing 'greenies', who are both concerned with protecting the countryside from 'townies', is a fascinating paradox. The following account is drawn from a range of sources, including the work of Ball (1994); the editor's research into implementation of planning policy and consultation related to the DoE *Quality in Town and Country* programme (DoE, 1995a); and governmental sources.

Hugh Barton has already listed a range of governmental documents which relate to sustainability policy. In particular PPG12 *Development Plans and Regional Planning Guidance* (DoE, 1992b), paras 6.3, 6.11 and 6.12 were highlighted by him, with reference to general principles and to the PPG's emphasis on climatic change and the implications for controlling CO_2 emissions and thus the motor car. But as Barton notes, because of separation of powers between planning authorities, highways authorities and public transport undertakers, the planners have limited powers of control. Indeed, curiously, such central government policy documents seem to be over-estimating the statutory powers of local government planners! In addition PPG1 *General Policy and Principles* (revised, 1992) paragraph 3 states that the government intends to work towards ensuring that development and growth are sustainable, and that it will continue (!) to develop policies consistent with the concept of sustainable development. It is recommended that through the preparation of development plans, local planning authorities can contribute to the objectives ensuring that development and growth are sustainable. Other governmental consultation documents are also showing the influence of sustainability principles particularly in relation to transportation planning, such as PPG13 *Transport*. The recent DoE (1995a) consultation document *Quality in Town and Country*, and the subsequent good planning campaign to which it is linked, as masterminded by John Gummer, Secretary of State for the Environment, strongly promotes sustainability sentiments in all but name, and on page 2 shows awareness of the problems of disparate zoning, and even acknowledges the particularly fragmented nature of women's journeys (to work→schools→shops→and back), which are so different from the traditional male commuter's 'journey to work', and which have been further exacerbated by growing distances between different land uses and facilities. Likewise *Transport: the Way Ahead* exudes 'sustainability' (Mawhinney, 1995). This document constitutes a set of ministerial speeches, given in response to participants in a consultation programme on transport policy, involving transport interest groups such as motoring organisations and community groups. Indeed as will be discussed in the next section, transportation policy is a key factor in achieving sustainability.

Local authorities have also been expected to formulate national sustainable development plans as part of the Agenda 21 programme (not development plans in the town planning sense note). Chapter 28 of the Agenda required all local authority areas in signatory states to produce a Local

Agenda 21 initiative by 1996 (Church and McHarry, 1994; Levett, 1994, and UNA, 1994). With time, presumably, the policies in these sustainability plans and those in statutory development plans will become more interlinked, if not merged, as apparently is already occurring in some Canadian planning authorities. Each new 'planning' tends to start as an add-on and with time its policies and agenda become more integrated within mainstream planning. But, as with 'women and planning' policies, sustainability policies may (i) be fully integrated into the main text, (ii) be added as a paragraph at the end of each main topic section or (iii) be relegated to a separate section or chapter in the statutory development plan document according to the importance attributed to them by the local planning authority and subsequent central government guidance.

Whilst PPG1 refers indirectly to 'material considerations' (matters of legal relevance) in determining planning decisions in respect of sustainability policy, it might still be argued that, like social and economic policy, environmental policy is a grey area which might be viewed as *ultra vires*, that is, not a land use matter. With time, case law will establish its relevance more strongly, as this is an evolving area, in which the legal boundaries are not yet clear, as highlighted by Tracey Merrett. Likewise in PPG12 *Development Plans and Regional Planning Guidance* (1992), local planning authorities are encouraged to incorporate 'environment in its broadest sense' into policy statements, but, para 3.8 states that plans should not include policies or proposals which are not related to the development and use of land. PPG22 on *Renewable Energy* and 23 on *Pollution Control* both contain statements implying these topics are material considerations in determining permission, although strictly not land use matters. Therefore guidance is still somewhat ambiguous, but the shift has started.

PPG3 *Housing* (1992) stresses the importance of using infill sites within existing urban areas, rather than spreading outwards, but there have been several appeals in recent years in which local planning authorities have not been supported by Secretary of State decisions in their attempts to enforce urban containment. Stuart Farthing in his chapter on affordable housing highlights the importance of recycling land, but land availability is always constrained by the question of land values and other economic factors, as discussed by Christine Lambert. So again, the chances of achieving sustainable settlements are linked to wider economic factors, and especially the demand for land, and nature of the property market in the area in question. However, PPG3 also mentions the use of redundant space in existing buildings for housing use, such as above shops, and LOTS (Living over the Shop Campaign) has certainly brought this issue to the fore in recent years. However, such accommodation may not be suitable for everyone and, apart from town planning legislation, there are other property law controls such as restrictive covenants and tenancy agreements which constrain the availability of such accommodation and thus the chances of achieving a little more sustainable policy implementation.

It has been shown (Farthing *et al.*, 1996) through research that it does not always follow that the most sustainable location is likely to be an infill site, or a central area location. Britain has a tradition of suburban development, much of which is still in proximity to local and district centres with their own array of shops and facilities (albeit undercut by out-of-town development nowadays). Therefore if the objectives of sustainable planning include reducing travel distances and encouraging walking, as well as avoiding building in dispersed green field locations, the compromise might be to build more in the suburbs, infilling and building up existing districts to slightly higher densities and thus providing more viable catchment populations for local centres. Indeed, one must be wary of what is termed 'town cramming', which is going to the other extreme and overdeveloping areas in the name of sustainability. As can be seen, therefore, different sustainability objectives might come into play in different situations and there is no one 'right' way of planning for sustainability as much depends upon the characteristics of the site and location. In relation to the local level of planning Hugh Barton and colleagues have produced a design guide for achieving sustainable development at estate and district level (Barton *et al.*, 1995). With time it is inevitable that the 'urban design' aesthetic agenda of the architect-planner will increasingly be modified by contact with the environmental planner's perspective, and the power of the sustainability agenda itself.

In terms of actually implementing sustainability-related policies through development control procedures, as indicated above there are problems as to whether sustainability-related requirements are material considerations. However, more positively in respect of certain categories of development, Environmental Assessment must now be undertaken. As mentioned in Barton's, Merrett's and Ludlow's chapters the 1988 Town and Country Planning (Assessment of Environmental Effects) Regulations, which are 'based' upon EC Directive 85/337 (Fortlage, 1990), require EA to be undertaken in respect of certain types of development, and the 1995 Environment Act has increased control. Suprisingly these include not just toxic industrial development, but also relate to large urban uses such as, for example, a major housing development, or out-of-town shopping centres perhaps, and to major development changes in the countryside which would not previously have come under British planning law, such as for example large-scale forestry and fishfarming schemes (see Circulars 7/94 Environmental Assessment: Amendment of Regulations and 15/88 Town and Country Planning (Assessment of Environmental Effects) Regulations. The GDO (General Development Order) has recently been revised to incorporate these changes, in the form of the 1995 Town and Country Planning (General Permitted Development) Order, which also consolidated a range of other revisions to GDO regulation modifications brought in over the last few years. The relationship between GDO and EA requirements is explained to the general public in the (free) booklet *Your Permitted Development Rights and Environmental Assessment* (DoE, 1995b). The role of development control in implementing and enforcing sustainability policy is discussed in Miller (1990), and Tyesley and Associates (1994), and was tackled by one of the University of the West of England School of Planning's postgraduate planning students in her dissertation (Ball, 1994).

It is evident that sustainability pronouncements are beginning to pepper PPGs, and a range of other governmental documents, particularly those related to transport, retail development, and housing. PPG1 was again revised in 1995 with more emphasis being put upon sustainable issues than previously. The idea of 'urban villages' with a mixture of shops, housing, offices and cultural facilities is promoted in the new PPG1, and segregation of land use is no longer relevant in such schemes. But, current UCO (Use Classes Order) Regulations and the whole tone of planning law still embody a historical planning discourse centred on segregationary zoning principles. The legal basis of implementation and enforcement of sustainability-led planning is still somewhat unclear as environmental planning does not fit easily into existing statutory planning structures, although, of necessity, the various EC Directives have had to be fitted in by means of amendments and additions to existing legislation. There is also some confusion, it would seem, as to the respective roles of town planners, and environmental health bodies, and other regulatory bodies, in respect of matters such as pollution control, energy conservation, waste disposal, and minerals policy.

Physical planning

It has been seen from the chapter by Geoff Walker on retail development that a key factor in determining development location, the scale and structure of urban form, and the preferred distances and relationships between different land uses, is the form of transport utilised, and therefore this section will discuss this aspect. Increased car ownership, and the apparent lack of power, or in some cases apparent complicity, on the part of the planners to prevent the consequent dispersal and decentralisation of erstwhile central area land uses, especially retail and office development, have led to our cities facing major functional, physical planning problems. For many years, especially in the 1960s and 1970s, when North American transportation planning theories were welcomed uncritically, town planning appeared to be for the benefit of the motor car rather than for people. Nowadays, too late, the pendulum has swung in the opposite direction towards controlling motor car use. This may be seen as 'shutting the stable door after the horse (or car) has bolted.' Since so many people are now dependent on the motor car, measures to reduce car use are likely to have major social consequences. For example the concept of road pricing is seen by many as a means of limiting road usage not according to need but on the basis of ability to pay. Also ideas of limiting car usage to 'essential users' are looked upon suspiciously by many. Transport planners in the past have had a reputation for not counting the sort of journeys women make, such as to shops, school, and for a hundred other household and family-related purposes as 'essential journeys' (Greed, 1994, Chapter 3). In fact it is estimated that nowadays in many cities more than 60% of all journeys over a 24 hour period will not be related to the 'journey to work' (and back) which for many years so obsessed transport planners, as they sought to cater primarily for the needs of the car-borne commuter. At a recent transportation conference a woman councillor commented if cars had just been invented they would be made available only for women with children, the elderly and disabled, as within our modern macho culture young men and the able bodied would not like to be thought of as being so unfit that they needed to use them!

Attempts to control the motor car often appear to create more problems than they solve, partly because the planners are trying to deal with the situation without adequate powers. PPG13 *Transport* (1994) argues for stronger integration of new development location policy with public transport planning, but the planners, as stated, have limited powers over its provision. PPG13 states that the location and nature of development affect the amount and method of travel, which is somewhat obvious. But at least this statement re-established the link between land use policy and traffic generation, and anchored the debate back into the realms of physical land use planning intervention. The PPG13 further argued that local planning authorities could reduce reliance on the private car and make a significant contribution to the environmental goals set out in the government's sustainable development strategy (Baker, 1995). But again it may be said this is expecting too much of the planners in the light of their somewhat limited planning powers. It would seem that it is easier for local authorities to introduce negative controls over parking and road use than to enforce positive policies which would prevent unnecessary relocation and decentralisation of land uses. Indeed it would seem that some local authorities have increased parking charges as a way to increase revenue but have pleaded a concern with sustainability as their reason, whilst doing nothing positive to attempt to solve their transport dilemmas.

PPG6 *Town Centres and Retail Development* (1993) also acknowledged the importance of achieving patterns of land use which minimise the need to travel, promoting transport choices which help keep down CO_2 emissions. In some local authorities (such as in Bristol to a degree), attempts have been made through development plan policy to encourage firms which want to leave the centre to decentralise, but only as far as district suburban centres, rather than going right out to an out-of-town location (cf. Farthing *et al.*, 1995). This strategy of suburban decentralisation facilitates the development of the sustainable multi-nucleated city (also proposed in Greed, 1994b, Chapter 11, and touched upon in Volume II of this series). Such a multi-nucleated policy, if adopted more broadly and supported by government guidance, would reduce commuting by providing more local employment, and also strengthen the economic base and the retail catchment area for local shops, businesses, clinics, schools, and services.

In 1995, because of the continuing decline of town centres, as described by Geoff Walker, a further draft revision of PPG6 was produced which pragmatically advised that coherent car parking strategies should be developed which do not discriminate against car-borne shoppers who choose to shop in town centres. Of course many people without cars have no choice but to shop in town centres. In order to keep these centres commercially viable, and socially vital, it is important to attract and retain shoppers who might be discouraged and go elsewhere, and so a 'villes sans voitures' policy is not practical in this context, particularly if there is no reliable public transport alternative. 80% of the single elderly do not or cannot drive (Mawhinney, 1995), and many of the older generation when young were simply not accustomed to using cars, for in 1951, for example, 86% of households did not have a car. In contrast, today over two thirds of households possess at least one car, and the figure approaches 80% in some cities, whilst over a quarter of households have two cars, and around a half of 17–21 year olds have a driving licence. Walking, according to Mawhinney (1995, p. 45), still accounts for 30% of all journeys, but looking at it the other way around, 75% of all journeys by any means are not by car (RTPI, 1991), whilst research by women and planning groups in London suggests that the percentage of walkers is much higher than government estimates indicate (GLC, 1985). In *Planning Week* (23.11.95) it was reported that a Department of Transport source had discounted walking as a form of transport, because, it said, 'transport' is something you get *in*!

At the local design level, traffic calming measures have, for example, proved a mixed blessing, particularly if they are done 'on the cheap' (Hass-Klau *et al.*, 1992). Trench and Ball (1995) comment upon the potentially lethal combination of bus lanes and traffic calming obstacles, which narrow the carriageway at certain points, with no space allowed for cyclists in between. Others have commented upon the dangerous policy of mixing pedestrian routes and cycle paths, a solution ideal for neither type of user (Greed, 1994b, Chapter 3). Installing sleeping policemen in roads (a primitive form of traffic calming using bumps in the road) has been much criticised by people with a range of medical conditions, such as those who have had detached retina operations, and spinal injuries, who have to avoid jolts. Much greater thought needs to go into the overall structuring, and the detailed planning of transport routes. If people are going to be encouraged (or coerced) into walking, cycling, and using public transport, there is a need for more provision of facilities to meet people's practical needs as pedestrians, as well as undertaking changes in road design and pedestrian accessibility. For example, if people are expected to travel around on unreliable public transport systems, where they may be standing around in cold bus shelters and waiting for perhaps an hour or more at a railway station or bus depot, it is vital that better seating, shelter, refreshments, security measures, lighting, and public toilets are provided at all transport interchanges and termini. Also the built environment should be made more accessible at street level, as most pedestrians are not able-bodied, burden-free people striding along without a care in the world, but rather they are composed of people carrying shopping, parcels or luggage, those with babies, children and pushchairs, the elderly, 'doddery', and disabled: all of whom may find narrow doorways, steps, sudden changes of level and badly laid, cracked or rough paving surfaces major hazards.

Mothers with pushchairs and young children have commented that they much prefer to use out-of-town shopping facilities travelling by car, even if they live within walking distance, or a short bus journey, of local shops, because they find the lack of childcare facilities and toilets, poor access in multi-level traditional retail buildings, the problems of traffic, difficulty of getting on and off buses with pushchairs, and fears of having to leave push-chairs containing offspring outside a shop whilst they go inside (because of the steps and narrow doorways) quite overwhelming and exhausting. In con-trast they can drive up to their local Tesco, or Sainsbury, and transfer the tod-dler to the supermarket trolley with childseat and whizz around the store without having to change level or negotiate narrow doorways. Admittedly this possibility is partly the result of campaigning by groups such as Women's Design Service, a group of women architects and planners, over the years, to ensure that aisles were wide enough, and that there were babychanging facil-ities available. The battles over planning gain requirements, and to change retailer and planner attitudes, in order to achieve such provision are now legendary and discussed in Greed (1994b).

However, many women do not have the use of a car, so this possibility is not available to them, and therefore traditional town centres must be improved to meet pedestrian users' needs, as well as sorting out car parking policies. 1995 changes to BS6465 Part I, Table 5 *Customers' Accommodation in Shops and Malls*, on public toilet provision (previously discussed in Volume II in this series) now make it compulsory for the first time, in the case of new build retail develop-ment, that customers' toilets must be provided in shops and shopping malls having over 1000 square metres of net retail floorspace on the following basis: 1000–2000 square metres, one male and two female WCs, plus one male urinal, and one disabled toilet. From 2001 square metres to 4000 square meters one male WC, four female WCs, two urinals and a disabled toilet, and above this provision should be in proportion to the size of the net sales area. It should be noted that the ratio of women to male customers in an average retail development is likely to be at least 60:40 and up to 80:20 on weekdays. Childcare and babychanging facilities are not specified in the new standards. For comparison, the following retail floorspace figures are given, and include details of the sizes of retail developments as given in Geoff Walker's chapter. An average traditional small shop is around 60 square metres or 660 square feet; an average supermarket is 500 to 2500 square metres or 5000 to 25,000 square feet; a Marks & Spencer is around 3000 to 8000 square metres, or 30,000 to 80,000 square feet, but ones in London are much larger; a super-store is at least 2500 square metres or 25,000 square feet; a hypermarket is at least 5000 square metres or 50,000 square feet; a regional shopping centre is 50,000 to 100,000 square metres or 500,000 to a million square feet; the Metro

Centre at Gateshead is 1.5 million square feet, or 144,000 square metres; a retail warehouse is at least 1000 square metres or 10,000 square feet; and a retail warehouse park is basically the size of a small village, as for example Clark's, Street, Somerset. (Conversion: 1 square foot = 0.09 square metres and 10.764 square feet = 1 square metre, i.e. divide or multiply by ten approximately to convert. Note all planning applications must now be submitted using metric measurements following the enforcement of EC regulations in 1995.)

Such matters are not just 'social' issues, but are totally germane to achieving sustainability objectives, which include (Blowers, 1992) not only conserving natural resources, but also achieving greater social equality and avoiding imposing risks and costs on future generations. In the longer term our current transportation problems may be transformed as a result of changes in technology. Many consider a growth in 'telecommuting' (teleworking) will lead to a reduction in the numbers of commuters, and to an increase in 'outworking', particularly of the large workforces which currently occupy high rise office blocks and undertake clerical, administrative, and routine white collar work (Huws, 1990; Adcock, 1994). Some enthusiasts consider the Internet to be a form of communication which will transform everyone's lives outside work too (Graham and Marvin, 1996). However one should not overestimate its effects, as at present only a small proportion of the world's population (around 50 million) are on the Internet; indeed there are millions who do not even have a telephone or electricity. In Britain, large sections of the population do not possess a home computer and many more are not computer literate. Nevertheless, non-work related Internet uses may involve changes in urban transport usage. For example concepts of 'virtual shopping' in which one sits at home and does one's shopping on the Internet, to save going to the out-of-town retail centre in person, will only work if there are vast numbers of delivery vans taking the food to individual houses (such as, after all, existed serving the suburbs before the growth of mass car ownership). Retail businesses may not find this to be financially viable, although it is probably more sustainable for the retailer to deliver to the shopper than the shopper to travel to the retailer. Also, as many disabled groups have pointed out, having access to a world of information on the Internet is small compensation if they cannot get out of their front door and into the city because of steps, lack of suitable public transport, and unhelpful public attitudes. Therefore they may become more determined to increase access to the 'real' rather than 'virtual' built environment, and perhaps at last the government will capitulate under pressure, and reform access regulations to cover all aspects of the built environment, including existing buildings and public transport, not just a few new ones as at present.

Social planning

Previous research has shown professional decision making by planners is not value-free or 'neutral' but is likely to reflect the personal views of those involved, and current professional preoccupations (cf. Healey *et al.*, 1988, p. 33; Howe and Kaufman, 1981; Greed, 1994a, p. 30 *et seq.*) As has been seen in previous volumes there is no one right answer as to how a city should be planned. That is too simplistic; it is a matter of what you want and are trying to achieve. It is foolish to imagine that the professional man is able to plan with sufficient disinterested neutrality for all groups in society (Dunleavy, 1980, p. 112). Because of the somewhat homogeneous characteristics and life-experience of the predominantly white, male, able bodied, and middle class people who constitute the majority of the membership of the built environment professions, demands made by so-called minority groups, such as those seeking better childcare provision, ethnic minority religious or cultural premises, access-sensitive urban design, or public transport provision for the elderly, might be deemed to be 'special' and therefore not of general interest or importance. Alternatively many groups have found that requests for such 'social' facilities may be ruled to be 'not a land use matter': that is they are seen as *ultra vires* (as discussed earlier in the chapter).

What is considered worthy to be included in or out of the different types of 'plannings' and why, requires close investigation. For example, the definition of what counts as 'social' (and 'special') and what counts as 'physical' or 'economic' (and 'normal') is highly gendered. For example childcare provision might be considered 'only' social when in fact adequate provision would have major land use and developmental implications, and availability of such facilities is a land use matter because it directly affects the way people use land, limiting or encouraging access to town centres and employment mobility (Cullingworth and Nadin, 1994, p. 251). In contrast, recreational and sports facilities, used predominantly by young men, have traditionally been seen to be valid land use matters, playing fields being shown clearly on traditional zoning maps as 'public' open space (WGSG, 1984).

Some consider there is as great a gulf between the environmental and the social dimensions of planning as some see between the environmental and economic discourses. This is because much of the environmental agenda, although 'very worthy' in intent, comes across as astoundingly 'peopleless' in spite of 'social equality' being one of the objectives of the sustainability agenda, and 'social equity' one of the related EC sustainability objectives. However, presumably, it is 'the people' who are 'to blame' for environmental decay in the first place, although they seem 'invisible'. A woman architect commented that it seemed odd to her that in order to measure human wellbeing for the purposes of Agenda 21, environmentalists were measuring the numbers of salmon in a stream (referring to an internationally known Canadian example), not the number of children with asthma in the urban area (cf. WDS, 1995b). Admittedly, wildlife is the 'global canary' providing warning signs of forthcoming environmental crisis (when no other signs are available), but this must be balanced by monitoring the human population too in relation to already manifest health problems. Curiously, although public health (and preventative medicine policy) were strong components of the

Victorian planning agenda they became somewhat detached from municipal town planning in the twentieth century. Social ecology groups and 'women and planning' groups are seeking to get the people dimension more fully integrated into the debate (WDS, 1995). Encouragingly, at the international level of planning there is a resurgence of interest in the relationship between town planning, environmental health, sustainability, and the creation of 'healthy cities', as spearheaded by the WHO (World Health Organisation) initiatives. Indeed 'health planning' may nowadays be seen as another of the significant 'plannings' which is shaping public policy and urban governance, and it is intended to pursue this dimension further in future research and publication.

Many women are involved at the local level in grass-roots activities, looking at ways of reshaping lifestyles and at collectivisation of household work, and nappy recycling, as a key to sustainability (for example WEN (Women's Environmental Network)). (It is of note that many of the old 'feminist' demands about childcare and housework have subsequently proved to be 'sustainable' too.) This mundane household level of sustainability is less 'glamorous' than saving endangered species or commissioning architect-designed green buildings, but it is crucial. Although one might get the impression from the media that the green planning is staffed chiefly by white, middle class people, in fact many poor, working class, and ethnic minority groups are aware of environmental issues, as they are the ones who have to face 'environmental discrimination' directly in their locality. For example, there have been several campaigns by Afro-American residents of certain North American states to prevent waste disposal sites, and toxic chemical installations, being located on their side of town. In Britain it is the poor and carless who have to bear the brunt of high bus fares (relative to their income), and expensive public transport privatisation measures.

Women are generally seen as more responsible, or culpable, for the problems of the planet, as the main 'consumers' – as food shoppers, users of washing machines and other labour-saving devices, electricity, household chemicals, and 'second' cars, and as buyers of disposable nappies for their babies. It should be pointed out that much of this activity is undertaken not for their own gain or benefit but on behalf of others in the household. Clearly women want solutions, rather than condemnation, and, in the meanwhile they cannot stop undertaking such duties and wait for the planners and green gurus to come up with solutions. 'Time' is probably the most valuable non-renewable resource for many women. Women cannot afford to spend a whole day doing the weekly wash by hand, just because it might be considered more sustainable to do so, according to some gender-blind sustainability viewpoint. If the only way that women can succeed in taking their children to the childminder of a morning, getting to work on time, and doing the month's shopping at the hypermarket on the way back is by using a car, they will do it. Women weigh the value of saving 'time' in choosing whether to use other non-renewable resources (by for example switching on the washing machine for a small load) in developing their personal sustainability and survival strategy (see Bhride, 1987, in which reference is made to classical 'time budgeting theory' as pioneered by Pred).

The solution to these problems needs to be sought at the macro level of spatial, economic and societal restructuring, not just at the guilt-laden individualised level. For example, reconfiguring urban land uses patterns to reduce the distance between work and home locations, and reconfiguring of spatial relationships between shops, schools and local facilities, as recommended in many 'women and planning' texts and spatial research (Farthing *et al.*, 1995) would create cities which were both more sustainable and more convenient to women. It may be limiting to think only in terms of planning space, since, as stated, time is such a key non-renewable resource to many women and all busy people in cities. For example, in Turin, Italy, attempts have been made to include a 'plan of times' as well as 'land uses' within the urban plan (Belloni, 1994). It was found that in order to increase women's satisfaction with, and access to the city, there was a need to ensure that shops, government offices, schools, clinics, and other facilities were opened and closed at times more convenient to women and all carers, particularly to those combining paid employment and childcare. Also, reorganising the timing of urban activities increased the efficiency of the use of road space and public transport. In Britain the move towards increasing the night time economy of cities as discussed in the chapter on city centre management (Montgomery, 1994) is a step forward, but we are a long way from the '24 hour city'. Incidentally such measures require improved street lighting and thus more use of electricity, but set against this is the social priority of achieving personal and road safety.

Clearly the social as well as the environmental impact of policies must be set alongside each other in the decision-making process. Whilst 'planning for minorities' has remained a popular topic among some planners, this has not been reflected in legislative requirements within the planning system. In contrast environmental planning in general, and the sustainability debate in particular, appear to have had a considerable impact upon the statutory planning system. It is now a requirement to undertake Environmental Impact Assessment in respect of certain categories of development for planning application purposes. Requests from women planners that Social Impact Assessment should be undertaken to gauge the human effects of large-scale developments on employment and housing opportunities for minority groups (as has been discussed at the international planning level, OECD, 1994) have not been heeded, although this procedure is not uncommon in some other developed countries. It is curious that in Britain, sustainability has been so centred upon the environmental dimension, when the original RIO statement (see Brundtland, 1987) states that sustainability had three equal components: economic self-sufficiency, environmental well-being, and social equity – and all these were seen as essential to achieving real sustainability.

Conclusion

At present, environmental planning, as epitomised in the sustainability movement, appears to have taken centre stage as the most fashionable form of planning, in terms of publications, planning school courses, conferences, and academic discussion. But, at the local authority level physical land use planning remains a key component, and recent PPGs reinforce the primacy of spatial considerations. Whilst somewhat 'negative' transport planning measures are popular, legitimised in the name of sustainability, environmental planning has not yet strongly been manifested in 'positive' strategic development plan policy implementation or development control (Ball, 1994).

Economic planning continues to be an area of great fascination for academics, and still has potential for those concerned with effective urban governance. Governmentally possibilities are structured around a policy emphasis upon *ad hoc* initiatives (such as City Challenge) undertaken in partnership with the private sector, rather than upon a commitment to state-led strategic urban, regional and national economic planning. Social planning, as a component of strategic planning, is somewhat limited in extent at present, and restricted to various worthy 'equal opportunities' type statements being inserted into statutory planning documents. However, implementation, as against mere policy statement creation, is much less successful (Little, 1994), chiefly because of lack of central government policy guidance and support, and the intransigence of an archaic planning law system in which 'social' matters are still likely to be ruled *ultra vires*. In contrast, there is still a great deal of research, writing, organising, and general activity taking place related to the 'social aspects of planning', and also a considerable amount of campaigning work being undertaken by minority groups and in the community.

In spite of the inconsistencies, unresolved dualisms, and lack of power identified in this book, the statutory planning system stumbles on regardless. In order to change the situation it is recommended, firstly, at the academic 'ideas factory' level of planning schools, that much greater research is given to investigating the interrelationships and potential conflicts between and among the different types of planning, that is a stock taking should take place to see exactly what this monster called 'British town planning' comprises. Secondly, there is a need to consider 'what we want', that is to develop strategic policy objectives. This is likely to be a fraught process, because there are probably as many different 'plannings' as there are planners. In particular it is important to consider how objectives can be set which reconcile and draw on the strengths of the different types of planning, not least which create and encourage productive synergy between 'planning for sustainability' and dealing with social and economic priorities, and transposing these through into appropriate physical planning measures.

Thirdly, the legal structure of town planning needs to be overhauled; in particular the tradition of basing planning regulations upon principles of 'sorting' of land uses and development, by means of legislation which is obsessed with separation, 'order', segregation, categorisation, and thus zoning, needs to be expunged. This needs to be replaced with a legal structure which encourages functionality, mixing, merging, and synergy among land uses and human users of land. It has not been a tradition in British planning legislation to include policies within statutes as is the case in some other Western countries, rather policy guidance is given in a somewhat understated, subtle manner through policy guidance documents; but this might be considered in the future. The scope of planning legislation and policy making needs to be broadened to allow for comprehensive policies which combine social, economic and environmental considerations in equal weight with physical, land use factors. There is a need for more pro-active, enabling, and policy-related legislation, as against the more negative, regulatory system in force at present. Lastly there is a need to restructure the agencies responsible for doing planning. At present in the wake of local government organisation there is a return to more localised unitary level authorities in many areas. Therefore there is a need for more consideration of regional and supra-urban levels and, in relation to environmental and economic planning in particular, a reopening of the debate about national levels of planning, which might provide a more meaningful planning unit to carry out high level policy. To balance this the role of smaller local *ad hoc* planning bodies should be re-evaluated. At present many of these have been set up with commercial agendas as part of the move towards urban revitalisation, but more socially motivated bodies at this level should also be considered to bring people and planners together in productive and equal union.

BIBLIOGRAPHY

Aaronovitch, S and R Smith (1981) *The Political Economy of British Capitalism: a Marxist analysis*. London: McGraw-Hill.

ACC (Association of County Councils) (1989) *Homes We Can Afford*. London: ACC.

ACC (Association of County Councils) (1991) *Towards a Sustainable Transport Policy*. London: ACC.

Adams, D (1994) *Urban Planning and the Development Process*. London: UCL (University College London) Press.

Adams, D, L Russell and C Taylor-Russell (1994) *Land for Industrial Development*. London: Spon.

ADC (Association of District Councils) (1987) *Housing Needs in Non-metropolitan Areas*. London: ADC.

Adcock, H (1994) Is Teleworking a Threat to the Commercial Office Centre of Bristol? unpublished BA (Hons) Planning Dissertation, Bristol: University of the West of England, Faculty of the Built Environment.

'Agenda 21' see UNA, 1994.

Aglietta, M (1979) *A Theory of Capitalist Regulation*. London: New Left Books.

AMA (Association of Metropolitan Authorities) (1993) *Local Authorities and Community Economic Development: A Strategic Opportunity for the 1990s*. London: AMA.

Ambiente Italia (1994) Urban Environment and Sustainable Development. Paper given at *Towards a New Development Approach*. Report of Conference Proceedings, 24–25 November 1993.

Ambrose, P (1986) *Whatever Happened to Planning?* London: Methuen.

Annis, K (1994) Strategies for Affordable Homes, *Planning Week*, 18th August.

Ambrose, P (1994) *Urban Processes and Power*. London: Routledge (relates to Chapter 1).

Anfield, J (1988) The role of the planner in national parks, *The Planner*, Vol. 74, No. 1, January.

Armstrong, P, A J Glyn and J Harrison (1985) *Capitalism since World War Two*. London: Fontana.

Atkinson, R and G Moon (1993) *Urban Policy in Britain. The City, the State and the Market*. London: MacMillan.

Audit Commission (1989) *Urban Regeneration and Economic Development: The Local Government Dimension*. London: HMSO.

Audit Commission (1991) *The Urban Regeneration Experience: Observations from Local Value for Money Audits*. London: HMSO.

Backwell, J and P Dickens (1978) *Town Planning, Mass Loyalty and the Restructuring of Capital: the origins of the 1947 planning legislation revisited*. Department of Urban and Regional Studies Working Paper No. 11, University of Sussex, Brighton.

Baker, J (1995) Turbulent ride ahead for strategic sustainability, *Planning*, No. 1123: pp. 1123–1124, 16th June 1995.

Balchin, P and G Bull (1987) *Regional and Urban Economics.* London: Harper and Row.

Baldock, D and M Wenning (1990) *The EC Structural Funds: Environmental Briefing, No. 2.* London: Institute for European Environmental Policy, June.

Ball, M (1983) *Housing Policy and Economic Power.* London: Methuen.

Ball, M (1988) *Rebuilding Construction.* London: Routledge.

Ball, M, M Harloe and M Martens (1988) *Housing and Social Change in Europe and the USA.* London: Routledge.

Ball, P (1994) How Far, and in What Way, is the Town and Country Planning System Incorporating the Concept of Sustainable Development in Practice? unpublished MA, Town and Country Planning Dissertation, Bristol: University of the West of England: Faculty of the Built Environment, School of Town and Country Planning.

Ball, S and S Bell (1995) *Environmental Law.* London: Blackwell.

Ball, R and A C Pratt (eds) (1994) *Industrial Property: Policy and Economic Development.* London: Routledge.

Barlow Commission (1940) *Royal Commission on the Geographical Distribution of the Industrial Population.* Command Paper 6153, London: HMSO.

Barlow, J (1990) Who plans Berkshire? Land supply, house price inflation and housing developers, *Urban and Regional Studies Working Paper 72.* Falmer: University of Sussex.

Barlow, J (1993) Paper presented at Planning and Environmental Training conference, London, 8 October (unpublished).

Barlow J and D Chambers (1992) Planning agreements and social housing quotas, *Town & Country Planning,* May, Vol. 61, No. 5, 136–142.

Barlow, J, R Cocks and M Parker (1994) *Planning for Affordable Housing.* London: HMSO.

Barlow, J and A King (1992) The state, the market and competitive strategy: the housebuilding industry in the United Kingdom, France and Sweden, *Environment and Planning A,* **24,** 381–400.

Barnett, A (1994) Building on recovery, *Planning Week,* 18 August, 16–17.

Barras, R (1987) Technical change and the urban development cycle, *Urban Studies,* Vol. 24, No. 1, 5–30.

Barras, R (1994) Property and the economic cycle: building cycles revisited, *Journal of Property Research,* Vol. 11, pp. 183–197.

Barrett, S and P Healey (eds) (1985) *Land Policy: Problems and Alternatives.* Aldershot: Gower.

Barton, H and N Bruder (1995) *Local Environmental Auditing.* London: Earthscan.

Barton, H, G Davis and R Guise (1995) *Sustainable Settlements: a guide for planners, designers and developers.* Bristol: University of the West of England and Luton: LGMB.

Bate, R (1994) Paper at RTPI Yorkshire Branch Minerals Seminar Wakefield.

BDP Planning and OXIRM (Oxford Institute of Retail Management) (1992) *The Effects of Major Out of Town Retail Development.* London: HMSO.

Begg, D (1991) Comment, *The Planner,* Vol. 77, No. 22, 7–8.

Belloni, C (1994) A woman-friendly city: politics concerning the organisation of time in Italian cities, Proceedings of *Women in the City: Housing, Services, and the Urban Environment.* Paris: OECD (Organisation for Economic Cooperation and Development).

Berry, J, S McGreal and W Deddis (1993) *Urban Regeneration: Property Investment and Development.* London: E & F Spon.

Best, R H (1981) *Land Use and Living Space.* London: Methuen.

Bhride, K (1987) Women and planning; an analysis of women's mobility and accessibility to facilities, Unpublished thesis. Dublin: University of Dublin, Master of Regional and Urban Planning Degree, No.182.

Bishop, K and A Hooper (1991) *Planning for Social Housing.* London: National Housing Forum.

Blincoe, B (1987) Demanding Attention; Why development Plans need to take account of market demand, *The Planner*, November, Vol. 73, No. 11, 37–39.

Blowers, A (ed.) (1993) *Planning for a Sustainable Environment*. London: Town and Country Planning Association and Earthscan.

Blunden, J (1975) *Mineral Resources of Britain*. London: Hutchinson.

Booton, C (1994) Factory outlet centre faces the inquiry test, *Planning*, No. 1079, 8–9, July.

Bramley, G (1988) *Access to Owner Occupation*. London: Association of District Councils.

Bramley, G (1989) Land supply, planning and private housebuilding: a review, *SAUS Working Paper 81*, University of Bristol, School of Advanced Urban Studies.

Bramley, G (1993a) The enabling role for local housing authorities: a preliminary evaluation, in Malpass, P and R Means (eds) *Implementing Housing Policy*. Buckingham: Open University Press.

Bramley, G (1993b) The impact of land use planning and tax subsidies on the supply and price of housing in Britain, *Urban Studies*, **9**, 1.

Breheny, M (ed.) (1992) *Sustainable Development and Urban Form*. London: Pion.

Breheny, M (1993) Fragile regional planning, *The Planner*, Vol. 79, No. 1, 10–13.

Breheny, M J and A Hooper (eds) (1985) *Rationality in Planning: Critical Essays on the Role of Rationality in Urban and Regional Planning*. London: Pion.

Brindley, T, Y Rydin and G Stoker (1989) *Remaking Planning*. London: Unwin Hyman.

Brinkhorst, L (1991) Environment Policy and the European Community, *Town and Country Planning*, January, Vol. 60, No. 1, pp. 18–21.

British Geological Survey (1994 and annual) *UK Minerals 1993*. London: BGS.

British Property Federation (1986) *The Planning System: a Fresh Approach*. London: British Property Federation.

Bromley, R and C Thomas (1993) *Retail Change: Contemporary Issues*. London: UCL Press.

Bruton, M J and D Nicholson (1987) *Local Planning in Practice*. London: Hutchinson.

Brundtland Report (1987) *Our Common Future*. World Commission on Environment and Development, Oxford: Oxford University Press.

Byrne, S (1989) *Planning Gain: An Overview*. London: Royal Town Planning Institute.

Burrows, R and B Loader (1994) *Towards a Post-Fordist Welfare State*. London: Routledge.

Burton, P and M O'Toole (1993) Urban Development Corporations: Post-Fordism in Action or Fordism in Retrenchment, in Imrie, R and H Thomas (eds) *British Urban Policy and the Development Corporations*. London: Paul Chapman, pp. 187–199.

Carson, R (1962) *Silent Spring*. Harmondsworth: Penguin.

Castells, M (1977) *The Urban Question: a marxist approach*. London: Edward Arnold.

Cawson, A and P Saunders (1983) Corporatism, Competitive Politics and Class Struggle, in King, R (ed.) *Capital and Politics*. London: Routledge.

CBI (1994) *Living with Minerals*. London: Confederation of British Industry.

CEC (Commission of the European Communities) (1973) *First Action Programme on the Environment*, Brussels: CEC.

CEC (Commission of the European Communities) (1977) *Second Action Programme on the Environment*, Brussels: CEC.

CEC (Commission of the European Communities) (1983) *Third Action Programme on the Environment*, Brussels: CEC.

CEC (1985) 'Directive on the Assessment of the Effects of Certain Private and Public Projects on the Environment' (85/37/EEC), *Official Journal of the European Communities*, L175, 5.7.85. Brussels: CEC.

CEC (Commission of the European Communities) (1987a) *Fourth Action Programme on the Environment*, Brussels: CEC.

CEC (1987b) *Single European Act.* Brussels: CEC.

CEC (1990) *Green Paper on the Urban Environment,* Brussels: CEC, COM (90) 218.

CEC (Commission of the European Communities) (1990) *Green Paper on the Urban Environment* (COM (90) 218) Luxembourg.

CEC (1991a) *Europe 2000: Outlook for the Development of the Community's Territories.* COM (1), Brussels: CEC.

CEC (1991b) *Draft Proposal for Directive on the Environmental Assessment of Policies, Plans, and Programmes,* Doc XI/194/90, Brussels: CEC, 10.01.1991.

CEC (1991c) 'Council Resolution of 28th January 1991 on the Green Paper on the Urban Environment' (91/c 33/02) *Official Journal of the European Communities* C33/4, 8.2.91, Brussels: CEC.

CEC (1992a) *Towards Sustainability: A European Community Programme of Policy and Action in Relation to the Environment and Sustainable Development.* Brussels: CEC, COM (92) 23.

CEC (1992b) *Proposal for a Directive on the Environmental Assessment of Actions Approved During the Planning Process.,* Doc XI/745/92, 17.11.92, Brussels: CEC.

CEC (1992c) *Treaty on the European Union,* Brussels: CEC.

CEC (Commission of the European Communities) (1994) *Growth, Competitiveness, Employment: The Challenge and Ways Forward into the 21st Century,* Brussels: White Paper, CEC.

CEC (1995) *Proposal for a Council Directive on Strategic Environmental Assessment,* Brussels: CEC, Draft, 16.5.95.

Cecchini, P (1988) *The European Challenge 1992 – The Benefits of a Single Market.* London: Wildwood House.

Cherrett, T (1993) Affordable housing in rural areas, *The Planner,* Vol. 79, No. 5, 28–29, May.

Cherry, G (1994) Comment on Cullingworth (1994 *ibid.*), *Town Planning Review,* Vol. 65, No. 3, 291–292.

Cheshire, P and S Sheppard (1989) British planning policy and access to housing: some empirical estimates, *Urban Studies,* **26,** 469–485.

CHICL (Campaign for Homes in Central London) and CPRE (Council for the Preservation of Rural England) (1990) *Home Truths: A New Solution to the Provision of Affordable Housing in Urban and Rural England.* London: CPRE and CHICL.

Chiddick, D and N Dobson (1986) Land for Housing – Circular Arguments, *The Planner,* Vol. 72, No. 3, 10–13, March.

Church, C and J McHarry (1994) Indications of Sustainability: the thinking behind a project which aims to develop a set of local sustainability indicators for use by UK local authorities, *Town and Country Planning,* July/August, 208–209.

CISC (1994) *Occupational Standards for Professional, Managerial, and Technical Occupations in the Construction Industry in Planning, Construction, Property and Related Engineering Services.* London: Construction Industry Standing Conference, Building Centre, London.

Clark, J (1988) Achieving affordable homes in the countryside – unlocking the land factor, in Winter, M and A Rogers (eds) *Who Can Afford to Live in the Countryside – Access to Housing Land.* Cirencester: Centre for Rural Studies, Occasional Paper No 2 Royal Agricultural College Cirencester.

CLES (Centre for Local Economic Strategies) (1990) *Inner City Regeneration: A Local Authority Perspective. First Year Report of the CLES Monitoring Project on Urban Development Corporations.* Manchester: CLES.

CLES (Centre for Local Economic Strategies) (1994) *Rethinking Urban Policy: Strategies for a Global Economy.* Manchester: CLES.

Clifton-Taylor, A (1987) *Patterns of English Buildings.* London: Faber and Faber.

Cochrane, A (1993) *Whatever Happened to Local Government?* Buckingham: Open University Press.

Colenutt, B and A Cutten (1994) Community Empowerment in Vogue or Vain? *Local Economy*, Vol. 9, No. 3, 236–250.

Collinge, C (1992) The Dynamics of Local Intervention: Economic Development and the Theory of Local Government, *Urban Studies*, Vol. 29, No. 1, 57–75.

Collins, K (1991) European Environmental Policy into the 90s. *European Labour Forum*, Spring 1991 (4).

Commission on Energy and the Environment (1981) *Coal and the Environment*. London: HMSO.

COM (1992) *The 5th Environmental Action Programme: Towards Sustainability*. Brussels: COM(92)23.

Constable, M (1988) Up-date on Section 52 agreements and local needs statements, *Village Housing*, No 3.

Cooke, P (1983a) *Theories of Planning and Spatial Development*. London, Hutchinson.

Cooke, P (1983b) Regional Restructuring: Class Politics and Popular Protest in South Wales, *Society and Space*, Vol. 1, No. 3.

County Planning Officers Society (1993) *Planning for Sustainability*. London: CPOS.

Cooper, D and T Hopper (1990) *Critical Accounts*. Basingstoke: Macmillan..

Council of Europe (1989) *European Seminar: Land Use Policies in Regional Planning; Economic Aspects*. Brussels: Council of Europe, European Conference of Ministers Responsible for Regional Planning, Seminar Report.

Cox, A H (1984) *Adversary Politics and Land: the conflict over land and property policy in post-war Britain*. Cambridge: Cambridge University Press.

CSO (Central Statistical Office) (1976) Cyclical indicators of the United Kingdom economy, *Economic Trends*, May, London, HMSO.

CSO (Central Statistical Office) (1993) *Economic Trends: monthly supplement*. July, London: HMSO.

CSO (Central Statistical Office) (1994) *Economic Trends: monthly supplement*. December, London: HMSO.

CSO (Central Statistical Office) (1995a) *Economic Trends: annual supplement*. London, HMSO.

CSO (Central Statistical Office) (1995b) *Economic Trends: monthly supplement*. February, London, HMSO.

Cullingworth, J B (1975) *Environmental Planning 1939–1969, Volume 1: reconstruction and land use planning 1939–1947*. London: HMSO.

Cullingworth, J B (1993) *The Political Culture of Planning: American Land Use Planning in Comparative Perspective*. New York: Routledge.

Cullingworth, J B (1994) Fifty years of post-war planning, *Town Planning Review*, Vol. 65, No. 3, 277–290.

Cullingworth J B and N Vincent (1994) *Town and Country Planning in Britain*. London: Routledge.

Davies, H W E (1993) Europe and the future of planning, *Town Planning Review*, Vol. 64, No. 3, 235–249.

Davies, H W E (1994) *The Impact of the European Community on Land Use Planning in the United Kingdom*, Reading: University of Reading, Commissioned Study for the RTPI.

Dawson, J and C Walker (1990) Mitigating the social costs of private development: the experience of linkage programmes in the United States, *Town Planning Review*, Vol. 61, No. 2, 157–170.

Dawson, J (1991) *Urbanisation and the Functions of Cities in the European Community: Linkages and Networks in Urban Europe*, Liverpool: John Moores University, European Institute for Urban Affairs, Working Papers, Liverpool.

Deakin, N and J Edwards (1993) *The Enterprise Culture and the Inner City*. London: Routledge.

DoE (1972, 1982, 1988) *Survey of Derelict Land.* London: HMSO.

DoE (Department of the Environment) (1976a) *Planning Control Over Mineral Working* (Stevens Report). London: HMSO.

DoE (1976b) *Aggregates: The Way Ahead* (Verney Report). London: HMSO.

DoE (1977) *Policy for the Inner Cities.* London: HMSO, Cmd 6845.

DoE (1980) *Study of the Availability of Private Housebuilding Land in Greater Manchester 1978–81.* Joint report by the DoE and the National House Builders Federation, London: HMSO.

DoE (October 1981) *Environmental Effects of Surface Mineral Working.* London: HMSO.

DoE (1986) *The Future of Development Plans.* London: HMSO, Green Paper.

DoE (1987a) *Action for Cities.* London: HMSO.

DoE (1987b) *Housing: The Government's Proposals.* London: HMSO.

DoE (1987c) *Land for Housing,* Progress Report. London: HMSO.

DoE (1989a) *Environmental Assessment: A Guide to Procedures.* London: HMSO.

DoE (1989b) *Planning Control in Western Europe.* London: HMSO.

DoE (January 1988) PPG6 *Major Retail Development.* London: HMSO.

DoE (1990) *This Common Inheritance: Britain's Environmental Strategy.* London: HMSO, Cmd 1200.

DoE (1991) *Environmental Effects of Surface Mineral Workings.* London: HMSO.

DoE (1992a) *Press Release,* No. 115. 18th February.

DoE (1992b) PPG12 *Development Plans and Regional Planning Guidance.* London: HMSO.

DoE (1992c) *Land Use Planning Policy and Climate Change.* London: HMSO.

DoE (March 1992) *Environmental Effects of Surface Minerals Working.* London: HMSO.

DoE (1993a) *Press Release* No. 731. 4th November.

DoE (1993b) *Good Practice Guide on the Environmental Appraisal of Development Plans.* London: HMSO.

DoE (1993c) *Development Control Statistics: England, 1991/92.* London: HMSO.

DoE (July 1993) *Town Centres and Retail Development,* PPG6 updated. London: HMSO.

DoE (1994a) PPG13 *Transport.* London: HMSO.

DoE (July 1994) *Quality in Town and Country: A Discussion Document.* London: HMSO.

DoE (1994b) *Housing and Construction Statistics.* June, London, HMSO.

DoE (1995a) *Quality in Town and Country: Urban Design Campaign.* London: HMSO.

DoE (1995b) *Your Permitted Development Rights and Environmental Assessment.* London: HMSO.

DoE and the Urban and Economic Development Group (May 1994), *Vital and Viable Town Centres: Meeting the Challenge.* London: HMSO.

DoE *et al.* (1994a) *Sustainable Development: The UK Strategy.* London: HMSO, Cmd 2426.

DoE *et al.* (1994b) *Climate Change: The UK Programme.* London: HMSO, Cmd 2427.

DoE *et al.* (1994c) *Biodiversity: The UK Action Plan.* London: HMSO, Cmd 2428.

DoE/DoT (1993) *Reducing Transport Emissions Through Planning.* London: HMSO.

DoE/SS/LGMB (1993) *Guide to the Eco-Management and Audit Scheme for UK Local Government.* London: HMSO.

Doling, J, V Karn and B Stafford (1986) The impact of unemployment on home ownership, *Housing Studies,* Vol. 1, No. 1, 49–60.

Donnison, D (1967) *The Government of Housing.* Harmondsworth: Penguin.

Donnison, D and C Ungerson (1982) *Housing Policy.* Harmondsworth: Penguin,

Dow, J C R (1970) *The Management of the British Economy, 1945–1960.* Cambridge: Cambridge University Press.

Doxiadis, C (1968) *Ekistics: An Introduction to the Science of Human Settlements.* London: Hutchinson.

Drewett, R (1973) Land values and the suburban land market, in Hall, P, H Gracey, R Drewett and R Thomas *The Containment of Urban England*. London: PEP and Allen & Unwin.

DTZ (1994) *Money into Property*. London: DTZ Debenham Thorpe.

Dudley Report (1944) *The Design of Dwellings: A Report of the Sub-Committee of the Central Housing Advisory Committee*. London: HMSO.

Duncan, S, M Goodwin and S Halford (1988) Policy variations in local states: uneven development and local social relations, *International Journal of Urban and Regional Research*, Vol. 12, No. 1, 107–28.

Duncan, S and M Goodwin (1988) *The Local State and Uneven Development: Behind the Local Government Crisis*. London: Polity Press.

Dunleavy, P (1980) *Urban Political Analysis*. London: Macmillan.

Dunmore, K (1992) *Planning For Affordable Housing: A Practical Guide*. London: Institute of Housing. The National House Builders Federation.

EC (1989) *Planning Control in Western Europe*. Brussels: COM.

EC (European Commission) (1990) *Green Paper on the Urban Environment*. Brussels: EC Fourth Environmental Action Programme 1987–1992.

EC (1994) *Growth, Employment and Competitiveness*. White Paper, Brussels: COM.

ECEG (European Commission Expert Group on the Urban Environment) (1994) *European Sustainable Cities*, Brussels: CEC, Part I, October 1994.

Ecologist (Goldsmith *et al.*) (1972) Blueprint for Survival, *The Ecologist*, January. Reprinted Harmondsworth: Penguin.

EEA (European Environmental Agency) (1995) *Europe's Environment: The Dobris Assessment*. Copenhagen: EEA.

Edwards, M. (1979) Notes for the analysis of land use planning, pp. 21–26 in *Bartlett Summer School Production of the Built Environment: Proceedings of the Bartlett Summer School*. London: University College London.

Edwards, M (1990) What is needed from public policy? in Healey, P and R Nabarro (eds) *Land and Property Development in a Changing Context*. Aldershot: Gower.

EIU (1975) *Housing Land Availability in the South East*. London: HMSO.

Elkin, T and D McLaren (1991) *Reviving the City: Towards Sustainable Urban Development*. London: Friends of the Earth and Policy Studies Institute.

English Nature (1994) *Sustainability in Practice Issue 1: Planning for Environmental Sustainability*. Peterborough: English Nature.

Ermisch, J (1990) *Fewer babies, longer lives*. York: Joseph Rowntree Foundation.

Evans, A W (1985) *Urban Economics: an Introduction*. Oxford, Blackwell.

Evans, A (1991) Rabbit hutches on postage stamps: planning, development and political economy, *Urban Studies*, **28**, 853–870.

Everton, A R and D J Hughes (1987) Minerals subject plans in action, *Journal of Planning and Environmental Law*, March, 174–84.

Faludi, A (1987) *A Decision-centred View of Environmental Planning*. Oxford: Pergamon.

Fainstein, S (1991) Promoting economic development: urban planning in the United States and Great Britain, *Journal of the American Planning Association*, Vol. 57, pp. 22–33.

Farthing, S, T Coombes and J Winter (1993) Large development sites and affordable housing, *Housing and Planning Review*, Feb/March, Vol. 48, No. 1, 11–13.

Farthing, S, C Lambert, P Malpass, R Tetlow, M Auchinloss and G Bramley (1995) *Land, Planning and Housing Associations*. London: Housing Corporation.

Farthing, S (1995) Landowner involvement in local plans: how patterns of involvement both reflect and conceal influence, *Journal of Property Research*, Vol. 12, 41–61.

Feinstein, C H (1972) *Statistical Tables of National Income, Expenditure and Output of the United Kingdom 1855–1965*. Cambridge: Cambridge University Press.

Florida, R and A Jonas (1991) US urban policy: the postwar state and capitalist regulation, *Antipode*, Vol. 23, 349–84.

Flowers Report (1981) *Coal and the Environment.* London: HMSO.

Foley, D (1964) An approach to urban metropolitan structure, in Webber, M, J Dyckman, D Foley, A Guttenberg, W Wheaton and C Bauer Wurster, *Explorations into Urban Structure.* Philadelphia: University of Pennsylvania Press.

Forrest, R (1991) The Privatization of Collective Consumption, in Gottdiener, M and C Pickvance (eds) *Urban Life in Transition.* London: Sage.

Forrest, R and A Murie (1986) Marginalisation and subsidised individualism, *International Journal of Urban and Regional Research,* **10**(1), 46–65.

Forrest, R and A Murie (1988) *Selling the Welfare State: The Privatisation of Public Housing.* London: Routledge.

Forrest, R and A Murie (1994) Home Ownership in Recession, *Housing Studies,* Vol. 9, No. 1, 55–75.

Fortlage, C (1990 and updates) *Environmental Assessment: A Practical Guide.* Aldershot: Gower.

Fraser, W D (1993) *Principles of Property Investment and Pricing,* 2nd Edition. London: Macmillan.

Friend, J K and W M Jessop (1969) *Local Government and Strategic Choice.* London: Tavistock.

Friends of the Earth (1988) *Slate Quarrying in the Lake District.* London: FOE.

Gaffikin, F and B Warf (1993) Urban policy and the post-Keynesian state in the United Kingdom and the United States, *International Journal of Urban and Regional Research,* Vol. 17, No. 1, 67–84.

Garner, J F and M P Brafells (eds) (1986) *Planning Law in Western Europe.* Amsterdam: North Holland.

Geddes, P (1915) *Cities in Evolution: An Introduction to Town Planning Movement and the Study of Civics.* London: Architectural Press (1968 reprint).

Geddes, M (1988) The Capitalist State and the Local Economy: 'Restructuring for Labour' and Beyond, *Capital and Class,* No. 35, 85–120.

Geddes, M (1994) Public services and local economic regeneration in a post-Fordist economy, in Burrows, R and B Loader (eds) *Towards a Post-Fordist Welfare State.* London: Routledge, pp. 154–174.

Gibson, M S and M J Langstaff (1982) *An Introduction to Urban Renewal.* London: Hutchinson.

Gilroy, R and A Castle (1995) *Planning for our Own Tomorrow.* Centre for Research on European Urban Environments, Department of Town and Country Planning, University of Newcastle, Working Paper 48.

Glass, R (1959) The evaluation of planning; some sociological considerations, reprinted pp. 45–67 in Faludi, A (ed.) (1973) *A Reader in Planning Theory.* Oxford: Pergamon.

Glasson, J *et al.* (1994) *Introduction to Environmental Impact Assessment.* London: University College London.

GLC (1985) *Women on the Move: GLC Survey of Women and Transport.* London: GLC.

Goldsmith *et al.* (1972) Blueprint for Survival, *The Ecologist,* January. Reprinted Harmondsworth: Penguin.

Goodchild, R and R Munton (1985) *Development and the Landowner.* London: Allen & Unwin.

Goodlad, R (1993) *The Housing Authority as Enabler.* Coventry: Institute of Housing and Harlow: Longman.

Goodwin M (1995) Governing the Spaces of Difference: Regulation and Globalisation in London. Paper presented at the Tenth Urban Change and Conflict Conference held at Royal Holloway, University of London, 5–7th September.

Gore, A (1992) *Earth in the Balance: Forging a New Common Purpose.* London: Earthscan.

Graham, S and R Marvin (1996) *Telecommunications and the City: Electronic Spaces and Urban Places.* London: Routledge.

Greed, C (1993 and 1996 2nd edition) *Introducing Town Planning*. Harlow: Longman.

Greed, C (1994a) The place of ethnography in planning: or is it 'real research'?, *Planning Practice and Research*, Vol. 9, No. 2, 1994.

Greed, C (1994b) *Women and Planning: Creating Gendered Realities*. London: Routledge.

Greed, C (ed.) (1995a) *Implementing Town Planning: The Role of Town Planning in the Development Process*. Harlow: Longman.

Green Books on minerals (see MHLG).

Guy, C (1994) *The Retail Development Process: Location, Property and Planning*. London: Routledge.

Hague, C (1991) A review of planning theory in Britain, *Town Planning Review*, Vol. 62, 295–310.

Hague, C (1994) Towards 2000: the responses, *Planning Week*, 29th September, 20–21.

Haigh, N (1987) Environmental Assessment: The EC Directive, *Journal of Planning and Environmental Law*, January, pp. 4–20.

Hall, D, M Hebbert and H Lusser (1993) The planning background, pp. 19–35 in Blowers, A (ed.) *op. cit.*

Hall, P, H Gracey, R Drewett and R Thomas (1973) *The Containment of Urban England*. London: Allen & Unwin.

Hall, P (1975 and see 1992 and 1994 editions) *Urban and Regional Planning*. Harmondsworth: Penguin.

Hall, P (1988) The industrial revolution in reverse, *The Planner*, Vol. 74, No. 1, 15–19, January.

Hall, P (1992, 1993 and 1994) *Urban and Regional Planning*. London: Routledge.

Hall, P and A Markusan (eds) (1985) *Silicon Landscapes*. London: Allen & Unwin.

Hall, P and P Preston (1988) *The Carrier Wave: New Information Technology and the Geography of Innovation*. London: Unwin Hyman.

Hall, S and M Jacques (1989) *New Times: The Changing Face of Politics in the 1990s*. London: Lawrence and Wishart.

Ham, C and M Hill (1993) *The Policy Process in the Modern Capitalist State*. 2nd Edition, London: Harvester Wheatsheaf.

Harvey, D (1973) *Social Justice and the City*. London: Arnold.

Harvey, D (1982) *The Limits to Capital*. Oxford: Blackwell.

Harvey, D (1985) *The Urbanization of Capital*. Oxford: Blackwell.

Harvey, D (1987) *Urban Land Economics*. 2nd Edition, London: Macmillan.

Harvey, D (1989) From Managerialism to Entrepreneurialism: The Transformation in Urban Governance in Late Capitalism, *Geografiska Annaler*, Vol. 71 B, pp. 3–17.

Hass-Klau, C, I Nold, G Böcker and G Crampton (1992) *Civilised Streets: A Guide to Traffic Calming*. Brighton: Environmental and Transport Planning.

Haywood, S M (1974) *Quarries and the Landscape*. London: BQSF.

Healey, P (1982) Understanding land use planning. The contribution of recent developments in political economy and policy studies, pp. 180–193 in Healey, P, G McDougall and M J Thomas (eds) *Planning Theory: Prospects for the 1980s*. Oxford: Pergamon Press.

Healey, P (1983) *Local Plans in British Land Use Planning*. Oxford: Pergamon.

Healey, P (1986) Emerging directions for research on local land use planning, *Environment and Planning B*, Vol. 13, No. 1, 103–120.

Healey, P (1988) The British planning system and managing the urban environment, *Town Planning Review*, Vol. 59, 397–417.

Healey, P (1989) Directions for change in the British planning system, *Town Planning Review*, Vol. 60, 125–149.

Healey, P (1992) The reorganisation of the state and the market in planning, *Urban Studies*, Vol. 29, 411–434.

Healey, P (1994) Regulating property development, paper presented to SAUS, University of Bristol, Seminar Proceedings *21 Years of Urban Policy*, September.

Healey, P and J Underwood (1978) Professional ideals and planning practice: a report on research into planners and ideas in practice, in London Borough Planning Departments, *Progress in Planning*, Vol. 9, Part 2, 73–127.

Healey, P, P McNamara, M Elson and A Doak (1988) *Land Use Planning and the Mediation of Urban Change*. Cambridge: Cambridge University Press.

Healey, P and S M Barrett (1990) Structure and agency in land and property development processes: some ideas for research. *Urban Studies*, Vol. 27, 89–104.

Healey, P and R Nabarro (eds) (1990) *Land and Property Development in a Changing Context*. Aldershot: Gower.

Healey, P, S Davoudi, M O'Toole, S Tavsanoglu and D Usher (eds) (1992) *Rebuilding the City*. London: Spon.

Healey, P, M Purdue and F Ennis (1993a) Planning gain and the 'new' local plans, *Town and Country Planning*, February, 39–41.

Healey, P, M Purdue and F Ennis (1993b) Development impacts and obligations, *The Planner*, July, 11–14.

Hebbert, M J (1977) The evaluation of British town and country planning, Department of Geography unpublished PhD thesis, Reading, University of Reading.

Herington, J (1984) *The Outer City*. London: Harper & Row.

HRH The Duke of Edinburgh (1985) *Inquiry into British Housing*. London: NFHA (National Federation of Housing Associations).

Hills, J and B Mullings (1990) Housing: A decent home for all at a price within their means? in Hills, J (ed.) *The State of Welfare: The Welfare State in Britain since 1974*. Oxford: Clarendon Press.

Hobbs, P (1992) The Economic Determinants of Post-War British Town Planning, *Progress in Planning*, Vol. 38, part 3. December, pp. 179–300.

Hoggett, P (1987) A farewell to mass production? Decentralisation as an emergent private and public sector paradigm, in Hoggett, P and R Hambleton (eds) *Decentralisation and Democracy*. Occasional Paper 28, School for Advanced Urban Studies, Bristol.

Hoggett, P (1990) Modernisation, Political Strategy and the Welfare State: An Organisational Perspective, *Studies in Decentralisation and Quasi-Markets*. Occasional Paper 2, School for Advanced Urban Studies, Bristol.

Hoggett, P (1991) A new management in the public sector? *Policy and Politics*, Vol. 19, No. 4, 243–56.

Hooper, A (1992a) The Economic Determinants of Post-War British Town Planning, *Progress in Planning*, Vol. 38, part 3, 179–300, December.

Hooper, A (1992b) The construction of theory: a comment. *Journal of Property Research*, Vol. 9, 45–48.

Hoskins, J (1955) *Making of the English Landscape*. London: Hodder & Stoughton.

Houghton, T (ed.) (1992) *Bristol Energy and Environment Plan*. Bristol: Bristol Energy Centre.

House of Commons, Environment Committee (1994) *Shopping Centres and Their Future*. London: HMSO.

Howard, E (1895) *Garden Cities of Tomorrow*. Reprinted 1974, London: Faber and Faber.

Howard, E and R Davies (1988) *Change in the Retail Environment*. London: OXIRM and Harlow: Longman.

Howe, E and J Kaufman (1981) The values of contemporary American Planners, *Journal of American Planning Association*, July, 266–78.

Humber, R (1987) Affordable Housing – the Unmet Demand, *The Planner*, Vol. 73, No. 11, 28, November.

Huws, S, W Korte and S Robinson (1990) *Telework: Towards the Elusive Office*. London: Wiley.

IPCC (1990) *Climate Change: the IPCC Scientific Assessment,* Report prepared by the Intergovernmental Panel on Climate Change, Working Group 1, WMO/UNEP.

Jackson A, N Morrison and C Royce (1994) *The Supply of Land for Housing: Changing Local Authority Mechanisms.* Cambridge: Discussion Paper 42, Department of Land Economy, University of Cambridge.

James, N (1994) Reversing the car culture, *Town and Country Planning,* May, 131–132.

Jessop, B (1994) The transition to post-Fordism and the Schumpeterian workfare state, in Burrows, R and B Loader (eds) *Towards a Post-Fordist Welfare State.* London: Routledge.

Jessop, B (1995) Post-Fordism and the State, in Amin, A (ed.) *Post-Fordism: A Reader* pp. 251–279.

Johnston, R J and V Gardiner (eds) (1991) *The Changing Geography of the United Kingdom.* London: Routledge.

Jones, A (1989a) Comment, on Healey (1989) *op. cit., Town Planning Review,* Vol. 60, 323–326.

Jones, A (1989b) Development control workshop: recent and emerging trends, *The Planner,* February, 75–80.

JRF (Joseph Rowntree Foundation) (1994) *Inquiry into Planning for Housing.* York: JRF.

JRF (Joseph Rowntree Foundation) (1995a) *Income and Wealth.* York: JRF.

JRF (Joseph Rowntree Foundation) (1995b) Evaluating rural housing enablers, *Housing Research Findings,* No. 141. York: JRF.

JURUE (1977) *Planning and land availability.* Report to the Department of the Environment, Birmingham: University of Aston.

Keeble, L (1969) *Principles and Practice of Town and Country Planning.* London: Estates Gazette.

Kennett, P (1994) Modes of Regulation and the Urban Poor, *Urban Studies,* Vol. 31, No. 7, 1017–1031.

Keogh, G (1985) The economics of planning gain, pp. 203–228 in Barrett, S and P Healey (eds) *op. cit.*

Keogh, G (1994) Use and investment markets in British Real Estate, *Journal of Property Valuation and Investment,* Vol. 12, 58–72.

Kirk, G (1980) *Urban Planning in a Capitalist Society.* London: Croom Helm.

Lambert, C (1991) New housebuilding and the development industry in the Bristol area, *SAUS Working Paper 86,* Bristol: University of Bristol, School of Advanced Urban Studies.

Lambert, C, S Jeffers, P Burton and G Bramley (1992) Homelessness in Rural Areas, *Rural Research Series No 12.* Salisbury: Rural Development Commission.

Lane, P and M Peto (1995) *Environment Act 1995.* London: Blackstone.

Langstaff, M (1992) Housing associations: A move to centre stage, in Birchall, J (ed.) *Housing policy in the 1990s.* London: Routledge.

Lasok, D (1991) *Law and Institutions of the European Community.* London: Butterworth.

Lawless, P (1979) *Urban Deprivation and Government Initiative.* London: Faber.

Lawless, P (1981) *Britain's Inner Cities: Problems and Policies.* New York: Harper and Row.

Lawless, P (1986) *The Evolution of Spatial Policy.* London: Pion.

Levett, R (1994) *Local Agenda 21, Supplements 1 and 2.* London: LGMB (Local Government Management Board).

LGMB (1992) *A Statement on Behalf of UK Local Government.* Luton: LGMB, in association with UNCED.

LGMB (1993) *Framework for Local Sustainability: a Response by the UK.* Luton: LGMB.

LGMB (1995 forthcoming) *Sustainability Indicators.* Luton: LGMB.

Lichfield, N and H Darin-Drabkin (1980) *Land Policy in Planning.* London: Allen & Unwin.

Lin, R S T (1987) Land taxation and land use in Taiwan (ROC) and the U.K., Department of Land Management and Development, unpublished PhD thesis, Reading, University of Reading.

Lipietz, A (1987) *Miracles and Mirages: The Crises of Global Fordism.* London: Verso.

Llewelyn Davies (1994) *City Living: Increasing the Housing Capacity of our Urban Areas.* Bristol: SAUS: University of Bristol, in association with JRF.

London Research Centre (1993) *London Energy Study: Energy Use and the Environment.* London: LRC.

Loney, M (1983) *Community Against Government: The British Community Development Project 1968–78.* London: Heinemann.

Low, N (1991) *Planning, Politics and the State.* London: Unwin Hyman.

Ludlow, D (1995) European Sustainable Cities Project, *The Urban Street Environment,* August/September, Issue 22, p. 34.

McKay, D H and A H Cox (1979) *The Politics of Urban Change.* London: Croom Helm.

McLaughlin, B (1986) The rhetoric and the reality of rural deprivation, *Journal of Rural Studies,* Vol. 2, No. 4, 291–308.

Malpass, P (1990) *Reshaping Housing Policy.* London: Routledge.

Manchester (1994) Papers Presented to a Conference on *The Night-time Economy,* Manchester: Published by Manchester Institute for Popular Culture Publishing, The Manchester Metropolitan University, Cavendish Building, Cavendish Street, Manchester M15 6BX, including 'The Evening Economy of Cities' by J Montgomery, and 'Two Urban Festivals: La Merce and First Night' by M Schuster.

Marshall, M (1987) *Long Waves of Regional Development.* London: Macmillan.

Marshall, T (1994) British planning and the new environmentalism, *Planning Practice and Research,* Vol. 9, No. 1, 21–30.

Massey, D (1984) *Spatial Divisions of Labour: Social Structures and the Geography of Production.* London: Macmillan.

Mawhinney, B (1995) *Transport: The Way Ahead.* London: Department of Transport.

Mawson, J, M Beazley, A Burfitt, C Collinge, S Hall, P Loftman, B Nevin, A Srbljanin and B Tilson (1995) *The Single Regeneration Budget: The Stocktake.* Centre for Urban and Regional Studies, School of Public Policy, University of Birmingham.

McDowell, L (1991) Restructuring Production and Reproduction, in Gottdeiner, M and C Pickvance (eds) *Urban Life in Transition* (Urban Affairs Annual Review. London: Sage.

Meadows, D *et al.* (1972) *The Limits to Growth.* London: Earth Island.

Meadows, D H, D L Meadows and J Randers (1992) *Beyond the Limits: Global Collapse or a Sustainable Future.* London: Earthscan.

Merrett, S (1979) *State Housing in Britain.* London: Routledge and Kegan Paul.

Merrett, S and F Gray (1982) *Owner Occupation in Britain.* London: Routledge and Kegan Paul.

MHLG (Ministry of Housing and Local Government) (1951 and 1960) *The Control of Mineral Working* (The Green Books). London: HMSO.

Miller, C (1990) Development control as an instrument of environmental management, *Town Planning Review,* Vol. 61, No. 3, 231–245.

Mills, E (1974) Recent developments in retailing and urban planning, *PRAG* (Planning Research Advisory Group) Technical Paper, No. 3, December.

Monk, S, B Pearce and C Whitehead (1991) *Planning, land supply and house prices: a literature review.* Cambridge: University of Cambridge, Department of Land Economy, Monograph 21.

Montgomery, J (1994) The evening economy of cities, *Town and Country Planning,* Vol. 63, No. 11, 302–307.

Moor, N (1983) *The Planner and the Market.* London: George Goodwin.

Morgan, P and S Nott (1988) *Development Control: Policy in Practice.* London: Butterworth.

Murray, R (1989) Fordism and Post-Fordism, in Hall, S and M Jacques (eds) *New Times*. London: Lawrence and Wishart.

National Housing Forum (1989) *Housing Needs in the 1990s*. London: National Housing Forum.

NEDO (National Economic Development Office) (1971) *The Future Pattern of Shopping*. London: HMSO.

Needham, B (1992) A theory of land prices when land is supplied publicly: the case of the Netherlands, *Urban Studies*, **29**, 669–686.

Neutze, M (1987) The supply of land for a particular use, *Urban Studies*, **24**, 379–388.

Oatley, N (1993) Realising the Potential of Urban Policy: The Case of Bristol Development Corporation, in Imrie, R and H Thomas (eds) *British Urban Policy and the Development Corporations*. London: Paul Chapman, pp. 136–153.

Oatley, N and C Lambert (1995) Evaluating competitive urban policy: the City Challenge Initiative. In Hambleton, R and H Thomas (eds) *Urban Policy Evaluation. Challenge and Change*, pp. 141–57.

OECD (1990) *State of the Environment Report*. Paris: OECD (Organisation for Economic Cooperation and Development).

OECD (1994) *Women and the City*. Conference Report, Paris: OECD.

O'Brien, L and F Harris (1991) *Retailing: Shopping, Society and Space*. London: David Fulton Publishers.

O'Riordan, T (1994) Environmental protection and sustainable development, *Town and Country Planning*, November, 291–292.

Owens, S (1986) *Energy, Planning and Urban Form*. London: Pion.

Owens, S (1991) *Planning Settlements Naturally*. Chichester: Packard.

Parker, R A (1967) *The Rents of Council Houses*. London: Bell.

Paumier, C (1990) *Designing a Successful Downtown*. Washington DC: The Urban Land Institute.

Pearce, P J (1992) The effectiveness of the British land use planning system, *Town Planning Review*, Vol. 63, No. 1, 13–28.

Pimlott, B (1992) *Harold Wilson*. London: Harper Collins.

Pinder, D (1990) *Western Europe – Challenge and Change*. London: Belhaven.

Plato (5th Century BC) *Critias*. Translation (1929) by Bury R G, London: Heinemann.

Price, D G and A M Blair (1989) *The Changing Geography of the Service Sector*. London: Belhaven Press. (Very relevant to Walker and Oatley.)

Punter, J (1991) *Property in Europe: The Investment, Development, and Planning Processes in Belgium, France, Italy, the Netherlands, Portugal, Spain, and West Germany*, Reading: University of Reading, Centre for European Property Research, Working Papers in European Property.

Raggett, B (1992) One small step for town centres, *Occasional Paper 8*, Hillier Parker.

Randolph, W (1993) The re-privatization of housing associations, in Malpass, P and R Means (eds) *Implementing Housing Policy*. London: Open University Press.

Reade, E (1987) *Town and Country Planning*. Milton Keynes: Open University Press.

Reading Report, see RTPI, 1994.

Rees, G and J Lambert (1985) *Cities in Crisis: The Political Economy of Urban Development in Post-War Britain*. London: Edward Arnold.

Reith Committee (1946) *Final Report of the New Towns Committee*. (Cmd 6759) London: HMSO.

Roberts, P and T Shaw (1982) *Mineral Resources in Regional and Strategic Planning*. Aldershot: Gower.

Robinson, F and K Shaw (1994) Urban Policy under the Conservatives: In Search of the Big Idea, *Local Economy*, Vol. 9, No. 3, 224–235.

Robson, R *et al.* (1994) *Assessing the Impact of Urban Policy: Inner Cities*. Research Programme, Department of the Environment, London: HMSO.

Roger Tym and Partners (1987) *Land Used for Residential Development in the South East.* Summary Report, London: Roger Tym and Partners.

Roger Tym and Partners (1990) *Housing Land Availability: Planning Research Programme.* London: HMSO.

Rogers, A W (1985) Local claims on rural housing – a review, *Town Planning Review,* Vol. 56, No. 3, 367–380.

Royal Commission on Environmental Pollution (1994) Report of the Commission. London: HMSO.

Royal Commission on Environmental Pollution (October, 1994) *Transport and the Environment.* 18th Report, October.

RTPI (Royal Town Planning Institute) (1988) *Planning for Shopping into the 21st Century.* London: Royal Town Planning Institute.

RTPI (1991) *Traffic Growth and Planning Policy.* London: RTPI.

RTPI (1992) *The Impact of the European Community on Land Use Planning in the United Kingdom.* London: RTPI, The Reading Report, Commissioned Study by Professor H W E Davies, in association with Reading University.

RTPI (1993) *Towards 2000: RTPI Education Policy for the 1990s.* London: RTPI.

RTPI (1995) *Planning in Europe.* London: RTPI, set of audio tapes.

Rydin, Y (1993) *The British Planning System: an Introduction.* London: Macmillan.

Saunders, P (1979) *Urban Politics: a sociological interpretation.* London, Hutchinson.

Saunders, P (1986) *Social Theory and the Urban Question,* second edition. London: Hutchinson.

SAUS (1991) *The European Community and the Urban Environment: Report of a UK Consultation Seminar on the Green Paper on the Urban Environment.* Bristol: School of Advanced Urban Studies, University of Bristol.

Schiller, R (1986) Retail decentralisation: the coming of the Third Wave, *The Planner,* Vol. 72, 113–115.

Scott, A J (1980) *The Urban Land Nexus and the State.* London: Pion.

Scott, A J (1988) Flexible production systems and regional development: the rise of new industrial spaces in North America and Western Europe, *International Journal of Urban and Regional Research,* Vol. 12, No. 2, 171–186.

Scott Committee (1942) *Report of the Committee on Land Utilisation in Rural Areas.* (Cmd 6378) London: HMSO.

Scottish Office (1986) *National Planning Guidelines: Location of Major Retail Development.* Edinburgh: Scottish Office.

Seymour, J and H Giradet (1986) *Far from Paradise: The Story of Man's Impact on the Environment.* London: BBC.

Shaw, M (ed.) (1994) *Caring for our Towns and Cities.* London: Boots the Chemist and Civic Trust Regeneration Unit.

Shoard, M (1980) *The Theft of the Countryside.* London: Temple Smith.

Short, J R, S Fleming and S Witt (1986) *Housebuilding, Planning and Community Action.* London: Routledge.

Shucksmith, M (1981) *No Homes for Locals?* Farnborough: Gower.

Shucksmith, M (1990) *Housebuilding in Britain's Countryside.* London: Routledge.

Simmie, J M (1981) *Power, Property and Corporatism: The Political Sociology of Planning.* London: Macmillan.

Simonen, L (1995) *Agenda 21 Briefing Sheets.* Available from Lin Simonen, The Create Centre, Smeaton Road, Bristol BS1 6XN.

Slater, J (1995) The accuracy of property performance forecasts, unpublished final year undergraduate dissertation, School of Valuation and Estate Management, Bristol, University of the West of England.

Smyth, H (1985) *Property Companies and the Construction Industry in Britain.* Cambridge: Cambridge University Press.

Smyth, H (1982) Land banking, land availability and planning for private housebuilding, *SAUS Working Paper 23*. Bristol: University of Bristol, School of Advanced Urban Studies.

Steer, Davies and Gleave Ltd (1989) *The Right Tracks to Europe: The Regional and Environmental Impact of the Channel Tunnel*, London: Steer Davies and Gleave, A Report for *Transport 2000*: The National Environmental Transport Campaign.

Steinem, G (1994) *Moving Beyond Words*. London: Bloomsbury.

Stevens Report (1976) *Report of the Committee on Planning Control over Mineral Working*. London: HMSO (see DoE, 1976).

Steward, F (1989) Green Times, in Hall, S and M Jacques (eds), *New Times: The Changing Face of Politics in the 1990s*. London: Lawrence and Wishart.

Stewart, M (1994) Between Whitehall and Town Hall: the realignment of urban regeneration policy in England, *Policy and Politics*, Vol. 22, No. 2, pp. 133–46.

Stewart, M and J Underwood (1994) Inner Cities: A Multi-Agency Planning and Implementation Process, in Smith, R and J Raistrick (eds) *Policy and Change*. Bristol SAUS. First published in Healey, P *et al.* (1982) *Planning Theory: Prospects for the 1980s*. Oxford: Pergamon.

Stoker, G (1989) Inner Cities, Economic Development and Social Services: The Government's Continuing Agenda, in Stewart, J and G Stoker (eds) *The Future of Local Government*. London: Macmillan.

Stoker, G (1990) Regulation Theory, Local Government and the Transition from Fordism, in King, D S and J Pierre (eds) *Challenges to Local Government*. London: Sage Publications.

Stoker, G and S Young (1993) *Cities in the 1990s: Local Choice for a Balanced Strategy*. Harlow: Longman.

Storper, M and R Walker (1989) *The Capitalist Imperative*. Oxford: Blackwell.

Thatcher, M (1993) *The Downing Street Years*. London: Harper Collins.

The Planner (1988) Local plans – the vital missing ingredient, *The Planner*, No. 6, p. 6, unattributed comment.

Theriral, R *et al.* (1992) *Strategic Environmental Assessment*. London: Earthscan.

Thomas, K (1990) *Planning for Shops*. London: Estates Gazette.

Thornley, A (1991) *Urban Planning under Thatcherism: the challenge of the market*. London: Routledge.

Thornley, A (1993) *Urban Policy under Thatcherism: the Challenge of the Market*, second edition. London: Routledge.

Trench, S and R Ball (1995) Buses and traffic calming, in Trench, S and O Taner (eds) (1995) *Current Issues in Planning*, Volume II. Aldershot: Gower.

Trench, S and O Taner (eds) (1995) *Current Issues in Planning*, Volume II. Aldershot: Gower.

Tucker, W (1978) *Environmentalism and the Leisure Class*. Washington: Georgetown University, Ethics and Public Policy Centre, Reprint No. 7.

Turok, I and J Shutt (1994) The challenge for urban policy, *Local Economy*, Vol. 9, No. 3, 211–215.

Tweedale, I (1988) Waterfront Redevelopment, Economic Restructuring and Social Impact, in Hoyle, B, D A Pinder and M S Hussain (eds) *Revitalising the Waterfront: International Dimensions of Dockland Redevelopment*. London: Belhaven.

Tylesley, D and Associates (1994) *Sustainability in Practice: Planning for Environmental Sustainability*. London: English Nature.

Tym, Roger and Partners (1987) *Land used for residential development in the South East*, Report to the DoE. London: HMSO.

Tym, Roger and Partners (1990) *Housing Land Availability: Planning Research Programme*. London: HMSO.

UN (1996 forthcoming) *Habitat II: UN City Summit*. Istanbul: United Nations, Report of Proceedings.

Uthwatt Committee (1942) *Final Report of the Expert Committee on Compensation and Betterment.* (Cmd 6386) London: HMSO.

UNA (United Nations Association) (1994) *Sustainable Communities Project: Local Agenda 21.* London UNA Sustainable Communities Project (Leaflet).

Van Duijn, J J (1983) *The Long Wave in Economic Life.* London: Allen & Unwin.

Verney Report (1976) *Aggregates: The Way Ahead.* London: HMSO; see DoE, 1976.

Walentowicz, P (1991) *Development After the Act.* London: NFHA Research Report 16.

Ward, S V (1994) *Planning and urban change.* London: Paul Chapman.

Ware, R and V Miller (1991) *European Political Union.* London: House of Commons Library, May 1991.

Wates, N (1976) *The Battle for Tolmers Square.* London: Routledge and Kegan Paul.

WDS (1994) *Are Town Centres Managing?* Broadsheet 12, London: Women's Design Service.

WDS (1995a) *Development Advice.* London Women and Planning Forum, London: Women's Design Service, Broadsheet 13 based on work by Lorraine Hart and Farida Makki.

WDS (1995b) *Sisterhood, Cities and Sustainability.* London Women and Planning Forum, London: Women's Design Service.

WGSG (Women and Geography Study Group of the Institute of British Geographers) (1984) *Geography and Gender.* London: Hutchinson.

Whitelegg, J (1993) *Transport for a Sustainable Future: The Case for Europe.* London: Belhaven.

Williams, A M (1994) *The European Community: The Contradictions of Integration,* 2nd edition. Oxford: Blackwell.

Williams, G and P Bell (1992) The exceptions initiative in rural housing – the story so far, *Town and Country Planning,* Vol. 61, No. 5, 143–144, May.

Williams, P (1992) Housing, in Cloke, P (ed.) *Policy and Change in Thatcher's Britain.* Oxford: Pergamon.

Willis, K G (1980) *The Economics of Town and Country Planning.* London: Granada.

Willmott, P and R Hutchinson (1992) *Urban Trends 1, A Report on Britain's Deprived Urban Areas.* London: Policy Studies Institute.

Winter, J, S Farthing and T Coombes (1995) Compact but sustainable, *Planning Week,* 8th June, Vol. 3, No. 23, 15–17.

World Commission on Environment and Development (1987) *Our Common Future.* Oxford: Oxford University Press (Brundtland Report).

Yeo, T (1991) Social housing and the planning system, *Royal Town Planning Institute/District Planning Officers Conference Proceedings.* November, London: RTPI.

Yiftachel, O (1989) Towards a new typology of urban planning theories, *Environment and Planning B,* Vol. 16, 23–39.

European Union planning controls

Article 119 of the Treaty of Rome 1957 established the principle of equal opportunities, and the Equal Treatment Directive 76/207.

1987 Single European Act.

EC Directive 85/337 on Environmental Assessment *The Assessment of the Effect of Certain Public and Private Projects on the Environment* is applied in Britain under Assessment of Enviromental Effects Regulation No.119 of the 1988 Town and Country Planning Regulations. (All EU legislation must be embodied in relevant domestic state legislation, and in case of dispute takes precedence.)

EC Directive 79/409 *Conservation of Wild Birds* and the EC Directive 92/43 *Conservation of Natural Habitats and of Wild Fauna and Flora.* These were applied in

Britain under the Conservation (Natural Habitats) Regulations 1994 (SI 1994/276) (see Chapter by T Merrett).

1992 Environmental Information Regulations and related EC Council Direction 90/3813.

Circulars and policy guidance notes

Minerals planning guidance

MPG 1 *General conditions and the development plan system* 1988 (revised 1995)
MPG 2 *Applications, permissions and conditions* 1988
MPG 3 *Coal mining and colliery spoil disposal* 1994
MPG 4 *Review of mineral working sites* 1988
MPG 5 *Minerals planning and general development order* 1989
MPG 6 *Guidelines for aggregates provision in England* 1994
MPG 7 *The reclamation of minerals workings* 1989
MPG 8 *Planning and Compensation Act 1991: Interim Development Order Permissions – Statutory provisions and procedures*
MPG 9 *Planning and Compensation Act 1991: Interim Development Order Permissions – Conditions*
MPG 10 *Raw materials for the cement industry*
MPG 11 *Noise at surface workings*
MPG 12 *Disused mine openings*
MPG 13 *Guidelines for peat*
MPG 14 *Review of mineral planning permission*

Regional planning guidance

1995 revision RPG3 *Strategic Guidance for London Planning Authorities*
RPG 1 Strategic Guidance for Tyne & Wear, June 1989
RPG 2 Strategic Guidance for West Yorkshire, Sept 1989
RPG 3 Strategic Guidance for London, Sept 1989
    (based on advice from LPAC)
RPG 4 Strategic Guidance for Greater Manchester, Dec 1989
RPG 5 Strategic Guidance for South Yorkshire, Dec 1989
RPG 6 *Regional* Planning Guidance for East Anglia, July 1991
RPG 7 Regional Planning Guidance for the Northern Region, Sept 1993
RPG 8 Regional Planning Guidance for the East Midlands, March 1994
RPG 9 Regional Planning Guidance for the South East
RPG 10 Regional Planning Guidance for the South West, July 1994
RPG 11 Strategic Guidance for Merseyside, Oct 1988

Important PPGs (Planning Policy Guidance notes) include:

1988
1. *General policy and principles* (revised 1992, and redrafted 1995)
2. *Green belts, 1988* (revised 1994)
3. *Land for housing* (revised 1992 as *Housing*)
4. *Industrial and commercial development and small firms* (1992 replacement is *Industry, commerce and small businesses*)

5. *Simplified planning zones* (redrafted 1992)
6. *Major retail development* (updated 1993, and revised draft 1995)
7. *Rural enterprise and development* (revised 1992 as *The countryside and rural economy*)
8. *Telecommunications*
1989
9. *Regional guidance for the South East*
10. *Strategic guidance for the West Midlands*
11. *Strategic guidance for Merseyside* (and see RPGs, regional planning guidance notes)
12. *Local plans* (revised 1992 as *Development Plans and Regional Planning Guidance*)
13. *Highways considerations in development control* (updated 1994 as *Transport*)
1990
14. *Development on unstable land*
15. *Historic buildings and conservation*
16. *Archaeology and Planning*
1991
17. *Sport and recreation*
18. *Enforcing planning control*
1992
1. *General principles and guidance*
3. *Housing*
4. *Industry, commerce and small businesses*
7. *The countryside and rural economy*
12. *Development plans and regional planning guidance*
19. *Advertisement control*
20. *Coastal planning*
21. *Tourism*
22. *Renewable energy*
1993
6. *Town centres and retail development* (was *Major retail development* and revised 1995)
15. *Historic buildings and conservation*
1994
2. *Green Belts*
13. *Transport*
23. *Planning and pollution control*
1995
1. *General policies and principles, revised*
6. *Town centres and retail development, revised*
N.B. Check current DoE lists for updates, current Circulars, and additional PPGs not referred to in this book (see The *Building, Housing and Planning Catalogue*, HMSO, Annual). Frequently, consultative drafts are produced by the Department of the Environment in an ongoing process of updating existing PPGs and creating new ones reflecting current policy issues.

Circulars

Please note this is a selective list, based on circulars mentioned in individual chapters, plus other key circulars. Nowadays key policy statements are more likely to appear in PPGs than Circulars or Command Papers (White Papers). Please note this is only a small selection.
42/55 Green Belts
24/75 Housing Needs and Action

4/76 Report of the National Parks Policies Review Committee
22/80 Development Control: Policy and Practice
38/81 Planning and Enforcement Appeals
22/83 Planning Gain (replaced by 16/91)
14/84 Green Belts
15/84 Land for Housing (cancelled by PPG 3)
16/84 Industrial Development
22/84 Memorandum on Structure Plans and Local Plans (See PPG 12)
1/85 The Use of Conditions in Planning Permissions (updated as 11/95)
14/85 Development and Employment
2/86 Development by Small Businesses
11/87 The Town and Country Planning (Appeals) (Written Representations Procedures) Regulations
3/88 Unitary Development Plans
15/88 Town and Country Planning (Assessment of Environmental Effects) Regulations
12/89 Green Belts
7/91 Planning and Affordable Housing (cancelled by PPG 3)
16/91 Planning and Compensation Act 1991: Planning Obligations
17/92 Planning and Compensation Act 1991: Immunity Rules
7/94 Environmental Assessment: Amendment of Regulations
11/95 Planning Conditions

Command papers

This only includes those mentioned in this particular volume. There are also many more specifically on town planning, although over the last ten years the trend has been to put key policy statements in PPGs rather than Department of the Environment Command Papers, but other departments and ministries also produce relevant White Papers. A full list is to be found in Cullingworth and Nadin, 1994; and in the HMSO *Building, Housing and Planning Catalogue (annual)*.

1971 *A Fair Deal for Housing*
1977 *Policy for Inner Cities*, Cmd 6845
1990 *This Common Inheritance Britain's Environmental Strategy*, Cmd 1200
1992 (and annually) *This Common Inheritance: The First Year Report*
1994a *Sustainable Development: The UK Strategy*, Cmd 2426
1994b *Climate Change: The UK Programme*, Cmd 2427
1994c *Biodiversity: The UK Action Plan*, Cmd 2428

British Standards Institute

BS 6465 Sanitary Installations Part I: Revision 1995
BS 6465 Sanitary Installations Part II: Draft Revision

Note that there are BSI standards on every aspect of construction, and most other industrial products too.

Acts referred to in this Volume

1945   Distribution of Industry Act
1946   New Towns Act
1947   Town and Country Planning Act
1949   National Parks and Access to the Countryside Act
1952   Town Development Act
1954   Town and Country Planning Act
1960   Local Employment Act
1968   Town and Country Planning Act
1969   Local Government Grants (Social Needs) Act
1970   Community Land Act
1971   Town and Country Planning Act
1972   Local Government Act
1974   Housing Act, (Housing Action Areas)
1975   Community Land Act
1975   Development Land Tax Act
1976   Local Government (Miscellaneous Provisions) Act
1978   Inner Urban Areas Act
1980   Local Government, Planning and Land Act
1982   Local Government (Miscellaneous Provisions) Act
1981   Minerals Act
1982   Derelict Land Act
1985   Housing Act
1986   Housing and Town Planning Act
1988   Housing Act
1988   Local Government Act
1989   Local Government and Housing Act
1990   Town and Country Planning Act
1990   Environmental Protection Act
1990   Planning (Hazardous Substances) Act
1991   Planning and Compensation Act
1992   Local Government Act
1993   Housing and Urban Development Act
1994   Local Government (Wales) Act
1995   Environment Act

SUBJECT INDEX

PERSON AND AUTHOR INDEX

South East Essex College
of Arts & Technology
Carnarvon Road Southend-on-Sea Essex SS2 6LS
Tel: (01702) 220400 Fax: (01702) 432320 Minicom: (01702) 220642